PRAISE FOR *L IS FOR LION*

"Annie Lanzillotto, the bard of Bronx Italian butch, is an American original, a performance artist and cultural anthropologist whose work is unique
in theme, sound, affect, and effect. This memoir reveals her to be something
more: an astonishing writer possessed of an utterly inimitable voice, a voice at
once as richly soulful as her mother's lasagna and as bracingly unsentimental
as her father's Marine masculinity. Lanzillotto's stories bounce and stretch
with the elasticity of her trusted Spaldeen, keeping us just a step ahead of
the flying emotional shrapnel of an intensely lived life as we move from
the mean streets of 1970s Bronx to the Ivy League, the Memorial Sloan-
Kettering cancer ward, the banks of the Nile, and the Italian mezzogiorno.
A landmark of ethnic expressivity, *L Is for Lion* indelibly portrays the iconic
Italian American spaces of kitchen, stoop, sidewalk, and street; the body as a
site of humor and tragedy; and, above all, the family war zone as an uncanny
intermingle of poignancy and brutality."

—John Gennari, author of *Blowin' Hot and Cool: Jazz and Its Critics*

"*L Is for Lion* is a book about a girl named 'Daddy' who goes to Brown
but never leaves the Bronx. This long-awaited memoir by lesbian storyteller
and performance artist Annie Lanzillotto traverses the distance from Arthur
Avenue to Cairo to Sloan-Kettering and back again in an ethnography of
the self and of an era. It's a book made of dismantled padlocks, and of doors,
opened and closed; of spoons clanking against radiators in an attempt to speak
or scream; of Ivy League classism and World War II racism; of language 'spoken
and broken.' Equal parts humor, guts, and grief, it's a disarming story of all
that a person—body, mind, and soul—can undergo without going under, in
which 'Bronxite' is a new kind of rock."

—Mary Cappello, author of *Awkward: A Detour* and *Called Back*

L is for lion

SUNY SERIES IN ITALIAN/AMERICAN CULTURE

FRED L. GARDAPHE, EDITOR

Me at the town limits of Acquaviva delle Fonti, Bari, Italia. I was jogging with my cousin Tonino out into the fields.
Photo: Antonio Lepenne, 1986.

L is for lion

an italian bronx butch freedom memoir

ANNIE RACHELE LANZILLOTTO

excelsior editions

AN IMPRINT OF STATE UNIVERSITY OF NEW YORK PRESS

Illustrations by Rose Imperato

Published by
STATE UNIVERSITY OF NEW YORK PRESS, ALBANY

© 2013 State University of New York

Printed in the United States of America

Excelsior Editions is an imprint of State University of New York Press
For information, contact State University of New York Press, Albany, NY
www.sunypress.edu

Production and book design, Laurie Searl
Marketing, Fran Keneston

LIBRARY OF CONGRESS CATALOGING-IN-PUBLICATION DATA

Lanzillotto, Annie Rachele.
    L is for lion : an Italian Bronx butch freedom memoir / Annie Rachele Lanzillotto.
        p. cm. — (SUNY series in Italian/American culture)
    "Excelsior Editions."
    ISBN 978-1-4384-4525-0 (hbk. : alk. paper) 1. Lanzillotto, Annie Rachele. 2. Italian American lesbians—New York (State)—New York—Biography. 3. Italian Americans—New York (State)—New York—Biography. 4. Bronx (New York, N.Y.)—Biography. I. Title.
    HQ75.4.L36A3 2013
    306.76'63092—dc23
    [B]   2012009553

10 9 8 7 6 5 4 3 2 1

for my Mother, my best friend

No matter where you go,
you have to suffer aggravation,
and you have to suffer joy.
—*Granma Rosa Marsico Petruzzelli*

You are a little soul carrying around a corpse.
—*Epictetus*

All things fade into the storied past.
—*Marcus Aurelius*

contents

part one
Bronx Tomboy

part two
Educationa Girl

part three
Kimosabe

part four

How to Cook a Heart

part five

Ánnie's Parts

Photo galleries follow pages 72, 200, and 256.

prologue

The Blue Suitcase

September 16, 1962, domestic violence cases in New York State were transferred from Criminal Court to the newly established New York State Family Court. Assault of a stranger outside your front door was punishable to the full extent of criminal law, while assault of a family member inside the front door was not. Marriage became a license for abuse. Two weeks later, I was conceived. I said, "I better go down and protect that woman, the courts ain't gonna do shit."

What better way to heal this family than a beautiful baby girl?

Family Court had no muscle. Victims were referred to civilian agencies for help. My mother's case was referred to the Salvation Army and then switched to Catholic Charities. Family Court did not have the power of the State of New York behind the plaintiff. This is the stage on which I was born, on Saint Raymonds Avenue in the Bronx.

Our street was named after Saint Raymond Nonnatus, or, the not-born; Raymond was taken from his mother's uterus postmortem. As an adult, he bartered for the freedom of slaves by trading himself into captivity, where he exuberantly preached. To stop his inspirational speaking, his lips were pierced and locked with a padlock. As an offering for Saint Raymond's intercession, supplicants leave padlocks on altars. My father, perhaps knowingly, did one better. The last decade of his life, while in a residential mental home, he dismantled padlocks that he found when he scavenged the neighborhood trash. It's not an easy task. Padlocks are built of two dozen intricately cut steel plates fashioned together by pins and a yoke. After my father was done with them, the last thing these wildly cut steel plates and pins resembled was a padlock.

My parents were married in 1947, after my father returned home from World War II. Anticipating the trips they would take, my mother bought a royal blue leather suitcase at Gimbels. It had hard walls and thick brass hinges that popped open with a catch. The blue suitcase stayed under her bed for fifty years, twenty-five with my father, and twenty-five after she escaped the brutal reality that had become *la vita quotidiana*, their daily life. With the blue suitcase, she ran for her life. She slid it under her bed, full of her keepsakes; my name bracelet from birth, all her children's oversize kindergarten diplomas, newspapers from the first lunar landing and of Joe DiMaggio's career milestones, old coins. Every few years she would open the suitcase to find a birth certificate or to look among her keepsakes, and have a coughing fit from the aged newspapers. This is close to the process of writing this memoir, for me.

My mother, who read me books every night, taught me, "Books open and close and the things inside them stay inside them." At two years old, I had no idea what she was talking about. I scratched and grabbed at the pages of my storybooks, convinced that I could pull the characters off and make them real. I was confused and upset when they didn't jump off the pages to play with me. Half a century later, I still grab at characters, only now, from inside my brain, and I transfer them onto blank white spaces where they can be real again and find you, beautiful Reader.

This book, for me, is one gorgeous rearrangement of all that otherwise would be locked. This memoir, like any other, is about how what we refuse to remember carves us into who we are. I place this book, unlocked and open, spoken and broken, into your hands.

Annie Rachele Lanzillotto
Yonkers, New York, 2011

Some names have been changed to protect the living.

part one

Bronx Tomboy

Eat with Guys You Trust

THE BRONX, NEW YORK, 1968

"War is full of smoke." Lanzi's laugh is a single gruff exhale. Cigarette smoke gushes out his nostrils and up into the light over the table. His eyebrows are thick and black and move up and down one at a time, fast as pinball flippers. His left eyebrow is interrupted by a hanging ball of skin. I shiver with laughter and duck under the thick stream of smoke. "You call this smoke, Daddy, you don't even know what smoke is." My father calls me Daddy. He belongs to me. He lays the cigarette down on a plate. The smoke rises in one white rope that curls around the wagon wheel chandelier and spreads out across the tin ceiling patterned like ten thousand *pizzelle*. We sit together most nights, just me and him at the maple table. My brothers and sister are old enough to be out. Rosemarie works at Macy's. CarKey and Ant'ny run the streets. My father says with boys, you don't need to know where they are all the time. I wanna be a boy. I put my feet up on the table, eat with my hands, get my clothes filthy, lean back on the hind legs of the chair. When the women do the dishes, I sit with the men at the table. I feel like a boy most of the time, but I'm not as free as real boys. I feel most free when I'm alone with my father. He takes the time to teach me things. He draws a circle around the name of a racehorse and underlines the jockey's name. He draws an arrow at the horse and writes "*sloppy at the start*," with a pencil the size of his cigarette butt. He sharpens the tip with a steak knife, the wood and lead shavings mix with the ashes. I cough. He spanks the curls of smoke that hang between us. We study the names of horses and jockeys. He points to a column of numbers and shows me how many races each horse has run on sloppy track dirt. Other columns list how much money the thoroughbred won this year, how many wins the jockey has, what's the horse's lifetime purse. He tests me on the different answers. On my father's knee I learn the words: *furlong, flank, platoon, kamikaze*.

"Cigarettes are staples," he says, "the military issues cigarettes in K-Rations. Two Chesterfields, a slab of cheese, and a couple of crackers. That's all the body needs. As long as you eat with guys you trust."

This is the Bronx. You learn your lessons early.

I learn to count with a deck of cards. "Ace deuce tree fo' fi' six seven eight nine ten Jack Queen King." He calls and I repeat. "The ace can come in high or low." He pushes aside his horse-racing binders, takes out two decks of cards and begins to shuffle. I run to get my jar full of coins from under the bed and dollars from my sock drawer and dump it all on the maple table. Lanzi shuffles the cards one hand to the other then makes the fluttering bridge between his two hands. My hands aren't big enough to do that. Lanzi's hands are massive. He crushes a walnut between the knuckles of his fore and middle fingers. Knuckle skin, underneath his nails, and the lines of his palms are etched in black, from oil stains built up over the years; his destiny is indelible. He smacks the deck onto the table. Blue streams of smoke gush from his nostrils.

"Cut, Daddy," he says.

I grab half and smack it down. He puts the stacks together.

"We'll bury one," he says, and takes the top card, shows its face, and puts it on the bottom. It's the deuce of diamonds. Lanzi raises one eyebrow at the steepest angle an eyebrow can go. He licks his thumb and flicks cards down, one to me, one to him, one to me, one to him, seven times. I fan my cards out in my hand. They are too many to hold. I put the fan of cards down in front of me.

"So Daddy, you're all Gung Ho 'bout kindy-garten, huh? Good. Good. Just remember, listen to me, keep your eye on the pavement and your mouth shut in the schoolyard. Be a listener not a talker. The guy who knows the most is always saying the least. Remember that. You, are your own business. Everyone else is an intruder."

He looks into the smoke he blows. The veil rises over me. I crease my dollar bills and make them face the same direction. He picks a card and throws one down.

"Walk directly there, one foot in front of the other. If someone looks at you in the street, you say nuttin', you keep walking. You must constantly be aware of who's behind you. If someone smiles at you, they want something. Stay away. Stupid things don't happen to those aware. Look both ways you understand before you cross even a one-way street. One-way street, one way, who says the one way? When you sit down in class, make sure you don't sit near the windows. A bullet coming in through the bottom of the window will cause the greatest shrapnel effect. You wanna duck below the window. You wanna cover your head. You never know. You hit the floor. Keep ya' mouth shut and if anybody aggravates ya', get rid of 'em."

Old dollar bills smell to me like fire. My father hands me his magnifying glass, and I pass it over the details on the bills the way he taught me, the signature of the Secretary of Treasury, the shadow on the head of the number one, the eye over the pyramid, the code of numbers that start with a capital letter to trace where the bill was born. Philadelphia. Denver. I pick a card and fit it into my hand.

"Don't pull your cards up so high. What if I'm in cahoots with a guy standing behind you? What if there's a mirror there? Hah? Be aware of what's behind you. Be aware of who's behind you."

Pennies I stack into towers of ten. "Wheat chaff" pennies, I put aside to save in my mechanical bank. I put the penny in the hunter's rifle, pull the crank, and he shoots it into a tree stump. Stacks of pennies I put into towers, towers I put into rows, rows into platoons.

"Throw down," my father says.

The King of Clubs looks like my father. He has a curl at the bottom of his hair and swings a club at anybody he wants.

"I knock," he says, and lays his cards down. My father gets all the points in my hand. "Loser deals."

Lanzi pushes all the cards in front of me. I try to shuffle them but they fall, some face up. That's a no-no. I turn them all over and begin again. There's one woman in a deck of cards and three men, the Jack, the King, and the Joker. The Jack of Hearts looks like my brother CarKey, blond with tender blue eyes. Ant'ny is the Joker. He laughs for no reason and I never know what to expect from him. Dollar bills disappear from my sock drawer. Quarters from my piggy bank. But he never means any harm and he tries to be entertaining. He makes blueberry pancakes, sings the melodies of songs by repeating "na na na" and "doop do doop do doop" instead of real words, and lets the batter drip freely over the stove. The Jokers we put on the side. They watch us play. Rosemarie and my mother Rachel both look like the Queen of Spades, blue eyes, a serious look. They hold scepters like long wooden spoons. The King of Hearts holds a knife behind his head, and I can't imagine why.

I flick a standing quarter. It flies across the maple table. I practice flicking my finger in the air.

"Concentrate Daddy. Are we playing pinochle or spinning coins?"

"I am concentrating. Just show me once."

I release my middle finger onto the edge of a standing quarter held up by the pulp of my left hand's forefinger. The coin falls.

"Try again Daddy, you gotta learn to have the right touch."

"My hands are small."

"It doesn't matter. You gotta flick the edge. You're hitting too much of the coin."

He gets five quarters spinning at one time. Ghosts of my father's spinning coins whirl in the maple table's shine. Mine fall flat or fly into the curtains.

"Curl the middle finger like this, see, into the pad of the thumb. Hold it tense, the whole top of the finger, so when the thumb lets go, the finger flies. And if you find quarters that are solid silver, they are older than you. Hold onto 'em."

"Whaddya mean?"

"Look at the side-wall ridges, Daddy. See the split band of copper and nickel? See if you can find one without that. Just silver. Those are the old ones."

The maple table is our rink. My fingertips blacken from playing with money and smell like copper. Later I will go into the bathroom and dip my hands in my father's can of grease solvent that's up on the toilet. I will rub the gritty solvent into my hands. I will look in the bathroom mirror and I'll say, "They don't make a soap can take the grease off these here hands. This is the history of New York. Who do you think fixed all the oil burners in all these here buildings? Who do you think brought all the ice up all the stairs?"

We play until eleven p.m., then we put the money and cards away. My mother Rachel walks over with her lemon oil rag, tells me to sit the chair up straight on four legs, and gives the table a rubdown. The maple table stands under the light like a race horse in a stall. My father pushes down on the table to get up from his chair, and the table grunts.

My mother says something.

And he says, "Shut up, you."

Rachel pushes the rag in circles with her bare strong arm, flips the rag, refolds it, and pushes circles to a slick shine. I kiss it and can see my lip prints in the shine. The table's legs bulge into shapely calves. Four strong legs she strokes up and down.

I follow Lanzi to the living room where we watch the news. The First Marine Division is in Vietnam and that's what he wants to hear about. My brothers are teenagers, and the draft is coming up. At midnight Lanzi and me make *sangwiches*, a piling of salami, provolone, ham, lettuce, tomato, mustard, on Italian bread. We watch *Alfred Hitchcock Presents*. We fill cereal bowls with ice cream. We watch the *Twilight Zone*. The tension in my body matches the tension in the stories. One episode replays in my mind for years. A prop plane with red markings on its wings crash lands into a house, rips through the living room walls, and lands next to the couch. The woman in the house has a past connection with the pilot. He's been lost since the war. She has waited. This is the episode that won't leave my mind. The lost soldier crashes into the living room and brings his war right to the couch. I can see my father as a young Marine, my father circles overhead, my father can demolish the plasterboard that surrounds our rooms at any moment now. The walls can split anytime now. I face the television set. I run my fingers in the corrugated-patterned terrain of our deep blue-green living room rug. I see ocean waves in our rug. I see the Pacific Ocean. I see my father on the islands of Okinawa and Guadalcanal in that sea blue. I see the First Marine Division cut the island of Okinawa in half. I see the Sixth Marine Division to the north. The army to the south. I say what my father would say:

"We landed on Blue Beach from the USS *Magoffin*. We called it My Coffin."

The television is the only light on, and the taillights of my Hess oil truck. Gray plastic dinosaurs from ESSO Fuel Oil Company stand in the truck's way. My truck drives over the sea, where the dinosaurs walk out of the water.

I lay down in the water.

My father carries me to sleep, sits on a chair next to my bed, and tells me a story.

"Once upon a time there was a white horse, and on the white horse was a princess named Annie. Princess Annie rode the white horse up a mountain. On the way up the mountain they met a goat. The goat said, 'Hey, where ya goin'?' And Princess Annie said, 'To the top of the mountain.' And the goat said, 'Can I come too?' 'Sure,' Princess Annie said, and the white horse and goat went up the mountain. And on their way up the mountain they met a lion. And the lion said, 'Hey, where ya goin'?' And Princess Annie said, 'To the top of the mountain.' And the lion said, 'Can I come too?' 'Sure,' said Princess Annie, and the white horse and the goat and the lion went up the mountain. And on their way up the mountain they met a rabbit. And the rabbit said, 'Hey, where ya' goin'?' And Princess Annie said, 'To the top of the mountain.' And the rabbit said, 'Can I come too?' 'Sure,' Princess Annie said, and the white horse and the goat and the lion and the rabbit went up the mountain. And on their way up the mountain they met a bird. And the birdie said, 'Hey, where ya goin'?'"

My father drifts off into silence and stares into the dark. "We went up the left flank of the hill. There was an explosion out the roots of a tree. I thought I got him. But he got you. I said, 'No Hewitt. No.' There was nothin' I could do. But I got him. I got the ear. I got the gold teeth. For you, I got him."

I fly through the living room and narrow hall outside my brothers' room. Soupy Sales flies behind me through the hall that leads to the kitchen. He chases me in between double doors that separate the kitchen from the rest of the house, a screen door and a glass door. Soupy Sales has a big smile. He wears a bow tie. His black-and-white houndstooth suit makes me dizzy. I shut him out with the doors. He flies right through them and chases me into the kitchen. I fly to the left, down the spiral stairs into the basement. The basement is pitch black. I am trapped. I fall into the black abyss, I fall. I clutch the mattress and it falls with me, and I fall back into bed.

Breakfast Is to Coat the Stomach

My mother starts me off with a hot bowl of farina—"It coats the stomach"—and burnt toast. She holds a shirt over my head for me to push my arms through, zippers my pants, ties my shoes. She even coats my insides. A square of butter shines steep roads winding up farina mountains to milk rivers and lakes. It all slithers through the tunnels of my throat, stomach, and guts. Mornings are peaceful. Lanzi and Rachel never fight in the morning. I love breakfast. I can eat breakfast morning, noon, and night. Farina, toast, waffles, pancakes, always feel good. Sunday mornings were our American rendition of the Italian *primacolazione* or before-breakfast breakfast. My father's sidekick Uncle Stanley came over with buns-n-rolls, which is what you ate if you were a Bronx Italian and it was Sunday: crumb cakes, jelly donuts, raisin buns, buttered rolls dunked in cups of coffee. Mom and I walked home the two blocks from Santa Maria Church, and Mom put on her indomitable pot of coffee. Lanzi and Stanley, who Dad called "The Big Pollack," sat at the maple table awash with newspapers, buns-n-rolls, horse racing sheets, and the voice of the television newscaster. Joey and Stanley always had a laugh. They were quite a pair. Once when my father had a flat tire, Uncle Stanley lifted the back of the station wagon and held it while my father changed the tire; the whole family sat in the car. Stanley had the girth of our maple tree. I hugged him from all angles but could never get my arms around even half of him. He laid cement and came up with other ideas for businesses, like the "homemade lunches for construction crews" idea, where Aunt Evelyn had to cook a pork roast and a specialty roast every day. The result was that we ended up having hundreds of Styrofoam to-go plates that he had bought in anticipation of the business's success. My mother aptly surmised his business plan, "The business would have taken off if he had had ten Aunt Evelyns." Evelyn was one of my mother's best friends from Jane Addams High School where they both had studied Beauty Culture. Evelyn and Stanley lived off Allerton Avenue and took us to the underground grotto at Saint Lucy's Church, where water poured in caves. Wet Madonnas stood straight up and blessed us. I held my hand in the flowing water, then touched my forehead, heart, left shoulder, right shoulder, and kissed the water. My Mom, Aunt Evelyn, and I had droplets of water on our foreheads. Back at their house, Aunt Evelyn reached deep into the washing machine where she kept a bottle of clear liquid she took swigs from. She saw me watching her and gave me a big smile, her dimples sucked deep into her cheeks. Her pork roast, mash' potatoes, and string beans were the best I ever had. When me, Lanzi, and Rachel went over there, we hung out for many hours, and these were the most peaceful and happiest nights of my childhood.

The X

My mother boils water on the stove. Water is always boiling. My father pulls a chair out to sit down and the chair falls apart in his hand. The captain's bar breaks off. *Ay!* he yells, and she turns on the kitchen faucet. The water runs on with his yelling. He curses the chair and hammers it together with his fist. He leans on the table to sit, and the table creaks. I have work to do. I am five years old. One day I will be allowed to play in the street and I better be ready for stickball. I have ball skills to practice. I kick the back door open. Penny slinks by me and runs out into the backyard. Penny is our Belgian Shepherd. Her fur is all black with a white messy diamond under her neck. Everywhere I run, she is underfoot. There are spots of blood on the kitchen linoleum.

My mother says, "The dog is in heat," and she wipes the floor with a rag and squeezes it out in the sink.

I don't know what my mother means, but I put a rag of cool water on Penny's forehead and kiss her nose.

I run out the back door, down the steps, up the alleyway to the back of the house where the alleys open up into backyards—back to back, two by two, up and down the whole block in a row, separated only by a wire fence gut-high that the neighbors talk across at the corners where four backyards touch beneath the fencing; where you can see that they really all are one, although each has been painted a different color that provides distinction all along the edges. The trees hang fruit over the property lines and in September drop them. In one corner Penny and Gigi, the tiny gray poodle, and Lucky Two Balls the Chihuahua, nose each other where their tails join their bodies; and in the other corner Penny and Cocoa, the giant poodle do. I jump from one big flat stone to the other. My father painted each stone a different color: orange, light blue, pink, red, brown, white, purple. Each stone is a different island I land on.

I break off a corner of plasterboard from scraps leaning against my father's garage and kick open the gate into our outer yard; a vast expanse of cement, on which he painted the lines for a regulation half-court basketball game. Our half-court rule is when the opponent rebounds a ball, he has to take it out past the foul line, before shooting. One day I will have my own full-court. I am the only kid on the block with a real basketball court. I practice shooting night and day. When I feel like it, I invite the boys over to play.

I chalk over the faint *X* on the side of the house with the hunk of plasterboard. The concrete walls of the house are high enough to throw against, and above the walls the asbestos siding is a color dead in the middle between pink and tan.

I throw the ball against the wall. I throw. I throw alone. I throw my pinky ball against the side of the house as if the force and accuracy of my throwing arm can change the world. The ball hits a leg of the X, spins off the wall, takes an odd hop. My parents shout. The house shakes with their yells. The rectangles of window glass shake, the windows my mother and I squeaked to a shine with white vinegar on sheets of my father's *Daily News* crumpled in our fists. My father's boots pound the underlying structure of the floorboards while my mother's slippers whisper across the linoleum. Her pots and pans bang and clap as his fist hammers together the struts, legs, and dowels of the maple chairs. My Spaldeen slaps the outside wall of the house to the rhythm of his yells and the crash of her pans.

"*Bafangool!* "

"Joe, don't come near me, Joe. I'm warning you."

"*Bafangool!* Cow! Snake!"

"Joe, please. I'll call the cops. Don't . . ."

"Say it again, Ray, say it again, Ray, say it. Gahead call the cops. Whaddo I care? What are they gonna do?"

I throw the ball. I throw the ball against the wall. I throw. I throw alone. I throw the ball at his head. I throw the ball in the soup. Through the window I throw. Into tomorrow. This ball bounces high so I can't see its top. The ball has an invisible top. I throw the ball and he catches it. I throw the ball and she stops to mark the place. I throw the ball and the rain comes down. All the doors open at once. I throw.

It's not their yelling that scares me, it's their lapse into silence. Silence means my father has run out of words. In silence is violence. I clutch my Spaldeen and run into the house. Penny follows me like a long black shadow. I open the door and it slams behind me. My father sits at the table looking up into the light. He swings the wagon wheel chandelier across the table and it catches my mother in the back of the head. She cries out. He laughs. The kitchen faucet runs. My mother slides down almost to the floor, she grabs onto the maple table and gets up. Her face is squeezed red tight. My father whistles the "Marines' Hymn," *From the Halls of Montezuma, to the shores of Tripoli* . . .

I pull my feet up from where they are stuck to the floor.

"Mom, you okay?"

I run to my brothers' room. I slam into the louver doors and they swing inward. There is a teaspoon hidden behind the heat pipe. I grab it. I bang on the pipe. Spoon to pipe spoon to pipe spoon to pipe *ppkink ppink pppink ppink*! Pulse alarm up the pipe's tall copper hollow. Alarm fast as pain to brain. *ppkink ppkink*! "Come down quick, Jesus Christ, he's gonna fuckin' kill her!" *ppkink! ppkink!* "Call the cops! Quick, quick. Hurry. *ppkink ppkink ppkink* I hack until I get a rapid tap back.

Two cops stand in our kitchen. One folds his arms over his chest.

My father sits in his chair like a bear. "Officer, I'm a hard-working man. I served my country."

My mother is red and holds her head. "Can't you do something? He cannot lay a hand on me!"

"She's going through her changes, Officer. You see? She's hysterical. She's imagining things. You want coffee?"

"Ma'am, have you been to the doctor lately?"

"The doctor? There's nothing wrong with me. Bring him down to the station house. I need protection."

"Ma'am, we didn't see anything."

Stoop

From the top of my stoop I watch the boys in all their freedoms, zooming up and down the street, running in and out of passing cars, peeling their T-shirts up over their heads and tucking them in the backs of their pants, whipping the air with their mothers' broomsticks, whacking Spaldeens far over rooftops, launching Spaldeens up into the sun.

I sit on the top step and smell my Spaldeen and dream of the day I'll be allowed to play in the middle of the street where the big boys play stickball. I hold my treasured Spaldeen. My Spaldeen is alive. It's made of electrons. My Spaldeen wants to roam, to hop down the stoop and take off under a car chassis, into the current of the street where a car can bump a Spaldeen for blocks. I am four, and confined to games that take me up and down the stoop. I must toss things that have no bounce: popsicle stick, bobby pin, small flat stone. Stoop, sidewalk, street; this is the order of progression of my entrance into the world.

Our stoop has eleven steps. Our last name, eleven letters. Our zip code is 10461. Numbers are the things I am sure of. It is war. One has to know exactly where one is in the world. I toss the bobby pin down a step. I learn to spell my name by going up and down the stoop, one letter per step, L A N Z I L L O T T O. If I miss a letter, I go back up and start again. Each step glitters, a cement mix of crushed glass crystals, white and gray pebbles, crushed stone bits with mica veins that course with the chrome sun

Our stoop is just behind the home-plate sewer cap, optimal for a tomboy such as me, a bleacher seat for the block's stickball game. Sewer caps are home plate and second. Chrome car-door handles are first and third. Spaldeens hit through windows past second base, are automatic doubles. Automatic homeruns are hit over the rooftops three sewer caps away, where Saint Raymonds butt-joints Zerega. In front of the stoop we have big even squares of cement, optimal for boxball with two or four players, and boxball baseball, which is played three squares in a row. To the left of my stoop is the johnny pump, so no cars will ever block my stoopball game for long, and my father's the one in the summers to open the hydrant water for all the kids to cool down. He walks down the driveway from his garage, pipe wrench in hand, and gives the wrench three two-handed pulls. The hydrant cap opens, falls, hangs by its chain, and out comes the glorious white force arching into the middle of the street. My father laughs loud as all the kids jump up and down and dance with the water. Cars slow down, roll up their windows as the rush of water crashes against their windshields, onto their hot hoods, and smacks their driver's side. Cars were our transport animals, they needed to cool off, too. The cold force of water was good for all our systems. We stitched in and out with fast little steps, barefoot on the asphalt, in and out of the forceful arch of water. We got bashed by water. We got bashed by each other. We got bashed by life. We stood as close as we could to the source of the water and still stay up on our feet. We ducked in and out, backed up into it. Cold water bashed our bodies back into the middle of the street. Anyone can learn how to swim, but not everyone can stand the sheer ice punch of all that water.

From my stoop, I watched every move Blaze made. Blaze is the most coordinated kid on the block. He rides up the street, lets go of his handlebars, stands up on the crossbar of the bike, and surfs it. I am amazed. I rehearse his moves in my body, the way he tosses himself the Spaldeen, double pumps his bat and steps into it, how he focuses his brown eyes on the pinky ball, the expression on his face before and after slamming a Spaldeen, and the way he pulls Yo-Yo up against him. Yo-Yo is the most voluptuous girl on the block. Blaze holds her with his right hand clamped over his left wrist, locking her into place against him, as he leans back against a parked car. Their mouths lock for hours, and he leans all the way back onto the hood of a car. When he releases her, their body prints are left behind in sweat on the car hood.

When there's nothing to do and no one around and Lanzi's not home to strip copper wire with, I gather long thick twigs from underneath our maple tree. The boys on the block talk about one Puerto Rican kid who dares bicycle up Saint Raymonds Avenue. Nobody knows what block he is from. Our block is our world. Defending the block is part of our job. Gangs of kids from other blocks are enemy tribes. When a gang of kids from another block raid our block, the boys on our block stand together like a wall. Nasty words and rocks and punches are thrown back and forth. One day I'm on my stoop and I hear the whizzing of gears. It's that Puerto Rican kid who dares ride down our block. I launch a twig at the spokes of his wheel, it gets caught in the spokes, locks the wheel, and flips him over the handlebars. I run up the stoop and into the house as if the maple tree had done this all on its own.

The Return of the Rust

Rachel comes out on the stoop to check on me. She eyes something off to the side. She wrings her hands on a striped dishtowel. I look down at the stoop. Nothing is unusual or out of place. Rachel is a hawk, eyes something that needs to be cleaned. She walks back into the house and leaves the front door open, she'll be right back. I close my eyes and watch the sun's psychedelic starbursts behind my eyelids. She comes back with a cup, dark-green lens sunglasses, and yellow rubber gloves. She steps down the stoop and waves me away with her rag. She sits on a step and pours a clear liquid carefully over a spot of rust that bleeds out onto the step from where the iron pole of the banister drills in.

"Acid. Don't go near, or it'll blind you."

We wait while the acid sits.

I stroke the scars that wind around my mother's knees. Scars the years make wide enough almost to talk. With my finger, I trace each scar. Scar flesh is the softest and shiniest skin.

"Mommy, tell me again, what happened?"

"What happened? Oh, that was a long time ago." She takes off her gloves, lifts the scapular around her neck, kisses it, and hesitates with the story. But I want to hear it, again and again. It's the story of the miracle of our family's existence. And no one ever says more than one or two sentences about it. I want to know more.

"There were no childproof window guards in those days." Her blue eyes swell and fill as if to spill over when she doesn't finish her story.

"How old were you?"

"A baby. All I know is the neighbor thought somebody threw a doll out the window."

I squeezed my eyes to picture her as a baby, tumbling down into the alley. The alleyway between our house and the next-door neighbors was just wide enough for metal garbage pails, and boys who could scale the houses, one leg and arm on our house, one leg and arm on the neighbor's house.

"Where was GranmaRose?"

"I don't remember. She must have been there."

"Where was Aunt Patty?"

"Annie please. All I know is, it was July sixteenth, the feast day of Our Lady of Mount Carmel."

La Madonna del Carmine. La Madonna di Monte Carmelo. I'd heard about the saint all my life. My mother's older sister, my Aunt Patty, was the only witness to my mother falling, but she would never tell me anything about it. My mother was two. Aunt Patty was four.

She takes her wire brush and scrubs meticulously around the post on the stoop.

"No matter how much I scrub, rust always returns, but this way it'll be clean the rest of the summer."

I bounced my Spaldeen on the top landing of the stoop. The Spaldeen went off on its own, down the stoop and into the street. I waited for it to settle underneath a car, and for one of the big boys to get it for me. The boys ran in the street around an oncoming car. Retrieving each other's Spaldeens was part of the play on the block.

I wasn't allowed off the stoop. I watched for the rust to grow back. Rust always returns.

A Good Eater

CarKey walked up the stoop and in through the front door. Something special was happening. My brothers usually shot in the back door and let it hammer close behind them. *Boom. Boom. Boom.* CarKey had shoes on, and a girl with shiny lips and a sweet smile walked in behind him as they came through the living room, down the hallway, past the bathroom, and into the kitchen, which was situated in the back of the house. This girl was important. Otherwise he wouldn't have brought her all the way into the kitchen. They would have leaned up against cars the way the guys on the block did with girls, laying their shadows down into the shine. Enza had a swell of hips, black bangs and hair up on her head and down in swoops along her neck. She smelled sweet, her eyes were bright and alert, and she held a pocketbook by her side. I crawled under the table with Penny. Sitting under the maple table was my favorite spot in the house. Cigarette smoke didn't come down there as much, and I could tell what people were really feeling by the way their feet moved under the table. Both my brothers' legs always shaked, nervous around my father. Enza smiled, said hello with her lips and her eyes, and hung her pocketbook by its strap off the corner of a maple chair. Penny offered her black wet nose and Enza's hand came down over the nose. Her shoes crossed and uncrossed and tapped the linoleum. My mother walked around and around the table and the floor whined under her steps. I pinched Enza's toes in her strap shoes and laughed as her feet tapped, lifted, and fell. Enza's toes had bright slick nails, and her feet kept tapping the floor, and her ankles crossed and uncrossed. Her shoes were the fanciest things I'd ever seen on our kitchen floor. My father had on white socks and brown leather strapped slippers; Enza wore high heels with a gold buckle and delicate black cross straps. The maple table jittered. My mother walked back and forth from the table to the stove in her penny loafers, clashing plates and cups and the aluminum coffeepot. She'd let me place the pennies in her shoes. I'd chosen pennies from the year I was born. My father slapped the table as he talked. I wondered if Enza knew it was important in our family to be a good eater and that afterward the adults would size up whether she was a good eater or not. I pinched her toes and her feet jumped and her hand waved playfully under the table. I knew my father was trying to see her teeth. He'd taught me:

"You can tell a good woman like a horse, by her teeth."

Enza's shoes tapped the kitchen floor like they were telling secret codes into the linoleum. Penny's nose pushed Enza's hand, and the hand came over Penny's head gently and around to her chin. Enza reached under the table and handed me two presents. I opened them under the table; an alligator soap dish named "Gaylord Gator," and a rubber clock filled with bubble bath. My mother had forbidden me to use bubble bath, saying, "It could burn you down there." Gaylord Gator stayed with me my whole life, as did Enza's sweet smile and warm hand reaching under the table. My father and brother were different when she was around. Even when they began to yell in her presence, their yelling was a bit held back, as if they had something to lose.

The Tin Ceiling

My mother doesn't just clean, she purifies. White vinegar and capfuls of bleach accompany her, and acid, when necessary. She performs an endless cycle of housecleaning. She is the kind of homemaker where no one can take a shower because curtains are being soaked in the tub, nobody can throw out a piece of trash because the garbage pail is soaking with white vinegar, you can't brush your teeth because underwear are soaking in the sink, nobody can put anything in the oven because when you open the oven door socks are drying inside, you can't take a nap because the pillowcases are off the pillows drying on the radiator and the blankets are airing out on the line. "Don't wash the pan. Let it soak. The sink is clean."

A speck of black on her kitchen ceiling bothers her. She paints the tin ceiling with Q-tips. One day she was up on the ladder for hours. I begged her to take a break. I wanted her to come down. The enormity of the task made me sad. First, she did the ceiling with a roller, but the golf-ball patterned recesses in the tin stayed black in places. So she went up with Q-tips, dipped one into the can of paint, and lifted it up into the holes. After a few hours, I whined for her to come down and be with me on the ground, but she wouldn't take a step down. I climbed up the weak side of the ladder to help. She let me fill in a few holes. I stepped up on the top step to reach the ceiling with the Q-tip. The batter of thick glossy white paint made me dizzy. I loved being high up, able to look down on the life of the kitchen. My mother made the ceiling pristine. I made her a ham sandwich with leaves of lettuce and tomato on rye bread. I painted the yellow mustard on the pink meat and brought it halfway up the ladder.

"Please, at least eat something."

"Thank you Tootsie-pie." She wiped her forehead with her sleeve and ate the sandwich up on the ladder. "How nice being served for a change. I feel like I'm out at a restaurant."

As long as she is up on top of the ladder, Lanzi can't expect her to answer the telephone for his oil burner business that is run out of her kitchen, or perk pot after pot of coffee. She can make everything perfect at least across her ceiling, a ceiling as shiny as a porcelain plate, so clean we could eat off it, if only we could all defy gravity.

Sidewalk

Rachel allowed me to play on the sidewalk. I played catch with the men on the block as they returned home from work. Santo next door played a gentle but challenging catch with me under the shade of the maple tree. He never threw the ball too high or over my head. Santo was the son of Sadie and Jimmy Petta. Sadie was the Mae West on the block. She had a hoarse voice, teased red hair, long nails, and ran the card parties. Sadie babysat me and Jimmy sang up to me at my mother's clothesline window, "*When I'm calling you oo oo oo, will you answer true oo oo oo.*" My mother said Santo had "a heart of gold." I pictured this. Most people had red hearts, but a few had glowing gold hearts. My parents talked about Santo at the table. This was the first time I heard the word *cancer*. Then I didn't see Santo around anymore and we never played catch again. Heart of gold and cancer.

Junkies were more gentle than marines. My brothers were very different from one another, and so were their friends. The one thing they had in common is that a lot of them died as teenagers. My brothers shared a room. Ant'ny had a mirror on his dresser covered in matchbooks from different clubs, and a poster of Jimmy Hendrix. I looked through his record collection: Jimmy Hendrix, Ten Years After, Joe Cocker. Once in a while, he'd wake up on Saturdays and make blueberry pancakes, my favorite, and sometimes at night he told me stories about a family of Saint Bernards he made up, called the Schultzes. He wore rings made out of bent silver spoons, and navy platform shoes with marshmallow heels. His windowpane dungarees were taller than I was. Ant'ny and his friends laughed all the time. Ant'ny came into the kitchen a couple of afternoons and said that another of his friends had OD'ed. He was sad and slumped on his bed. I didn't know what OD'ed meant, just that his funny teenage friends stopped coming around the house to call for Ant'ny. He looked at the floor a lot and kept asking me for money, swearing me to silence. I was five and good at making money. I beat my father in poker and did chores for quarters around the house.

"Gimme fi' dollars. Don't tell nobody. Ya got fi' dolla's? Don't tell Mommy or Daddy. Keep ya' mout' shut."

I walk up and down the sidewalk with my Spaldeen and keep an eye on the block. Saint Raymonds Avenue between Zerega and Westchester Square Hospital is a small street of two-family houses separated by thin alleyways. Alleyways are full of argument. Backyards are crisscrossed with laundry. Our block is Italian and Irish families, twenty kids are out at night to play Manhunt in two teams of ten. I become expert at counting off perfect seconds. "Ten Mis-sip-pi, nine Mis-sip-pi, eight Mis-sip-pi, seven Mis-sip-pi." Five Italian sisters live on our block in houses to either side of us. Greengrass is the neighborhood boy to be feared and Bow is the dog on the block to be feared, and Bow and Greengrass fear one another. Greengrass with his red hair, skinny wiry body, and his terrible motor and Bow with his ears swiveling just ahead of the roar. Bow is the shepherd dog outside the white house down the corner on Saint Raymonds at Zerega. They keep Bow on a chain they call a choker. Whenever anyone walks by, Bow shoots out as if the lengths of chain will never end but chains do, and Bow gets yanked back up into a twisted leap and chokes. That's why they call that chain a choker. I count on that chain for my life I count the years I count the links I count the rust, one day that chain is gonna break and Bow will fly right out over that little white wall two cinderblock high and land dead in the middle of our street just as Greengrass in his white hot rod is burning rubber round the corner onto St. Raymonds from Zerega the way he does without looking.

The night of the blackout, everyone was out on their stoops at once. My father filled the maple table with thick wax candles, tin foil, and Mason jars filled with water. He lit a candle with his match, and taught me how to drip hot wax into the bottom of jelly jars and stand the candles upright in the hot wax. Then we put the jelly jars inside Mason jars of water. We added pennies to the bottom of the jelly jars until they sunk. The light magnified into a round glow of a lantern. Lanzi wrapped one side of each Mason jar with a piece of tin foil. The light reflected bright. We carried these outside and sat on our stoop. We had the brightest lights on the block. The Italian sisters all came to see my father's ingenious magnified light.

Licking Batteries

At the maple table, my father taught me to see. He never took out a coloring book, or read any story to me from a book, he made them up, and took out blank paper. He turned it sideways and filled a page with interlocking circles. He didn't lift his blue BIC pen from the paper until the page was covered in circles over circles. Then he hands me the pen.

He asks, "What do you see, Daddy?"

I say, "Circles."

"In the circles. Look between them, in them, around them. You gotta see what's not there. Here I'll show you." He takes the pen and outlines curves. He thickens parts of the walls of circles until a set of eyes appears, and above them, a crown. "You see the Queen's face?" Round eyes he fills in with blue ink. The eyes looked sideways.

"Now what can you see?"

I take the pen and draw a mouth. Faces and crowns and castles, whole kingdoms appear out of connecting the curves of circles. Once we're done we start all over again with a new blank page.

Lanzi is color blind. I run to get the Life book that has a full page of colored circles. I open the page and say, "Daddy, what do you see?" but he never sees the number fifty-seven, which is so clear to me. I wonder how this can be, how my father can see something so different. I follow him around the basement and garage and he puts me to work. He gives me a thick black round magnet that he got from the insides of a speaker he took apart, and tells me to pick up screws and nails from the basement floor and add them to his bucket. Then he tells me one of life's great lessons that I would apply to a thousand situations throughout my life; my first lesson in metallurgy and all things precious.

"If it doesn't stick, keep it."

He pulled a handful of coins out of his pocket and passed the magnet over them. Nothing. "See?" Then he lifts it to my gold holy medals. Nothing. "See?"

Lanzi gave me a bucket full of batteries and said, "Daddy, test them there batteries." He told me to figure out which batteries had a charge and which were dead and to separate them. I knew batteries held a secret power, and that this power runs out. The batteries were all different sizes. I looked around for a radio or something to get started. I looked for this gadget I'd seen him use, which had a red wire and a black wire to test electrical circuits.

"Get back here. I tole you test the batteries."

"I am. I'm looking for the whaddyacallit."

"Sit down, over here, I'll show you. You don't need anything. You just gotta lick 'em."

He sat me on an overturned bucket. I picked one up and licked it with a wide flat tongue like an ice-cream cone.

"No," he said, "you gotta focus the tip of your tongue on the cathode to taste if there's a charge there." He demonstrated how to point the tip of the tongue and only touch the tip of the nipple on top of the battery. "You taste it? Hah? The energy is salty and will sting." I could feel the sharp pinch of volts on the tip of my tongue, and soon I became expert at licking batteries. Dead batteries just tasted metallic, cold. Live ones connected to me, I could feel the voltage from the tip of my tongue to way down inside.

Teaspoons and Heatpipes

It was me who hid teaspoons behind the heatpipes. I was too young to reach the telephone, otherwise I would have called the cops myself. I lifted my mother's solid silver teaspoons and hid one behind each heatpipe, in the shadow where no one would find them, not even my mother when she vacuumed. I placed the head of the spoon almost touching the pipe, its tail in line with the shadow, so when I grabbed it, the scoop was my handle, the tail swift to swing into action, out of the sheath of the pipe's shadow. I tapped the pipe for help from whoever upstairs heard me.

Heatpipes are an urban form of communication. On heatpipes neighbors tap invitations up and down, from apartment to apartment—simple social messages, like Hey coffee's on, come up when you're ready; or, I'm going shopping in five minutes, you need somethin', meet me in the hallway; or, He just left, come on up, now—We got a half an hour. My code was much more urgent, an SOS: Come down quick, Jesus Christ, he's gonna fuckin' kill her. *ppkink ppkink!* Call the cops. Wake up. Call the cops. Wake up quick! *ppkink ppkink ppkink!* I can't stop him."

First my godparents lived upstairs, Aunt Archangela and Uncle Orazio and their four kids. When they moved, my father rented the apartment to strangers, an Irish cop and his family. One day the cop's daughter played with me on the stoop. We tossed a bobby pin up and down the steps, asking each other questions to advance. We called this game "Teacher." The cop's wife called the girl's name. She went running when she heard her mother call her name, and I blocked her at the front door. I wouldn't let her pass. This new game was, you want to pass, and I block you. Finally, I let her go and she ran up the stairs. I walked down the stoop. The boys were in the middle of the street playing stickball. My forefinger slid down the white wrought iron railing, which ended in a three-layer curl. The cop's wife came down pulling her daughter by the arm. She stood at the top of the stoop with a wild look in her eye and yelled down to me, "She says she didn't come when I called because you were blocking the doorway. I said, I'm gonna ask Annie, she always tells the truth. Were you blocking the door? Were you?" The front wooden doorway framed their two bodies. The cop's wife was right, I was in the strict practice of telling the truth. Less to go to confession for, plus we had a cherry tree in our backyard that I equated with "George Washington never told a lie." Every July my Dad covered the tree with netting so the birds wouldn't get every single cherry. I ate those cherries like they gave me the strength to tell the truth. The arm of the cop's wife was cocked up high and ready to strike. She had a long white cigarette out the side of her mouth that shook as she talked.

"Were you blocking the doorway?"

She trusted my word over her daughter's. I felt pure fear, I knew I'd catch a beatin'. I shook my head "No." She beamed at my verdict, showed her teeth, said, "Thank you." The hand swung down and slammed her daughter's rear end so hard the girl swung up and out over the stoop. She smacked her again and the girl shouted a wild cry. I watched the whole beating, the kid's pale Irish face turned horribly pink and her mouth opened in a full-lung wet cry. It was my fault she caught a beating. All my fault.

Kitchen Bird

A bird flew into our kitchen through the window my Mom left open at her clothesline. I watched the birdie's wings flutter as it rose over the table, through the wagon wheel chandelier, into the orange curtains with green and white daisies, then over towards the sink. The birdie landed on the silver arm of the faucet, then flew up and hit the glass of the closed window. The bird knocked into the glass three times. It flew back and forth, gained speed, and aimed for the closed window. My father rolled up a newspaper like a bat and swung at the bird. Rosemarie yelled, "Don't kill it," and ran out of the room.

"Birds carry disease," Rachel said. "Just get it out of my kitchen, Joe."

I stood against the cold tile wall. Lanzi swung the newspaper and hit the cabinet. The bird jumped to the wall. I yelled, "This way, come here bird, come here." The birdie flew high, near the tin ceiling, and made a series of quick darts in different directions away from my father. The birdie smacked into the glass over the kitchen sink. I ran to the other side of the kitchen. "C'mere birdie. Come over here." I hoped the birdie would follow me to the clothesline window. Lanzi swung and cursed the bird.

"Son of a bitch."

He rolled his newspaper bat tighter and closed the clothesline window. The birdie hopped across the countertop. I jumped and swung my arms. "Bird, this way." With two quick swings Lanzi knocked the bird into the cupboard and the bird fell onto the countertop. The bird reached up onto the wall. Lanzi charged the bird, and brought the newspaper hard against the wall and pressed. He grunted, dropped the newspaper on the counter and walked away. A stream of red and black and blue hot guts splattered down the wall.

"Hey you, Coffee."

Kindergarten, Boot Camp: 1968

CarKey's number came up for the draft. I started kindergarten the same time CarKey left for boot camp. Enza became what my father called "a permanent fixture" on our couch.

I was five, vigilant, well trained. The big boys on the block chose me to be the Lookout. I sat on the hood of a parked car at the corner of Saint Raymonds and Rowland, and aimed my sight over the line of parked car roofs in three directions to skim the car tops for cherries. The boy next door taught me how to do this. I could pick a cop car out easily that way. "Cop cars can come from any direction," he trained me, "they don't have to obey the one-way signs." Cop cars were like Queens in a chess game. The boys raced go-carts and minibikes in the intersection. The boys were always lighting something that exploded.

To prepare me for kindergarten, my mother sat me down on the piano stool and put a plastic cape around me. "These are special scissors," she said, "very sharp, from when I was in the beauty parlor. You have to hold your head still and sit up straight, or God forbid . . ." She left her sentence hanging and walked around me. The scissor made sharp slices next to my ears. I wondered if she knew about my father's friend in the war who had a jar of ears.

"Put your head down forward. I'm giving you what they call a Buster Brown." She combed the hair on top of my head to the front, pulled strands up between her fore and middle fingers, and snipped straight across.

"Mom, how'd you first meet my father?"

"Stay still."

"Okay, so . . ."

"I saw him washing the windows of his father's business. That's where I changed trolleys to go to school. One of my girlfriends said, 'Look at him, he's so handsome.' We were impressed by his muscles as he cleaned the windows. Now put your head straight, and close your eyes."

"Where was the trolley transfer?"

She carefully snipped bangs, protecting my eyes from the scissor with her hand. I wiggled on the stool. "On 161st Street, where I changed trolleys."

"Where were you goin'? Why was he right there? What's a trolley anyway?'

"*Madonn'!* Let's see, I was going from where we lived, over at 165th and Teller, to Jane Addams High School on Tinton and Union. That was a vocational high school. We dressed like nurses, in starched white uniforms and got inspected every morning—hair, nails, everything. If you had dirty fingernails you got sent home. That's how serious they were. Now tilt your head to the side. You have a natural wave to your hair. The cut has to go with the wave."

She stepped away, pulled the hair near my two ears to make sure it was even. She should have put a level on my head; that's what my father would have done. I loved to watch the green bubble in my father's level. Haircuts never felt even on my head. My mother pulled my hair to curl under, but the hair stuck outward like a wing off the side of my head.

As soon as I turned five, my mother signed me up for my own library card, and I memorized the route to Westchester Square Public Library. Up

Rowland Street, down Glebe, across Saint Peter's Street. We walked with our pinkies linked. Our pinkies are crooked in an identical way, they take a sharp turn inward at the top knuckle. I belong here with her, our pinkies linked. I gathered a big stack of books, as many as I could carry, put them up on the check-out desk and handed the librarian my new card. The librarian looked at me and said, "There's a maximum limit."

"What's a maximum limit."

"You can only take five books at a time."

"You have to put some back," Mom said.

"Why? I promise I will read all these."

"For now, choose five, Tootsie-Bell, then we'll come get more."

I kept the book about Egyptian mummies and the pyramids, setting off an obsession that would last my entire life. And I kept a book on Greek mythology and *The Five Chinese Brothers*. I grab at the pictures and try to scratch them off the page. I don't understand why the illustrations don't come off the page.

"Books open and books close, and the things inside them stay inside them," she says. She points her pink polished fingernail at the words. Her fingernails look like flower petals. When she gets to the end of the book, I ask her to read it all over again. I love this story. Each of the five brothers has a superpower that he can use to survive capital punishment. One has a neck of iron. One can hold the whole sea in his mouth. One holds his breath forever. One's legs grow so tall so he can stand in the center of the ocean with his head above water. One is immune to fire. Each brother takes a turn to stand in for the one brother who is sentenced to death, for the accidental drowning of a boy. The townsmen fail when they hang, drown, burn, and guillotine, the condemned. Finally they give up, concluding he is meant to be alive.

"You see," my mother says, "everybody has something unique to contribute."

I showed my father the book and told him about *The Five Chinese Brothers*. He looked at the book and said, "That's right Daddy. I was on the Great Wall of China. They're good people. I was in Peiping on R&R after the war. One day you'll go there, walk the Great Wall. We're survivors. Lanzillottos are survivors. Remember that. You can get knocked down, as long as you don't get knocked out."

My mother made me wear a dress for the first day of school. She opened her sewing machine and had a stack of aqua cotton scraps of fabric that GranmaRose brought home from the garment factory where she sewed ornamental piecework in Manhattan. "I'm making you an A-line dress." I watched her push the aqua fabric under the fast silver needle of the machine.

Her foot pressed the pedal for speed, and her hand backed up the wheel to pull the needle out of the fabric when she was done with one line of stitches. She had a spool of aqua thread. My mother had a basket of spools of thread in every color. She cut the aqua thread. She licked the end of the thread. She pushed the thread through the needle. I allowed her to pull the dress over my head. She had pins in her mouth. The color was real good. The same color the Virgin Mary wears. I didn't want to make her sad. The night before the first day of school, she held up the aqua dress and a matching beaded purse. My mother's passion showed in her eyes whenever she sewed or knitted something for me to wear. Her blue eyes actually sparkled with love and I couldn't take my eyes off them when she held the dress up for me to see, so I let her pull it over my head without a fight. I just had to wear a dress for the first day, I told myself. I loved seeing my mother smile. Her hem on the dress was straight. My bangs were straight. All was in order. This pleased her. When my mother is happy, and her blue eyes shine, my world is good. Her eyes hypnotize me. They are the color of morning glories with a dazzling luminosity. When my mother was a little girl her teacher took her by the hand from room to room to show all the teachers her eyes, and she grew embarrassed. In high school boy after boy became sullen around her when she paid them no attention. "They'd get heartbroken and I didn't do anything," she said, "I felt so bad all the time." When her parents' landlord's son insisted he take her to the movies, to appease him, she finally told him he could give the money to a boy she was more fond of so she could go to the movies, and he did. According to her, "He was happy to do so." Lanzi was the lucky boy to win her heart and I was lucky to be her baby, to have her intense and loving deep blue eyes stare down on me was a balm to my soul.

On the big day, Lanzi saw me off from the top of the stoop. "Daddy," he said looking up at the Bronx sky, "you never know. Keep your eyes open. There's always a stray Jap." I looked up beyond the sneakers and birds on the telephone wires, and at the maple tree branches. What I thought was a small branch broke off into the sky and flew away. My Mom's crooked pinkie linked around my crooked pinkie, and we walked down the block, arms swinging. Bow shot out at us, barking, ran the length of his chain and got twisted up into a leap as he choked. We crossed the street, taking a left on Zerega Avenue. I jumped off the curb, and looked back at the men standing outside Carly's Candy Store. We walked past the pharmacy, Paul's Junk Store across Zerega, and the big fenced-in schoolyard. Other kids were dressed up and walked with their mothers.

   "Don't drink chocolate milk if they give you a choice," Mom said, "it'll stain your dress. Stay with white milk."

I scanned each piece of jagged baby-blue sky cut out by the buildings. I thought of my father's words. I took my chances and walked in through the gate of the chain-link fence, kissing my mother good-bye. She wore white gloves and stood there for a long time, waving. I was about to enter the school building, tan brick with steel lettering: Santa Maria, a small Catholic school I knew could blow at any moment.

Sister Rosaria

Sister Rosaria, my kindergarten teacher, looked as tall as Meadowlark Lemon, my favorite Harlem Globetrotter. She had a vast forehead, silver-topped eyeglasses, and a soft hairline tucked inside her black-and-white habit. She held a brass bell in her hand and shook it by its wooden stem, so the bell rang out over all of us. "Come, children!" She corralled us into a line in a fenced-in yard attached to the back of the school building. Fencing around cement: I was about to enter the world of schedules and work and rules and order. Sister Rosaria marched us silently and contained through a red door held open by a tiny wooden triangle shaped like a ramp. I counted twenty-six of us. Twenty-six felt like a good number. Maybe my father would play it. One boy immediately stood out to me; his black hair was slicked back, and he wore a red bow tie over his white shirt. Enter Johnny Denaro. The desks were pushed together into group tables. Johnny Denaro asked, "Can I sit next to you?" I nodded, "Mmm-hmm." His hair had a crisp, white side-part. The first time I heard Johnny Denaro laugh, all my nervousness flew away. He laughed louder than anyone in the room.

I did what I was told on cue. Folded my hands. Put my head on the desk. Stood up. Sat down. Whatever Sister Rosaria ordered. There were a couple of kids in the class who already looked like little old Italians at five years old. I will never forget them. One girl stood at the windows all morning and cried, "Mamma! Mamma!" Sister Rosaria couldn't console her. I gently tapped the girl, and tried to coax her away from the windows. She wouldn't budge. She stood there looking out at the last spot she had seen her mother, and would continue like that until noon when we were released. I was worried for my mother. No one was home to look after her except Penny, who hid from my father with her nose under the radiator. Penny wouldn't bark or intervene, she'd just slink away.

Sister Rosaria asked, "Who knows how to count?" My arm shot straight up. "Miss Lanzillotto," she said.

The first thing out of my mouth was, "Ace deuce tree fo' fi' six seven eight nine ten Jack Queen King." Johnny Denaro burst out laughing. Sister Rosaria's eyebrows flattened and she called on someone else. I added, "The ace can come in high or low."

Sister Rosaria handed each of us a yellow paper nameplate to put on our desks. The block letters were handwritten in green marker on pale yellow triple-lined paper; the middle line of dots served to grid the height of the limbs of each letter. *Lanzillotto* was spelled wrong. I couldn't believe it. Here I was officially on the first day of school where I'm supposed to learn how to read and write and they can't spell? I knew how to spell my name. Double *l*'s, double *t*'s. Eleven letters. Sister Rosaria missed one *l*. I counted ten letters. I knew better than to contradict a nun. Nuns didn't make mistakes. I never said a word to anyone. I snuck the nameplate home and added a faint *l* in green marker on the outside of the contact paper.

Quicksand

Me, Mom, and Enza took an eleven-hour train ride to South Carolina to visit CarKey at boot camp at Parris Island. My mother sewed matching A-line aqua dresses so we all matched. When she finished she said, "It took me four days to put the zippers in straight."

Enza and my mother pulled frittata sandwiches and Ring Dings out of their bags. I puked on the train. Enza handed me Italian hard candy. She had lots of flavors all wrapped in shiny colored cellophanes. *Anise, Espresso, Mandarino, Limone.* I chose the orange ones. As we entered South Carolina, pale red mud was on the side of the train tracks. A man on the train saw me looking out the window.

"Watch out for the quicksand," he said.

I stared at the pale-red dirt, wanting to dip my finger or foot in to see how powerful the suction was. How would I pull myself up out of it, or pull my mother or Enza out if they needed a rescue? Any one of us in our aqua dresses could be sucked down in the red sand and swallowed up whole. I asked the man, "So if I step innat stuff whaddo I do?"

"Just remember," he said, "the more you fight it, the faster you fall."

I nodded. That sounded like something Lanzi would agree with.

At Parris Island, I saw CarKey standing in a pack of soldiers. He was holding onto a long rope pulled across the sky between two poles like a giant clothesline. One by one the soldiers had to climb across the rope, holding on with their legs and arms. Underneath was a mud swamp. CarKey hung under the rope as he pulled himself across. Enza bit her polished nails. "I can't look," she said, and she curled her arms into her breasts and held her own hands. In the middle of the rope, CarKey's legs slipped. The mud was brown, I hoped normal mud. He fell through the air and the mud swallowed him whole. I was sure it wasn't quicksand, his head popped up. I recognized the shape of his muddy head. He climbed up out of the mud with full gear on.

We took photos in our aqua dresses near the statue of the Marines lifting the flag at Iwo Jima. Lanzi's face wasn't carved into any of the statues, but I knew he had a flag. Once in a while at the maple table, my father would take his sun mark flag out of a manila envelope and unfold it on the table. The flag had a big red circle in the center, and black brushstroke characters on the sides in Japanese, that told the whole family story of the man whose flag it was. I looked at the flagpole in the sun, our white stars on a blue sky and red-and-white stripes like tape over bloody wounds. I imagined Lanzi as he took the Japanese flag off the pole, replaced it with the American flag, and pushed the pole back into its diagonal place in the hill.

I looked for the quicksand on the train ride home, but the train started out at night, so I couldn't distinguish the pale-red patches. By the time daylight came, we were out of quicksand country and back north.

Lasagna Vows

With CarKey in boot camp, my mother made a vow.

"I'm not making the lasagna until my son comes home."

She took me by the pinkie, and we walked down the block to Frank & Joe's. She tells them, "I'm placing the order on reserve for my CarKey's homecoming. I'm placing this on reserve you understand. I'm not making lasagna until CarKey comes home. I can't. It's his favorite. I can't. So, I'm placing this order. Whenever I get the call he's coming home, I'll pop my head in and you'll know what to do. Here's what I will need. Two large tins of *ricott'*, basil, better give me four *mozzarell'*, the long strips of pasta, six cans crushed tomatoes, tomato paste, and everything for the *antipast'*: the good salami sliced thin, ham, *prosciutt'*, *capicol'*, provolone, swiss cheese, black olives, artichoke hearts, give me a pound and a half of the cold cuts each. You hold this order. The day I get the call he's coming home, I'll let you know. *Capishe?*"

The deli guy behind the counter wrote the list of foods that was my mother's vow, with his short pencil and taped the paper up on his wall. That paper was a promise for CarKey's safe return. While he was overseas, life seemed on hold. I remember those years like a still life. Enza sat on our couch and watched the television for news of the war. Everyone ran to the kitchen every time the telephone rang, and my father sat in his cloud of cigarette smoke in his boxer shorts and tank shirt at the maple table. One afternoon my father walked into the kitchen with a little black box that he plugged into the telephone with a black suction cup. When the phone rang, we all stared into the black box. The voice was now on speaker. CarKey's voice came out, "Hello everybody," and his voice buzzed all over the countertop, toaster, and the tin ceiling. Mom cried. We all shouted at once at the black box:

"You eatin' okay?"
"Is it hot over there?"
"You doin' okay?"
"Did you get the tin of cookies we sent you?"
"Hi CarKey."
"Hi CarKey."
"Take care of yourself."
"Where are you?"
"We love you.
"Come home. Come home."
"Take care of yourself."
"God bless you."
"Watch your head."

Then we waved at each other to shut up, to let his voice come out of the black box. All we wanted was to hear his voice. Then we parted, pushing Enza to be nearest the telephone, and have a few words with him alone.

CarKey mailed us colored photos of him hugging Vietnamese children. Across the bottom of the photo he wrote, "Me and my rice-powered pals." The greens and browns in his uniform matched the hills and sandbags behind him. The edges of his lips were upturned, but I didn't see a trace of a smile at the sides of his eyes, only along the line of the lip, the forced edges. His head was tilted to the side. His eyes were squinting. The sunlight there was direct. His shadow fell in line directly behind him. The children stood up to his thighs that were thicker than their stomachs. Nine Vietnamese boys stood. There were more than nine. The tenth boy was cut in half by the edge of the photo.

Ravioli, Homing Pigeons, and Teletype Machines

The women gathered on a mission to make ravioli and mail them to CarKey. My mother and I walked up to Ralph's Butcher shop in The

Square, and she asked for ground sirloin and some pork. She taught me, "When you go to a butcher and they know you, you know what you are getting. He knows just what I want. He has only top-grade stuff." I watched the butcher's wet hand push the meat into a silver grinder. The meat came out in wormy red strands like out of a shower head, swirling onto white paper. The butcher wrapped it tightly like a diaper, dropped it on the scale and wrote the price in thick black pencil. My mother nodded in approval, and he tucked the pencil back behind his ear, his hands wet with meat.

Enza lived in Throggs Neck across from Saint Raymond's Cemetery, where all our relatives this side of the Atlantic were buried, and one day we all would be. I saw the gray ocean of gravestones in the distance as we turned up the Bruckner Expressway ramp. Our family came from the blue water ocean and ended up in the gray marble ocean. We parked on the street. My mom held onto the brick wall as she walked down the steep driveway into Enza's basement. I ran down the driveway and slammed into the garage door, which shook in its frame. We walked through the door then down a long, dark hallway to the left, and down two more big steps into a cool plaster-walled kitchen. In the basement kitchen, three tables were pushed together to roll out the dough for the ravioli. The first thing I had to do was to run over to Enza's grandmother, Lorenza, and kiss her twice hello. The second kiss was for where we came from. Every time I saw her she was in her chair, all crushed blood velvet and deep mahogany. It had a straight back and stiff arms with glass balls. She held onto these balls. She'd push the arms of the chair down to try to raise herself up out of it. A silver candy dish stood at attention by her side, filled with butterscotch balls, and in her lap butterscotch-colored cellophanes, like shiny fallen leaves, twisted tightly. The feet were mahogany claws that clasped glass balls. Enza's grandmother Lorenza said very little. She held these glass balls. Her kisses were loud as firecrackers in my ears. When she did speak, it came straight from her heart—forget vocal chords—just heart riding on air, *"Mangiamangge."* She held a butterscotch ball up at me from across the room. The planes passed low overhead. Her chair was in line with a runway at La Guardia.

For one day, Enza's house became a ravioli factory. This was the women's war effort. Enza, her mother Florence, her grandmother Lorenza, me, my Mom, and GranmaRose, that's who I remember being there. I'm sure Rosemarie was working at Macy's that day, as Rosemarie was always working to save for a future. Each woman slung a *mappine* over her shoulder and wore a sleeveless housedress or an apron with long strings tied in a bow behind her back. Gravy bubbled on the stove with garlic, bay leaves, oregano, red pepper, parsley, basil. Mom took out the ten pounds of ground sirloin wrapped in white paper she got at Ralph's butchershop. Enza set out empty bowls and they started to mix the meatballs, eggs, breadcrumbs, fresh parsley, chopped garlic, grating cheese, onions. Their arms were deep in the bowls. Granma shaped meatballs quickly in her hands. Florence lifted the tin of golden olive oil with two arms, and poured it into the gravy and frying pan. Enza fried the meatballs. I crawled under Grandma Lorenza's chair and stared at the feet of the chair, each mahogany leg ended in a claw around a glass ball. I looked into these crystal balls. I could see the whole kitchen upside-down, the steam streamed down from the white tin ceiling into the hand the wooden spoon circled the great aluminum pot. Fleshy calves and arms pointed and moved around the table. Rags wiped sweat from foreheads. The women breathed hard. The whole kitchen breathed.

On one side of the basement was the kitchen, the other side was stacked with machines with green screens that emitted high pitched tones. Enza's father Gaetano was a contact between soldiers and their families. He delivered messages stateside. He smoked a pipe, got messages from the screens, and didn't hear a word we said. He shouted answers at his wife when he knew she addressed him directly. His Teletype spit up long pages of words all on its own, intermittently throughout the day. The machine hammered letters with its automatic metal fingers striking black ink onto one long continuous paper. He ripped off long scrolls of paper and telephoned a family with the message. His green screens had heartbeats and made pennywhistle sliding noises as frequencies tuned in and out. Transmissions became words on paper.

Gaetano asked me, "Wanna come with me to feed the pigeons?" I walked out back with him and into the pigeon coop he built with his own two hands with wood and chicken wire. The pigeons had their own little rooms.

"They sure do a lot of talking," I said.

"Hah?" he said, and I repeated loud, slow, and clear, what I was saying. He shoveled feed into the trough. "They race hundreds of miles. They always find their way home."

"How do you know which are yours when they fly?"

"I know my pigeons. And they have these bands on their legs. These pigeons can find their way home from anywhere," he told me and smiled.

"How do you time them in a race?"

"A racing clock. I'll show you in the house."

We went back into the house, and went upstairs, where I was never allowed to play. At the top of the stairs was a pristine living room; a red couch covered in plastic, a dark cherrywood table shined as if it was covered in glass, the hutch with statues and knickknacks behind glass doors. I stood still as if there was an invisible velvet rope, like I was looking at a diorama at the Museum of Natural History. I knew I wasn't supposed to go in there. We walked to the back where there was another kitchen. Gaetano sat down and took out a special brass clock he used to time pigeon races. He explained how his pigeons get released far away at the start of a race, and the serial number and time code is set in the clock. Then he takes the ring off the first pigeon to return and presses it into the clock for the time-code stamp. The clock looked like something off an old ship. I didn't understand how it worked, so I asked him to repeat it a few times.

Back downstairs I ran to tell my mother about the pigeons, how they know how to find this house all on their own. My mother whispers in my ear that Gaetano knows all about animals. "He's a direct descendant of Saint Francis of Assisi," she told me, "they have the same last name. Bernadone." I looked over at Gaetano who sat facing his Teletype machine. I never realized that saints had last names.

The pasta water boiled on the stove. The women took turns boiling the Mason jars and lids, and stirring the gravy; tall wooden spoons reddened all the way up the handles. They sprinkled the table with flour and rolled out the pasta dough with rolling pins. I tugged on my mother's apron, "Can I help?"

"Yeah," she said, "you can help fill the ravioli."

Deep silver spoons ladled mounds of *ricott'* from bowls down onto the sheet of pasta. My mom handed me my own tablespoon and showed me how to scoop the creamy *ricott'* and plop it down with precision. Everyone's hands were busy. Soon the whole table was filled, and Florence cruised the wheelie knife down the length of the table to make long strips of scalloped edges. Then she went across the table, so we had a giant grid of pasta. She covered row by row with a long strip of pasta that she gently laid on top. Soft strong fingers quickly cut squares and pinched the edges together, sealing hundreds of ravioli with pouches of precious *ricott'*. I helped press the edges together. Our fingerprints all were in the dough.

Two thick cardboard boxes were packed tight with jars. My mother added a chocolate cake she baked in a cookie tin. Somehow my mother knew how to get CarKey the ravioli.

"Mommy, how do you know where exactly to send everything? Do you just put WAR on the box and the mailman knows?"

"No, but a mother knows how to find her son. Your brother is in the jungle, not a barracks." She wrote a lot of numbers on the box in black marker. Those were CarKey's numbers.

Ravioli was our women's war effort to pull my brother's soul back. CarKey would feed all the Marines he could. The women wept for him but not when they cooked. Enza's white T-shirt was marked with the Italian women's stigmata: gravy stains over the chest, and this stigmata appeared on her, each Sunday for as long as I can remember.

"Hey Ma," Enza said to my mother, "you always said you cooked enough to feed an army, now you have."

Grandpop, the Hook, and the Eyebrow

BLIZZARD OF '69, THE BRONX

Blue snow, winter sky. Deep-blue dusk suffused the kitchen, snow drifts muffled all sounds. Penny, under the radiator in the hallway, breathing. The orange flower curtains, beveled waves of shadows. The oval of shine, the expansive maple table. I pressed into her, the weight of my body over her chest, my fists squeezed the long thin bars, my head at rest on her shoulder. She never rocked dangerously back. If I fell asleep she would stop rocking and lift me into bed at once, and so I gripped the bars and pulled and pushed the chair to and fro, keeping myself awake with this blissful rocking. I pumped the bars with my arms for more thrust. With the rhythmic cracking of wood to and fro with a silence in between, I imagined I heard the chair ask a question then answer itself. I know there is something behind there. I know answers lie behind there, somehow within the wood of the rocking chair and the bones of my mother's chest vibrating as she sang, "*Que Sera, Sera.*"

The back of the rocking chair faced the doorway, so I had the bulk of the responsibility. Penny guarded the outer door. I had the inner door. My mother, the window. We were covered. As she sang, the dark rose all around us. I held the bars and roused myself from sliding into slumber. I moaned and lifted my head. We were safe here, my mother and me and Penny. I watch over her shoulder out through the wooden bars of the chair. I never want the rocking to end. The moon comes up over the clothesline and stares at us through the kitchen window.

The telephone rang, and the ring skidded through the house. My father's heavy footsteps thudded up the basement stairs and into the kitchen. He answered the telephone and turned his back. The phone cord curled around him.

"Whatsamatta?" he said into the phone. "No. O, God. No." He hung up and slid his arms into his coat. "Papa died."

"What happened Joe?"

"Shovelin' snow. I'm goin' to my mother's."

In my half-awake state, I said to my father, "What's died? I won't see Grandpa no more?" and he assured me I'd see Grandpa one last time, and that's when the blast of yelling started. My mother took a firm stand, "Children don't belong at funerals, Joe. She's too young."

"Too young fa' what?"

"I don't want her getting confused."

"All her cousins will be there. We're a family. Always a problem with you."

He walked past Penny and out the back door.

My mother continued the rocking. "Shh, try to get some sleep."

I fell back to sleep thinking of my grandfather's house in Morris Park. To the left of the house was a long driveway, which widened into an outdoor workstation. Above this workstation, way up high, hung a steel meat hook. Whenever we went over the house, my grandfather would meet us at the beginning of the driveway, bend down, and say to me, *"You'a good'a gherl'a?"* and his eyebrow pointed up at the hook, *"or else, I'ma put'a you up'a dere."*

Made of Rubber

"**Y**ou think you're made of rubber," my mother yelled at me.
      In my mind, I was Evel Knievel, red white blue and reckless. Spaldeens bounced high. Spaldeens had life inside them. They were made of electrons. Spaldeens ricocheted off the sides of cars. Spaldeens hit the point of a step and flew clear across the street. Spaldeens got bunked by oncoming car grills and ran to the next block. Spaldeens ran the curb all the way to the sewer. On my block there were two corner sewers, one down by Zerega, and another half a block behind home plate, at Rowland. Corner sewers swallowed our treasured Spaldeens. I'd lie over the grate and extend a wire hanger down into the muck, and listen to the sound of water striking the iron pipes. The ringing sound of sewer water soothed me. Spaldeens rolled and hid behind car wheels. I'd stick my leg under a parked car to kick my Spaldeen out from under it. Spaldeens were like my body parts, when one split open, I suction cupped the halves onto my cheeks and elbows. Spaldeens took on the smell of the street. Spaldeens sweated and got dirty. Spaldeens taught me soul; to find adventure, to fly, to roll, to hide, to float, to be buoyant, to bounce back even after you rolled down the sewer. I felt my inner bounce. I jumped and flew and rolled and ran down the block with the force and resilience of my trusty Spaldeen. I slammed down on the sidewalk and jumped back up. My skin broke open into red flowing cuts, scrapes, bruises. I soared down the banister, hit the concrete hard and ran. Yes Mom, I am made of rubber.

Maria Nextdoor has a world of Barbies. Her mother Dorothy even looks like a Barbie. She has white hair spun high on her head, long glittery robes, thick mascara, long white cigarettes, and a kitchen table made of glass. Their plastic placemats are green on one side and blue on the other and smell like cheese. Maria Nextdoor knows I rather play with itchy balls than with Barbie. Barbie has no life inside her. There's a great big itchy ball tree in her cement yard. The balls have spikes. They fall off the tree and are good to throw at your opponent or smash them open and slip the pods down each other's shirts.

It was cruel, but not as cruel as knucks; a game where you make a fist, and your opponent slams the edge of a deck of cards onto your knuckles. You take turns doing this, until both your knuckles are scraped and bloody and one person gives up.

Maria's father Carlo is a butcher. One day she says to me, "You wanna stay here and play with Barbie or go to the butcher shop and watch my father make sausage?"

I yell across the fence to my mother, "Ma! Can I go watch Carlo make sausage?" and my mother waves to me from her clothesline window and says, "Okay, and bring a nice wheel home."

I run around the butcher shop in circles as he fits the white sleeves of cows' intestines over the silver nipple of a hand powered machine and pushes the meat mixture in. He cranks and cranks and the meat blows up the guts like skinny balloons. I run and run, giggling and out of breath and then, for no reason at all, I run straight for the door, I leap and fly through it. I broke through the screen and got caught across my belly by the hard metal edge of the bottom half of the door. I was stuck up there, hanging from the door, folded in half at the belly. Carlo lifted me off the door. My gut was black and blue.

"Why'd you run through the door?" Carlo asked.

"I dunno. I ran and ran and let the running take me."

We ran. The world bounced. She bounded with the lure of a superball. What's that pile of mattresses? We found them on the street. Why are we jumping off the side of the stoop onto them? Because it's fun. Dangerous? Mom who cares! Where'd we get that cardboard refrigerator box? Out of the trash down the corner. Somebody got a new refrigerator. We make the box into a tank. Knock it down, get inside, and crawl so hard it races down the sidewalk over everything in its path. We don't stop until we ram into a brick wall or a parked car. Then we break into laughter, breathless.

Ramps we built with pieces of plywood or planks stacked on crates. We took turns bicycling over the ramp to see who could catch the most air. We flew. My knees and elbows were covered in scabs. I fell, got lumps on my head, bled, got up again, bounced, jumped. I was Evel Knievel. I was a Spaldeen. Yes Mom, I am made of rubber. I got a pink rubber soul.

At four and a half, my mother allowed me on the sidewalk alone. I mounted my bicycle and went all the way around the block. This went on for a couple of years. As long as I didn't cross a street I was within my bounds. Down Saint Raymonds, right on Zerega, where a dope fiend who called himself "Jesse James" sat on the sidewalk in a black cowboy hat against a brick wall covered with thick red paint, nodding out in a puddle of sun, telling me, "Don't worry Sweetheart, everything will turn out alright, things have a way of working themselves out." I stopped at Carly's Candy Store for two salted stick pretzels and a vanilla fountain soda. I stretched to reach up to drop my coins onto Carly's counter. Carly was an entertaining neighborhood figure; he had one blue glass eye and he always touched his unlit Tiparello cigar to my knuckles as if he was going to burn me. The faster I pulled my hand away, the heartier he'd laugh. Back on my bike, I continued down Zerega, curved right on Dorsey Street, pedaled hard up the block, jumped the lip of the curve, then right on Seddon Street, past Westchester Square Hospital, and made a quick right on Saint Raymonds down to our driveway gate, the finish line, where I skidded to a halt, burning rubber, leaving a black stripe on the sidewalk. It was harder to burn rubber with handbrakes than a pedal brake. I had to jam the brakes so the bike skidded out from under me.

When the streetlights came on, we all ran home. I'd wash my hands and face, and my Spaldeen. I scrubbed it in the sink with soapy water and a washcloth. It smelled clean, ready for the next day. I slept with it under my pillow.

Sister Giuseppina

FIRST GRADE, SANTA MARIA SCHOOL, ZEREGA AVENUE, THE BRONX, 1970

In first grade I had a crush on an eighth-grade girl. She stood in the schoolyard, long brown hair, dark eyes, dark Italian skin, a big beauty mark on her cheek, and full breasts under her white ironed blouse. She wore her navy blue wool socks pulled up to just below her knees. I was amazed at how good our school uniform looked on her, the green and blue plaid with gold pinstriped pleated skirt just hung off the rest of us. She wore it short, the pleats opened in the wind. I saw her every day in passing in the schoolyard on Zerega, where I was dizzy with passion, as sweet Sister Giusepp' lined us up after recess where we ran around a fenced-in asphalt yard. The older kids lined up on the sidewalk to have their turn in the yard. One day she smiled down at me. Then I noticed, there was two of her, she had a twin sister who stood next to her. I wanted to do something, but I had no idea what, so I just stared. They graduated and disappeared. I never saw her as I biked around the neighborhood, riding with no hands, sure I would spot her one day sitting on one of the stoops.

Sister Giusepp' walked around the class and put two long Stella D'oro cookies, one chocolate, one vanilla, on each of our desks, and drilled phonics

into us. At home I ran my finger under the words in Rosemarie's college
books and sounded out the biggest words. Three-syllable words fascinated me.
I asked Rosemarie, "What does it mean? How do you say it? Do you really
talk with these words or do they just live in books?" Rosemarie knew Latin,
so she knew a lot about syllables, and she taught me many three-syllable words.
With Rosemarie I learn the words: *increment, typewriter, incognito.*

My things began to go missing from our bedroom. One day my guitar was
gone, another day my coin collection from under my bed. My mother said,
"Keep looking you will find everything." But I knew Ant'ny sold them for
dope. After a while I didn't want to have anything that Ant'ny could take. I
stopped wanting things that could be stolen and sold. I began to draw still
life pictures with charcoal sticks. I drew the bowl of fruit on the table, I
drew a pumpkin. The charcoal sticks made my hands as black as my father's
and I was happy. With Ant'ny I learn the words: *junkie pride, dope fiend, track
marks, trestle, psychedelic.*

I needed my own bank book so my money would be safe, out of the
house. I snuck out and walked up to the bank in Westchester Square with
my life savings in my pocket, eight dollars. The air in the bank was so cool,
and the ceilings so high. I felt like my money could grow, just standing there.
I told the teller I wanted to open a bank book. She said I was too young
and needed an adult's signature. I asked her for a pen. I walked around the
block, forged a signature and went back into the bank. The teller caught on
and called my house. She didn't understand how desperate I was to put my
money somewhere safe.

Sister Ercolina

SECOND GRADE, SANTA MARIA SCHOOL,
ZEREGA AVENUE, THE BRONX, 1971

Sister Ercolina left the classroom to go to the bathroom and appointed my
friend Faith, the tallest girl, as class monitor. Faith stood in front of the
class with a piece of chalk in her hand, her eyes scanning each of us. "Don't
even let them scratch their heads," Sister Ercolina ordered menacingly as she
walked out the door, pulling a tissue out from inside her sleeve at the wrist.
We put our heads dutifully on our desks, bending our arms into a pillow, and
rested our heads in the caves of our folded arms. I stared at the class monitor
mutely. Faith was a friend of mine. We played basketball together. She came

to my birthday parties. After a while, one boy let out a soft giggle, and the monitor scrawled his name on the board. As her back was turned, writing on the chalkboard, two kids protested in favor of him because he wasn't causing a stir, he'd just naturally giggled in the silence, and their names went up on the board. Silence reigned once we saw how rigid and literal Faith was in her position as class monitor.

I rested my head on my arms and stared into the dark cave my elbows made, smelling the wood finish of the desk and rubbing my finger along the pencil groove. I drew my finger back into the cave. But then, all of its own volition, my obstinate forefinger poked out of the cave and cranked two tiny scratches on my head. Instantly I heard the chalk moving up and down the board, making a lot of letters. I could tell by the endless sound of the chalk that it was my name. I could hear the double loops of the two l's. My name was up on the board. I looked at Faith with astonishment. She knew how Sister Ercolina punished us if our names were up there. Faith opened her eyes back at me, arching her eyebrows—she had become a little Mother Superior. She had the chalk. Lanzi was right when he said, "Your best friend's your worst enemy 'cause he's the guy you trust." I had given up a birthday cake for Faith. It was my seventh birthday party. My Mom asked me what kind of cake I wanted, I begged her not to have a cake because my friend Faith was diabetic. "I want a watermelon," I said. And so, my mother carved an elaborate basket out of the watermelon, to hold all the grapes—green and purple, pineapple, apples—golden and red, cherries, strawberries, blueberries, cantaloupe and honeydew scooped into tiny balls, and the fuzzy miracle of kiwi, brought to our house by a local Marco Polo named Capozzi, who ventured as far away as Amish Pennsylvania. "Bite right through it," Capozzi encouraged me, "you don't have to wash it." I bit through the furry head of the kiwi, surprised to find a banana-like mushy core with seeds like strawberries. My mother put candles in the watermelon and carried it toward me, while Lanzi lifted the small, black wrought-iron coal shovel and tossed platefuls of coal into the potbelly stove in the backyard to make a barbecue for my friends.

Sister Ercolina walked back into the silent class, her eyes winced and she smiled when she saw a substantial list of names up on the board, as if she relished punishing us. She went down the list naming the names and assigning punishments. "For homework, write five hundred times, I will never talk in class." When she came to my name she said, "Lanzillotto! And Lanzillotto will say that she wasn't even talking!"

"But Sister, I wasn't talking!"

"You see? What did I tell you. Go stand in the coat closet!"

"But, Sister!" I looked at Faith after my sentencing and said, "Tell her!" but Faith didn't offer a word, she just arched her eyebrows silently mouthing, "Don't scratch your head."

I walked to the back of the class and dutifully stood in the coat closet. Sister Ercolina ordered me to stand deeper in the closet. I backed all the way up until the brass hook on the coat rack dug into my spine. She carried on with her lesson. I stood for an hour. Then two. I stood on one foot, then the other. Johnny Denaro snuck a turn of his head and flashed me a supportive smile. Sister Ercolina declared it was such a beautiful day that she'd take the class for a walk. Row by row the kids came back and got their coats. Some avoided my gaze. I was a criminal; the closet was jail. The brass hook pressed against my spine. When Johnny came to get his jacket, he whispered to me, "Aren't you coming?"

"She didn't tell me to," I said. I was terrified to go against Sister Ercolina's word. As the class filed out, my back against the hook, I began to cry. All the shame and all the injustice burst out of me. I stood straight and cried, the hook pushing into my spine. Now that the room was empty, I could cry fully, noisily, not hide my tears. I expected at any moment that Sister Ercolina would look back at me and tell me to come along, but she didn't. I stared at the clock. I stood tall as a soldier, the hook felt like the shaft of a rifle stabbed into my back. After a half hour, a nun from the upper classes walked by in the hallway and heard me sobbing. She walked in and asked me sternly, "Why are you in the classroom alone? What are you doing here? You're not allowed to be in the classroom alone."

"Sister Ercolina told me to." I was hot with tears.

"Follow me," she said.

We walked down the hall to the Mother Superior's office. Mother Superior gave me a tissue and a drink of orange juice. I went to the bathroom to wash my face.

When the class returned, Mother Superior walked me to Sister Ercolina herself, and said something to her. Sister Ercolina took a step back, and became sweet, "Miss Lanzillotto, why didn't you follow us?"

"Sister, you told me to stand in the closet."

I stayed home after that. In second grade I was home a hundred and two days out of the hundred and eighty days of the calendar year. I got mono. Johnny Denaro brought my schoolbooks over. With the mono, he couldn't come into my room, but he stood at the doorway and talked to me, then he'd go home and call me on the phone and go over the lesson plan with me, especially the math. I kept up with all the assignments this way. My mother gave me a tiny antique brass bell to ring for her. It had a gentle sweet ring. I rang it throughout the day. It meant she had to make two trips for every ring. One to see what I needed, and the second to get it. My father then put a telephone in my room with an outside line, and a special second phone that was a direct line to my mother's kitchen. I ordered whatever I wanted night and day. As long as I was sick, there was peace in the house. My father left my mother alone. "Go take care of your daughter," was all he said to her. The sicker I was, the more peaceful the house became.

Sister Ercolina gave me straight A's and promoted me. I was at the top of the class, from my sickbed. At the end of the year, I went in to take the national standardized tests. There's one question I will never forget: *Which rhymes with dog? A., B., C., D.,* and the impossible answer for a Bronx kid, was *log*. I sat there so angry. No one could help me out of this. How could *dog*, which off my tongue rhymed with *morgue*, match up with *log?*

Playing War

"**N**o I ain't dead. You didn't get me. I got you first."

"No way."

"Yes way. I got you right between your eyes. You're dead die. You're dead die you're dead die."

"Did not."

"Did too."

"Okay. Do over."

"Do over. Oh man, this stinks. I quit."

"Okay I die. I'm dead. I'm dead."

"Not fair you didn't die."

Steven Upthecorner's father had also been in World War II. He and his brother had all kinds of plastic artillery, so when we played War, we made a big deal out of choosing our weapons. We had many "Choose Songs" to figure out who would go first. All the players stood in a circle. One player called the song, accentuating each syllable, so that the corresponding hand slap progressed from player to player. Whoever the last syllable landed on, was out. The last one standing, chose first. My favorite Choose Song was: "My mother punched your mother right in the nose. What color blood came out?" You called a color and spelled it out. "P-u-r-p-l-e." My other favorite was: "Ink a Bink a bottle of ink. The cork fell out and you stink. Not because you're dirty. Not because you're clean. Just because you kissed the girl behind the magazine." For this song, everyone put two fists in the circle, thumb-side up. The caller smacked the underside of her chin with her fist on the first word *ink*, then fist to fist. This sequence was passed around the circle: Ink (chin) a bink (fist) a bottle (switch fists) of ink (next players fist).

In the game of War, I was a good shot and I knew how to die. But when Steven Upthecorner got shot, he got sullen and refused to hit the ground.

We decided we should stop playing War, and we made up a game called Demolition Squad, where we blew things up. I heard my parents talk about an explosion one day when I was under the table, and it stuck in my mind.

My mother said, "I don't know how she survived. I would've cracked. To lose four sons in an explosion. She's made of stone. Not cement. Cement cracks. It's a mixture of different things. Stone wears out around the edges. Stone doesn't crack. It becomes weather-beaten. You actually have to dynamite it."

"Dynamite is right," Lanzi said.

"What are you talking about? It was an accident. They cleaned the floor with kerosene. All it takes is a spark. God knows what chemicals they had baby blue.

"That was no accident. That was an execution."

"Oh, I don't believe it."

Steven and me asked Lanzi for some thermostats, and he pointed us to a crate in his garage. He had dozens of them, rectangular, circular, flat, and dome shaped. I chose the copper dome that had a dial. Steven chose a rectangular unit big as a walkie-talkie. We lay in the dirt behind my front yard fence, and pointed at the apartment building across the street. It had to come down. We synchronized our timers and counted down from ten, "Ten-mis-sip-pi, nine-mis-sip-pi, eight . . ." as we dialed up the numbers on the thermostats, slowly raising the temperature gauge. We made explosion sound effects with our voices, as we watched the apartment building explode into a flying heap of rubble. Bricks broke and flew into the baby-blue Bronx sky. We ducked and hid for cover in the dirt. Then did it all over again. "Let's see what we can blow up next." When we got bored of Demolition Squad, we walked up the block to Westchester Square Hospital and told the nurses, "We go to Santa Maria School, and we need test tubes for experiments." For some reason, the nurses were happy to give us bags of glass test tubes. We had all the test tubes we ever wanted. Then we ransacked our mothers' cabinets for yellow, red, blue, orange, and green liquids, and my father's garage for coveted black oil, and poured them back and forth the rest of the day for our experiments.

Lead Pipe, Montezuma, Icicle

I knew when my father came home by the entering screech of the gate. He came and went at all hours. Lanzi was the Heatman, willing to go anywhere in the Bronx and Harlem at any hour. Whenever a boiler broke down and the people needed heat, the Heatman was on his way. He kept a cutoff lead pipe under the driver's seat of his van. My father told me that in Harlem, guys sat on their stoop and eyeballed him as he pulled up in his van to enter their building at night. "So Daddy, I grab my pipe in one hand and my toolbox in the other and I walk straight at them. I say—you want heat! And they move away." I thought of life as one big fight with thousands of rounds and God ringing the bell. I am Lanzi's kid, and I am always ready to fight.

When the gate screeched, my mother Rachel put a light on in back of the house, stretched her spine from sleeping on the couch, put a foot into each slipper and shuffled over the blue rug and the kitchen linoleum to the stove to put on a pot of coffee before he even yelled. She reheated the steak and onions in the frying pan or began to cook no matter what time it was. She held a Tareyton cigarette with her teeth and bent down pointing it into the ring of blue gas that threaded the burner's cold metal holes. The cigarette lit unevenly and made a lot of smoke. She drew a fist to her yawning mouth. Penny hid under the back of the stairs. I stared at the moon. The teaspoons were in position.

To this day, I hate the sound of slippers across linoleum, it reeks to me of subjugation, and I beg whatever woman I am living with, please, lift your feet.

My mother always told me, "Go outside and get some air." In the winter, giant icicles hung off the garage. Lanzi stared at icicles. He reached up and broke off a big one, and turned it in his fingers. The heat of his hands melted the shape. He turned and turned it, sharpening the tip.

"You can kill a man by sticking this through his temple," he told me.

"What's a temple?"

He demonstrated by lifting the icicle to the side of his head, just behind the eye socket. "You push it in right here and it spikes the brain."

I was curious about death. The *Daily News* was on the table every day, the words *RAPED* and *SLAIN*, in bold-type headlines. I pointed to the words and asked my father what they meant.

"Daddy, don't worry 'bout that. This one guy here killed this other guy by bashing him in the neck and knocking his Adam's apple in. It has nothin' to do with you."

"What's an Adam's apple?"

"This thing here in your neck."

"Why do you die if it gets knocked in?"

"Hah?"

"If you get killed, do they write *slain* instead of *died* on your gravestone?"

"No, they just put *died*. What are you thinkin' about?"

"You're telling me newspapers are more specific than gravestones?"

"Hah?"

Lanzi sang around the house. I sat at the upright piano in our living room and pecked on the keyboard. I opened the piano bench full of odd scraps of sheet music. I loved opening up the secret compartment of the bench and decoding this language of music onto my fingers. I pulled the music sheets out wildly. I looked through the books. I translated the notes into letters. I drew with crayons the letters on the ivory keys. I drew the letters on my fingers, so I knew which fingers were supposed to hit what keys. I had them all color-coded; the *A* was blue, the *G* was orange. I translated the melody to the "Marines' Hymn" one note at a time from a songbook, notes to letters to keys. I pressed piano keys down with determination, and stretched to reach the foot pedal to reverberate the sound.

> *From the Halls of Montezuma, to the shores of Tripoli,*
> *we will fight our country's battles in the air, on land and sea.*
> *First to fight for right and freedom and to keep our honor clean;*
> *we are proud to claim the title of United States Marines.*

I even said my prayers to this tune. *Our Father who art in Heh-eh-ven, hallowed be thy name. Thy kingdom come—Thy will be done, on earth as it is in Heaven.* At seven, to make Holy Communion, I memorized the words for how to go to confession: "Bless me father for I have sinned," I chanted and marched around the house, "Bless me father for I have sinned, bless me father for I have sinned." Being Catholic meant I had a guardian angel and a legion of saints who witnessed everything I did and thought. Saints were specialists, like doctors, you called on a certain saint who specialized in the kind of problem you had. I felt patrolled by saints and angels. Thinking something bad was as bad as actually doing it. I learned to say "no" to my thoughts. When I stood in the confessional I imagined being alone with my sins, horizontally, in a coffin. When the lid was closed, it was just you and your sins.

Hand to Hand

"This is my Jap flag, Daddy. You keep it. I want you to have it."
　　　Lanzi held the manila envelope. He unwound the string in a figure-eight pattern around two dime-sized circles, put his hand in gently, and slid out the flag wrapped in Saran Wrap. He unfolded it on the maple table. The flag had a big red circle in the center of it, and Japanese characters written in black brushstrokes all around the sides.
　　　"This here tells the whole story of the guy's family. They were naval engineers. Here's his name."

I read, "Toshiharu Kotani. Who is he, Pop?"

"Hah? Your sister brought the flag to one of her professors at whaddycall Queens College to get translated. That's what these are here." He pointed at a lined yellow sheet of paper with English words next to Japanese characters. "Maybe one day you can get the translation checked out. Figure it all out. You're one smart cookie Daddy."

I read the words out loud that were big, down the side of the flag: "Pleasure. Today. Emperor. Heaven. Earth."

"Daddy the way them Japs believed, to die in battle was the best your soul could do. They had that right. The best your soul could do. Kamikazes were smart. *Kamikaze* means Divine Wind. And believe me, when one hits, the divine wind blows right through you."

He pulled out a certificate from the U.S. Marines, dated August 1945: *Private First Class Joseph Lanzillotto captured and is authorized to keep: one Jap flag, one bayonet, one sword.*

"To get it, did you have to climb a flagpole?" I pictured him shimmy up the tallest pole, wave to the other Marines, tear the flag off, and slide down.

My father laughed in one big exhale. He didn't laugh at me. He laughed at life. "Hmmmph. Climb a flagpole. Yeah, I climbed a flagpole."

"Why is it all ripped? What are the brown stains? What do all the words mean?"

"Schoolin', schoolin', civilian life schoolin'. Flagpoles are figments of civilian imaginations. A Jap kept his flag right here." He patted his chest. "He was a pipsqueak. But he was an officer."

That Halloween, when I was eight, I wore Lanzi's Marine uniform and medals. I wanted to be him.

"You're smart enough to be an officer," he told me.

I came home with two huge bags of candy from the neighbors. My parents dumped them in big silver bowls and inspected each piece for razor blades and puncture marks. I looked down at my chest. Two medals were missing from the uniform, they'd fallen off. I looked up at my father. "Pop, I'm so sorry," but he just laughed and shook his head. I hadn't gone far trick-or-treating. "I'll take a walk," he said, and he went out looking down at the sidewalk. When he came home, all he said was, "Somebody must have picked them up."

The Return of the Lasagna

CarKey telephoned and said, "I'm coming home." I felt his voice buzz in the palms of my hands on the aluminum stripping around the counter,

"I'm coming home." Mom ran down the block to Frank & Joe's and yelled, "Place the order! He's coming home!"

It was time again to make the lasagna. I grated *Parmigiano Reggiano* until my knuckles bled. I rubbed the hunk of cheese up and down the tall aluminum pyramid grater. I kept looking up and asking my mother, "Is this enough?" over the fluffy mound of cheese grated like soft snow. My mother eyed the hunk I had left in my hand and said, "a little more." Even when my knuckles were pricked with blood from the grater, and the cheese was down to the rind, she eyed the rind and saw more cheese to grate. Next I got my glitter out. We didn't have any glue, so Mom showed me how to make glue paste with flour and water. I rubbed the paste into the shape of a big star and the words "Welcome Home" on a posterboard, poured red glitter on the lettering, and blue glitter on the star. I could never draw a star straight. One leg was always skinny and *shangaith*. Mom hung the sign in her bedroom window. I ran down the stoop and looked up at the sign in the window. It would be the first thing CarKey saw when he walked up the stoop. The *antipast'* took me two hours to arrange. Mom gave me the giant round silver platter and ten pounds of cold cuts. I rolled each slice of Swiss cheese and arranged them one next to the other in a fanning-out pattern. I kept them in place with my left hand so they wouldn't unravel, while I rolled Genoa salami with my right. I placed the reds in the meat next to the pale yellow. Then pink ham, and *capicola,* and olive loaf. I had to roll them tight to fit the perimeter of the circle of the platter. I alternated the colors, four areas of red, pale yellow, and the varied pinks, tight in formation. Roast beef was juicy and harder to roll tight. I imagined I was decorating an ancient Egyptian sun disc. In the middle of the platter, I put square chunks of provolone with yellow, blue, red, and green toothpicks, a mound of black olives, green olives stuffed with red pimento, shiny red roasted peppers with hunks of garlic, marinated artichoke hearts. Then I put a second layer of the meats and cheese. The provolone smelled so sharp and the red peppers so sweet.

At JFK airport the Marines walked down the ramp one after the other. I looked at every soldier to see if it was CarKey. After many soldiers who weren't him, there he was, walking toward us, quiet, skinny, with a shaved head, carrying a duffel bag. Everything turned bright. My family hugged one another. Everyone around me hugged a soldier. The whole airport seemed to be hugging. For the first time in my life I felt the peace of prayers answered and dreams come true. A balm of gratitude like a warm blanket covered us all. We piled into Dad's green station wagon and drove home where we all sat around the oval maple table once again. Enza, CarKey, Mom, Dad, Rosemarie, Ant'ny, me, and Penny underneath. This is the day Mom prayed two years for. Champagne came out. Enza drank champagne and slid off the chair and under the table. My mother carried the lasagna to the maple table. The lasagna took center stage. Rosemarie cleared a spot in the center of the table and put down hotplates. My mother heaved the great pan down and looked back with accomplishment at the nicely browned edges of the curled pasta. Eating the lasagna was a ceremony to celebrate men; the birth of Christ, the return home of CarKey from Vietnam, big things like that. I refused to eat it. My mother leaned over the table to divvy it up. She cut the lasagna into heaping squares big as city blocks. Her spatula carefully craned it toward me. She plopped a whole city block onto my plate. The lasagna was the only food to not share a plate with anything else. There was so much in there all at once. Layer after layer. Stratification of *mozzarell'*, grating cheese, pasta, *chop meat*, garlic, parsley, basil, *ricott'*. I refused to get my mouth around it. The inside squeezed out like lava. I put pieces in my hand and held my hand under the table. Penny's warm slow licks took the lasagna down to the palm of my hand, and between my fingers. The adults loved it. The black lasagna pan emitted a force field around it pulling them to the table. They made out with it. They let it slide down their open throats. They breathed it in and hummed their bliss in its lusciousness, making sounds around the table. Nobody fought. Nobody ever fought during the lasagna. The long tongues of pasta sedated them after only a few mouthfuls. CarKey went off in the backyard and didn't eat any.

When CarKey unpacked, he gave me three T-shirts, one with the Marine insignia in blue, one in red, and one of Alaska where he stopped for R&R. I pulled the blue Marine shirt over my head and didn't take it off until it was full of holes and I looked like I'd been through the war, and my mother said it was ready to be a rag. When a T-shirt became a rag it was some sort of domestic blessing. My mother said the cotton was soft as skin, just right to polish the maple furniture. The Marine insignia was big across my chest; a globe with an anchor through it like an arrow through a heart. Those first few weeks he was home, CarKey and I wrestled until I couldn't breathe. His arm around my throat felt big as a tree limb, and as unmovable. Did he know how strong the war made him? On his knees, he was about my height. He boxed me. I needed brass knuckles like Ant'ny showed me, but I had none. I ran to the freezer and pulled out a can of frozen solid orange juice. I socked CarKey in the jaw. His mouth bled. There he was, on his knees on the sea-blue rug, shaved head and muscles, holding his jaw.

CarKey got a job building the Twin Towers. He sat with my father at the maple table and talked about the Twin Towers being built. It was 1970. I sat underneath the table with Penny, breathing into her fur, in the safety of our maple cave, and listened to every word the men said.

"Count 'em, for every foot of aluminum, Hoodycallit gets a nickel."

I pictured CarKey climbing to work every morning up the outside of the building up to the seventieth floor. I thought how tired he must be, just by the time he got to work.

"Hoodycall won the contract bid."

"Who got the air-conditioning contract?"

"Who got the plate glass contract?"

"His pockets are jingling."

My father talked of people "lining their pockets," and of a mafia hit over a fight about a contract and a union. The dead guy's corpse was laid in the foundation of one of the towers. The corpse was somebody big, and whoever dumped him there knew they'd never in a million years exhume that body under the hundreds of thousands of tons of concrete and steel. I imagined all the floors of the towers stacked on top of one guy's body. I grew up thinking of the Twin Towers as a huge grave marker, like the pyramids are gravestones to kings, the Twin Towers were gravestones to this one racketeer whose name I was too young to remember.

Street

My mother gave me the go-ahead to play in the street. Her oldest child was safe, so she could afford for her baby to begin to take risks. I was seven. From the top of my stoop I watched as the two strongest stickball players on the block faced off for *The Choose*. This was the last *Choose* on Saint Raymonds Avenue that would begin without me. The stickball bat was tossed up into the air. Blaze took a step forward, and snatched the bat on its descent with one hand. I held onto the cool white wrought iron handrail and made my way down our eleven sparkling steps. The Sullivan boy clamped his right fist above Blaze's and their fists climbed one on top of the other toward the top of the stickball bat. Blaze scissored his two forefingers flat over Sully's fist so his last grab didn't quite reach the top. Blaze's fist triumphed, his thumb topped off the stickball bat. He tightened his grip knuckle-white around the bat, while Sully took a step back and landed three hard kicks at the midsection of the bat in a fierce attempt to knock it out of Blaze's hands. Blaze's grip prevailed. The stickball bat absorbed the shock of the black Converse sneaker-clad foot, the bat swung in a high arc three times. Blaze grabbed the middle of the stickball bat and pushed it diagonally up into the air like a spear. He proclaimed his advantage of picking first and third out of the pack of boys. With his chin Blaze pointed at the heavy kid whose bottom lip hung open slightly drooling and whose swing could launch a Spaldeen through third-story windows. Blaze summoned him, and he stepped forward and stood behind and slightly to the side of him. Sully spun his loss of *The Choose* to his advantage, "Alright man! We got first ups!" He winked and pushed his jaw up at a boy who tightened his fist affirmatively and ran behind and to the side of him. I took three steps down. I held onto the strong white railing. I had the strongest father on the block. These guys would never *fhuck* with me. I jumped up on the railing and slid down to the sidewalk. I knew this game. I was ready to play. I knew the players. I'd practiced Blaze's moves in my body. I knew it would be his call ultimately whether to accept a girl into the game or not. I never saw any other girl play out there in the middle of the street. I was determined to play stickball. No boy would stop me. I took a deep breath in. I was Lanzi's kid. Who would *fhuck* with me? I had two brothers that were older and bigger than these boys put together. I marched over the two cement squares of the sidewalk, stepped off the curb, slid my finger along the chrome bumper of a parked car, and strode onto the black asphalt toward the pack of boys who stood, hands on hips, waiting to be chosen. I stood next to the pack.

"You in?" Blaze called me out. Up close he had Dean Martin good looks and one dimple dug deep into his cheek.

"Yeah I'm in."

"Good, that evens up the sides."

There were some grumbles. I heard the word *girl* moaned, and "oh man." One boy stomped his foot on the asphalt in protest. *The Choose* continued. As the girl, I automatically ranked last. Blaze took me on his team.

Here I was, in the middle of the street at last, that's all that mattered. I bent my head back. The sky was huge up there. I looked as high as I could. A bird coasted way up high, then flapped its wings across the sky. When it was my turn up at bat, I took a few swings at the air. My swing was strong and level. I saw the ball connect with the bat in my mind, I heard the kiss of wood on rubber. The pressure was on. I had to connect. The pitch came in. I watched it go by. I took another practice swing. The pitch came in. I swung. I hit the Spaldeen solidly, dropped the bat, and ran toward first. The Spaldeen took off up the street, ricocheted off a car, then a hand, and rolled down the block until it settled under a car. The bat struck the asphalt three then four times, then rolled like a giant drummer's stick. I touched the chrome car handle with my hand, and ran to the second base sewer cap, where I stood with my hands on my knees, ready for the next up to bring me home. My mother stood tall on our stoop, wringing her hands in a dishtowel. I felt free and powerful when I saw my pinky ball zoom off in its own direction, and disappear on its own. The boys on my team laughed at the other team, because a girl made it to second.

We played until the street lights flashed on. That was our cue. We all ran back to our stoops, took the steps two at a time, hoisted our bodies up the railings and into our houses. I'd done the work of a tomboy. I'd sent the Spaldeen on its way all over the block. I pushed open our front door, then the hall door. I made my way through the dark foyer, through the living room, and into the kitchen to get a drink of water. Once I stepped into our house I felt like I was in quicksand. The force pulled me down. My father sat in a haze of cigarette smoke under the wagon wheel chandelier at the maple table, in his white thermal shirt, boxer shorts, black-rimmed eyeglasses, his elbow on the table, cigarette pointed up at the ceiling, giving off smoke. A clear blue light came in from the window and saturated the room in a royal blue glow. Lanzi was in a deep study of his horse-racing sheets. My mother made noise in the sink, the glasses and pots clanked. Those were the loudest sounds I heard her make in the house as if the pots and pans spoke up for her. The television newscaster spoke of Vietnam, Muhammad Ali, and Watergate. My father had the news on constantly. The evening light streamed in from her window above the sink. I bounced my pinky ball against the refrigerator and hopped up on the counter to sit. I stuck my mouth under her stream of water at the sink and she turned it from hot to cold.

"You're all sweaty." She wiped my neck with a dishtowel. "Go wash your face. You'll feel better."

I jumped off my perch on the countertop.

"Go wash your hands. They're filthy."

I bounced my pinky on the floor and it came right back into my hand.

"Why are you coughing?"

I sat on the floor where Penny lay, and she took my pinky in her mouth and struck out a paw to my chest. All I wanted was to get back in the middle of the street where only the sky was above me. Tomorrow, I thought.

"I saw you out there," my mother said as if I had done something wrong. "You think you're made of rubber."

It was time to make my own stickball bat. I took one of my mother's old mop sticks and broke off the metal end that held the rags she used to clean the floors. I marched down the spiral staircase to the basement. Lanzi wrote WATCH YOUR HEAD in thick black letters on the underside of the stairs overhead that curved down to the basement. I slapped the sign as I walked under it.

To make a stickball bat, you had to know where your father kept his electrical tape. For me that was easy. Lanzi was methodical. He could locate the exact tool he needed and not just the tool but the most obscure piece of hardware in the exact size that someone needed at a moment's notice. In my father's basement workshop, order was always paramount. I found his electrical tape. I spiraled the black tape around one end of the broomstick, this was my grip. I gave it a good twelve inches so I could choke up on the bat. Tomorrow I would rub the edges smooth against the concrete. With my own stickball bat, I was ready to face the world.

How to Catch a Flyball in Oncoming Traffic

I grew up playing in traffic. Under the arcs of balls, balls hit high—'til they became small and black in the sky. The ball's going back and all the while you have your inner ear on the car at the intersection. You don't miss the ball. You don't get hit by the car. With a car coming at you, you face the open sky. You never miss a pop fly because a ball is coming at you. You listen. You turn your ear to the horizon. The ball is in the air. Your feet are moving beneath you. Your ear tracks the speed the car is coming at you. Your eye you keep on the ball. You know a car is coming without needing to look. You don't want to stop the car, just like you don't want the car to stop the play. With your throwing arm you flag the car around you. You figure which side of the street the ball is favoring in the wind. You wave the car to the other side of you. You may temporarily halt the car 'til the ball is square in your hands. The car inches forward 'til the ball is in your hands, then the car proceeds. The car is your audience rushing to find you. The car came all this way, down this particular street, around several corners, jumped the exit ramp, to back up 'round the corner to see you make this play. The car in the middle of the play is part of the play. It's all in the timing.

The Names of Horses

I agreed to be the flower girl at CarKey and Enza's wedding, with one caveat; I wasn't going to wear a dress. Enza compromised and let me wear culottes in her bridal party instead of a gown. She wanted me to hold hands with the ring bearer to walk down the aisle, but that's where I drew the line. My father and CarKey worked hard fixing the upstairs apartment for them. I got to paint the baseboard moldings, pick up nails, and watch my father and CarKey build walls and hang drop ceilings. We got full of sawdust and plaster and I learned the words: *router, miter box, wood plane.* Curled wood shavings, plasterboard dust, and cigarettes made me wheeze, but felt like home.

Penny's belly was big and hung low to the ground. "Bow raped her," my mother said, "she's pregnant." Penny was nowhere to be found. It was my father's worker, Willy, who said, "They go somewhere they never been before, somewhere special when they're ready to give birth and when they're ready to die."

My mother looked around the house, and found Penny in her bedroom up on the blue chair that folded out into the bed where I used to sleep. Penny wasn't allowed there, and my mother chased her away. She went back to her dark cave in the hallway off the kitchen. Her whole body bucked as if her hips were on a hinge. One by one, each puppy covered in a slimy juice slid out of her. Penny licked each one of them clean as they fumbled around and blindly sucked the air. Six puppies, one slimy mass jockeyed into position each on one of Penny's six teats. After three days, Penny had no more life to give suck to, she bit at their necks to pull their mouths off her teats. Willy brought in an empty cardboard box from the garage and settled the puppies underneath Mom's clothesline window. The puppies' collective mission became to climb over one another to stretch for the top of the box, to try to get back to their mother. Penny joined her shadow on the floor and never got up. My mother got baby bottles and made a feeding schedule. I came in from playing to feed the puppies five times a day. Puppy smell was my favorite smell in the world.

My second favorite was the smell of rain on our front aluminum fence. I pressed my nose on the crossbar and my lips around the chain links. Cold metal in the rain, smelled like blood. Rainwater gushed along the curb to the corner sewer. I watched the sky through the rings of rainbows in the puddles on the street. Birds soared through those puddles. I heard Lanzi's van rumbling from a few blocks away as he came down Rowland, past Frisby, past Glebe, and cheated a bit on Saint Raymonds, by driving the wrong way on the one way to get into our driveway. Lanzi was a juggernaut. Water tails spit up behind the tires. He sped up the lip of the driveway and threw the van into park. The van lurched forward. He got out of the van and left his driver's door open. The front gate he kicked in the wire gut like a dog. The gate swung open, scraping an arc in the sidewalk, a white scar that recorded my father's entrance. The screech of the gate was louder than the squeal of her clothesline. That cry of friction jerked the wide-eyed squirrels into trapeze feats, securing them out of sight, branches trembling in their wake.

Lanzi gunned the van up the yard and threw it into park just beneath her clothesline window.

"Coffee," he hollered up at her. "Coffee!" He yelled with long open vowels, almost singing. My father called my mother, Coffee. I knew this wasn't her name.

"Coffee!"

This time she ignores him. This time there is none, and she knows he knows there is no more. This morning he wouldn't give her a nickel, "No, not fi-cents," he said on his way out to work, afraid she'd go to Frank & Joe's, where Frank or Joe or even Pete might squeeze her hand as she slid the five-pound bag over the counter to be ground, and slip her a thin slice of salami to tuck inside her cheek to chew on the walk home. "It don't make sense," Lanzi said, "if they went giving salami out to everybody they'd be broke in no time."

I wheeze all the time and Dr. Ricciardi says I'm allergic to puppies. Adults are dumb. He doesn't say cigarettes or fighting has to go, just the puppies. The puppies are my only peace. The puppies and my Spaldeen.

My father wants to give them all away. The men are coming over to take a look. One man will take two. The other men at least will take a look. There is no coffee in the house. My mother is leaning out the window, reeling his clothes in just ahead of the rain. The clothesline squeals as she reels it. Sock by sock she unpinches and drops into the brown plastic basket on the kitchen table and the basket fills.

I am feeding Blacky. He pushes the nipple of the baby bottle out with his tongue and looks for her with his mouth he looks, but days ago she slinked away, curled up in the light coming in through the screen door, curled up like days do and dust—beneath the radiator Penny laid down in that diamond cut-out of sun there patched on the floor. She had six pups two weeks ago. Every day since she's moved less and less. Now only parts of her move. Her tail, for instance, slithers out of the diamond onto the cool dark floor, and her fur—when the hall door is opened, her fur lifts with the wind, and her eyes, as I feed the puppies she is too weak to feed, her eyes follow my hand to their mouths, then fall away. With the day the sunlight stretches across the floor and she, toward the back of the staircase. The stairs there lead nowhere, spiral up into the ceiling. My father had that way closed off years ago. I toss circles of meat at her, things she used to jump for. I touch salami to her tongue and it drops. I walk away. I come back. It still lies there. The sun has climbed the underside of the stairs.

My father wants to give them all away before they're named, but each I've named already I've whispered their markings into their little twitching ears: Blacky, Spotty, Whitey, Rusty, Patches, Shep. Blacky's all black like his mother black with a white streak up the belly to the neck, and a white tip on the tail as if the tail had been dipped in paint. The others look like Bow.

"Coffee!"

She yanks the rope. The puppies all huddle in their box. She yanks the rope and the basket fills. There is no coffee in the house. His shorts by the crotch she rips off the line.

The houses are almost touching, the alleyways are thin and filled with argument. Laundry crisscrosses the backyards from second and third story windows. My mother's clothesline is the grandest on the block, spanning our cement yard on a diagonal, from her second-story window out over my basketball court way out to the pipe my father rigged atop the roof of his garage. At night my mother's clothesline is a thick white vein the moonlight rides until morning. Then the rope begins its daily rounds again from window pulley to garage pulley, her world to his world. All the sun and all the wind work with my mother's rope to help her purify the clothes. My mother has a rope to the sun.

She yanks the rope. She yanks the rope. The knot catches the groove of the pulley at the far end over his garage. She pushes the rope out the other way. She yanks the sun. His shirts come down together. She yanks the rain. The green shoulders clamped to the line, march in the air, their arms swinging, falling, swinging toward her, elbows bending. And the basket fills.

"Coffee!"

My mother doesn't flinch as she unpinches a clothespin. "You know there ain't none." She yanks. "There's no milk, there's no sugar. If you want, give me money. I'll go to Frank & Joe's. You know that."

The garage door he hoists up like a great white sail. Black gaping holes, the clean-cut lips of so many copper pipes stacked into pyramids stare out of the garage, taking aim at him from head to foot. I see them shoot him full of clean holes so the light comes right through his body. He whistles the "Marines' Hymn," and walks through the holes of light.

If he wanted to keep them he would have named them all by now. He would have given them the names of horses, taken a binder down from one of his two shelves lining the kitchen-long wall, spread the racing forms out over the kitchen counter and let each paw drop onto a name.

"You name what you keep. You keep what you name."

When he wants to scare me, my father messes his hair, loosens his dentures so they knock up and down, and runs at me with a gargled yell, "I'm gonna get you." I run for my life. My father makes a terrifying monster, he can be so scary. I never know when he switches back and forth from being scary or just playing. He puts coins over his eyelids and orange skins over his teeth. He loves to scare me. He thinks it's funny. I stay close to him. From close up, it's easier to see his eyes and tell where he is. Sometimes he's here. Sometimes he's off fighting the Japs in his mind. I'll cough or yell to snap him back to our card game. When I go to sleep, I am scared of the boogeyman, and ask my mother to check the closets. Nights, I fly. Soupy Sales is flying, chasing me. I fly through the living room over the blue rug, through the hallway with the giant mirror, past my brothers' room, into the kitchen, down the spiral stairs into the black darkness of the basement, and I fall into the abyss and back into bed. I clutch the sides of the mattress as I fall endlessly.

"Coffee!"

"I have a name."

"Hey You!"

"I have a name!" the words spit out of her defiantly. Willy is with him. Somehow this protects her. "I have a name!" she says again. And I hear a trumpet call.

"Hey Meatball!" he calls up at her, laughing out his mouth.

She yanks the rope. The sun and rain come down together. "I have a name!" Her words hang in the air, damp, with pinched corners. The drums are not far off now, and the men lifting their knees in unison.

Willyboy stands half in the garage and half out, the rain darkening his shirt in spots. "Hiya Mrs. Lancilotta," he calls up, taking care with each soft sound. And before he can even finish, she says, "Willy! Call me anything but that!"

"Okay Miss Ray," he says, widening his eyes and wrapping his lips around his teeth to hold back from smiling. My father is walking around the back into the house. There are two gates and three doors my father has to pass through to get into my mother's kitchen, our fort. The first door is a screen door, never locked. The second door leads into the small foyer where Penny lies. The third door has a diamond-shaped window through which we can see his head a split second before he plows into the kitchen, uproots the *Daily News* out of his back pocket, and tosses it at the face of the table. Then he begins to shed. One boot scores the heat pipe, the other the wall. My mother scratches her head, concentrating on where things land so she can find them later when he says he doesn't know where anything is, and where'd she hide them? He tracks to the bathroom in damp socks, pressing water out with each step. I follow him close behind. I watch his every maneuver. I'm careful not to get in his way. Everyone is in place: the puppies in their box, Mommy at the kitchen sink, Daddy at the bathroom sink, Penny in her shadow. He leaves the bathroom door open. I watch. He dunks two fingers in the can of grease solvent. His hands chew it, blackening the sink. Watching my father wash his hands after he came home from work was frightening. Hand–cups full of hot water splash his face, head, up his nose, neck, ears, gargling all over the mirror and walls. It sounds like a gorilla is drowning in the bathroom. The grease never comes off his hands. The black never comes all off. There are roadways in my Daddy's hands. A whole map. He points to the markings on his hands. He shows me his open palm.

"I know the Bronx like the palm of my hand."

I study the black lines etched in the palms of his hands.

"Never get that grease off," he tells me, "they don't make a soap that can take the grease outta these here hands. This is the history of New York. We built this city, each brick, each block of ice, each coal, every frame of sidewalk."

He measures my height against the kitchen doorjamb and digs a line with the point of his BIC pen, into the pine. He goes over it and over it, 'til the blue ink fills the grooves he made.

When my father sings, it is a refusal to talk. He sings loud and ignores the rest of us. He laughs as he sings. He towels his whole head furiously and finger combs his hair through with Vaseline hair tonic, getting wet at the crotch from leaning against the sink. He walks back into the kitchen with the big white towel around his neck like a muscular peasant shouldering a dead lamb. He taps a new pack of Lucky Strikes on his wrist twice fast, ripcords the red cellophane band with his teeth, spits it out onto the floor, and pulls a cigarette out with his teeth. My mother's eyes follow the red cellophane band as it floats to the floor. "I get any calls!" There is little question in my father's voice.

"No, I don't think so." There is a tentativeness in her tone of voice. This provokes him.

"What do you mean you don't think so! It's yes or it's no!"

"What am I your secretary?"

Lanzi laughs. That was never a good sign. It meant he was running out of words. Willyboy comes in, and stands in the doorframe, half in the kitchen, half out, ducking a little to fit under it. Willy's hands are in his pockets. My father says that's a habit from years of Willy thieving. My father walks past Penny and steps down to the basement, ducking his head as the stairs spiral down.

"Miss Ray, would you be so kind as to put away my earnings this week?"

"I'll tell you what, Willy," my mother says, "I'll bless your money." She takes his dollars to her Bible. She layers the bills in between the pages of the big colorful pictures of Moses walking through the Red Sea bed. "Now your money's blessed," she says to him with conviction, "now it has to go to your wife and kids." My mother is always blessing things, even my forehead she touches with the sign of the cross when I leave the house.

Willy nods. "That's just where it's going Miss Ray, that's just where it's going." My father stomps back up the stairs. The phone rings. I run to it, climbing on the step stool to reach it. The voice asks for Joe. I cover the mouthpiece as he has trained me to do since the business is run out of the kitchen, and I whisper-shout, "Daddy, are you home?" The voice on the phone laughs. My father takes the phone, exhaling a gruff laugh.

"Sure," he says into the phone, "right six," he says, "come on over for coffee. Right. I'm here. Right. Sure bring hoodycall." He hangs up and takes a sandwich of folded money out of his front pocket. He opens up a sweaty twenty, and hands it out toward Willy, the bill's edge woven around his thick, middle black-etched finger. This bill he doesn't fold into a tight little square hidden in his palm the way he hands me money, no, all flat open and showy. "Ga' head, Shine, go on down the corner and bring back five cups of coffee and buy yourself an egg cream."

My father doesn't come home from work until late. I go to bed early so I can get up again when he comes home and hang out with him. After dinner, Lanzi and I play poker with Gold Medal chips. He peels the skin off an orange or an apple in one shot, one long curly helix strip. He smashes a walnut with his open palm coming down on the table. He cracks a walnut between his knuckles, by squeezing the knuckles of his forefinger and middle finger together. I try to do what he does. Impossible. I smash my hand down on a walnut, but just hurt my hand. A walnut feels hard as a tree. Lanzi helps me by squeezing starter cracks in some walnuts so I can smash them open and build my confidence. With practice I crack a few, learning to slam the meat and bones of my hand down through the walnut shell. I slam my hand hard, as if I'm going to chop the maple table in half.

Willy takes the twenty, walks out the back door and ducks through a hole in the fence to go get the men coffees. My mother bends down to pick my father's clothes up off the floor. She tosses them down the basement steps like unwanted fish back into the sea. She takes the brown basket full of dry clean clothes and tosses it down the basement steps. My father walks outside whistling the same tune he was singing, "Bless Them All." My father's whistling has a whole dictionary of meanings. This particular whistle means my mother doesn't exist and should stay out of his way. He bunks into her as he exits, as if she's a piece of furniture he has to walk around. She leans against the great white refrigerator and slides to the floor covering her eyes with her hands. I pull at her arm to get up. She walks directly to his shelves as if something is guiding her. His shelves are the only place in the kitchen that's off limits to the rest of us. His shelves of binders. She grabs at the binders and one falls open to the floor. His binders are full of horse-racing statistics. His system. His hours and hours of thoughts and strategies. His gambling with our lives. His "one day my horse is gonna come in" promises. Hours of his handwritten notes and scrawls surround the names of horses. Some of the names are crossed out. Other names are heavily underlined. There are words written thick in the margins: SCRATCHED. JOCKEY CHANGE. SLOPPY AT THE START. She grabs at them, her hands do the thinking, her hand grabs a bundle of a hundred tickets held together by a rubber band. I know it's a hundred. I help count them at night. Money. It is all money spent, she thinks as she grabs a fistful of pages. She goes to her window. She does what she knows how to do. She grabs the wooden clothespins. She snaps a page onto the clothesline. She pushes the rope. She rips more and more pages, clothespinning horse race sheets to the rope, pushing them out over the yard into the soft rain.

"Here," she shouts, "here's where all the money goes. This is what he does. This is where he disappears. This is where he goes. This is where all the money goes." She pushes the rope. My father looks up at her and laughs. Then all the men there laugh. She shouts the names of horses down onto them, as she pushes his pages out over their heads, "Stage Door Johnny! Forward Pass! Dancer's Image! How much did that one pay?" She pushes the rope. "Captain's Kid. Gleaming Sword. Verbatim. Top Knight. Here's the milk." She pushes the rope. The sun and rain come down together. "Majestic Prince! Shams! Ocean Roar. Here's the sugar. Here's all the coffee you want! Hey you! Here! You want coffee!" She grabs a pack of ticket stubs and flings them out all over the men standing in the yard. The stubs flutter and whirl down onto the wet cement. There is a different color for each race each day of the week. Stubs from Belmont. Stubs from Aqueduct. Stubs from the OTB. My father has years of stubs. My father always says never throw away a racing stub.

He looks up at her, "That's some stunt," he murmurs under his breath, "snake. Cow. Bitch." He laughs. Then all the men there laugh. And the troops seem not far behind.

My mother closes and latches her window then the shutters, then slides down the wall to her shadow on the floor. She swallows her tears in the back of her head as if the tears do not exist if they do not exist. But I know mountains from ground shells and time. I want her to let it out. I lift Blacky to her neck and he licks. She passes her eyes over Penny's wilted belly, then her hand. She calls Dr. Ricciardi. While she's on the phone with him, her hand passes over Penny's belly and stops quietly over one spot. She bows her head. "I'll be damned," she says into the phone, "there must be a seventh still in there." She instructs me to run down the corner to the drug store on Zerega and Saint Raymonds to buy CN, the disinfectant. "Go now," she instructs, "and get the money off your father."

I hear Blacky yelping. I tilt the box. I reach down through all that softness. Blacky is nowhere in the box. I follow the sound of his yelp. I race to the hall. Blacky is in Penny's mouth. The radiator is silent where she lay. Penny is pressing Blacky's head against the iron bars. I clap at her 'til she drops him.

"Mom! Penny is slamming Blacky into the radiator!"

"Keep the puppies in their box."

I kneel by Penny and shout, "Open your eyes!" But if salami didn't move her, I thought, fagetaboutit, words ain't gonna do what salami can't.

I run down the block past Bow. Bow runs out at me and gets twisted up in the air and chokes. He barks through his choking like he's underwater. At night Bow is kept in his backyard free.

"Seven fences away from Penny, seven fences he jumped to get to her. He raped her twice," my mother says. "In the puppies you can see his markings clearly."

I don't need money, the guy down the corner store knows who my father is. I pull the murky brown bottle with the red letters *CN* off the shelf and the clerk nods at me and tries to hand me a paper bag, but I have the bottle by its neck and am out the door running back up the block, past Bow still barking; you can hear his vicious baritone for blocks. My father is carrying a big black piece of wood out of the house wrapped in my mother's new plaid comforter. Black wood like a cut-out of Penny. I shout her name. Her pink wood tongue is out the side of her black wood lips.

"One. You can keep," my father yells, and the back doors of the green work van slam shut.

This unborn pup, still inside her, made Penny die. We fed the puppies Similac in baby bottles. A whole box of puppies soft as dandelion flowers. I'd push my nose into the fur of each of them and just breathe there. They smelled safe to me. Blacky we kept. I'd bury my nose in Blacky's fur. I sat on the kitchen floor and pushed the nipple of the baby bottle in his mouth and let him suck. He smelled safe to me.

My Mom sprinkled *CN* ritualistically everywhere Penny had lain, as if a magnificent power was present in that one bottle of liquid, as if she was blessing the dog's presence, and releasing her at the same time.

I sat on the fourth step of the stoop and cried. My father's sister, Apollonia, walked up. She had a way of just appearing. She walked up the block and made a visitation. She saw me crying and held her two fists out in front of me.

"Pick one."

I was in no mood for games. I slapped her right hand. She opened her right hand. There was a stone.

"Here. You know what this is? *Il Malocchio*. This'll protect you from the evil eye."

Mucus dripped from my nose.

Aunt Apollonia. I knew from my Greek mythology book that her name came from the god Apollo and means rational, ordered, self-disciplined, but she talked circles around all of us. I let her words wash over me, like rain:

"You know the four-three cops don't come round no more. I don't know why. Somebody was tampering. That sneaky Charlotte. I saw her double working at the bank in The Square. You wanna hear a story? You know my wristwatch is at City Hall, with two Brooklyn precincts inscribed on it. What's it doing there? I was going to the cops reunion to see cops I worked with in front of City Hall, there was somebody in plainclothes who resembled a motorcycle cop. That sneaky Charlotte. Beatin' my chances and grabbin' my opportunities. I walk into the diner but they're closed, so I walk in I say, 'You know me. I want a cup of ice. You know me. I used to be the Crossing Guard on the corner.' I say, 'You see that phone booth? You can thank me for that phone booth.' They look at me. Ooooh. I don't think these same people are still here. I don't forget Saint Raymonds, my post. I put a phone booth here I say. I had stock. I wrote to the company that I was the only crossing guard without a callbox or a phone booth. They came down because I had stock. There was a phone booth. That phone booth is there because of me. That is me helping the community over there. Because a' me you have that phone booth. Gimme a cup a ice."

My father drove up in his van and shouted, "Stop botherin' the kid."

"Don't get funny with me," she said, "you're my kid brother."

"Come inside. Come on inside. Come inside."

The chill of the steps went up into my back. I stayed there with my head on my fists.

In the backyard behind the rows of tomato plants, my mother found six holes dug deep, like for planting. Six holes Penny dug to bury her just-born.

"She knew she couldn't take care of them, she knew she was dying," my mother said, as she strung the tomato stalks up into the light with white ribbons in bows tied to the sticks. We watched the globes turn green for weeks and grow to orange, pink, rose, then red, then red, then red red red.

It is the smell of *CN* now not of death that I remember. *CN* was sweet. Awful. Sweet.

Rook to Queen Four

Bobby Fischer and Boris Spassky played out the cold war on the chessboard, and I sat in front of the television set, copying every move they made on my carved wooden chess figures. Chess was played in silence, it was the wrestling of two minds. Rosemarie came in and out of the living room, with her friends Linda and Gene, who stopped to play me in chess. I told him, "Don't let me win. I can beat you on my own." I had a couple of Bobby Fischer's opening move sequences memorized. The rook pawn moved way out front. The bishop pawn. The bishop. The knight. Then the king and rook switched places for protection. The other pieces moved in for the kill as I aimed to triangulate the opponent's king with any combo of my bishop, rook, knight, pawns, and queen. I loved to topple the other guy's pieces and sweep them off the board, back to the velveteen box. I recorded Fischer's moves in my notebook as my parents yelled in the kitchen. I dug the absolute focus and patience of the chess players. I sat there for a week.

Rosemarie let me sit on her lap as she read her college books. She travels all the way to Queens College. Her words are so big, she picks them apart for me. She points to each syllable with her long, clear, polished fingernail, and helps me sound it out. Her electric typewriter is called a Royal. It fills our evenings with the rhythmic buzz of the keys hammering ink onto the paper. Rosemarie has a box of onion-skin paper and tiny sheets of white Ko-Rec-Type, like Band-Aids for misspelled words. Rosemarie has slender fingers that skid masterfully over the keys. When she reaches the end of a line, she hits return and the roller slams back to the beginning of the next line. I love the smell of the typewriter ribbon and the buzz of the machine. Rosemarie's typewriter makes its own rhythm, like my mother's sewing machine, or my father punching the speed bag in the basement, or me bouncing my basketball against the cement. We all make big noises. With Rosemarie I learn that words can appear and disappear on pages of paper, and that strands of words can be perfected.

Burning Rubber and Penmanship

Mrs. Norton, my third-grade teacher, held up a page of a little girl's magnificent penmanship. Mrs. Norton was tall and stout and walked around the room in solid heels striking the shiny floor. She held the paper up high like a flag for the whole class to see the round curvy lettering. The girl died of leukemia. The nuns gathered in our classroom doorway, touching pages of her penmanship, like holy relics. "Perfection," the nuns said, as they slapped silver staplers at the hallway bulletin board with the open palms of their hands, for a shrine to the little girl, with gold waves around her handwritten alphabets. I stood at the shrine and admired the curls of her capital Qs and Rs. Penmanship was Godly. Santa Maria School beatified her. Illuminated penmanship was a sure way of getting into Heaven. I sat at home at the maple table for hours every afternoon practicing with my pencil, tracing the printed dashes of the skeletons of the alphabet. I did love God. I put hours into my lettering. Penmanship was a form of prayer. I did this to the sound of cars crashing. Two blocks away, Rowland and Glebe, was a notorious corner for cars that didn't stop and couldn't get out of each other's way. Cars swerved to a halt and crashed into one another, while I went over my Qs, which were far from illuminated. No matter how hard I tried, I could not make a capital script Q, not the fancy way the nuns wanted. A bulbous callus formed on the top knuckle of my middle finger from squeezing the pencil, a callus that would stay my whole life as a writer. After the police cars and ambulances cleared, I rode my Raleigh Chopper into the intersection. I followed the long overlapping skid marks and tire tracks from the unstoppable cars that burnt rubber on that corner. In those intricate patterns, I slalomed, weaving in and out and around the massive skid marks, a drawing I was sure, was made by some swerving black rubber God.

Trestles and Love

Rosemarie shared her room and single bed with me. I got scared for her if she had to leave the room to go to the bathroom, or get a drink of water in the kitchen, because she'd have to walk through the living room, and my father could come at her with a barrage of curses like a machine gun. The way he said her name it sounded like "Rosary." My mother called him a "Doctor Jekyll and Mr. Hyde." His words shredded Rosemarie. She came back to the room, fell on the bed and cried. I wished I could console her. Most nights we went to sleep to the sounds of our parents yelling and screaming.

One night I opened my eyes and the full moon stared at me through our window. The moon was a skull in the sky. The moon's face bounced off our neighbor's window across the alleyway, to look at me in our room. The moon spoke loud and clear:

"I was like you once. Until my people fought and fought and struck and fought and blew us all up into cold dark ash, smithereens. Stop the fighting before it's too late."

I jumped up. Rosemarie got startled, saying, "Whatsamatta?" in a sleepy voice. I needed to make sure our mother was still alive. The room was full of dead bodies slumping over the door, the chair, and the floor. I squeezed my eyes to adjust to the dark, and I could see the bodies were just piles of my teenage sister's clothes. I hurtled over the clothes and ran for the door. Mom was asleep on the couch. I stood over her and watched her breathe.

"Ma, Ma."

"What?"

"Nothin'."

I brought Johnny Denaro down to the basement to play. I reached up and slapped my father's sign WATCH YOUR HEAD. We were warned as we went down, walking the spiral down into the dark basement. I showed Johnny the white rat my sister kept in a maze for her college psychology experiment. The rat tried to smell her way out. Only by banging her head against a dead-end wall could she make progress and go another way. I showed him the pool table and how to keep score by moving the number line of wooden markers strung up over the table in black and tan wood colors. The portraits Lanzi put up of Indian chiefs in sepia tones in framed glass surrounded the pool table, and the speed bag. My father and my brothers punched in a fast rhythm with their fists and elbows. Lanzi put a wooden crate there for me to stand on and practice my speed bag technique by not looking straight at the bag.

To get into a rhythm, my father taught me, "Look past the bag. Not at it. You can't keep your eye on the bag. It's too fast."

I understood this already. My Spaldeen already taught me that kind of oneness. I could see where the ball was flying and run for that spot. I applied that same principle to punching the speed bag.

I grabbed the handles of the weight set attached to the back wall, and punched outward into the room. I showed Johnny my father's tools and workbench, his calendar with black and red numbers, the pagoda he brought me from a basement. Lanzi worked in basements, and people gave him all kinds of junk. He'd pack his truck and unload his antique finds back at the house. My mother loved when he brought home hurricane lamps, pot belly stoves, milk pails, and the blue-glass telephone pole insulators. Our basement floor was cement painted in ship-deck gray. For some shots around the pool table, you had to shoot around a pillar. I showed him the elaborate system of trestles which supported the tracks for my brothers' motorized toy cars. The smell of engine oil and the sparks of the motors as I held a car upside down in my hand, will always stick with me, and the knowing if you raced 'em too fast around bank turns they'd spin off the tracks and fly into the wall. And trestles. Trestles held the whole thing up.

Me and Johnny Denaro played hitchhiker. He pedaled the exercise bike and I stood to the side with my thumb up. He said, "Hey, where ya' goin'?" And I said, "Gimme a ride, Mac. I'm headin' west." I got on the back of the bike and held him tight. I was in love with him. We were seven. He stood up as he pedaled and I sat on the seat, holding his waist as his hips moved from side to side. I held him as his heart beat fast and he got sweaty. Then we'd switch and I'd be the biker and Johnny would hitchhike. I'd try to move my hips like he could. We went upstairs for a drink of Hawaiian Punch, and I played my record on the Victrola while we sat on the floor, singing our lungs out to the Partridge Family's "I Think I Love You." On his way out, we stood at the top of my stoop. He asked me, "What boy do you like in class?"

"Guess," I said.

He went through all the boys names, to which I replied, "No, no, no, no," until it was down to two names, his and the other John in the class. Since we were born in 1963, a lot of boys were named after John Fitzgerald Kennedy. I told him to keep guessing, but he wouldn't go any further. He had a big smile on as he backed down the stoop.

"There isn't anybody else," he said.

"You're leaving someone out. Think."

"Who?"

"Think."

Peter gave Rosemarie a diamond ring, and she lifted her hand up for everybody to see. My mother, Roe, and I sat in the living room and stuffed hundreds of envelopes for her wedding invitations. Five pieces of paper had to go into each envelope in a certain order. Peter and Roe drew a circle for each table on a piece of oaktag, and penciled in names of where everyone would sit.

"Impossible," my father said, "Hoodycallit can't sit wit' Whaddyacall. You wanna have a war?"

"Andrew!" Peter hollered from across the intersection. He put his hands up to indicate for me to throw him the ball. I threw my Spaldeen up over the street.

He caught it, came onto the sidewalk, and tossed it way up high in the sky for me to catch. "Hey Andrew. Let me just tell your sister I'm here." He ran up the stoop, and called into the hallway to let Rosemarie know he'd wait for her outside, while he played catch with me. Peter called me Andrew. He saw my true nature. Nobody questioned this or minded that he called me by a boy's name. He threw the Spaldeen all the way straight up in the sky. Nobody threw the ball as high as Peter. His reached way back with his throwing arm, almost down to the sidewalk, and catapulted the pinky ball straight up over the sidewalk, over the telephone wires, higher than the maple tree. I watched the ball go up up up, then slowly arc to a descent. I positioned my body beneath the ball and put my two hands up at the last moment to bring the Spaldeen down, back into my chest. I threw it back at him, and he launched it straight up again. We didn't have wide fields, in the Bronx we had sky.

Playing catch with men was like having a conversation. Peter was the most fun. He taught me how to put English on a Spaldeen. He'd steal the pinky ball out of my hands, bounce it a few times and then play his best trick on me. His throwing arm went into a dramatic wind-up as if he was going to throw me a line drive. The arm came down overhand but the ball vanished. I was stupefied. Peter had released the ball behind his back and caught it with his other hand. He taught me boxball baseball, a special game played with three contiguous sidewalk squares. One guy pitches, and the other guy bats by slapping the Spaldeen. When Peter pitched, he pushed his knuckle into the Spaldeen, giving it an errant hop, impossible for me to hit. Peter's last name meant little boy of the mountain, and that is how he played, with a fresh sense of finding adventure in life. I was happy he dated my sister. Rosemarie came down the stoop, her long, light-brown hair washed and combed, her blonde streaks hung to the sides of her face. She was all pretty with mascara and lip gloss for her date with Peter. "See ya' later, Coolie-Pie," she said, and kissed me on the head. The two of them walked down the block holding hands. I bounced it and bounced it and bounced it and bounced it, until the streetlights came on. Then I ran up the stoop and into the house.

Rosemarie bought herself *The Culinary Arts Institute Encyclopedic Cookbook*, in preparation for becoming a wife, and the two of us read recipes in bed at night, before turning off the white milk glass hobnail lamp. I'd reach up and feel along the bumpy glass until I found the push-stick to turn the light off. We giggled to sleep, long after the light was shut. In the morning, her radio would blare on to wake us—with Harry Harrison telling all the girls of New York he is zippering up their dresses. Every morning I heard: "*Zzzzzzzzip.* Thanks Harry. Thanks Harry. Thank you, Harry." The cookbook had a red cover and was bigger than our family Bible, almost a thousand pages, with pictures of fancy looking foods. Every night we read different recipes before we shut our eyes, said our prayers, and went to sleep, but there was one recipe we read over and over. I begged Rosemarie to read it. We laughed until we couldn't breathe. We read it so much that the book began to bend there, at that page. The recipe was for "Headcheese." The name threw us into uncontrollable hysterics. The ingredients were one hog's head, one hog's tongue, salt and pepper, sage, and chili pepper. *Clean and scrape hog's head*, at which Rosemarie and I started screaming. *Wash and trim tongue*. Is this what married life meant you had to do? Married life was full of gross things. What if the tongue began to yell and curse? Then, the direction that we couldn't bear to read without crying laughter, *Cover head and weight it down. Let stand three days.* This sent us over the top. Rosemarie and I thought this was the funniest thing in the world. We'd make "what if" jokes. What if the head talks, what if the head pops out of the jar, how many tongues do you need? Doesn't the head come with a tongue? How do you weight the lid on? Why? You need people to push down on it? Let stand three days? Our mother would never leave meat out for five minutes. She'd swipe your plate out under you if you didn't eat fast enough. Who ate this stuff? What did cheese have to do with it? We didn't realize that our grandmother, and our great grandmothers, had relished the heads and offal of animals. They sucked the marrow out of bones, these people, while we buttered our white bread and got colds easily.

When Rosemarie picked the day of her wedding I got white oak tag, cut out a giant bell, and drew 365 polygons the size of my thumbnail in different colors. This was my "countdown to the wedding" calendar present for her. I carefully drew a number from 1 to 365 in each of the polygons. I hung it over our bed. I didn't know it was a countdown to the saddest night in my early life, and that my mother and I wouldn't last long in the house without Rosemarie. We couldn't survive on our own, with my father's vile wrath. The night of her wedding, Rosemarie came back to our room to get her bags. I waited up in bed, reading, ready for her to come to bed, so we could go to sleep. She walked in, and Peter was with her. She lifted her suitcases.

"Where are you going?"

"I'm married now."

"So?"

"Well, where will Peter sleep?"

"Where he always sleeps."

"I'm going to sleep with Peter from now on."

I cried. No one had told me that marriage meant we had to worry about where Peter would sleep all of a sudden. I thought I'd never catch my breath again. Rosemarie sat on the bed. She held me. I wouldn't let go. She talked to me. I was sure I could convince her to get back into bed and go to sleep. I held onto her for my life. How could she leave me alone with these people?

Silence, Violence

It was the silence that woke me from sleep. I ran past them, trying not to look at what will never be forgotten. My father had my mother's head bent back over the radiator. In his other hand was a steak knife. I had to break them apart. I yelled, but it did no good. I grabbed his knee and bit his kneecap as hard as I could. My baby teeth were sharp, but only ripped his green work pants. His leg kicked me off and I fell across the floor next to the piano. I ran for the heatpipe, for the teaspoon behind the pipe. I ran. I tried not to see. Through tears I did look. I couldn't take my eyes off them. He shook her head like a rag doll. I ran into louver doors, fold-pushing them open. Slotted light raked the rug. My hands dropped and knees down onto the rug. The moon bounced across the alleyway through the window and off the heatpipe to cast the pipe's shadow across the rug. I stomped my hands and knees onto this long shadow and raced to the pipe. Lying frozen silver, I clutched it. So tight, bone white flesh. I spooned the pipe spoon to pipe spoon to pipe *ppkink*. I hacked his spine spoon to pipe *ppkink ppkink*

ppkink ppkink! I hacked 'til feet clapped heavy down the stairs. The rug was hot against the friction of my knees.

CarKey came down. The two Marines faced off. Lanzi and CarKey's faces were one inch away from each other. They yelled and the inch of space buzzed between them. It was an invisible barrier.

"You're not gonna be happy until you kill her!"

"She's an actress, your mutha! She's got some imagination. What a' you the big man now?"

Neither my brother nor my father advanced across that one inch that held them apart. I wanted CarKey to punch him. I wanted to have a strong man's body like CarKey. One day I would grow up and be muscular, and then I would punch my father and knock him out cold. I might even kill him for hitting my mother like that. One day I would be big and no one would ever hit my mother again.

The Blue Angel

"There's something wrong with the baby." Lanzi's open hand rested over my whole head to estimate the heat, and flipped from front to back on my forehead, cheek, forearm. He measured the heat inside me with his hand.

"Okay, let's see." Rachel slid the thermometer out of my mouth and held it up under the light. She turned it until she could see the red line. The thermometer's verdict?

"A little over a hundred and four."

I scored well. She held her hand to my forehead. Their hands almost touched for an instant, crossing over my body.

First, he turned to ice. Lanzi marched to the bathroom and twisted on the cold tap; as the bathtub filled with cold Bronx water, he marched to the kitchen and pulled three trays of ice cubes out of the freezer. I followed him, my feet were hot against the cold floor. He pulled the silver lever that cracked loose the cubes from their racks, and I felt the crack through my spine. He shook the cubes into the tub. Some of the cubes stuck to the tray. "Damn ice," he said, shaking it.

I heard my mother turn on the television set and switch the channels until she heard high-pitched singing. My father told me to climb into the tub. A headache had grown like a claw around my brain. I called to her, and she came in and held me up by my arms. She helped me stand. She adjusted the blue washcloth on my forehead. The singing voice came into the bathroom above the sound of the rushing water into the white tub, as if the voice was coming out of the shiny tiles. My father ordered me into the tub. I put one leg into what felt like fire. The leg came right out. The ice water cut my leg right off. There was no way I could get my torso into the tub.

"The fever has to come down," he coaxed me, reasoned with me, and then the Marine in him came out and he gave me the ultimatum: "It's just a body. Get in the tub!" I let my bones drop under their skin, and collapsed onto the cold bathroom floor. "Okay, we can try an ice enema, that always works," he said.

"Ga'head, Daddy," I eked out of my throat in surrender. He cradled me with one of his hairy tree-branch arms and plopped me into the ice water. My breath iced my lungs. My body cut away from me. Then he craned me up out of the tub with one arm. Rachel helped my body take a standing shape. He wrapped a pink towel around me. He dunked the pink towel into the tub of the ice water, strangled the pink towel, twisting the dripping water out and wrapped my pink body in the ice-cold towel. The towel immediately absorbed my heat. My mother refilled my water glass on Lanzi's command and put it to my lips. I let a sip enter my mouth and mechanically swallowed. The water felt hard as marbles going down. He unwrapped me and dunked the large towel again in the ice bath, wrung it out and wrapped it around my naked pink body. This he did repeatedly to extract the red heat out through my pink skin. Again the towel went into the ice bath, got wrung out, and wrapped around me. Again, my body heated up the towel. Next he wrapped two layers of ice towels around me and carried me to the couch in front of the television set, covering all parts of me.

"Daddy," he said, "I'll give you a dollar for every glass of water you drink."

My father always had dollars in his pocket. I downed a glass of water, and he took one dollar out. I downed glass after glass. The first few went down sharply as if water were shards of glass against my swollen red throat. I drank to the old warped music coming from the television set, where I saw the curved roofs of a small town, and a woman serving a big man his coffee. The man sits down to the coffee and whistles to his bird. On Lanzi's order, my mother brought a pewter pitcher of water and a tall jelly-jar glass. I drank, and Lanzi went into his pocket and placed another dollar on the tray. I drank another and asked my mother to keep the water pouring. She brought me more glasses, glasses my father had gathered from gas stations with insignias of football teams, blue helmets, orange helmets, Miami Dolphins, New York Giants, Dallas Cowboys, New York Jets. I had glasses all around me filled with good Bronx water, the best drinking water in the world. I downed two and a half glasses more. My father felt my neck and head and let me see he had a whole sandwich of dollar bills in his pocket. The television is loud: the man whistles for his bird. The man has a goatee and round glasses. The bird doesn't answer the man. The man whistles, drinks his coffee. The bird is dead in the cage. The man calls. A woman appears. The woman lifts the bird by its tail and tosses it into the wood-burning stove and walks out of the room. Lanzi wrung out a new ice towel and brought it to me. The cold water was numbing the inside of my body as it mixed with my heat. The man in the movie enters a classroom of boys that are huddled together and disperse on his arrival. He is the professor. He grabs a card from one of the guilty boy's hands and lifts his eyebrows at the enticing woman bent with her rear end facing the viewer. The professor looks at her closely.

"That's hoodyacall," my father said, "Marlene Dietrich, that's who it is." My mother helps me walk to the bathroom, and I sit down to pee. She feels under my armpits, on the back of my neck. Nothing came out, my body was using all the water. She supported me, walking back to the couch. Lanzi puts another iced pink towel around me. My teeth are knocking. I am shaking. Marlene Dietrich sings about love.

"That's the kind of woman that will ruin you," Lanzi warns.

He dunked the towel back in the ice water and wrapped it around me. I drank three glasses of water fast. I couldn't feel the water going down anymore. I went to the bathroom by myself and dumped out two glasses of water in the sink. I announced I drank two more.

"That was quick," he said.

My father knew me. He got up off the couch and dunked the towel back in the ice water and wrapped it again around me. I drank another glass fast and with his help, collapsed back onto the couch.

On the TV, a clown in full whiteface, stares at the professor. Clowns frighten me. The clown bunks into the professor. Clowns are warnings. The clown is silent. My father changed the towel, my mother shook down the thermometer. I dropped a glass of water onto the tray; it felt too heavy to lift. My mother held the glass to my lips and my father's eyebrows evened out. I sat with the pink iced towel wrapped around me. I cried burning hot tears on my cool cheeks. I held the cool water in my mouth.

"Steer clear of that one," my father says to the professor who is smiling at Dietrich. Her dressing room is full of mirrors, dancer's clothing: feather boas, a top hat, silk stockings, makeup.

I got up and walked alone to the toilet. I dropped the pink towel and grabbed a dry white towel around me. I was shivering. A tiny burning hot trickle came out. I walked back to the living room.

The professor is now in clown makeup, and squawking like a chicken.

My mother raised my legs onto the sofa. "Marlena Dietrich," she says, "didn't she entertain the troops?"

Lanzi looks at her and his words came out straight and smooth without edges, "Yes," he says, "Hoodycallit saw her. Dietrich went all over Africa, Europe. She didn't come to the Pacific."

"Imagine going against your own country?"

"Well, when your country's involved in wrongdoing."

I broke into a massive sweat. "I'm sweating," I said with triumph.

"Good, good," Lanzi said.

"*Finalmente*," my mother said, "thank God. I prayed to Saint Anthony, 'Please make my daughter well.'"

My skin had been peeled off. I was broken open. I struggled to throw the towels off me.

"Seventy-five glasses of water," I declare. I am able to cry dry hot tears that evaporate soon as they hit my pink cheeks. My father pays me in full. We defeated the fever. He counts out a whole pile of dollar bills. I lift the stack of bills and hold them up to my nose, fanning the paper. Old bills, a familiar fire. We were safe that night, all of us, in our rendition of peace.

Bronx County Family Courthouse

My mother handed my father an "order of protection."

"What's this? A piece of paper?" he laughed.

She didn't want to put me on the witness stand, so I stayed in the hallway all day. She packed baloney sandwiches and cans of apple juice, and I took my Spaldeen and my plastic motor scooter. The doors were thick and heavy with windows embedded with wire cross-hatched in the glass. Designs and letters had been scratched into the glass, by others who waited in this same spot as me, for the same number of hours. I tried to add a scratch to the pattern, but I had nothing sharp enough. I bounced my Spaldeen in the stairwell and sat on my scooter. To get my scooter to zoom forward, I had to pull it backward to wind up the wheels. I pushed with my feet. I backed up the full length of the smooth shiny hallway. The farther backward I went, the faster and farther forward I zoomed.

My mother came out from behind a closed door and said, "The judge wants to see you, in chambers." We all sat down. My father, the judge, my mother. The judge leaned down over me and asked me one question that would ruin the rest of my life:

"Whose fault is the fighting?"

I looked up at the judge. I looked at my mother. I looked at my father. The judge urged me on: "Give me a percentage."

I looked back and forth between my parents.

The judge offered me options. "Eighty-twenty? Sixty-forty?"

I looked at my father's brown eyes. Pure fear seized me. If I gave odds that weren't in his favor, he'd blow up. He was a Marine. *No better friend. No worse enemy.* He might even hunt us down, kill us, or he might just never talk to me again. If I said "A hundred-zero," which I knew to be true, he'd cut me out, or worse. I looked at my mother's blue eyes. I knew one thing for sure, my mother would never turn her back on me. I weighed the odds and ramifications. Numbers jumbled in my head. I loved them both equally and I didn't want to live without either of them. I counted in my head the number of words they each yelled at each other.

"Fifty fifty," I said. What else could I say? I didn't want to betray my father. How would I ever look at him again if I picked an uneven number?

"Fifty-fifty? How could you!?" My mother looked at me as if I had smacked her, as if I was Judas, as if she was going to be crucified, as if I was the executioner.

"What. Ma? Should I have said eighty-twenty?"

"How is it my fault?" She was distraught.

Now, all the Petruzzellis would stand against me. I would have to live in her world. But I would always be his kid.

Parkchester *Poseidon Adventure*

One night, not long before the divorce, I insisted the three of us go to the movies. My father acquiesced to my demand. We had never been to a movie theater together. I needed the movie to express to them what I was feeling but didn't know how to say. Rachel, Lanzi, and I drove to Parkchester to see *The Poseidon Adventure.* I sat between them. I was drawn to the television commercials of people running for their lives from a capsized ship in the vast ocean and the one giant wave, that like a divorce, turned everything upside down. I pictured our whole house upside down, like the ship. I was nine. The theme song "The Morning After" promised, *"There's got to be a morning after. If we can hold on through the night. We have a chance to find the sunshine . . ."* I held both of their hands. Lanzi bought the biggest popcorn, Raisinettes, and soda enough to drown in if you dunked your face into it. Rachel laughed at the size, but she loved Raisinettes. The tidal wave came, the ship flipped. Shelley Winters plodded through the water-filled corridors. Water burst into the engine rooms. I cried throughout the movie, and my mother insisted we leave.

"No, I want to see who survives," I whined.

Rachel was fierce. "The movie is too upsetting. Movies should be entertaining. I leave my house for this?"

She got up and walked out. We followed her. Out of the theater into the dark night.

"Let's go eat. I'm starving." Lanzi drove us in the blue Chevy Malibu to the Flaming Grill, near Saint Raymond's Church. Outside was a neon sign in the shape of a raging fire. It made me want grilled meat. We sat in a booth in the back. Lanzi and me ordered T-bone steaks.

"I'll just have some of yours," my Mom said.

"I want my own."

"It's good for her."

"You know how big these steaks are?"

When my steak came, I picked up the bone with my bare hands and chewed it.

"That kid's got some appetite," my father bragged to the waiter.

"She's a good eater," my mother agreed, "but use a napkin for God's sakes."

I chewed that steak bone as if for survival. I sucked on the crisp fat and the marrow. I ripped the bone apart with my teeth.

The waiter brought me more napkins. I stripped the tendons from the bone.

My father picked his teeth and smoked a cigarette. He was proud of me, steak bone in my mouth and meat drippings all over my hands. When he was finished, he pushed his cigarette butt out in the dried steak fat wax on his dinner plate.

The Lady in Black

When me and Mom walked to Parkchester to clothes shop, we always stopped at the fountain where I was mesmerized by the statues spitting water into the pool. I could spit thick but I couldn't spit far. I spit on the sidewalk all the time. Getting rid of phlegm seemed like a Bronx duty. One day as I stared at the figures spitting in the fountain, I turned around and my mother was gone. I spun around crying "Ma!" in all directions. She was nowhere. She always told me, "If you are ever lost, stay in one place." I didn't move an inch, so she could find me. I pivoted around in a circle. I cried. The fountain people spit. I cried hot tears. A woman dressed all in black walked up to me. She had a black skirt and black sweater, a black umbrella, and she pushed a black pushcart. She walked right up to me and told me to come with her. I did not move my pivot foot. She blocked my view. I wanted her to move so I could see. I heard my mother calling my name.

"Mom! Mom!" I yelled.

"I was so scared. I looked down and you were gone."

I reached up, took my mother's hand, and turned my head. The lady in black had vanished.

Fast Break

Johnny Denaro was with me the night I found out we were moving. Rachel set up snack tables for us kids to eat in the living room, and served us each a bowl of lentils and a glass of Hawaiian Punch and Italian bread.

Lanzi and Rachel yelled in the kitchen. She stomped into the living room and announced, with Johnny as my witness:

"I just want you to know we're leaving. We're going to live in Yonkers."

I gagged. Lentils and the red Hawaiian Punch shot out my nose. Johnny and I laughed. I spit all over the place. Lentils and Hawaiian Punch went over the snack tables and carpet. I couldn't catch my breath. We laughed and laughed.

A few weeks later, our fifth-grade teacher, Sister Lorraine confirmed what was true. "Class, I have an announcement to make. Today we have to say goodbye to a very special student in our class. We all will miss her. But she is moving away, and she will attend another Catholic school, where her family is moving. We love and will miss her. That student is . . . Annie Lanzillotto." Sister Lorraine's crooked index finger definitely pointed at me. Her hand pointed toward the first row, but the crooked finger veered toward the second row where I was seated in the second seat. I felt hot inside. I could not believe I heard my own name. My body stood up, while my soul stayed seated, resolute to not move an inch. And it didn't. My soul stayed in the Bronx. My Bronx accent set in stone. I stayed glued inside to every kid in that class, and especially to Johnny Denaro who whisper-shouted, "No!" from the back of the third row, and stretched his arm over his wooden school desk as if he could grab me and never let go.

I mouthed to him, "You knew You were there. You heard my mother."

My mother and father had one last fight. My mother picked me up and ran out the front door, which she swung behind her as my father ran after us. She slammed the door and the brass peephole hit my father in the middle of his forehead. She ran down the stoop carrying me. My father stood at the top of the stairs. He felt his head with his hand, looked at the blood, shook his head and laughed. The peephole cut a round wound like a shot between his eyes.

My mother packed cardboard boxes and drew a big *U* on a piece of paper and handed it to me, "We're moving to a big court. It's like this, all the people live around the court. We will live here, in Number One." A basketball court, I figured. We would live on a big basketball court where I could play night and day. How cool, I thought, to build apartments all facing a giant basketball court. The word *court* pacified me.

It was Saturday morning, November 23, 1974. Our Santa Maria basketball team had our first scrimmage. I trained with the team all season. Faith's mother was the coach, and Faith was the second string center. There were things I could do on a full court with a team that I couldn't do alone in my backyard. The fast break is the best feeling in team ball. The fast break is style, speed, forethought, vision, risk, bravado. It's about beating time. Not honoring time. Pushing time. Stunning the opponent. I'd snatch the rebound under the boards. Pivot. See my teammate who ran down the aisle of the court. I fire the ball over everyone's heads right to her. She is alone for a layup.

I pulled on two pairs of tube socks, one over the other, and laced my sneakers up tight.

"Don't go far," my mother said, "Aunt Patty will be here in a half hour."

"Mom, I got my first game today."

"What are you talking about? Today's the day we're moving."

"I have to play. I'm on the team. I can't just not go."

"You can join a new team. In Yonkers there's plenty of teams."

Aunt Patty pulled up in front of the house in her shiny 1970 gold Mustang. It was the sharpest car I'd ever seen, and the most gold. She wore dark Jackie O sunglasses and blew cigarette smoke sideways out of her red lips. She came to rescue her baby sister, but to me she was the angel of death. A truck pulled up behind her. She bossed the two men around, and they came up the front stoop and into the house. They carried the cardboard boxes out of the house and down the stoop. They carried the maple table, four legs up. They wrapped it with a blanket and laid it in the truck on its back. How would I ever sit at that table without my father? Everything I loved, we left behind: Blacky, the piano, the garage full of tools, the basketball hoop, Johnny Denaro, and most of all, my father.

I walked down the stoop for the last time. I got in behind the bucket seat of the Mustang and felt sick to my stomach. Aunt Patty made a sarcastic comment, including the word *finally*. I watched my block go by. I watched the Bronx go by, block by block, out the back window.

My mother handed me a tissue and said, "We have no choice. What choice do we have? Your father sold the house right from under us. What man does this? What's the sense of talkin'? Stop crying, you're gonna make yourself sick."

By car, from the Bronx to Yonkers is ten minutes, but we might as well have crossed an ocean. The Bronx became as far away and mythic as *Acquaviva delle Fonti*. Now I had two phantom lives, one with my cousins in the fields of grapes and olives, and the other on the stoops, sidewalks, and streets of Westchester Square.

Top: Me popping a wheelie on my Raleigh Chopper outside the house, 2433 Saint Raymonds Avenue, The Bronx. Eight years old, 1972. *Photo: from the author's collection.*

Bottom: Me in the Nevada desert, still popping wheelies, this time raising consciousness for A.I.D.S. on a cross-country bike tour. 1986.

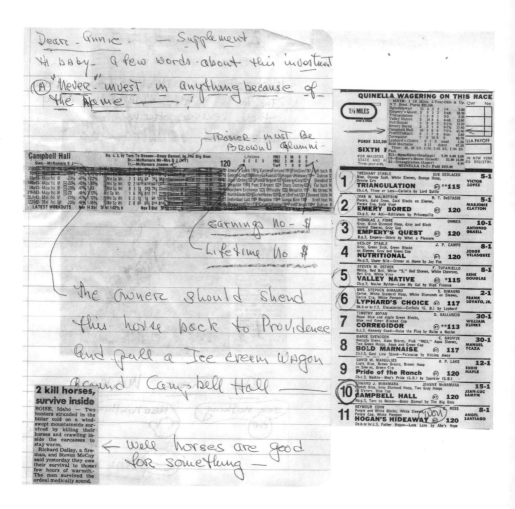

Dear Annie — Supplement

Hi BABY— a few words about this investment

(A) "Never" invest in anything because of
the Name —

Trainer — must be
Brown Alumni

Earnings no — $

Lifetime no $

The owner should send
this horse back to Providence
and pull a Ice cream Wagon
around Campbell Hall —

← well horses are good
for something —

2 kill horses, survive inside

BOISE, Idaho — Two hunters stranded in the bitter cold on a wind-swept mountainside survived by killing their horses and crawling inside the carcasses to stay warm.

Richard Dailey, a fireman, and Steven McCoy said yesterday they owe their survival to those few hours of warmth. The men survived the ordeal medically sound.

A letter from Dad, with horse race sheet.

My Dad, Joseph Rocco Lanzillotto, U.S. Marine boot camp, Parris Island, South Carolina, 1946.

Me and Dad in the backyard. I learned how to strip copper wire, under Mom's clothesline. The Bronx. *Photo: Rachel Lanzillotto, 1967.*

Mom and Dad at Glen Island, 1947.

Mom and Dad's wedding, Audobon Ballroom, New York City, where in 1965 Malcolm X was killed.

Standing, from left to right: Dad's brothers and sisters, Nicky, Sammy, Laura, Tony (Apollonia's husband), Apollonia, Orazio (Archangela's future husband) Archangela, and Tessie.

Sitting, from left to right: Grandpa Carmine, Joseph (Dad), the cream puffs, Rachel (Mom), Grandma Anna.

Mom and Dad's wedding day: Rachel and Joseph Lanzillotto. November 2, 1947.

Standing are Tony and Apollonia. Mom and Dad handed out hundreds of cream puffs at their football wedding. Mom wore the "illusion veil."

The day I fell in love with mummies at the Met, 1972. *Photo: Rosemarie.*

Santa Maria School, Kindergarten Graduation. Sister Rosaria, me, and Father Caldarola. Zerega Avenue, The Bronx, 1969.

Me and Blacky in our backyard, The Bronx, 1971.

Blizzard of 1969. I'm on my sled under Mom's ever-present clothesline. The Bronx.

Me and "Enza" with Penny's litter on the kitchen floor.

Me and my sister Rosemarie outside the Met. *Photo: Peter.*

Me and Mom. The Bronx.

Japanese sun-mark flag, my Dad captured in battle. The characters
on the flag tell the story of Toshiharu Kotani, a soldier my Dad
killed in Okinawa. He gave me the flag when I was eight years
old. *Photo: Andrew Perret.*

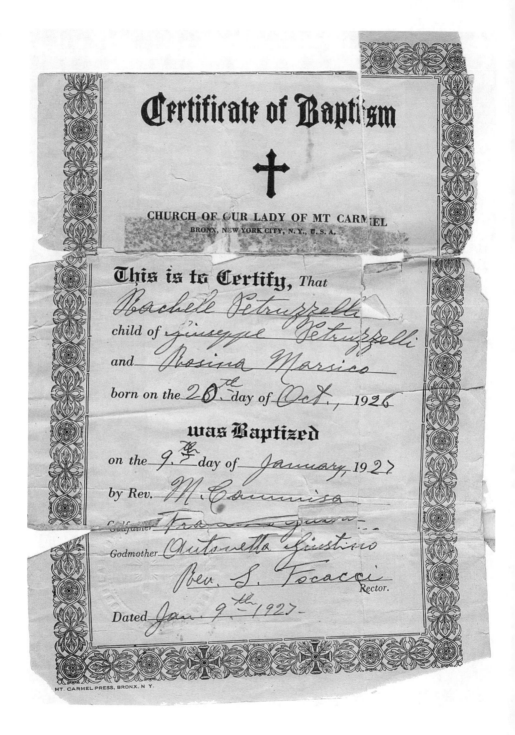

Mom's Bronx Baptism certificate from the Church of Our Lady of Mt. Carmel. Mom was baptized by Father Focacci! Severino Focacci.

part two

Educationa Girl

The Temporary Apartment

Dead End, the street sign read. We turned down the hill and drove to the bottom. I followed my mother up a strange set of concrete stairs set into the side of a grassy hill. The stairs leveled off every four steps onto a flat plateau, but the flat parts slanted downward. It felt stupid. Where was the thinking? First, we had to drive down the hill, only to walk back up the hill via these crooked stairs. The banister also had the strange up flat up flat up flat up flat shape, so it wouldn't even be good to slide down. Stupid. At the top was a large rectangle of grass with two story brick buildings attached in a horseshoe pattern around the grass. A single lane cement path was laid in a loop around all the doorways.

My mother came up behind me, "This is it."

"This is what?"

"Think of it as temporary."

"Where's the court?"

"Haah?"

"Where's the hoop?"

"What hoop?"

"You said we were moving to a huge court."

"This is a court."

"What? Where's the hoop."

"Not that kind of court. A courtyard."

I slammed my basketball down hard onto the cement path and it stopped dead in the useless grass. I could trust nothing any adult said ever again. This was an inside-out block. In the Bronx, I walked around the block on the perimeter of the houses and kept watch on the neighborhood. Here, in Yonkers, what could I do but walk around this empty field of grass, the apartments watching me?

The doorways were all identical. A sign posted on the brick wall read: NO BALL PLAYING all in white capital letters, as if the very wall was shouting at me: DO NOT EXIST. My perfect hell. The apartments were built over a giant indoor garage. Foul odors came up through the garage windows to our bedroom window. We didn't have a stoop. Only three steps. I threw my Spaldeen at them anyway. I hit the point of the stairs and the Spaldeen fell onto the grass without a bounce. I walked over to retrieve it. There was no more chase. I throw. The Spaldeen bounced up and banged the glass hallway door. I looked around. I felt conspicuous. Two old men played cards on a bench and smiled at me with big teeth. I throw the ball. The Spaldeen sails over my head into the grass and stops dead. I walk slowly. I throw the ball. I throw. Into her soup I throw, into tomorrow. I throw down onto a square of cement. The ball bounces high so I can't see its top. The ball has an invisible top. I throw the ball and she stops to mark the place. The temptation to hate her exists. I throw the ball. I throw the ball through the wall. I throw. I throw alone. There were no sewer grates up there, but I knew the Spaldeen would find crevices to hide in. The Spaldeen bounced up, hit the awning over the steps and landed in a bush. I grabbed it, got pricked by the bush, and walked down to the large white wall that slanted steeply into the garage. This was the closest thing to a handball wall I would find. I threw my ball against the wall. The garage was cold and full of fumes. Fumes didn't make me sneeze as much as grass.

The next day I tucked my basketball under my arm and walked around looking for a hoop. The only hoop I saw was across the six-lane Central Avenue I was way too young to cross. I was miserable. Rosemarie lived with Peter five hours away. She decoupaged us a plaque with a quote and pastel butterflies and sent it in the mail: *"Remember, no human condition is ever permanent. Then you will not be overjoyed in good fortune, nor too sorrowful in misfortune."* Socrates. My mother hung the plaque up in the kitchen. I yelled and kicked and threw my Spaldeen inside the house. The upstairs neighbors banged on their floor. "Shhhhh. The neighbors," was my mother's new thing to say. I rode my blue Raleigh Chopper in rectangular laps around the court and tried the Yonkers hills that were new to me, but Choppers weren't built for the hills. I pulled hard on my handlebars to make it up the hill and my front wheel popped up. I was in a perpetual wheelie.

My father picked me up in his Chevy Malibu. I sat with him in the booth of a big bright diner, ate triple-decker turkey club sandwiches and read the *Daily News* and horse sheets. When he dropped me off, he gave me my height chart, a strip of wood that had stood in the kitchen doorjamb my whole life.

"Here, you forgot this, Daddy."

"Who's gonna measure me?"

"I don't know, Daddy, I don't know. You're with the Petruzzellis now."

I carried my height chart up the grassy hill, refusing to use the stupid stairs. The height chart was a lot taller than me. I put my key in the door. It was tricky to turn. I never had to use a key before. Mom went back to school and was out every day. When she came home, she saw my height chart and said, "I don't want you nailing that thing to the wall. This is an apartment, and we'll only be here temporarily. Aunt Patty and Uncle Joe put a thousand dollars under the table just so we could be here. We can't put holes all over the walls."

I leaned my height chart against a wall. It slid down the wall to the floor. I stuck it in the closet. I hated the word *apartment*. All I heard was *apart, apart, apart*.

Permanent Wave

Mom got the okay from the Yonkers Welfare Office to go back to school to renew her New York State Hairdresser's License. She was expert at permanent waves, finger waves, cold waves, the hairstyles of the 1940s. Now, after a quarter century of marriage and motherhood, she needed to learn the shag haircuts of the 1970s. Aunt Patty, our new neighbor Amelia, my mother's cousin Lucy, GranmaRose, everyone came for Mom's permanent waves.

"Aunt Patty's coming over for a perm. I have just enough time to give you a haircut. I'm learning feather cuts and I need heads to practice on. You're starting a new school. Let me give you a nice cut." She put her hand under the water in the kitchen to test the temperature. I bent over the sink and stuck my head under the faucet. She massaged my scalp with shampoo. I sat down and she snapped the plastic cape around me.

"How's school going, Mom? You making friends?"

"Friends? I'm old enough to be their mother, but yes. There are these two young guys. They're very effeminate. We have so much fun. Larry showed up one day without his uniform jacket. I told him borrow mine, I'm an old lady, what are they gonna do? You had to have the white jacket or you get points taken off. P.S. today he gives me the jacket back. Our stations are next to each other, we're cutting our models' hair. Larry says, 'Rachel, a roach just fell out of your pocket.' I nearly jumped out of my skin. I thought he meant a bug, what do I know that's a drug term? He bent down and picked it up. He could have gotten me in trouble. They laughed and laughed, how I jumped."

"A roach is marijuana."

"Now I know. How do you know that? You're eleven years old!"

"Ma, your son's a junkie, you don't know what a roach is? Anyways I wanna meet these guys."

"Yes, I already told them. One Friday night we're going out for *a pizz'*."

"All the techniques are different now. I got a lot to study."

"How are they different?"

"Put your head down. I want to do the front. See this is the new way they feather cut now. How are the techniques different? That's what Larry asks me. Everything's different. It's a whole 'nother ball game. He wants to know how it was done in the old days. He's fascinated, like it was the year one. Permanent waves were the big thing; the way I learned, the old-fashioned way, you wash the hair and dry it, then you block the hair with small pieces of felt. The felt had a slit in it, perfect for the size of the roller. You clamp it, and block the hair. The felt was rubberized on the back, it protected the scalp when you applied heat."

"Heat? How'd you apply heat?"

"Electricity. I'm getting to that. Hold still. You section the head. Like bricks. Curl by curl. Like this see. This is one section of hair. This is another section. The rollers all fit. If the hair needs a trim, you cut it while it's blocked. If you see the wave's going a certain way, you cut into the wave. You have to look at the head to see the way the hair naturally goes. Then you moisten the head with permanent wave lotion. You take a piece of cotton, and it has to be saturated, each piece of hair. Then you take end paper, you comb the hair nice and smooth and you put the end paper near the end of the hair. You take the metal roller and you roll the hair up, smooth and flat. The roller clamps. After the hair was all rolled up, you put the lotion to soften the hair, it broke down the molecules in the hair. It smelled. I don't know what the hell it contained. It smelled like ammonia. You plug the head in. You put on the switch. You left the electricity on five minutes, then you take it off and the hair has to cool off. Then you take everything off, all the plugs, all the clamps, all the curlers, all the papers, everything, and the hair's curly. You take the rods and felt off gently so you don't stretch the curl. You rinse the hair off to get the lotion out. You don't wash it, you just rinse it out. And you set the hair however you want. We used to do them with the pin curls. Pin curls, you had to go around the finger and you put the two hair pins. Usually the sides of the head take about four. The top, going back is four or five. Maybe one extra here and there for a larger head. You lock the curl with the naturalizer. You plug the apparatus in. We'd put the electric clamp on each roller, for heat. Each roller had a clamp that was wired to the apparatus. And you turn on the switch."

"Sounds like the electric chair."

"The electricity goes through the wire to each clamp, and each clamp was placed on a roller on the head."

"You ever electrocute somebody?"

"No. But I burnt a woman's hair. I was still in school. I worked for nothing at the time. I made my own apprenticeship. The shop was called Lou Bud's. It was on Ahun-Fiftieth Street offa Third Avenue. It was above a bank. I walked into the shop and said, 'I want to work.' I told him I'd work for nothing. I wanted experience. He gave me a chance. He saw I was neat and clean, efficient. I knew what I was doing, I just needed experience. I did a permanent wave, and I started kibitzing with the girls; we used to have a lot of fun. I forgot to shut the machine off. The customer said, 'Miss, it's getting hotter and hotter.' I said, 'That can't be, because it's off.' I went running to the back, I saw smoke coming up from her head, and I yelled to my boss across the shop, 'Mr. Bud!' And I motioned to him to help me. We pulled everything off—one, two, three—and put the cool dryer on. We took the curlers off, *boop,* the hair came right, off, *boop,* the hair came right off. But it was all in here at the base of the neck. I was very fortunate. She had exceptionally thick hair, what we used to call like a horse's hair. She never knew. She was very happy. I learned that lesson good. Next time I paid attention. It never happened again."

"That's what you're going to do to Aunty Patty?"

"No, now we do cold waves. First came machineless waves, then cold waves. Machine waves had individual packets that had a chemical that provided the heat, which activated the chemicals in the lotion. No more plugging the head in. The chemical broke down the shaft of the hair and moistened it. The head would get hot. That process softened the shaft of the hair, so it adheres to the curl. The hair that's wrapped around the curler took on the shape of the curler. The neutralizer hardens the hair. Think of concrete. When you pour it, it's still soft. When it dries it hardens, and it remains that way. And that's how the hair would then harden with the contour of the curl that had been softened by the chemical, and it stays curly until it actually grows out. Then came cold waves, done strictly with chemicals. No heat whatsoever. That has a very strong smell. That's what I'm gonna do for Aunt Patty later."

Mom passed her hairdressing test, got her license, and walked into a beauty parlor in Bronxville called, "The Gramatan."

"I belong here," she said to the boss.

He said, "I think you do. I'll start you off as the receptionist." Then she got promoted to manicures, thinking the tips would be better.

Now she held the hands of the rich for a living.

Useless Expertise

"Yo. Talk. We want to hear you talk. Say, yo. Say, what's up man? How ya doin? Say water. Say corner. Say water. Come listen to her say water.

Yo man. What'sup? Gimme five. Watch out. Annie from da Bronx. Say yo. Say fagetaboutit."

Nobody had a Spaldeen. Nobody knew how to play. I taught the kids boxball in the schoolyard, and organized a boxball tournament at lunchtime, which I won. One boy learned quick, picked up my moves and my "English" on the ball. By the second tournament, he sliced the ball, pushed his thumb into the rubber to get an unpredictable hop on the first toss, and beat me. Nobody played stickball. They had aluminum bats and protective pads and helmets and leather mitts and baseballs with fancy red stitching and colorful uniforms with numbers, all official. Play was organized into teams with coaches and umpires and referees. Gone were the shirts against the skins. Rules were made by adults with whistles. Stickball was supplanted by the hegemony of Little League baseball and softball. I had to play with girls. I had to play on grass. We were cut off from traffic by a tall fence. Cars in Yonkers didn't know how to play, anyway. Cars came in spurts after the green light, and went past me on the other side of the fence. I was disoriented, thrown off. I had no need any more to sense what was behind me. What was I supposed to do with this useless expertise of catching fly balls in oncoming traffic? I had the urge to be in the middle of the street, to swipe my finger along the chassis of a passing car, to feel the tension run through me, knowing I could break at any moment.

I keep running back and listening behind me, but there is nothing coming at me. No cars coming at me. Nothing coming at me. I turn to look but there is nothing coming. Just the sound of water, running water, an ocean laughing down upon me. Each drop so delicate from the sky. A penny dropped from the Empire State Building, they say, acts like a lead bullet in your skull, but not the rain, the rain can fall all the way down from the clouds and never harm you. The rain will fall on you in drops, the waters pour down from the sky. The sky is an ocean, down so delicate, an ocean, a wall in the sky. The water lifts and falls so life giving, so delicate. The rain has always been my favorite. Wash the streets clean rain. Make rainbows rain. The rain will never harm you.

Hunger Beats *Agida*

Lanzi was right. I spent all my time with the Petruzzellis now. I hardly heard from anybody on my father's side. I felt like my mother and I were traitors excommunicated for crimes. At Christmas my father's sisters sent me cards with the Blessed Virgin's picture and angels on the outside and folded money inside. Once in a while my father would pick me up and take me to one of their houses to eat, but hardly anyone ever asked me how my mother was. Her name was not spoken.

Despite their divorce, there were things on which my warring parents agreed. Empty stomachs, empty pockets can kill you. You can't accomplish much on an empty stomach, and all you can accomplish is garbage on a stomach full of garbage. "Don't give me *agida*," I've heard all my life. *Agida* can be a combination of acid and agitation. GranmaRose took it a step further. Foods from the outside, like people, were held suspect. Anything grown on fire escapes and in backyards passed. Items from stores were triply inspected with the coordination of eye, hand, and nose. A few Bronx stores were implicitly trusted, Frank & Joe's on Zerega, and anything from Arthur Avenue, a short pilgrimage from our old neighborhood of Westchester Square. Foods and people had to pass inspection to come into her kitchen. Every walnut had to be young, and it's an art to be able to peg the age of a walnut. She did not let my mother or me touch her dough. She refused to teach our fingers to make *cavateel* jump like grasshoppers off the fingertips on her rolling board. She mocked my mother's attempts, scoffed at the misshapen pasta, poked fun at our AmeriCAHN know-nothing hands. Handling dough is like handling a horse; the dough can scare just as easily and, being a living thing, needs the right balance of handling and solitude to find its full rising.

GranmaRose grew up holding crops. I grew up holding crap, things that never lasted. This was the difference between us. She handled every single thing like there was life inside it. Even plastic she held like an egg, plastic she held like it grew right out of the ground she stood on. My hands could never make what her hands made. My hands opened books. She never read a book in her life. "*Fa'what!*" she'd say. She was too busy making and fixing every little thing. I threw my sneakers up on the telephone wires every couple of months, GranmaRose's shoes lasted for decades. She conserved her shoes. "When I walked to the school, I carried *le scarpe*, and put them on once I got inside." She told me this as if that was what I should do. As if it was my fault the soleS of my sneakers wore out. My mother trained me differently. My mother was a cripple as a child. When she bought me new sneakers, she had one directive, "Wear them out."

GranmaRose went to school up to the second grade, "*È basta.*" That was enough. She worked the fields. They didn't own any land, they worked it and gave shares of the crops to the *padrone*. As a youth, they called her Rosina. I thought of her girlhood years as often as she repudiated mine.

With my mother's side of the family, I was a Lanzillotto, loud and tough like my father, the brutal enemy. With my father's side of the family, I was a Petruzzelli, the intruder.

GranmaRose voiced dissatisfaction at me, "Watchayou gonna fall down. Then don't acome acrying to me. That's a no nice, the way you sit. Bah! Crossa you legs."

"I can't."

"Crossa you legs."

"You never tell Ant'ny or CarKey to cross their legs. They sit with their legs open wide and shake the whole table." Both of my brothers always sat with one leg shaking.

"Crossa you legs. Mavatheen. Educationa Education."

GranmaRose went into the kitchen, opened the faucet and let the water run. In her eyes, I didn't sit right, walk right, talk right, eat right, dress right, do nothin' right. She muttered, "Educationa Education." She gave me four nicknames each full of derision: "Educationa Girl," "Study Girl," "Educationa Education," and the worst of all, "Educationa Girl Accomplishmenta Nothing." I studied for hours every night. The more I studied, the more I achieved hundreds of American indecencies in her eyes. She made fun of my studies and athletic pursuits. The more she made fun of me, the more I tried to understand her. I asked her a lot of questions. Tell me what it was like where you were born. Why were you the one to come on the boat? How many brothers and sisters did you have? GranmaRose hated talking about the past.

"Bah. Tell me somea'tinga new."

"Where were you born Granma?"

In reply, she tapped the heel of her black strap shoe.

And that's all I knew of *Acquaviva*. The heel of the boot. The archipelago of Italy.

I continued my inquiry with my mother and her cousin Lucy. They told me that GranmaRose had a brother named Gennaro who emigrated in the early 1900s and worked in Union Twist Drill factory in Athol, Massachusetts. The available factory work up there was in Union Twist, the shoe factories, and the comb factory in Worcester. Gennaro sent money home for the next two in line to come live in *L'America*. GranmaRose was not the next in line, her sisters Lucia and Maria were. But the Great War came and by the time it was over, her sister Maria had turned twenty-one, and deemed herself too old to venture to a new land, and in my grandmother's words, "She didn't want to go. So my mother Rachele said, 'You go instead.'" And so GranmaRose got on the boat, the *Duca degli Abruzzi* in 1919, with her sister Lucia. I sat her down throughout the years, and asked her questions about the boat on which she sailed to America.

"Thirteen days I didn't eat," she said. She kept saying over and over, "Rrroccoahgeeballt." My mother and I had no idea what she was saying. We started guessing, asking her if it was some guy named Rocco she was talking about. I closed my eyes and repeated and repeated *Rrroccoahgeeballt* over and over with accents on different syllables. Then I thought it might be a place. I opened my Almanac and traced with my finger the route of the *Duca degli Abruzzi*. GranmaRose rode a donkey cart out of *Acquaviva*, got to *la citta di Bari*, took a train to *Napoli*, where her ship left port. They sailed into the Tyrrhenian Sea into the Mediterranean Sea through the Strait of Gibraltar, past the tip of Spain and Morocco. And there it was, "The Rock of Gibraltar." Finally I understood, of course: *Rrroccoahgeebrrrallta*. How could I not have heard it?

Sistemazione

At night, even the simple act of peeling the skin off an apple was the loneliest act in the world. I remembered the skillful way Lanzi patiently skinned fruits in one long spiraling skin, turning the fruit around the knife blade. Sometimes to entertain me, he reformed the skins into spheres stuffed with napkins and stuck them into the freezer until they hardened. Then he'd trick people with the empty spheres of fruit skin.

One winter night, before going to bed, I sat in my mother's living room, in the "temporary" apartment, peeling an orange. The orange unpeeled in one long curled strip of skin. GranmaRose sounded her shrill alarm, "Eeeeee!" with her right arm straight up, indicating that I'd broken one of her secret codes of eating.

"What? What I do! What I do now? I can't do one thing right. I can't eat a piece of fruit, sit in a chair, something's always wrong. I was born in America. What do you want from me? I don't know better. What can I tell you. I am an American."

This time, she spoke the rule. I was lucky. It was clear.

"*L'arancia di mattina é oro puro, nel pomeriggio argento, di sera piombo.* An orange in the morning is pure gold, in the afternoon—silver, in the evening—lead." I never ate an orange again at night. GranmaRose had a *sistemazione*, an order in which things can be eaten, and *i sfraganizze*, a peasant wisdome saying, for the many *sistemazione*.

Sistemazione applied to naming also. Girls were named after their grandmothers, father's side first. My mother grew up in one apartment with four girls: her cousins Lucy Petruzzelli and Rachel Petruzzelli, her sister Lucy Petruzzelli, and herself Rachel Petruzzelli. The Rachels were born Rachele, and the Lucys were born Lucia. They distinguished themselves from each other with nicknames. They called my mother Lilly, and her sister Patty. Patty grew up and married a man named Joe O'Brien. And that's how a Lucia Pettruzzelli became a Patty O'Brien.

In 1919 GranmaRose was nineteen. She was the youngest of six children. She boarded the *Duca degli Abruzzi*, with her older sister Lucia. On the boat, a *paisan'* showed the two sisters a photograph of two brothers, Franco and Giuseppe Petruzzelli, who had already immigrated to Massachusetts. As GranmaRose told me so many times, "Lucia said, *'I lika dis'a one,'* and pointed at Franco. And I said, *'I lika data one,'* and pointed at Giuseppe. "*Ci siamo sposati.* We send the money to our mother, you know, so they could have a celebration over there. Then the babies came. Daughters, and according to the custom, we named the daughters after their grandmothers, my mother Rachele Lerario, and Grandpop's mother, Lucia Armenti."

My mother says that her family took this to an extreme. She tells me of her cousin who I never met. "Giacomina they called Kiki. This is a cousin on my mother's side. Giacomina had a brother Giacomo they called Jack. Giacomina and Giacomo had a Giacomina for an older sister who they called Giacomina, and a Giacomo for an older brother they called Giacomo. Their mother, we called Aunt 'Tse. She had been married twice, and had two kids by two husbands. It must have been that both sets of her in-laws were a Giacomina and a Giacomo. There was a system for naming, you know, you had no choice, you didn't deviate from it. They had a system for everything. *Sistemazione*, there was a *sistemazione* for everything you did and how you did it from the time you opened your eyes to the time you went to bed. Kids had to be named after the husbands' parents first, that was the system we used, alternative names came in to keep everyone straight, after all, four kids growing up in one house all with the same name, when you yell for your kids how are they supposed to know who you're referring to? Aunt 'Tse had no choice in the naming, but the nicknaming, okay. Come to think of it, I don't know what Aunt 'Tse's real name was. We call her 'Tse 'cause that means aunt, from *zia*, that's all we ever knew. I never thought to ask."

Walk Softly but Carry a Big *Pockabook*

Mom held my hand and we took the bus up Tuckahoe Road to Getty Square to the welfare office and applied for food stamps, Medicaid, and welfare. The welfare office was crowded and loud with kids screaming. We sat around and waited for hours, and for the first time, I felt awkward that we were white-skinned people. There was only one other white-skin guy in the place, who wasn't a worker. Mom said the social worker asked her the same questions over and over because she didn't believe her. "She looked at me like I was too pretty to lose a husband. They think I'm a floozy."

Food stamps came on stiff paper in bright denominations like Monopoly money; purple, blue, orange, green, gold, brown. Were we poor, or were we playing poor? Checking out at the supermarkets was always a hassle. Food stamps didn't flow out of the hand as fast as dollar bills. We walked to the A&P on Tuckahoe Road with our pushcart, and when we went to pay for the food, my mother struggled to rip the food stamps out of their booklet along the perforated edges. The perforations never worked cleanly. Food stamps always got stuck in the book, or ripped, and the supermarket cashiers didn't want ripped bills. My mother tried strategically to pre-rip them, but the cashiers wouldn't take those either.

"Your ID has to match the number printed in black on the outside of the booklet. How do I know you didn't steal loose bills?"

My mother settled on pre-ripping each bill most of the way but carefully preserving their attachment to the booklet. The people stuck behind us on line stared and grumbled and made faces like, 'Why'd we get stuck behind the food stamp people?' I grew to hate shopping and couldn't wait to get out of the store. I felt like we weren't supposed to eat cookies on food stamps, just meat and vegetables. Mom grumbled that we weren't allowed to buy a bar of soap with food stamps, because you couldn't eat it. I hid the box of Oreos down in the bottom of the cart. I didn't want me and Mom looked at as the Floozy and the Cookie Eater.

In stores, my mother looked at the prices, and muttered, "We're getting robbed blind." Price tags that could be peeled off in one piece, she peeled and switched with lower prices. Expensive items were put in cheaper boxes. This was the normal way she shopped now. Stems were broken off the *broccoli rabe* and other vegetables that were weighed by the pound. Anything to lower the price. Anything to survive. Anything to not feel ripped off every day of our lives. I stared at blades of grass that grew in cracks between the sidewalk. I'd heard it said about people who "fell between the cracks," and somehow I knew this now applied to us. The only way we would survive was on Mom's diligence, fortitude, and street smarts.

Ant'ny took shopping up a notch with junkie street smarts. He was proud when he used Windex on a pair of worn sneakers and returned them to a store they weren't bought from. They both doctored receipts, and had it down to a science. Once, my mother was caught. I'd wanted apricot face scrub, so I put it in our shopping cart. We needed a light bulb for the refrigerator. The prices brought her to a quick boil, "I'll be damned they think I'm giving them five dollars." I kept my distance as she took the face scrub and light bulb out of their packaging, and stuck the packaging in the cereal aisle behind the boxes. The store detective met us at the register with the packaging. He let her off with a warning. The advent of price tags that had jagged pre-cut pieces curtailed her activities; you couldn't peel them off in one piece. Bar codes put her out of business.

Beyond coping to survive, there was something very anti-establishment about the way they "shopped." Aunt Patty did the same things. Every chance she got: sugar packets from diners, rubber gloves and rolls of white tape from hospitals, coffee packets, cups, and saucers from a cruise ship that had double rings to stabilize the cups on the saucers. In the Bronx, they had a *paesan'* whose house was like a store full of hot items for sale: Bulova watches, clothes, illegal fireworks, the newest shirts with raised lettering. When you walked into the house you had to walk around stacks of boxes. She even had a clothing rack, like Macy's. She whipped women's outfits out, covered in plastic, in different sizes, on their hangers and draped them over the bed for people to try on. Come Christmastime, my mother would always say, "Let's go see what Hoodycall has," and we'd go shopping in her house.

As with all things, GranmaRose took this to an extreme.

GranmaRose carried a big *pockabook* that snapped shut with a click loud as a pistol shot. She refused to pay for life itself. Garlic was as elemental as air and water. *L'aglio*, garlic, she silently fisted and tucked in her coat pocket. *Il prezzemolo*, parsley, she folded like money and pushed into her pistol shot pocketbook, decisively clicking it shut. Expensive peaches she would mix with cheaper ones on top and tell the cashier they were the "ones outside." When open salad bars hit the East Coast, and the rest of us filled our plates with cut cubes of provolone on toothpicks, GranmaRose took the whole ten-pound hunk and stuck it in her white leather *pockabook* underneath the table, wrapped in a navy blue linen napkin. Granma, my mother, Aunt Patty, me, and Uncle Joe all sat through dinner with church smiles on, cracking up from time to time so that we could hardly chew or swallow our dinner, knowing the giant provolone sat inside Granma's white leather pocketbook with the gold clasp. In the supermarket, she maneuvered up and down the aisles, stopped at the *arugula*, muttered about the price and quality of the leaves, and moved on, smelled each peach at a microphone's distance, pocketed garlic, snapped parsley into her *pockabook*, rummaged through the tomatoes, the bananas, held artichokes up to the neon light, weighed the bags of vegetables on their scales and then reweighed them on her own scale back home. The daily preparation of fresh greens, the companionship of fruit ripened to perfection in brown bags in the bottom drawer of her fridge and along the windowsills, her fire escape tomatoes and *basilico*, August fried zucchini flowers; GranmaRose lived with this medicine only. She needled me with derision for not carrying a pocketbook. Without a pocketbook, a woman couldn't hunt and gather.

"What no pockabook!"

Lunch Is to Clean the Blood

GranmaRose wanted me to be American, but she wanted me to eat well. It was understood: if you are born in America, you must learn how to eat. I watched her standing by the window rolling dough. Flour dust kicked up into the arm of light reaching in through the window. Pulling the sunlight into the dough on her wooden board, her fingertips dexterously jumped back and forth. She was making homemade *cavateel*. My mother's *cavateel* were mere hopeless forgeries, small lumps that Granma pulled back into the large ball of dough with her deft fingertips. I walked into the kitchen pushing my sleeves up to the elbow, splashed my hands under the running water in the kitchen sink, and reached into her dough. Water is always running. Rachel leaves the kitchen faucet running. Rosa leaves the kitchen faucet running. I leave the kitchen faucet running. Running water is the life force we live by, the voice of water calms our souls and quiets our minds. This is our *Acquaviva delle Fonti*: Living Water of the Fountains, for now, here, right where we stand.

"Granma, show my hands how to make the little circles."

She dismissed me, and banished me from the kitchen.

"EEEeee! Whatsada use Study Girl, go make a coupla more pages."

She sneered with derision at my baloney sandwiches, while she ate bitter greens with garlic broth and a hunk of hard crusty bread. GranmaRose ate dandelions, *dente di leone*, the teeth of lions. She took walks with empty paper shopping bags and her shoemaker's knife, and stared into the grasses of the courtyard. I followed her to learn how to forage for dandelions. I looked at the grass and weeds. She bent down and pointed out the difference between *cicoria* and other weeds. I hunted for the lion's tooth leaf pattern, pulled up a bunch to show her, and she shook her head with a sharp "Ttt Ttt." She filled two bags with *cicoria*, brought them into the apartment, and filled the kitchen sink with water to soak the greens. Granma could forage greens on the sides of streets and highways and empty lots. Out came her little aluminum pot. I threw the windows open while she sat alone by the kitchen window boiling *cicoria* with garlic and oil. I ran around the apartment opening windows.

"It smells like she's boiling dirty socks!"

"Bah! It cleansa da blood."

Lunch is to clean the blood. Her blood she scoured, like her floors with Ajax, on her hands and knees. Blood was one more thing that needed to be cleaned.

Slow, Loud, and Clear

"Lanzillotto, you have a big mouth. Come by my room after school today." Sister Raymond Aloysius was the most feared nun. What could she want with me? Staying after school was like going to prison. She predicted who among us would end up in Sing Sing, and who on death row. She had a hook nose and a man's name.

I walked into Sister Raymond Aloysius's classroom and she handed me "The Gettysburg Address." "Memorize this. I want you for the Speech Team. We begin practice next Wednesday after school." Then she gave me two containers of white milk. "Take this milk home to your mother."

I came home and opened a package I'd received from Alaska. It was the Bicentennial year. I was in the seventh grade. All over town people painted their johnnypumps red, white, and blue. I'd called my father and asked him how I could find out what celebrations were planned state to state. "Write to the Chamber of Commerce," he told me. I'd written letters to all fifty states, posing as a family of six who wanted to travel to their state. For months, I had been getting packages in the mail.

I read over the words of Abraham Lincoln, and told my mother, "I don't know if I want to do it."

"She picked you. She must see something in you. If you don't try, you'll never know."

Wednesday, I showed up at practice. Sister Raymond had me stand at the front of the room.

"Begin."

"Four score and seven years ago our fathers brought forth on this continent—"

"Slow."

"Four score and seven years ago—"

"Slow."

"Four score and—"

"Slow. Elongate your vowels. Fawww scawww and . . ."

"Faww scaww . . ."

"Good. Now raise your right arm in a pointing gesture."

She hammered out my syllables for weeks.

"Liberty."

"There's no *D* in Liberty.

"Lib-er-ty."

"I can't hear the *T*."

"Lib-er-tttee."

"Slow. Loud. Clear."

"Lib-er-ttteee"

"Slow."

Sister Raymond smiled. She was more proud of me than anyone had ever been.

"America."

"Again."

"Uh-mair-rick-uh."

"Slow. Spread your right arm as you extend the second syllable, as if you are looking over a vast plain."

"Uh-mmairr-rick-uhh."

"Say it softer."

Every syllable of the word *America* posed problems for my Bronx tongue. The opening *Ah* came out of my mouth *Uh*. *Mer* was cut short. The ending *ca* was lost. *Mer* had to be filled with expansive hope; *ca* had to be kind of sung, a crisp hard *c*, and *ah* had to bring all the audience in together. I should have been saying *Amerigo* in an Italian accent; that would have been easier on my tongue. The word *beautiful* was impossible. I couldn't hear the *ttt*, and softening the *fff*, and including the last *l* was like trying to curl my tongue into a right angle.

Sister Raymond took me and Mom to New York City and on the tramway to Roosevelt Island. It was my secret that she was wonderful.

In my first speech contest, I won first place. Me, Sister Raymond and my mother, marched in the Yonkers Memorial Day Parade, and went to a dinner for the Gold Star Mothers who had lost a son or daughter at war. Yonkers Mayor Angelo Martinelli sat next to me and put his arm around me. I got up and delivered the Gettysburg Address. By now I felt linked with Abe Lincoln and drew our initials A.L. on my composition notebook. Then Sister Raymond had me write my own speech about why people should "answer the call" to become nuns and priests. We came home with trophy after trophy. When I delivered a speech, my Bronx accent went somewhere else. We traveled all over the county and state together. My heart raced through my body, as I sat in the front row and waited my turn. I stood up at the podium, took one deep breath, looked out over all the audience and made eye contact, the way Sister Raymond taught me. I opened my mouth: "Ladies and gentlemen, brothers and sisters, honorable judges, friends . . ." I felt the crowd responding to my every word and gesture. I felt in command. I surfed the waves of energy of the crowd. I could visualize the pages of the speech turning in my mind. I always knew exactly where in the script I was, and where I had to go. Being on stage alone, delivering words, was the best place in the world for me to breathe.

Before each contest I got nervous and threw a tantrum. My mother was my ballast. She was right when she reminded me, "Once you open your mouth you are fine."

Asthma, Green Money, and the Feast

My father and Uncle Frank took me to the feast of *San Gennaro* downtown. Uncle Frank shook my hand. There was a twenty-dollar bill folded into a tight square in the palm of his hand. I put it in my pocket. "Thanks Unc." My father held me by the hand and yanked me through the muscle-bound crowd taking up the width of Mulberry Street, where the men and women walked as wide as can be; biceps, breasts, asses in tight Gloria Vanderbilt dungarees. I inhaled the sweet powdered sugar off the *zeppoli*: the white powder went up my nose and in my mouth and into my lungs. At the same time, the air was thick with sausage and cigar smoke. The muscles across my angel wings tightened. I wanted to win my mother a prize. I loved hanging out with my father and Uncle Frank. I felt like a boy. My father didn't treat me like a girl. He didn't treat me like a boy either. I was in my own category. Waves of sausage smoke stung my eyes. I forced air in and out of my lungs. I sucked air in, I pushed air out. Deep breaths brought deeper knots of phlegm. My lungs were creaky basement doors in a dark damp dusty room. *La Madonna* floated down the street, her dress covered in green money. Uncle Frank pinned a flat open bill onto her dress. Tip your saints well. We stepped inside the church. We dropped coins into the slot in the metal box under *San Gennaro*'s feet. I prayed for the success of my basketball team. I put my hand on his foot and made my prayer clear. "Please let Saint Eugene's win." The sound of a coin hitting the collection box, the coin hitting the other coins, was the first sound of a prayer to me. Coins were prayers. I took my inhaler out of my back pocket and sprayed it into my mouth. I didn't like the bulge it made in my back pocket, but I knew my inhaler was a body part I had to carry around.

Back on the loud street, Uncle Frank shouted to me, "Whaddyawant! Whaddyawant! Whaddyawant!"

I didn't know if I wanted everything or nothing. I had to choose something, one thing. I saw a man in a white cowboy hat. "I like the white cowboy hat."

"The one on that guy's head?"

I nodded.

"Mista, how much for ya' hat!" Uncle Frank loved Mulberry Street. He could make anything happen with a magic word and a handshake. He had wild passionate brown eyes filled with adventure, ideas, and magic.

"Mista, how much for ya' hat."

"It ain't for sale."

Uncle Frank looked down at me and laughed, as if to say, how dare that guy think the hat on his head ain't for sale. His head's for sale, if that's what you want. I took a step away to look for something else to want. His grip pulled me back. He shook the cowboy's hand slowly, smiled, and whispered into his ear. The man took the hat off his head and Uncle Frank put it on my head.

To celebrate the conquest of the white cowboy hat, now on my head, he bought me an antique brass horn. One squeeze on the black rubber ball plunged air out through the brass spiral, making a loud obnoxious honk.

"Remember," Uncle Frank bent down and shouted into my ear, "everything has a price tag."

Brakeman

I won the spelling bee in my class and came home to tell my mother I was one of two kids going to Washington, DC for the National Spelling Bee. That night the phone rang. Mom said I had to go into a runoff with one of the kids I beat at school. "The twin brothers are rich," she explained, "we don't pay tuition. We're on charity. It's an Irish parish, not like Santa Maria. Monsignor Rigney got a call from the twins' parents. They're all Irish. Sister Raymond said there was nothing she could do. Their parents want the boys to go to Washington, DC together."

I walked up the hill to school on a Saturday for an emergency spelling bee with the Irish twin brothers. All I had to do was beat one of them, which I did every time, but every time I won a round, Sister Raymond upped the odds, 2 out 3, 3 out of 4, 5 out of 7, 7 out of 9. We were there for three hours before I missed a word. It was a setup. The Monsignor was in cahoots with the parents, and Sister Raymond was complicit. How many hours would she keep us here? Sister Raymond looked me intently in the eye and gave me the word *brakeman*. I'd never heard that word. I spelled it *breakman*. She declared the game over as if it was a sudden death round, as if it was a tiebreaker. The twins would go to Washington. Sister Raymond gave me four white milk containers as a consolation prize to take home to my mother. That added up to a whole quart of milk. I brought the white milk home and handed it to my mother. Sister Raymond should have just explained to me that I had to "take the fall," like a boxer. I would have understood. My mother didn't make me go to church after that, but I needed proof that I attended mass for school, so I had a friend bring me an extra bulletin and tell me the gist of the sermon. I never forgot the word *brakeman*, and I never wanted anyone forcing the brakes on me again.

Outfield Greens

The beauty parlor kept Mom as a manicurist, but didn't promote her to hairdresser. Mom told most people, "I'm a widow," so no one would think she was a whore, which she pronounced *hoo-wah*. Divorce was leprosy. In school I had conversations like this many times:

"You're father is dead."

"My father is not dead."

"Yes he is. Your mother told my mother."

"I should know. He's my father. See this magnet? He gave it to me last week."

My mother came home from work, threw on a hamburger, boiled and mashed potatoes, opened a can of peas, buttered some bread.

I scooped mashed potatoes out of the bowl on the table. GranmaRose, who was staying with us for a few days, yelled her shrill alarm. "Eeee!" and her right arm shot straight up in the air.

"What!" I yelled. I pulled my spoon back quick. With GranmaRose I didn't have a chance. "What I do? What?"

"Take a from here!" she said. She turned the bowl. I was so confused. It was a round bowl. I asked my Mother to serve me. Maybe I dug too deep in the bowl? I dunno. "I give up."

"Bah! What good a' you!"

GranmaRose didn't *capishe* sports in general, and did not understand my newfound commitment to softball. When my mother and I focused on the television during Mark Spitz's record-breaking seven gold medal swims in the '72 Olympics, GranmaRose sat on the couch, tried to watch, then stood up and yelled, "Ay! Back ena forth, back ena forth. What's ada use?"

My mother brought GranmaRose to my city championship softball game. I had my own cheering section: Mom, Rosemarie and her two kids, Enza and her two kids, and GranmaRose. I was behind the plate. Catchers have swagger, and I had more swagger than most. I threatened base runners with my arm cocked behind my ear ready to fire, and taunted them, "Don't even think about it." Behind the plate, I talked to every batter. I talked to my pitcher. I talked to the ump. I signaled to my team. This particular umpire chewed tobacco and spit brown juice over my shoulder. The batters thought this was disgusting, but I didn't mind. I liked the guy. He had a good eye. The sun was bright over first base and right field. My mother cheered loud for us from the bleachers. It was the only place she let loose and yelled. The ump jumped up behind me and waved his arms to halt the game. Someone was walking around in the outfield. It was GranmaRose, picking *cicoria* in left center field. I jumped up from a squat and waved her off the field, "Granma! Get off the field! Granma!" She waved at me, and waddled off with her two shopping bags full of greens. She found a use for my big game. Greens. Greens you can eat.

My Mother, the Plaintiff

There was a knock on the door. My mother looked through the peephole, and said, "What do you want?"

A man's voice said, "Hi, Rachel, how are you?" It had to be someone on my father's side of the family. The Lanzillotto's called her Rachel, the Pertruzzelli's called her Lilly. She opened the door halfway. I hid behind the open door listening. The door had three hinges thick with brown paint, a fat space to look through between the hinge of the open door and the doorframe. It was one of my uncles. I don't remember which one. What I remember is my mother, in all her glory and rage, as she stood up for herself.

"How do you think I am?" my mother said. "You are serving me papers? Are you out of your mind?" Her rant sped up hills and dove down valleys, all the while she held the door in a tight grip. She could swing it closed in his face at any moment. I've heard my mother retell this rant so many times over the years that I can recite the lines by heart. "You were a kid brother to me. I cooked you how many meals how many years and you have the nerve to serve me papers? I thought at least I'd be entitled to half the house. But he had people write testifications that he owed out big money. So when he finally sold the house he wrote them all checks. That's how I got nothing after twenty-five years of marriage but a good kick you know where. I ran from that house like a refugee. I never even told my mother the details of my troubles. But she knew in her own way. I had to stop inviting her over. He didn't want anyone over the house." She slammed the door, put a cigarette in her teeth, dipped it over the stove, and dialed the telephone.

"Hi Sis, I was just served papers. I nearly passed out. There was a knock on the door. P.S. It was his kid brother who came to my door and had the nerve to try to hand them to me. I threw him out. I says to him, after all these years, you're going to hand me this crap? You should see this list. All I can think is they are talking about some other woman. That's all I keep thinking, who are they talking about? He fabricated a whole story. Plaintiff this and plaintiff that. I was in disbelief. The brother says, 'Rachel, don't take it personal.' Don't take it personal? Who's he kidding? He dropped the papers behind the door and left. He couldn't look me in the eye. I said, 'Stop looking at the floor. What are you doing?' Then I made the mistake of reading those papers. '*Plaintiff insisted on sleeping on the couch in the living room. Plaintiff refused to have relations with the defendant, saying she did not love him. Plaintiff failed to prepare meals. Defendant objected. When Defendant came home from work, he would find that supper had not been prepared, that the house had not been cleaned and that Plaintiff had neglected all household duties and chores.*' I can't believe what I am reading. I cooked I cleaned I listened to his horse crap for what? '*Plaintiff called defendant vile names such as baldy, toothless, ugly, and old, and said, "I could get another man in a minute."*' Sis, you gotta see this crap he fabricated with his lawyer. I keep thinking I am reading about someone else."

My mother was quiet, listened for a while then said, "Okay, Sis, that sounds perfect, just what I'm in the mood for. No, we'll walk. I need a little fresh air." Then she turned to me and said, "We're going over Aunt Patty's for pesto."

Aunt Patty's Bullfight

Aunt Patty lived in a big house with her husband Joe, on top of a hill a mile away. They lived on the edge of a forest. Behind their backyard was a row of mansions. Across the street from their front yard were modest brick houses. It was a good long walk up the side of what felt like a mountain. "Not a soul out," my mother said. "You can walk here for hours and not see one person. In the Bronx you'd run into everybody on the sidewalk. In the Bronx everyone's laundry hung out on their clotheslines and you knew all their business. Three traumatized World War II combat veterans lived on our block who were nuts," my mother said, "I wouldn't be surprised if all those women got smacked around. Behind us, across the street and down the block." Our family, even with all the violence fit in. People up here in Yonkers didn't call for one another, or tap on a pipe, or come in and out for coffee. One person was stalwart. Aunt Patty's daughter-in-law Tova. She called my mother every single morning at seven a.m. to check in, make her laugh, and make plans to pick her up and take a ride to a store. She had strong swimmer's shoulders and a short blonde pixie haircut. Tova was a loving, tough, straight talker, earning the highest accolades from everyone who knew her as "a pisser," which meant if you hung out with her, you'd definitely have a good time. Tova grew up in Parkchester. She had all the best of Bronx mores, and always made me feel at home. In her house was the first time I sat in a swivel chair, and the first time I heard the words penis, cock, and balls regularly. I spun around and around in her blue swivel chair and let the sexual language swirl around me, penis cock balls penis cock balls.

When we got to Aunt Patty's, we rang the front bell, and heard her yell, "Come around back." She wanted to save her carpet "wear and tear."

I went into the kitchen to help her bring the dishes to the dining room table. For a moment, it was just the two of us. "Aunt Patty, I got to ask you something."

"What is it Butchie?"

"I want to know details about how my mother fell out the window when she was a kid."

"Change the subject. Here, bring these to the table—watch out, it's hot," she said. I walked away and began to cry. I went to the guest bathroom to wash my face and walked into her living room. It was a room for display, not for comfort. She had a stiff couch and two stiff thrones. Glass cabinets filled with her Hummel figurine collection. Old vinyl records stood in the fireplace: Sinatra, Tony Bennett, Jimmy Roselli. A baby grand piano on which Aunt Patty played "Torna a Surriento," and her cherished pink champagne color carpet that none of us were allowed to step on. If we left by the front door, we had to walk on a narrow plastic runner across the living room, one foot in front of the other, like walking the plank. Above the stiff couch were four paintings of a bullfight. The toreador swirled his pinkish red cape up for the bull to attack the low curl of the cape; then he turned his back into the bull coming around him; next, he stepped away, the bull's horns just missing his chest; and finally, in the fourth frame, struck a bloody blow down the side of the bull's spine. I stared at the pinkish red cape and wondered what all the mystery and silence surrounding my mother's fall was about.

I rejoined the adults at the table.

"Why's your face all red?" my mother asked.

"Allergies."

After we ate, Aunt Patty put a green plastic poker table over her kitchen table to convert it for her evening card party.

You're Just Like Your Father

In lieu of a divorce settlement, my mother held onto all her good furniture. She salvaged the maple dining room table set and her bedroom set, which was way too large for the apartment. The wings of the chairs stabbed me every time I walked by, repeatedly giving me a black 'n blue in my gut. The chair dowels still pulled out of their holes. She continued to sleep on the couch, which relegated me to my parents' bedroom set. So instead of my father in that bed with my mother on the couch, it was me in that bed with my mother on the couch. I took my father's place, both as my mother's escort and tormenter.

"You're just like you're father," was my mother's continual *tremolo*, and now she had her sister's and mother's choral support. "You're just like your father you're just like you're father you're just like you're father you're just like your father you're just like your father. Go! Live with him!"

You're just like your father you're just like your father you're just like your father. You're just like your father you're just like your father. My mother's accusation rang inside my soul along with the fears my father drilled into me. You have to learn to know what's behind you. You're just like . . . Don't look now, you must be aware constantly of what's behind you. You're just like your father. Don't trust nobody you have to learn to look behind you. You have to learn to know what's behind you. Don't let life take you down for nuttin' stoopit. Don't let life take you down. You can get knocked down your whole life, as long as you don't get knocked out. Don't tell anyone whatchyou got. Stupid things don't happen to those aware. Avoidable mishaps. You have to learn to look behind you. We're survivors. Lanzillottos are survivors. Look both ways, you understand, before you cross even a one-way street. One way one way who says the one way. The old breed. You're just like your father you're just like your father you're just like your father go live with him!

Every time the phone rang, my mother let it ring three times. Two rings was Aunt Patty. One ring was Cousin Lucy. Only my mother had an unlimited local phone plan, so she would have to dial them back. If she fell silent and pushed the receiver away from her body, placing it down on the counter, then I knew it was my father.

Lanzi picked me up in his Chevy Malibu. Sometimes he drove out to New Jersey and took me shopping in the mall in Paramus. He liked to be on the road and talk, cross over a big bridge and philosophize, and have a destination to use the bathroom. My father was never a drinker, but during this period after the divorce, he kept a pint of whiskey under the driver's seat. This was the only time in my life I ever saw him drink. One day, some poor schmuck was driving too slow in front my father. Worse than that, he was in a white Cadillac. And on top of that he had a war veteran bumper sticker. To top it all off he had Jersey plates which is bad enough, but this guy had special Purple Heart license plates. This set my father off on an explosive rant.

"You should see this *chibobi*! Drives around in his green Caddy sportin' a license plate that says Purple Heart. Every day he takes up the disability spot at the diner. I take one look at him I know who he is. He was in the rear. Took the million-dollar bullet home. In the rear they had sleep. They had sleep, they had food. They had food, they had liquor. You could even get a woman in the rear. Same time we was digging the front in through a layer of dead Jap earth. Didn't take our boots off for tree weeks, then we traded socks and moved on. On the front you had to dig foxholes. You had no choice. If it rained you sat in mud all night. And it always rained. You take this here entrenching shovel. You dig in right through the bones in the earth, you dig. Establish a perimeter zone. You dig. Who knows what you come up with. You dig. Eventually you come up with earth. If I could sleep, I'd sleep but who could sleep? You sleep with one eye open."

In the mall, I picked out clothes and shoes in big sizes so they would fit my mother. I stood in the aisles of the women's department, and picked shirts with the sleeves that hung over my wrists. I picked belts with extra loops. I tried to buy my mother a new coat. Lanzi knew what I was doing. He appeased me. On one trip he bought me twenty pairs of shoes, in all different sizes. When he dropped me off, I ran up and down the grassy hill four times with packages. My mother rolled her eyes. She examined the shoes to see if she could return some of them locally, for cash.

"I feel like throwing them all out," she said, "this is ridiculous. He bought all this to spite me. He never paid child support."

I felt like a pirate with bounty. Money. Money. Money. Who had what? Who owed who? Who? Who? Who?

Junkie Pride

In high school I earned GranmaRose's rancor by taking showers every day. She'd stand outside the bathroom door and mutter with derision as I blow-dried my hair, "Educationa Education, you scrub all'a the oils off'a da skin." My mother would have liked me to do more curling and combing. She was a hairdresser to the core. In that house I couldn't win either way. Sporting holes in my dungarees, going outside with a wet head, eating three-colored ice cream out of a soup bowl, pulling fringe on my dungaree shorts around my thigh, all earned me the extra gesture of a twist and shake of GranmaRose's shoemaker knife, an old scythe-like blade meant to cut leather heels, which cut everything from Granma's hunk of provolone to pears to her sentences. That blade was an extension of her; curved, sharp, and without any shine. It could curve slices right through you like sliced peaches in the can.

The minute I turned sixteen I got my driver's license and became the get-away car. Aunt Patty bought a new Cutlass Supreme and gave Mom the gold '70 Mustang. I got to drive it. I got vanity plates that read LANZO and raced around high school. That car had pick up power. Ant'ny lived right up the hill from us with his new wife Diana. To get engaged my mother handed Ant'ny her wedding ring. He got a new setting for the diamond and began his life. The wedding party was in Aunt Patty's backyard. Diana was a Bronx Italian who worked at the Bainbridge Diner. In heels she was over six foot tall. She was blonde and wore her hair short with spiky sideburns. She knew how to dress and was fast with a comment. She always wore nail polish and hanging gold earrings. All my siblings were now married to Bronx Italians. Ant'ny never asked me directly for a ride to score dope or to steal things. He just came up with coercive cockamamie tales. To coax me into driving him places, Ant'ny told me stories. "Hey Annie, I bought a muffler, but it don't fit and my car's in the shop. I have to go get a part from this guy, would you drive me? But we gotta go now. Now. Now."

"Right now?"

"Now. The guy's waitin' for me."

"Where's the muffler shop?"

"Down the Bronx. It'll take twenty minutes back and forth."

When I pulled up into a seedy residential street, I said to him, "Where's the shop? I don't see any muffler shop."

"Stay here. Keep the engine running. Stay right here. Lock the doors. Don't talk to anybody. Don't look at anybody. Keep the engine running. You understand?" His thick forefinger pointed in assertion. He walked, almost in a run, holding the two flaps of his maroon colored leather blazer together, his other hand patting his jacket pocket. When he returned, he got back into the car as fast as he could, always looking around, and with urgency yelled, "Go. Go. Go. Let's go. Let's go. Take a right. That's it. Let's go."

"Did you get what you needed?"

He acted as if I wasn't there.

Ant'ny examined the contents of his little paper bag. There were no car parts in it.

Mary Perry

I had romantic friendships with girls. I put on my best cream-colored corduroys, and with my savings from three jobs, took one Italian girl on a helicopter ride around Manhattan, and dinner at Tavern on the Green. I was sixteen. I was so impressed the way the waiter could tell when our water glasses were empty from across the room. Water came out of nowhere over my shoulder, poured into the crystal tumbler. The water bearer stood at attention across the room. That was his job, pouring water. This blew my mind. The after-dinner entertainment was sitting in the bucket seats of the gold Mustang, looking through *Screw* magazine. I held the left page, she held the right page. We each came in a little closer. I felt a deep longing in my heart that I couldn't name or quench. Love became about wanting something I couldn't identify. We held hands for a year and sang Carole King songs, then she went with the high school quarterback and I fell into my first lovelorn despair. A dark fist resided in my chest. I drove around in the Mustang, and played James Taylor on my boombox. I didn't know what to do about the dull ache in my heart, but sing and cry.

I worked a series of jobs that gave me pocket money. Paper route. Babysat. Did the neighbor's laundry. I worked at Kentucky Fried Chicken on Central Avenue when I was underage, just fourteen, and got fired after a series of mishaps: first I slipped on chicken fat and dropped a whole tray of baby coleslaws, then I was early to work one day and sold chicken to a family who got sick from it. I didn't know the bluish chicken was being saved for some old guy's blind dog. I scrubbed that kitchen on my hands and knees like the good Italian American woman I innately was. After I got fired, I crossed Central Avenue and got my next job at Roadside China. I was the "duster" for all the imported crystal, china, and bone china. Not a good job for a bull in a china shop. I lost that job because I sneezed. Allergic to dust, yes I was. This was confirmed when I was on the top rung of a ladder in The Rosenthal Room; twenty feet of place settings stacked along shelves like dominoes, and that's exactly how they fell when I sneezed and knocked one down. Broken crystal and porcelain everywhere. Next I went to the Department of Parks and Recreation. I became the ID checker at the local tennis court. For the local dentist, I developed tooth films. Ambitiously, I worked three jobs at once. I'd wake up, develop the tooth films, drive up to the tennis court, then go to Central Plaza Cinema, where I sold popcorn and candy for the matinee. Then I'd take a break and drive to the tennis court to see if anybody was there. I left a lawn chair and an ice tea to make it look like I'd be right back. Eventually the checker of the ID checkers figured out that I was never really there. That's how I lost that job. My boss at Central Plaza was a bodybuilder and model. To interview to get that job, I had to stand on a desk in a short skirt and turn around in front of all the men who worked there. "Not bad Lanz," the boss said, "you're hired." But the worst job of all was telemarketing from the apartment, which my mother made me do at night, since I was about thirteen.

"Our name is too long," she explained, "so instead, use the name Mary Perry." Years later when I asked her where she came up with the name Mary Perry, she elaborated, "My best friend in high school was Mary Como. I used to call her Mary Perry's Sister Como. Perry Como was very popular at the time. So somehow that name popped into my head, Mary Perry." And that's how I became Mary Perry, telemarketer extraordinaire. I opened the thick Westchester White Pages in the kitchen on a piece of pull-out wood at our counter that served as our breakfast nook. I sat on my mother's antique milk pail, dialed one number at a time on the rotary phone, and made my way through the phonebook.

"Hello, my name is Mary Perry from Lawn King." I was not convincing as Mary Perry. I never made one sale. I would never be convincing as a Mary Perry.

College Entrance

I was eighteen and it was time to leave my mother. She was peaceful and dating a man named Bill who she said was "neat and clean." I had my heart set on going to college in the mountains. All my life I needed good air. This was my chance. Rosemarie and Peter and my goddaughter Melissa were living in the mountains in upstate New York. Roe picked me up in her orange Volkswagen Beetle and took me on a college road trip along beautiful country roads. She encouraged me to consider schools where I'd feel at home, and to study to be an engineer. I honestly thought engineers drove locomotives. I wore a blue striped engineer's cap all the time. One day I went to the public library, which always attracted all the perverts in Yonkers; nonetheless, I went there to look at college brochures and spread them out. This cute older guy I knew from the ball fields walked by my table and saw my brochures with Colorado skies and red tile rooftops of Spanish-style dorm buildings, and challenged me: "You want to work hard or go to a country club?"

"I wanna work hard."

"Well? What are you doing?"

I folded the big skies up.

A few nights later, I was at a bar with my friends. We drank Kamikazes at the Ground Round. I ran into another older guy I knew from high school. Jon Ebinger had been Roosevelt High School President and Captain of the ice hockey team. He was a scholar athlete, and I looked up to him.

"Apply to Brown," he said, "you'd love it."

"What's that?"

"Just apply. Trust me."

Both these guys seemed serious, smart, successful, and intent on giving me a message. For some reason, I heard it loud and clear.

The essay question for Brown's entrance application asked, "Who do you most admire and why?" I wrote about GranmaRose. At my age, she left her family forever, and started something new. That sounded very good to me, brave and independent. Who was as strong as GranmaRose? I wished I had half her gumption. I sat at her feet with my tape recorder and asked her questions about *Acquaviva delle Fonti*, and the boat *Duca degli Abruzzi* that she took to Ellis Island. "I don't want to think about that boat," she said. What most impressed me is that she left at eighteen and never saw her mother or anyone in her family again. She found her own adventure. I wondered what that would be like. I wondered if I could leave my mother. I knew once I left for college I'd never come back. I felt I had completed my mission. My name Lanzillotto comes from Sir Lancelot. My grandfather Carmine, spelled the name Lanzillotta, derived from the Italian *Lancialotta, Lancillotto,* in French *Lancelot du Lac*, and in English, Lancelot. Lancelot's missions were based on pleasing the Queen. I was clear that all my life 'til this moment, I had tried to save my mother. Now it was time for me to move on to my own adventures. Save myself. Somehow GranmaRose had done that. She got on the donkey which took her to the train which took her to the boat which took her across the ocean and she built a life in the Bronx, and she never saw her mother again. I didn't write all that in the application essay, but that was the gist. My grandmother amazed me.

The thick acceptance letter from Brown University was in the mailbox when I came home one day to change into my softball uniform. I pulled on the tight white-with-red-pinstripe pants and red stirrups and opened the envelope. "Cool," I said to my teammate who was with me. I tossed the envelope on the bed and didn't think too much of it. I finished getting dressed. I wore jersey number 31 in honor of CarKey who wore that number in his men's league. He wore it for his daughter's birthday. CarKey was a powerful hitter, respected by the other guys on the team. I put on my red suspenders, red-and-white striped engineers cap, red bandana around my neck, threw my cleats over my shoulder, and walked across Central Avenue to Andrus Field.

The next day at school, the guidance counselor celebrated when I walked in.

"What's the big deal?" I asked.

"This is the Ivy League. This is the big time."

At Central Plaza Cinema, an Italian guy named Joe who had a grand skill of whistling, was so ecstatic over my acceptance that he gave me a gift: a cassette tape of Mozart's, *Eine kleine Nachtmusik*. "You're going to the Ivy League," he said, "you gotta know this stuff. Wait 'til the kids hear Annie from da Bronx whistling *Eine kleine Nachtmusik*." I played the cassette on my boombox in the gold Mustang that had brought us from the Bronx eight years before. I practiced whistling Mozart's four movements everywhere I went. It made me happy.

I telephoned my father.

He said, "You got a shot."

It was as if I had entered a pole-vaulting competition. I was supposed to pole-vault further into the American dream; run, stick my pole in the dirt, reach for the sky and never come down.

Strike One

SUMMER VACATION, JERSEY SHORE, 1981

Zing was my pitcher, and I was her catcher. We could anticipate each other's every move. The ball was incidental between us. She wound her arm back overhead and, snap, the ball was in my mitt. We'd done this motion thousands of times. Curveballs, knuckleballs, pitchouts, sinkers, fastballs, wild pitches. Our signals were refined. But that summer of 1981, our playing together was over. I was going off to Brown, while she still had two years left at Roosevelt High School. Her sister rented a bungalow on the Jersey Shore and they generously took me with them. I'd never been on a vacation before. Zing and me worked out every day. I caught a hundred of her pitches twice a day: twenty-five warm-ups, fifty full-speed, and twenty-five cool downs. She sprung her arm back and came at me. By the end of a pitching session, a red welt appeared across the top of the palm of my catching hand. As a catcher I worked on my pop squats, throws to second to nab the steal, plays at the plate, tag outs of runners sliding home to the accompanying yell of "Out!" Each day I did two hundred pop squats barefoot in the sand. Each day turned me a bit more blonde, more fit, more tan, ready to jump into action in college, where I was a softball recruit for the varsity team.

For two weeks, we'd played and wrestled and at night spooned each other. We were inseparable, but there was a barrier in me that I wouldn't cross with a girl. I thought it was wrong. I thought I was wrong.

Our last day, I took one final walk alone down the boardwalk. College would be the first time my mother and I were separated. I wanted to buy a memento for her to mark this passage in time; a great present, not the crap that filled the New Jersey boardwalk stands: silk-screened Elvis mirrors, air-brushed T-shirts of palm tree paradises, stuffed ETs that were popular that summer. I wanted more of a forever keepsake, something my mother could remember me by, something to stand for this point in time. My mother and I believed that college would change everything. Since I got into Brown, my family treated me like I was "made." I would be an earner, I would be protected by being part of an institution, a system, a bigger-than-you place, I would become a somebody, I would be friends with doctors and lawyers. Life was a gamble and I had a shot. My odds were good. A shot was all one could ask for. I knew I'd never come back home, never return to Yonkers. Maybe one day I'd live in the Bronx again.

I went to the batting range. I loved the feeling of the ball connecting solidly with the heart of my bat. I swung ahead of some fast pitches, behind others, and connected solid-line drives up the middle. I walked up the boardwalk past the portrait artists who shouted at us day after day, flashing drawings of Marilyn Monroe and John Travolta, saying, "It won't take long," as if they could bring out the Travolta and Monroe in each of us in ten minutes. I never saw a portrait of anyone in my family before, and I was the first one going away to college, off to the Ivy League, and the Ivy League was all about portraits in stately rooms. Why not one of me? My mother would love it. That's a special gift, I thought. A portrait was a suitable way to celebrate this juncture of life; I was at my peak with all my potential before me. I wore dungaree overalls over a blue-green shirt with a low-cut lace neck and tassels that matched my eyes. I walked toward the portrait artists, some of whom were hawking. One sat quietly. A woman in a big yellow sun hat, a Bella Abzug–type hat that created a round arena of shade around her head. I walked up to her. I had fifty bucks left in my pocket. We agreed on fifty bucks. "Plenty of detail for fifty bucks," she guaranteed me, "not a pen–line caricature. Name's Rhoda. What's yours?"

I unsnapped the top of my overalls, fixed my shirt around my neck and sat for her. I couldn't see what her hand was doing. Her arm moved at a rapid speed, bending automatically at the elbow like the pitching machine in the batting cage. Rhoda asked me questions about my life as she chose reds and yellows. I told her of my bright future as a trial lawyer, that my talents were in public speaking and writing, that I loved to shadowbox. I threw a punch combination into the air. Rhoda's eyes landed on different parts of me: cheek, eyes, neck, hairline, nose. I felt appraised, sized up, like she was peeking inside me and also around me to see what was there. Her questions were pointed, and I answered them in detail and full of promise. I was primed.

"Good luck with your future," she said. She turned the portrait to face me, quickly, as if on a hinge. Rhoda Shapiro had drawn a girl a little more feminine and gorgeous than I was, with feathered hair a little blonder than my own, and eyes a deeper blue, and a glow—a white thin halo surrounding the whole bust. Pleased, I rolled up the portrait like a bat and brought it back to the cabin.

"Lanzo, it looks nothing like you!" Zing fell on the floor laughing. Her brother said it was beautiful. "It looks like what you think you want to look like," she added. Zing kept laughing, and wrestling me, but I could see the resemblance, even if she couldn't. The portrait was a culturally idealized version of me, some iconic combination of the Mona Lisa magnetism of John Travolta drawing you in, and the full-bursting-lipped ripe beauty of Marilyn Monroe enticing you to take a bite. Rhoda drew a corner of white light on my lips like I'd seen in a still life of an apple. And that's just what this point in my life was all about; my college application essays and recommendations were as blonde, blue-eyed, and with an exaggerated and energetic virgin's glow. The eyes she made soulful, soulful as the ocean she stared at day after day, waiting for her customers to sit in the slatted heat of the boardwalk.

That night, we had one last catch on the beach. Neither of us had the sense that this would be the last catch of our lives, but it was. I imagined we'd always be friends, even as old ladies. I held the white ball in my hand. We started far apart. I threw the ball with all my might in a high arc. I threw as far as most players could hit. This is my throwing arm. My one arm to throw, my other arm to receive. I throw. I throw with everything inside me. Zing ran down the beach chasing the ball. She threw it back high. I couldn't see it anymore. The blue sky was turning black. I inferred the arc the ball made and stood under it, 'til it was in my hands. I bent over, threw the ball to her from between my legs and did a tumble-sault in the sand. I released the ball far off to the side so she had to run for it, dive, and snatch it in midair before crashing down onto the sand. She sprang back up, and the ball was back in my mitt. Nothing got by her. I threw to one side. She dove, got it. I threw far overhead and she sprinted, reached, stretched into a dive, glove up, got it. Snap. Zing threw hard. I felt a pang on the pulp of my catching hand. I smelled the leather of the glove, and the salt of the sea air. Seagulls squawked and hovered nearby. I squatted and made a target. I inscribed the strike zone with my bare hand. Zing moved in closer. We struck out invisible opponents. Three up, three down. She threw it between us and the ball stopped dead in the sand. We both sprinted for it. I dove on top of it. She dove on top of me. She grabbed me, hugged me around my belly. The ball got away. We wrestled for it down into the sand. Her long black hair was in my mouth.

"I can't believe you're leaving," she said, and spit sand out of her mouth. Her lips were red and had a freckle. I pushed her shoulder. She grabbed my neck.

"Rhode Island's just a couple of hours away," I said, "you could swim up the shoreline."

"Very funny. I'm serious."

Her arms encircled me. She kissed me on my cheek. I kissed her nose. She kissed my forehead. I kissed her chin and the corner of her mouth. We both breathed hard.

"Damn," she said, jumped up and threw the ball out into the water. She was crying. The waters were ribbed like the sky. The full moon reached over the black water, right to us, over the pounding waves. The sky pulled the waters. The moon held the reins. The ocean was chomping at the bit. The moon rode the waters as they cantered. The moon was in the saddle. All was pulled by the moon. The ball had a cork center. I could see it bobbing up and down, a white ball in black water. I stood up to go after it. I stood at the edge where the water met the sand. I could float. I could dog-paddle. But I couldn't swim.

"Go ahead. Ah, you wouldn't."

"I won't?"

"I dare you Lanz. I bet you a hundred kisses."

"Five hundred."

"Bet."

I tore off my shirt, dropped my shorts and kicked them up in the air. I whooped and hollered and ran straight for the ball. I dog-paddled to the ball, grabbed it, held it up to the moon, and yelled in the cold, cold black cold water.

"You're crazy Lanzo, you know that? You're crazy!"

"C'mon in! I'll up you another hundred kisses."

"I must be crazy."

Just then her brother appeared, walking down the beach. "I been looking for you two," he said.

"Crazy," she called me.

I threw her the ball and she threw me a towel.

"You owe me," I mouthed to her.

I pulled on a shirt, wrapped a towel around my waist, whipped water onto Zing with my hair, and the three of us walked back to the cabin.

That night Zing delivered the kisses she bet, staring deep into my eyes, landing her lips all over my face and head and neck. But our lips never fully met. We spooned all night long. There was a barrier inside me I wasn't ready to cross, and didn't know how.

When I got home, I handed the scroll to my mother. "Mom, even though we haven't been getting along very well lately, I know I'll miss you, and although I'm moving on to new horizons and going off on my own, I won't ever forget all you did for me. Thank you for everything. These past years you've been a mother and a father."

My mother unrolled Rhoda's portrait of me and all she said was, "What's this lump on your neck?"

She looked at the portrait and touched my neck, where her hand landed on what Rhoda Shapiro had drawn and only my mother noticed, a bulge on the right side of my neck. Rhoda outlined in red and yellow, a diagnosis, a misshapen neck, a lump like a stop sign amid a blonde waterfall. As it turned out, Rhoda's eye had the accuracy of a sonogram.

Fontanelle Aurelius

One night when I was half asleep, I felt my soul like a silvery white tornado spinning inside me. It pulled up through my body and out the top of my head. I was scared. My soul wanted to leave my body. It was heading for the window. I resisted. I didn't want to leave my body. I heard this loud spinning vibration as my soul revved up. The next day I walked to the Yonkers Public Library to try and find out what happened to me the night before. I found a book on "astral projection." It seemed a lot of folks left their bodies at night, flew around, and hung out. Was astral projection like sex? Something adults did and never told me about? Several nights I laid there and tried to make it happen again. I hummed buzzing noises. I tensed the muscles around my spine. I pictured a silvery white tornado inside me. The spinning feeling did come back, though with less velocity. It was like the fontanelle on my skull was an open portal for my soul for one night, and then closed up tight again.

I got an invitation in the mail for a party in Scarsdale for all the kids going to Brown from Westchester County. I drove in the Mustang to the Scarsdale mansion. I wore my best sneakers. I felt lowbrow and out of place. I was the only one in sneakers. The girls were in "cocktail attire," a new phrase to me, and the guys wore casual suit jackets. If Brown was like this, I'd be lost in the sauce. I got through the party by talking to a cute hippy musician named Eric Applebaum. He had freckles and a red glint to his hair, and even though he was a Preppy, he was smart and a musician and a new kind of guy for me to hang with. I actually overheard one of the girls in a dress say, "Oh, drinking Coke from a can, how uncouth." If I didn't have Eric to talk with, I might have run out of the mansion screaming, revved the

Mustang, and shot down the Bronx River Parkway as fast as I could. I mean, I am Lanzi's daughter. There's only so much I can put up with.

I let my Mom give me a manicure, a soft perm, and a curling iron. She was so happy as she held my hand in warm soapy water and pushed back my cuticles. Rosemarie took me shopping to get the things she said a young woman needed to be on her own: mascara, eyeliner, Jean Naté body splash, an eyelash curler, pocket tissues. I was all set.

Mom and her boyfriend "neat and clean" Bill drove me up to Providence. I packed all my belongings in Hefty trash bags and filled his powder blue Cadillac trunk. Soft spoken, dull-witted, "neat and clean" Bill, was the antithesis of Lanzi and I hated being with him, but I was just glad to get the hell outta Yonkers. My father was sick. He was recovering from quadruple bypass surgery and had to take it easy. I took the ride in the Caddy and focused on where I was headed. I put blinders on and thought of Lanzi's words, "The fastest horse runs alone." I arrived at Brown with a red-white-and-blue basketball tucked under my arm and a lump on the right side of my neck, that a couple of doctors said was nothing serious. I wore dungarees, a short tight red-quilted sweater, and white sneakers with red-and-blue-striped laces in a box weave. I whistled the allegro *Eine kleine Nachtmusik,* and spoke in a thick Bronx accent. I walked around College Hill carrying my basketball under my elbow. I felt alive with its strong tight bounce; it hit my new sidewalks and came right back into the palm of my hand.

I loved the buildings at Brown. I felt I could hug them. They were chunky four-story brick and brown stone, and they really were covered with ivy. Flocks of birds whistled between the ivy and the brick walls. Students played frisbee on the Main Green. Frisbee wasn't a Bronx game, you need wide open fields for frisbee. In the Bronx, we had sky We threw straight up as high as possible, or we threw overhand at the X chalked on a wall. I had great aim. I kept my eye out for the chalked palimpsest of an X, to tell me against what walls kids threw here. I didn't see any on campus, but in Fox Point, a Portuguese neighborhood, I found chalked Xs on the walls of houses, clotheslines, big churches, and narrow side streets. I knew I was home. The sidewalks echoed the bounce of my basketball across the street, the way it did all those years ago on Saint Raymonds Avenue.

I sat on my basketball and leaned back against the base of the statue of Marcus Aurelius on campus in Lincoln Field. He held his arm out over the hill. Brown was an intellectual candy store, and I ordered the most exotic things on the menu. I chose one class called "Anatomy of the Soul," and another called "Mars, Moon, and the Earth."

I wanted to get away from all things Italian. I wanted to be American. The joke was on me. Rhode Island was the most Italian state, and Providence was run by the mob. I found this out because a lot of the working-class jobs on campus were filled with Italians. Big Tony G's job was to man the campus gym's laundry room and wash all Brown's sports teams' uniforms and towels. Big Tony G had twenty washers and dryers all going at once. He reminded me of Sonny Bono, short and skinny with endless energy, quick jokes and stories, big sweet brown eyes under brown bangs and the thick moustache. I found myself hanging out a lot in the laundry room talking with Tony. Then there was Joanne The Trainer who tended our athletic injuries. She was focused and diligently wrapped our knees and ankles while she clued us into how to take better care of ourselves. As we iced our joints, we listened to her stories and hard earned wisdom. Joanne The Trainer *capished* the things of life. Between the two of them, I had an instant family that stripped away any fantasies I'd had about my new life in Providence. I would eat at Caserta's Pizza and Angelo's Restaurant on Federal Hill, and I'd understand Mayor Buddy Cianci's legendary trail of extortion. Just a few blocks off College Hill, Providence was a seething hotbed of Italian-American *mafiosi*, anti-intellectualism, cronyism, and all the closed-minded attitudes I thought I'd fled far away from.

I ate ice cream at every meal. I waited on line with my tray at the "All You Can Eat" eating hall called, "The Ratty," filled my plate, and always went back for seconds. I tasted avocados for the first time. GranmaRose would have had a shopping bag. She never made it up to Brown to visit me. She had just returned to *Acquaviva* for the first time in her life. She was eighty, and her sister Maria was a few years older. Maria, whose place she took on the boat when they were teenagers.

I watched the freshman leave our dorm to go jog every morning. I watched them run off toward the river or Blackstone Boulevard, but I felt I couldn't make it all the way. My powerful thighs could do it, but not my lungs. "C'mon Annie!" they yelled as they jogged away from campus. I was confused, these kids dressed in clothes full of holes, had fresh complexions, jogged, and laughed and spoke of other countries with ease. They knew the characters from *M.A.S.H.* in all their nuances, they were social, and organized to rent a house for the summer in Newport. I was baffled. I stood on the roof of my dorm and held my arms straight out like wings. I was ready for some gust of wind to take me into their realm. I dove into college life with a vengeance. "Taste everything in the garden," Uncle Frank told me. Freshman week I made out with guys from three different continents. I knocked on professors' doors at random and asked them what their expertise was. I told my freshman dean, Bruce Donovan, "I just don't want to miss anything while I am here."

I made two good friends with working-class New York accents and attitudes. Debbie Gorney and I were softball recruits, she was a pitcher. We threw a hundred pitches a day in the off-season, and we took jobs as managers of the varsity women's soccer team, so we could throw on the sidelines all fall. Sue Maloney was a basketball recruit and a pre-med student. I felt at home when Maloney called for me up at my dorm room window, hollering, "Lanzillotto!" One day I met Maloney at the gym to play in a pickup game of hoops. I stood on the balcony of the gym, overlooking the basketball courts and saw Maloney's blonde ponytail hustling under the boards rebounding a ball. Maloney was an inspiring player. There she was, the only girl on the court keeping up with all the guys. A tough blonde New Yorker with an Irish twinkle in her eye, a sexy gap in her front teeth, and bravado, she wore a jacket that read "Empire Games;" she was a champion class athlete.

I walked down the stairs and onto the court to join the game. I was used to playing ball hard, past the point of discomfort or injury. From the start I couldn't keep up on the court. I couldn't get the ball into the hoop. Fifteen minutes in, Maloney heard me wheezing beneath the backboard. I lagged behind the play, making it downcourt after the other team already scored. This wasn't like me. I was used to pushing fast breaks, anticipating the play.

Maloney said, "What's up?"

"Nothin'," I said, "asthma."

Maloney looked at me on the court and jutted her chin out to check in with me, and to get me to sit down. She knew she couldn't get me off the court. She knew I wouldn't pull myself out of the game. After a respectable amount of time, she said, "Okay guys, that's it. I gotta go study." She called the game. Everyone dispersed. Maloney put her arm around my shoulders. "Lanzillotto you better get that checked out."

"I know. I know. I'm off. I'm off. I never been this off."

I lost my touch. I couldn't get the ball into the hoop. Normally I'd relish side-court shots where the ball whizzed through the hoop. I could feel it through my fingertips. I was off. My touch was off. The spin I put on the ball. I stretched my arms out and pressed my thumbs across the tops of my fingers. Then I pressed my fingernails into the pads of my thumbs. Something was wrong. I could feel it. I was off.

At Brown University's Varsity Basketball tryouts, my shots hit the backboard like lead, and my feet were heavy on the floor. I watched the ball miss, and thought, Whose shot is that? Where was my arc? My throw? The spin I put on the ball? The coach put her arm around me, walked me to the side and said, "Let's put you on JV. Play there a year and see how you do."

CarKey called me on the phone. He talked nice with me on the phone. He took the ball. Saved my life. A Marine takes action like nobody else. "Yeah Annie, what's going on with your neck."

"Nothing. I went to Health Services. Nobody knows nothin'. The doctor said it was an infected lymph node. I took the antibiotics. He sent me to a dentist who said, 'It could be wisdom teeth. Time will tell.' He sent me to

another doctor who said, 'It's your age. You're growing.' I can't sleep at night.
I take Tylenol. I wake up sweaty."

"You been to how many doctors and still no diagnosis?"

"Five. And I can't wake up in the morning. I can't stay awake in class."

"What class?"

"International politics."

"Yeah, well. And the thing didn't go away on its own?"

"No. It definitely didn't go away. It didn't get any bigger, but it's there.
It don't hurt. It don't bother me. It's hard as a rock. I'm off. I'm off. I've
been playing pickup games. I can't get the ball into the hoop."

"That's it."

"I know."

"That's it."

"I know. I'm off. I can feel it."

"I talked to Nicky, come Thanksgiving we're getting this thing resolved."

"Who's Nicky?"

"A kid I went to school with."

"What school?"

"Yeah, I know him from Saint Raymond's High School. He became a
doctor. An ENT. He says the lump has to come out. I'm scheduling it over
Thanksgiving."

"What's an ENT?"

"Whaddyacall. Ear, nose, throat."

"Okay. Alright. It didn't go away on its own, let's take it out. See what
it is."

I lifted my left hand and fingered the hard lump like a plum in the right
side of my neck, just under the bone of my chin. Soon it would be gone.

The Miracle Worker of 233rd Street

THANKSGIVING VACATION, 1981, THE BRONX

When a neighborhood kid makes good, the neighbors become his
customers for life. CarKey brought me to Nicky, a boy from the
neighborhood who made good. Dr. Nicky Daniello, an ear, nose, and throat
specialist who fixed the noses of boxers. Dr. Daniello said the only way to know
for sure what was going on, was to biopsy my neck. So, while my school friends
packed into cars to go to classmates' houses in Maine and New Hampshire for
the short vacation, I was going back to the Bronx, to 233rd Street, where Dr.

Daniello operated at Misericordia Hospital, and where a bouquet of flowers awaited me, on the window ledge of my hospital room, from Maloney.

I took off my white baseball shirt with the maroon long sleeves and put on a hospital gown. Down the front of my shirt the word BROWN was silk-screened five times in a progressively faded color palette from a strong deep maroon to a pink that was barely visible.

"Happy Thanksgiving," I said to the anesthesiologist. The next thing I knew I woke up after the surgery. I was surrounded by a blurry vision of nuns in white habits standing over my bed. Three nuns looked down on me with shiny crucifixes dangling from their necks, refracting the light that was too much for my just opened eyes. This must be Heaven, I thought, the light was so bright. Then I felt tremendous pain in my head and neck, like I'd been stabbed and stuffed. I could not breathe through my nose at all. Someone gave me blessed Dilaudid, and I fell back to sleep.

I recovered at my mother's apartment in Yonkers. No one told GranmaRose that I was in the hospital. They told her I was on vacation. That I'd stayed in New England. This appeased her "*Stay in one place, Dolly, don't go back ena forth, back ena forth*" pragmatism. A week later CarKey drove me and Mom down in his work van to talk to Nicky. I sat on a crate in the middle of the two bucket seats. Nicky Daniello had an office just up the hill from Misericordia. On the walls of Nicky's waiting room hung portraits of boxers with big flat noses, their fists coming right at me. Articles with headlines, "Miracle Worker: Dr. Nicholas Daniello," were framed on the walls. The boxers' photos were signed, "Dr. D., You're a miracle worker. Forever, Lefty."

I'd always wanted to be a fighter. I'd wanted to get into the ring. I felt one step closer. Dr. Daniello waved us right into the back.

Being sick is waiting; yet you don't have us wait in the waiting room. Why? You usher us instead into your back room private office ask me how I feel. Then you take your time in telling me. You spray something up my nose to get the breathing easier. You ask me when am I planning to go back to school, you stall, as if you want one lasting look at my face before you tell me what you have known for a week. You know something in my face will change once you tell me there will be an instant silence. You must fill it in with names of new treatments and doctors and hospitals—here's a phone number I've already arranged you'll say, a consultation. You cannot give me a minute to let it sink in. You yourself did the surgery and double checked the pathology when it first came back negative; you had a feeling something had been overlooked, something told you, you listened. You look at the scar you made on my neck and now with the same hand you touch at it; with your finger quietly pet it. You comment that it's healing nice although it isn't and will continue to bleed for the next few years.

"It's of a Hodgkin's type," you say without giving me a chance for any response, and my head does not jerk toward my mother so I do not see the expression on her face, and I do not look away from your lips for three beats waiting for you to retrieve what you said—to reel it back into your mouth, take it back and say, Oops, what I meant to say was everything's okay and until now the thought of cancer has not entered my mind, I've had the lump never thinking. It was not something thought about at eighteen; I believed what you told me all along: "It is a swollen gland, chances are it is nothing. Ninety-nine percent of the time people get pockets of pus," and now you are telling me this is the one percent, the rare percent, with your fingers pinching the air, but not to worry 'cause the doctor you are sending me to has a ninety-nine percent cure-rate batting average for Hodgkin's. It's the most curable cancer. It's almost in vogue this particular cancer; this year was very successful and doing well and after a year of treatment, a year of sickness, a year out of life, a year of one year being surrounded with only a year everyone who has cancer, I will be back, you tell me, to normal, "It will soon before you know it, all be over."

I walked out of Nicky's office first. The boxers' fists, ready to throw a combination of punches, aimed at the heads of the old people sitting in chairs along the walls, their sinuses dripping. On the way out, 233rd Street was different. When I walked in I didn't notice anything; nothing was worth noticing. When I walked out, everything hit me at once; the way the tire rubbed against the curb—CarKey had parked too close to the curb—and the unsure sky, pewter and bulging. I walked out with cancer and several pieces of paper with new names and future dates and things to remember and a little brown paper bag with a salve for my neck scar. There was lots to do but nothing somehow mattered. I closed my eyes and shook my head. As a kid I had an Etch A Sketch. I'd make a picture and then shake it until it was gone. I want to do this now. Shake this picture until it disappears. Then make a new one. Start from scratch. I close my eyes and shake and shake my head.

I telephoned Rosemarie first. She dropped the phone and started to cry.

"How can it be cancer?" my mother said. "You've gained weight at school." And as soon as she asked, the answer came to her: "Maybe gaining weight is God's way of protecting you in case you got sick."

As soon as my friends from high school learned I had cancer and wouldn't be going back to college, a buddy of mine came over and presented me with a gift. German Pete was one of the kids who, like me, went to public high school after Catholic grade school. I remember Sister Raymond Aloysius making us stand up in class, we were traitors to the religion, the kids they lost to the general population of society. German Pete was one of those kids.

"Everyone chipped in," he said, and gave me PONG, a digital handball game to play on my mother's television screen. German Pete and I both knew what Hodgkin's disease was. Our chemistry teacher, Chrystyna Hubickyj died of it the year before. We called her "Bic." I sat beside her in the hospital the night she told us, "Today my veins collapsed." Coach Cal, my beloved softball coach, and me sat there. I squeezed the bicep of my throwing arm. I felt so strong. Invincible. And I was so sad. Bic wore a wig, drank coffee after coffee in her ceramic mug that looked like the earth, showed up in class on time and stayed late into the night to tutor us, so we could all pass the Chem Regents. It was an act of devotion and sacrifice. I didn't understand, at the time, why she pushed herself, in her dying days, to help us. I remember asking her, "Why don't you relax? Go see another country? Do something you want to do? Why push and push yourself to get us through this exam?" And I remember how she looked at me with a ferocity of spirit, she was brutally honest and no-nonsense, with a wide open expression on her countenance and for years I was convinced all Ukranians were so open and honest, and Bic said to me so simply, "How else are you all going to get through?" And at thirty-three, she died, and we gave her our own hero's funeral; we all passed the New York State Chemistry Regents.

Now, I was back on my mother's blue couch hitting a green dot across the television screen. Hours and hours and hours, I honed my skills. I hit the green dot on bank shots, and sped it up by aiming it at tight corner ricochets. I used my Spaldeen techniques. I sliced it, put English on it, alone on the couch, trying to not contemplate the utter meaninglessness of life. With my little white dash paddle, I hit the digital ball. It returned at different speeds. The electronic beep sped up with the smack of the ball. The speed increased with the length of the volley. I wasn't going back to Brown. I'd have to start chemo. And at night, I would sit on my mother's couch, hitting a green dot *back ena forth and back ena forth* across the television screen.

part three

Kimosabe

The Best Place to Have Cancer

MEMORIAL SLOAN-KETTERING CANCER CENTER, NEW YORK CITY, DECEMBER 1981

I woke up at four a.m. and found my mother at her face mirror in the kitchen. She unwound the rollers out of her hair. She smacked the air frantically. Whirls of cigarette smoke surrounded her. "There! It's gone." She was the kind of smoker who made clouds of smoke above her, too much for one woman with four inches of cigarette. Rosemarie called her The Chimney.

"Even today!" I yelled. "Can't you not smoke even this day?"

"It's all gone."

"It doesn't just go away!"

I did an about face. To me, her smoke was a tall wall of spikes. I went back to bed, pulled the louver doors shut, hung a towel over the door. There was no way of keeping the burnt smell out through the slats and in my nostrils. I put my head under the covers. I got back up at six. All the floors were wet. I could smell her pungent mix of bleach and white vinegar. I squeezed my eyes from the fumes. My mother was mopping the kitchen and foyer.

"Do you want to take a vitamin?" she asked. She pulled two black, triangular tablets out of the bathroom closet and handed them to me. "Here is some iron."

"Now, all of a sudden you want me to take vitamins? My whole life you never gave me a vitamin. Now you're giving me vitamins? That's like antithetical to who we are! GranmaRose never took a vitamin in her entire life. Where'd you even get these?"

"Erica Upstairs."

"Erica Upstairs. Why don't you get me the whiskey she downs the vitamins with."

I swallowed the iron tablets.

"I made farina," Mom said, "at least two tablespoons to coat your stomach."

I dressed extra that day. Put on more layers. Curled the front and sides of my hair. Even though my mother enraged me, I still did what she said. She was my mother. Her suggestions had power. I stuck a ball in my pocket. A fake Spaldeen. I couldn't find real Spaldeens anymore. I wondered where all the real Spaldeens were. On rooftops, in sewer pipes, all over the city. Maybe one day I'd search for them, climb the Bronx roofs and hunt down all the automatic homeruns. They had to be somewhere. They don't just disappear. They're made of rubber.

It was close to seven when the taxi horn beeped for us. I asked the driver her name. She said, "Maisy." She drove nonchalantly, elbow out the window and one hand on the wheel. As we passed Yonkers Raceway, my mother shut her eyes. Just looking at a racetrack gave her *agida*. The digits 7:02 flashed above the cut-out jockey leaning back in his sulky being pulled along by a horse. She reopened her eyes as we passed the Hillview reservoir, a flat open expanse of blue water that calmed her as her eyes passed over it. A wide sheet of seagulls turned the light side of their wings then dark side down over us. Above the birds, a white scar stretched across the sky. I didn't know if it was clouds or a jet way up high.

We sped into the Bronx. The posted time flashed 7:28, as we passed the Stella D'oro cookie factory.

"Smells good huh?" My mother looked out her window.

"Yeah, Bronx air's sweet. Who cares, Mom."

"Stella D'oro should have put her picture on her packages," my mother went on, "after all, Julia Waldbaum is on all her products, even the pasta. Why not Stella? Am I right?"

Maisy laughed. "Honey, I hate to be the one to tell you, but there ain't no Stella. *Stella* means star. *D'oro*, means gold. *Stella D'oro* is Gold Star cookies. Get it? Like *Medaglia D'oro* coffee. There is no lady, Stella."

"Holy Shit. Mom, how could that be? The words are so simple. Mom, could it be true?"

"I don't know. I never thought about it. All these years I'd pictured some sweet apron-wearing lady, Stella. I never thought about it in Italian."

"We don't know nothin' 'bout nothin'," I shot at my mother as I stared out the window at a row of Bronx apartment buildings off the side of the highway. Flowerpots and window shades were pulled to different heights. How could we know nothing about Italy? I pictured my cousins in *Acquaviva* bending in the fields with weathered hands and strong laughs, drinking dark wine, with donkeys and goats, women with strong calves and eyebrows walking up steep hills into vineyards, and scrutinizing new lengths of zucchini. Did they have bathrooms? "How come I don't know nothin' about Italy, and nothin' of my cousins, *fhuckin'* nothin'. I don't know the word for *gold* or *star* for Chrissake. How could that be? Fagetaboutit. We don't know nothin'."

"That language."

When I said the word *fhuck*, my mother tuned out everything else I said. That's all she heard, one word. I loved the word and the hearty way, in the Bronx, we said it: like the word *huck*, with an *F* in front of it,

"Mom, why don't we know any Italian?"

"Annie, please."

"Please what? Please shut up?"

As we made our way down the Deegan, I notice the apartment buildings off to the left. Something was strange about them. All the window dressings were identical. One window was broken. I saw clear through the whole building: sky to sky. It was burnt out. The windows had all been covered to conceal that this entire strip of buildings was burnt out.

"Who put the fake fhuckin' curtains and geranium illusions up on burnt-out buildings?"

Maisy knew. "Koch. Koch had the windows of the empty buildings covered with sheet metal and painted to look like people lived there. Cost the city plenty."

"What? You gotta be kidding me," my mother said.

"He did it for the Russian diplomats. They're driven from their suburban hills into the UN. Now they can look at friggin'—pardon my French—the true shit and pretend their kids ain't inside those buildings, the rats outnumbering them as they shoot up and who knows what. But I remind them when I drive them. Look at those curtains I say. It's a goddamn joke."

My mother was incensed. "Whadda they think we're idiots?"

"They think what we don't see won't hurt us."

Yankee Stadium. The time was posted: 7:53.

My mother kept talking: "To think I grew up, you know, practically in the shadows of the stadium. Back then the players would stand around outside the clubhouse and talk with us girls. It was like from here to there, you know? And from the Paramount and the Strand I had everyone's autograph, I mean everyone. Sinatra, Dick Haymes, Xavier Cugat, Jimmy Dorsey, Tommy Dorsey, Harry James, everybody, Helen O'Connell, Bob Eberly. He had a brother, I forget his brother's name, I had his autograph too. Glen Miller, The Modernaires. And when I got married my mother just threw my album out. What did she know? Imagine what that'd be worth today? I had all the singers, Sinatra, I mean everybody. I don't know if I had Louis Prima. I really don't remember."

"Not today. It's not like that."

"No, not today. Back then in this neighborhood you never even heard cursing. If we ever saw a curse we ran away from it. One time there was the four letters scrawled on the sidewalk near the school on Teller Avenue, you know *F-U* . . . Someone must have found a piece of plasterboard. It was 1939, no one had chalk. I looked at that and actually ran away. I ran all

the way home. Could you imagine? That's how unusual it was. I told Papa.
He told me to stay away from the school. I remember he looked at me so
serious: '*You better off you don't know how to read.*'"

Maisy put Car 5 in low gear and sped around Willis Avenue. "Hold on
ladies, I don't want to be buying one of my own hubcaps, you know what
I mean? Here they'll sell you your own socks before you know they took
them off you. I don't begrudge nobody, and I don't mind paying for my
windshield to get cleaned, but whatever's in their spray bottles they just push
the dirt around." She wove in and out of two guys in the street holding up
squeegees and spray bottles. "Nobody hustles that much except for drugs or
love and drugs is love. Hold on." She swerved through the red light. "How
fast are these guys? Once I stopped at that light and they sold me a hubcap.
I didn't realize 'til I got where I was going that they took it off the passenger
side of my car."

Maisy floored Car 5 and passed three trucks to get up the ramp at
Bruckner to the FDR Drive. We appeared as a gray blur in the silver side
of an oil-tank truck, as we went up the curved ramp and left the mainland
behind.

In the center of traffic on York Avenue and Sixty-Eighth Street, I stared up
at Sloan-Kettering. We idled at a green light. I could see the guard standing
in York Avenue up to his chest with hands gloved white; he paddled the
cars apart to either side of him. Behind the guard, the windows were ablaze,
dashing nineteen stories up the eastern face of the building. Nineteen stories
and that was just what was aboveground. Further underground it extended
into interconnected tunnels like roots. New York Hospital across the street
stood much taller, but Sloan-Kettering was filled with cancer, nineteen stories
high. It took up the whole block. Streams of people went into entrances on
either side of the building. I walked on a diagonal through the traffic and
up Sixty-Eighth toward the side door. Across the street was a church next to
an awning that read: *FLOWERS BALLOONS GREETING CARDS FOR
WEDDINGS SWEET SIXTEENS FUNERALS*, as if you could take care
of your whole life on one block, with a church across from a hospital down
from a river lined by a highway, and all life was made of was occasions in
mixed order. Weddings may come before sweet sixteens, funerals do.

Those who walked in alone were hired. Those involved were in clusters. I
wish it were a foggy day. I wish I could say the sky reflected my temperament,
but it didn't. It was sunny. It was clear. I walked in enough steps in front
of my mother. Three steps were enough. No one would know. They would
think I was there to visit my grandmother. Ha! GranmaRose didn't even
know. No one had told her. "Why tell her?" Mom had said. "Why make
her worry?" GranmaRose, who had crossed an ocean at my age, she out

of all of us could know. What would I tell her? "*Ciao GranmaRose, come stai, bene, eh menza menz.* I got the cancer. No, I didn't eat nothin' today. I don't care about that. *No mangia niente.* I took a vitamin." And what would she say? "Educationa Education, now you got the cancer and you're taking a vitaminsa. That's a no nice. *Prende l'aglio.* Get the garlic. Everything be'a nice'a nice."

A small ramp to walk up. A pregnant woman knocked into me. She wore a flowered shirt. I looked down at my chest not knowing what was inside it, what strange difference I held, what life form in my chest, something else, not a child, but something had taken root and grown wild and rampant within me, flowering in my neck and chest and maybe lower and wider. I spelled my name out three times: *L* as in *Luck*, *A* as in *Angry*, *N* as in *No*, *Z* as in *Zeppoli*, *I*, *L*, *L*, *O* as in *Other*, *T* as in *Tomorrow*, *T* as in *Tomorrow*, *O* as in *Opposite*. I realized for the first time the word *ILL* is spelled in the center of my name. Maybe Sister Rosaria tried to do me a favor back in kindergarten with the dropped consonant, maybe she could have altered my fate.

I make eyes at the guy selling buns-n-rolls and good morning coffee from the portable cart in the ground-floor lobby. Rosemarie appears. She drove all the way up from Cherry Hill, New Jersey. She offers to take my coat. She folds my jacket over her arm, never has she been so willing to hold my jacket. Another small ramp to walk up. The secretary hands me the red ID card. Blood red with my name raised in white lettering. I don't want to hold it. The guy selling buns-and-rolls sees her hand it to me, and his eyes back down into the white paper bag his hand pushes in up to the wrist. I hold the red ID card long enough to check the spelling of my last name and then hand it to my mother. Let her carry it. My name's spelled right for once. I roll up the sleeve of my throwing arm. This I am sure of. This is my throwing arm. To send. To aim. This arm can get the ball far over rooftops. This arm can throw. I pull the one blond streak of hair out to the front, what's left from of my summer vacation on the Jersey Shore. Rhoda Shapiro, the boardwalk portrait artist was right. She was the first to see the tumor. I keep three strides between my mother and me as we get into the elevator. I eye the guy selling buns-n-rolls 'til the doors come together in the middle. I look straight ahead at the crease in case the doors reopen the way elevator doors sometimes do. My mother says how nice the buns look, how nice the rolls, she pats the wall beside her, "Nice fresh paint. Nice." Later she says I can come back down for a little bite. The way he handles the buns, tosses the rolls into small paper bags, presses lids on the coffee cups, he is the only one in the place who seems carefree. My eyes bounce from my shoelaces to the light hopping the number line above the door. I press 4 but it opens on 2. A line of wheelchairs. One girl shoots a glance right through me. The girl sits in the front chair, gripping the armrests as if she was in the

front car of a roller coaster at the crest of the longest drop. The sign above
her states: Radiation Therapy. The doors snap shut. No one got on or off.
The doors open up into a long rectangular room, white like a box with a
low drop-ceiling and gold molding trim. Orange cup chairs are arranged in
clusters row by row, four aisles thick. One in each cluster has the cancer. I
count to three hundred by tens. All are waiting to be chosen, like chocolates
in a gift box of candy. I try to guess who in each cluster has the cancer and
who is there for accompaniment, like guessing which chocolates have the nuts
inside. I look first for lumps. My mother, the licensed hairdresser, is attuned to
more subtleties; a lack of hair on head nape necks arms lashes. "That's some
toupee," she says nodding at a man. By *some* she means expensive. "Probably
never had that much hair in all his life." I take my place on the back of a
long line leading to a desk with a woman sitting behind tall fresh-cut flowers.
My mother stands close behind me. The flower arrangement looks as if it has
lived in the deep sea, thin branches painted white poke out from flowers that
look like they could bite. A name is called over a loudspeaker. A man nudges
another man awake. They are not twins. Are they twins? The one slumped
in the chair under a baseball hat looks prone to a different gravity than
his brother. Asleep, he faced away from his brother. He wears a brand new
sweat suit, signs exaggerating health, new sneakers, no scuffmarks, everything
fantastically clean. 9:48. The clock is in the center of the room high above
us all. No second hand. I cannot watch time passing. It is just gone. Gone.
Gone. 9:50. Waiting rooms are appropriately named.

Ant'ny comes out of the elevator, eyes the surroundings, then strides
toward us. A doctor comes out and stands beneath the clock. She has long
blond hair pulled away from her face in a ponytail. She has the quick steps
of an athlete, she darts around a cart of medical charts, as her eyes scan the
faces responding to the names called. She winks both eyes affectionately at
a cluster. Their heads turn toward her. They have not yet been called. Her
eyes pass over me without stopping. My father comes out of the elevator
and makes a beeline directly for my mother, as if he were in the middle of a
conversation with her that they never finished. He has not seen her in eight
years, since Bronx County Family Court. He starts mid-sentence.

"She lives wit' you, look where she ends up!"
"She's your daughter just as much as mine! What's the use—"
"Ma, don't even bother answering him."
"Stay out of this, Rosemarie. She's a failure, ya mutha. She did some job."
I can't stay out of this. "Dad, let's go down for a coffee."
"*Madonn'!* Hiya Pop, how you doin'?"
"You're a failure as a mother!"
"Dad, please."
"Oh, hiya Daddy, don't worry 'bout nothin', you're gonna be okay."

Ant'ny launched into a nonstop street corner rant. He was high on crack. "Dad, you know the last four days, I missed the number by one number, you believe that? Every day, I played 7·8·9. I tell my bookie, 'Look, my daughter was born eight seventy-nine, so I play seven eight nine.' It came out seven eighty-four, seven eighty-six, seven eighty-two. You believe that! Seven eighty-two, seven eighty-four, seven eighty-six, and yesterday seven fifty-nine! Can you believe that?"

My mother switches her coat from arm to arm. Rosemarie takes her coat and covers an empty chair. They both look in magazines. My mother says, "There's no sense in talking."

"First it came out 7·8·4."

"Geez," I say, "not even today you can keep peace? Pretend peace? What's it got to come down to?"

"Next day 7·8·6 comes out."

"Everybody's looking at us," Rosemarie says, gets up and walks away. She walks toward the water fountain, looks at it and decides not to take a drink. She glances at the pamphlets that line a rack on a wall. She chooses one. She takes her time, and finally returns after making a whole lap around the waiting room, and hands the pamphlet to my mother who looks my way.

"And in Jersey, it came 7·8·2."

"Tell ya mother that. What are you telling me for, I'm peaceful."

"Don't you think you've done enough talking for one day?" my mother shoots at my father.

"You believe that? Seven eighty-two! Seven eighty-four! Seven eighty-six! And yesterday, seven fifty-nine!"

"Dad, let's go down for a coffee," Rosemarie insists. My father takes out his Lucky Strikes.

"Dad, don't light your cigarette in here."

"Don't tell me what to do. I'm the father."

"Go outside with it," I say. "Rosemarie, go take a walk with Daddy, will you?"

"You, stay with your mother. You're her son. See where you end up."

My mom stands up. "Coffee sounds good to me," she says, "c'mon Rosemarie, I'll go with you."

My sister leads my mother by the elbow toward the elevator. I stood up next to my Dad. The clock posted 10:30. Gone. Gone. Gone. 10:50. My mother and sister returned with white cups of coffee and a white bag with a donut. CarKey was with them. He walked in like a linebacker. Here we were all together, the nuclear family, emphasis nuclear, two marines, a junkie, a corporate executive, a battered housewife survivor hairdresser, and me the asthmatic scholar athlete with the giant tumor flailing around her chest. King of Clubs, Joker, two blue-eyed Queens of Spades, Jack of Hearts, and yes I finally understood that old King of Hearts jamming the knife behind his head. The knife was at my head and it was big as a sword and would never go away. I would learn to live with it, duck from it, dance with it. The six of us separated into two clusters, and sat back to back.

Before my number was called, I stepped toward the door where people went after their number was called. I leaned with my back against the wall next to a woman who looked straight ahead. I only saw half of her face. A doctor walked up to her and said, "It's still oozing? It's been a year." Her face turned. Half her face was gone.

"Eighty-six." That's my number.

The technician squeezed the pulp of my middle fingertip, wiped it with a small square sterile gauze, asked, "Are you Shirley MacLaine?" and pricked it with a thumbtack. This little prick hurt. A red dot appeared on the tip of my finger. He squeezed it, making the blood drop out. He caught the blood drop by drop into a tiny plastic trough. One drop he put on a glass slide and scraped it skillfully with another slide to spread the blood. My blood was dark, the color of black cherry soda. He gave me a square of gauze to pinch. When I walked out, my parents and siblings all looked at my finger and wanted to know if it was okay. Something like our last name came over the loudspeaker. We all jumped up at once. We were led into a small room. Dr. Sanford Kempin looked down at his notes, then up at all of us and asked, "Who's the patient?" We froze as if we weren't sure. As if we didn't know. As if the cancer was inside all of us. And just by him asking, he confirmed all our fears, that it was true. Up until then, I had hoped he would say, "There's been some mistake, some switching of blood and tissue."

"I am. I'm the patient." I looked him directly in the eye from behind my feathered hair. He looked like a big blue-eyed teddy bear. His doctor eyes shot right through me like he didn't care if I had hair on or clothes or not. I had the cancer. All that mattered was that *it* was inside me. I didn't want to be there. I didn't belong there. I had hair on my head and a smile. I belonged on a baseball field, the whole field set out before me like a thing known, nine players waiting for my fingers to signal set the target, inscribe the strike zone with my hand, bare hand. I belonged barehanded somewhere with others, barehanded beside me in a field someplace with other fields, these fields known, these fields combed, these fields patterned. I belonged scrutinizing new lengths of zucchini.

"I am. I'm the patient."

Dr. Kempin stood up, extended his arm out to the curtain and said, "Let's take a look."

I left the chair empty between my mother and father. My mother looked at Dr. Kempin's hair. I knew what she thought. He had nice thick wavy hair, he could make everything okay. I crossed to the other side and in one quick motion, Dr. Kempin swiped the curtain closed.

"You get undressed, and I'll be back in a minute."

Bits of my image reflected in the shine of utensils and canisters around the examination room. I saw my parents' features in me. My father's blunt nose and one of my mother's blue eyes appeared in the stainless steel towel dispenser. My mother's shapely lips in the faucet neck. The red from my quilted shirt showed in a series of cylindrical canisters. I pulled my shirt over my head, the red repeated up and down the cylinders. I tossed the shirt at the stool under the mirror and put the gown on with the ties to the front, which left me to get a chill on my chest. I took the gown off and put it on the other way. I unbuttoned my dungarees and pushed them down, kicking off my sneakers with the red-and-blue double laces. How would the doctor know I was a basketball and softball player without my sneakers on? I pushed the sleeves of the gown up over the bicep of my throwing arm. I sat up on the table. I looked down at my thighs. I scratched my head hard, then finger-combed my hair and looked in the mirror on the wall. I turned the gown around again. It didn't close either way, just split open. On the other side of the curtain, Dr. Kempin asked them if anyone had any questions.

"We don't have any questions," Rosemarie said, "but we sure need some answers."

"How're you doing, Kiddo?"

"Okay."

"Just relax and we'll see what's what. I want to listen to your lungs and heart, okay?" His stethoscope was cold. He listened to my heart beating really hard. I couldn't calm it down. He asked me to breathe five different ways. I tried to breathe deep and calm like I was taking foul shots. He asked me to cough. What was he hearing? He said "good" a couple of times and silently listened with concentration. The stethoscope lingered on my back on the left side and his eyes opened a bit as he listened there. "Okay," he said, "there's definitely some congestion. There it is. How's your breathing been?"

I never had a man look at me with such seriousness. He wanted to know. He looked me in the eyes with a caring intensity. He wasn't like my brothers, he didn't make fun, he didn't make stupid comments. His eyes were open, receptive, inquiring. He wasn't like my father, his eyes were soft and stayed on me. He asked me questions and waited for the answer, and if I couldn't answer then he asked another way. His hands pressed into the crevasses of my neck. He pinched lumps out of the tissues of my neck. He held the lumps. His fingers ran around the bones along my clavicle and shoulders. He found lumps hiding beneath the clavicle, he pulled them up like plums from below the bone. Under the jaw, he found it twice, pea sized, prune sized.

He rolled them between his fingers. He touched every pore of my skin for something not quite right. I didn't know where these were coming from, but he pulled them up. I'd had swollen glands before, but this was different. Then he pressed deep into armpits, and asked me to breathe, and I couldn't breathe but I made my chest go up and down. I got goose bumps. I could hear my mother coughing. She had no water. No one would think to get her a glass of water and she wouldn't get it herself. She had candies, maybe she'd unwrap one if she wasn't afraid to make the noise of the wrapper. With his eyes fixed on the ceiling, he pushed into my breasts one by one. His hands made circles. I tried to make eye contact with him to acknowledge his hands were on my breasts, but his eyes were fixed on the white ceiling. As he pressed the center of my chest I felt a sudden flood of *this is the worst feeling for me*. I remembered the rocking chair where my mother held me when I wouldn't sleep.

"Does this hurt?"

"I don't know."

"Okay. Lie down."

He pressed into my abdomen and knocked one hand on top of another in some places. "Do you feel pain here?"

"No."

He pressed on, named my spleen. "Here?"

"Well, kind of."

"Where?"

"There. Wait now it moved. There. No it moved again. No."

He pressed, bladder. His blue eyes looked at my eyes. Then he looked at my belly as if he could see through the skin. "What are you studying in school?"

"Well, I was taking one class called: Mars, Moon, and the Earth." I could hear my brothers thinking, what good was school? What kind of job would that lead to?

"What department's that in?"

"Planetary geology."

"Does it hurt here?"

"No."

"Here?"

"No."

"What are your other classes?"

"Anatomy of the Soul. Søren Kierkegaard."

"Anatomy of the Soul?"

"Yeah. Religious Studies. Brown's an intellectual candy store; I'm determined to try everything, and at these prices I choose the most exotic things on the menu. I like Kierkegaard. Do you know what he says the opposite of freedom is?"

He considered this and looked deep into my eyes with understanding. "Let's see, the opposite of freedom, well slavery would be an overt answer, captivity, on a subtle level, I'd say; if freedom is choice in life, then the opposite would be fear, a freezing of choice, a lack of options."

I felt my family listening behind the curtain. "Guilt," I said. "Isn't that interesting? According to Kierkegaard the opposite of freedom is guilt." I aimed my voice at the curtain. "Guilt."

He pressed on. "Hmm. That's interesting. I will have to think about that."

I pressed my thumbs to my forefingers. "I know something's wrong, Doc, but I didn't think cancer. Something isn't right. I feel it through my whole system."

No one had listened for so long. Now suddenly everyone was listening, with stethoscopes even.

My mother held in a cough. No one would pat her back. She coughed into her fist and held it. She took out a tissue and squeezed her cough into it.

Dr. Kempin pressed into my groin on either side and pushed back and forth to feel for lumps. I didn't know my body had so many hiding places. My mother coughed and squeezed the tissue tighter. She was looking to get rid of it, but she couldn't see the trash pail under the desk of the doctor, so she held it, tightening it.

"The pail is under the doctor's desk, Mom," I spoke at the curtain.

"Okay, get dressed, and let's talk," Dr. Kempin said.

I sat up, put on my clothes, and walked to the other side of the curtain. "Stop staring at me," I said to all of them, and added sarcastically to Ant'ny, "take a picture, it lasts longer."

Dr. Kempin asked what felt like a million questions and wrote everything down. I could hear my father thinking, 'What's he writin' a book?'

"Now, tell me, is there any history of cancer in the family. Parents, grandparents."

"No," I said.

My mother interrupted. "My father had a tumor."

"He did? I never knew that."

"Yes. Bladder cancer."

"Did he have treatment?"

"No."

"No?"

"No."

"Okay. Grandfather. Anyone else?"

"No."

"My cousin had a breast removed," my mother interjected.

"Okay. Cousin. Anyone else?"

"Anyone else, Ma?"

"No. That's it."

Rosemarie took notes. Dr. Kempin told us about Hodgkin's disease and said I was a perfect candidate for his study of 150 patients randomized on two chemotherapy protocols. "You mean you don't choose what chemo I'm gonna take?"

"It's randomized."

"So, who picks?"

"Well, you call Susan, my secretary, and she'll tell you which protocol you are assigned."

"But how do I get assigned?"

"Computer."

"I don't want a computer picking my chemo. I want you to pick it."

"We don't know that one protocol is better than the other."

"I want to try the T.B.V. I don't want M.O.P.P. I want to stay away from that Nitrogen Mustard shit. Let's see if T.B.V. works."

I joined the study, hugged him good-bye, and was the first to walk out into the hallway. My mother asked him something in private, and I heard him say words that she repeated the rest of her life when speaking of him:

"You are never, ever to worry about money."

We got out of there as soon as we could. I felt nauseous. "I need to take a walk. Ma, you never told me about Grandpa. How did he have cancer and no treatment?"

"He walked out on the doctor. He told the doctor, "You make'a mistake'a. You gotta da wronga guy."

"You're kidding me."

"Swear to God."

"You think that's what I should do?"

"Don't be stupid."

"Hey Coolie-Pie, while we're in the city, I'll buy you new sneakers if you like."

"Thanks Roe. I'm too tired. Boy, you haven't called me that since I was a kid."

I stepped off the curb and into the crosswalk of Sixty-Seventh Street. I bunked into a blind woman with a Seeing Eye dog.

"Just cause you got cancer doesn't mean you can walk into the blind," Roe said.

I didn't laugh. I wasn't ready for cancer jokes just yet. A seagull was flattened on the asphalt, it had been run over by a car tire. Its top wing lifted with the wind, white feathers catching air.

Room 621

Mom and I stayed off the phone for two weeks while we waited for a bed to open up in Sloan-Kettering. Waiting with this mass growing inside me felt like an enormous waste of life-given time. My mother cut phone callers off with, "We're expecting the hospital to call." We finally got the call from a smooth well-oiled voice with a southern accent, "Good-morning-this-is-Donna-Andrus-from-Memorial? Yes, we-have-a-bed-for-you. If you check in by eleven-thirty, the dietician will see to it that you get a lunch. Okay? Good."

I was terrified to check in. Just the name of the place elicited fear. Who were these guys Sloan and Kettering? No one in my family ever heard of anyone walking out of there alive. I had the impression it was an old-school slice 'em and dice 'em cancer ward from the last century. But the first three people we met changed everything. Cecil Rowe, the Jamaican doorman made us feel like we were entering a grand opera house. He wore a pressed uniform and his smile lifted our hearts. "Don't worry," he said to me, "we're gonna take good care of Mama."

"Not her," I said, "me."

"You? You're young and strong. You'll be fine." He held each of our elbows and ushered us in through the automatically sliding doors into the cooled air. Cecil laughed like Sebastian Cabot as Mr. French on "Family Affair," a show I watched as a kid. 1275 York Avenue, the front entrance, was his post, and from then on, as long as this sacred gatekeeper worked there, I walked in through the front door. Cecil guided us to take a quick right to the admissions desk. There sat Donna Andrus. She was young and charming with that southern accent. She could have been one of my college friends. She exuded an extremely friendly vibe, wore tan corduroy pants and a soft cotton button down shirt with tiny blue flowers. She had a pixie haircut and big dimples. Her eyes had an extra openness to them, and the thought came to my mind; she is an adorable dyke. I told her to come visit me up in my room.

"I'll stop by," she said, "and see how y'all are doing."

Donna took us to Flavio Martinez who had important papers for me to sign. Flavio was short and extremely well groomed, a perfectionist with the air of a yacht commander. He was Ricardo Montalbán of *Fantasy Island*. Over his desk he had a framed certificate for perfect attendance at work. As I signed the papers, I asked him where he was from.

"Colombia," he said.

"I'm confused with who to pick to be my Medical Proxy."

"Someone you trust to make decisions for you," Flavio explained.

I didn't want to start a civil war in my family. I put my sister and my mother down. Lanzi might be upset, but I didn't know what else to do. I pushed up my sleeve of my throwing arm up above my shoulder and I signed more papers. I was an eighteen year old jock. I had muscles. Sign me up for cancer. I felt like I had enlisted. Cecil, Donna, and Flavio made me feel right at home. I had packed my things in one of CarKey's old duffel bags from Vietnam. I lifted the duffel bag and we headed for the elevator upstairs.

I tossed my duffel bag on the bed. A curtain split the room in two halves. I could see the whole other side of the room by reflection in the window at the foot of the beds. A woman sat upright in a high-backed chair. She saw me through the reflection in the window.

"Hiya."

"Hello there."

"Is it okay if I open up the curtain in between us?"

"Yes, please."

"Hi. I'm Annie. I have Hodgkin's."

"Connie Robinson. Leukemia."

"This is my Mom, Rachel."

I looked at the yellowness inside her IV bottle. "What's that?"

"That there is Shake 'n Bake. You'll see."

Connie Robinson was beautiful. Super tall. African American. Two big dimples, one on each cheek.

I looked at the name tag at the foot of my bed, "Who is Greta Trost?

"Nice woman. She passed this morning."

The phlebotomist walked in. I read her whole name off her name tag. "Call me by my first name," she said, "I am Minerva." She pressed the inside of my elbow with her forefingers. "Make a fist." Minerva had orange-painted fingernails long enough to get the blood herself. Deep-red lipstick. Copper-tinged hair. For the first time I noticed I had a strong blue vein. It flexed up the center of my arm. Minerva chose this one. She aimed the needle at the blue vessel beneath the flesh surface and nailed it. She could harpoon whales, I thought. She pulled back on the syringe with her thumb. Plain dark-red blood filled the tube in seconds. I expected my blood to look strange now that I had cancer, have white spots in it, or to be very thin or an off color. Minerva put another tube into the cylinder and another and another until she had six warm red glass tubes of my blood, all with different color caps, some she flipped upside down twice before placing them in her tray on her cart. "Six today because you are new, tomorrow only two. I promise."

CarKey walked in bearing gifts, a brand new pair of running sneakers and the hottest invention just out—the Sony Walkman. I put on the sneakers and the headphones and played the demo tape, a piano instrumental that transported me as I walked around the hospital floor. I walked rectangular laps. I went into the stairwell and walked up and down the floors. Only staff ever used the stairwell. There was a sign next to a pipe: Sound of Horn Indicates Water Flow in Fire Line. Check for Fire Then Turn Off Red Hydrant. I wanted the warning on my life to be so clear. I found myself in a hallway painted with bright colors, with little red wagons with IV poles. I saw a kid staring vacantly out, sitting in the wagon outside his room. I bent down. "I'm Annie," I said, "you wanna thumb wrestle?" He said, "I am Diego." We thumb wrestled. He beat me. I took the Mount Carmel scapular off my neck and gave it to the little boy. He smiled. The nurse came by and gave him a lollipop. I walked around the floor, and peered into every room. There were clusters of family around beds, televisions on. I walked down more flights, and around halls and found portraits of Charles Kettering and Alfred Sloan. Who were these guys? Doctors? No. I was surprised to learn they both worked for General Motors. Sloan was one of the pioneers of "planned obsolescence." That did not comfort me, and I needed to be comforted. I decided to call this place Charlie & Al's Cancer Center. When I go to the mechanic I go to Tony & Jimmy's. When I go to the deli I go to Frank & Joe's, when I go to the cancer center I go to Charlie & Al's. I chuckled.

Shake 'n Bake

Nights are the worst time in hospitals. All who do not sleep are united. Nights are the times when in quiet I can hear the pain seep under the doorway from down the hallway in muted moans. When through the thick window glass that does not open to the streets, the distant howl of a siren calls me to the state of my soul, while inside, the tumor knocks at my chest. There is a long groan down the hallway, flowing over the long shine in the floor into my room. I leave my room and walk around the hallway in rectangular laps like I do at home around the courtyard. I stop in front of each of the paintings that line the halls as if I am praying the Stations of the Cross on Good Friday. I stare at van Gogh's "The Langlois Bridge at Arles." A woman walks across the bridge alone. She wears black and holds a black umbrella. She is one step away from the midway point. The riverbank is a steep grade down into the river. All the houses are a distance away. She is alone. The yellow ripples on the water are uniform, striped, reflecting the brickwork of the bridge. The bridge, like eyebrows, can lift open so easily. I expect the bridge to rise at any moment. The bridge has a simple lever system to raise it for when boats pass. There is only one cloud in the sky. She is on a long walk. Definitely on her way out, not returning home. Yellow stripes of light on the water.

I walk into the patient lounge and stare out a window; lean my forehead against the cold glass. Tonight I have the vantage of the rich, looking down on Manhattan. There is nothing looking down on me. Everything looks clean from up here. The city looks like a village. The city is tolerable from this perspective. Distant lights twitter. I cannot sleep. There is no one to call. There are no faces in the windows facing me. The sky is black, the buildings, in silhouette.

I go back to room 621, and sit in my bed with my head raised and look out at the East River. There is a shine upon the water. I do not hear the waves or the traffic. It is not apparent which way the river runs. The river seems to run several ways at once. Streaks of light are bent on the moving water. Three long streaks kneel toward the little fourth streak of light. The sky changes all night long. At two in the morning, Connie gets up. She is on all her hands and knees in bed. She shakes and whips off sweat.

"Connie, what can I do?"

"Better go get me some new sheets."

I go down the hall to find her dry sheets. Van Gogh's cloud has changed position. I rummage around the sixth floor, and come back with a pile of sheets.

"Now you know what Shake 'n Bake is."

"Should I call the nurse?"

"No, no bother. I am a nurse, a nurse practitioner. I just need dry sheets."

"Okay Chief," I said, and from that moment on I called Connie, Chief, and her nickname was born. We changed her sheets eleven times that first night.

The second night, Chief called to me from the other side of the curtain: "Annie come see what I did." I expected her IV lines were caught in the telephone cord again and she needed untangling. I tugged the curtain. It slid along its track on the ceiling and folded up within itself. Chief sat up in the bed. Her brown curly Afro stayed down on the pillow like a nest. I could see the indentation where her head held onto the hair all those years. "Annie, I closed my eyes to go to sleep, and on the Lord, I just scratched my head and the hair came right off into my hand as if there was nothing ever holding the hair onto the head in the first place. When I raised my head, the hair stayed down on the pillow. The rest came off in handfuls so easily, I hardly had to touch it." The imprint of Chief's head was clear on the pillow. I stared at her smooth head. She looked relieved. Her bald head was so soft, like dandelion flowers I blew on as a kid; made a wish and blew their floaters up into the air in a thousand directions. I could blow on Chief's head and the patches of Afro left on her head would rise up and float away all over New York City. "I want to see my bald head in the mirror." Chief got up fast. Blood fell from the cave of one nostril onto the white fuzz of her slipper. She backed into the bathroom wheeling the IV pole in behind her and plugged her nostril with her thumb. I helped her pop the wheels of the IV pole over the lip in the floor where the linoleum met the bathroom tile. Her IV pole cleared the doorframe as she pulled it in behind her. She put the bloodied slipper in the sink under a steaming jet of hot water. I slid a towel under her bare foot. Her knees bent so the top of her head would fit in the mirror. She parted the steam with her hands, and wiped the dampness off the mirror, patting it onto her dry head. She shed the last remains of her hair and wrapped it in a white shroud of toilet paper, burying it at sea, by flushing. I looked back at the man standing barefoot on the rocks. When I first picked this painting from the volunteer cart that came around, I wondered how heavy the canoe was. Now, I wondered, how strong is the man? I walked up to the painting. I grabbed it from the wall, held it in my hands, turned it upside down, and hung it back up. That was better. Now, he's doing a handstand on the canoe. Much more interesting.

Chief knew this day would come since she was a nurse herself. She purchased a white terrycloth turban in advance that pulled on over her head like a hat. She knew her arms wouldn't have the energy to wrap a real turban all around her head. Terrycloth absorbed the heat and sweat coming out the head. She pulled at the plastic vein on the price tag. She set the turban low over her ears and the back of her neck so you'd never know she didn't have hair, you'd just think she liked to wear scarves and look majestic. The plastic vein scratched at her neck. She shifted the turban low to her eyebrows, then back high on her head. The baldness was noticeable only when it popped over her ears, so she kept alert to this. When the heat from the chemotherapy seeped up and heated the bones of her skull, Chief would wring out the sweat, rinse the turban, and once dry, slide it back on her head.

The next morning, the lymphangiogram technician cut a little cross on the top of each of my feet, pulled up a lymph vessel with a silver tool, and hooked up my feet to two calibrated syringes full of blue dye. I laid there alone for over an hour listening to a Kenny Rogers' *The Gambler* cassette on my Walkman. I watched the blue dye slowly, steadily enter my lymph vessel. I could feel the dye make its way up my feet, legs, torso, into my chest, neck, and arms. "It won't cross the blood-brain barrier," the technician told me. I pictured the Great Wall of China between my brain and the rest of my body.

The next morning Minerva complained she couldn't find any veins in Chief's arms, hands, or feet. Chief looked down at her arms, bruised from Minerva's needle and stained in spots from chemo burns. She pulled the skin here and there, in search of a good vein. She soaked her arms in warm salts and spread the skin with her fingers. There was an oval like a deep hole that stayed on her arm for a month, darkening. That's how I knew time was passing. We wore time.

Minerva came back and informed her, "Shunts serve as a permanent open vein. It's plastic. I have to draw my daily blood. Shunts provide direct access to the blood. I can't find any veins; I looked in your hands, your feet."

The next day Connie told Minerva, "Okay, let's go ahead with the shunt, Nurse, but do not insult me with your simple explanations. Remember that I too was a nurse, and a Nurse Practitioner."

I tossed my voice over the curtain that separated us: "*Are.* You *are* a nurse. Right! Right Chief?" Connie smiled back at me. The whiteness of her teeth banked off the window at the foot of our bed.

Bone marrow biopsy was the hardest test of them all. "It'll feel like a corkscrew," the nurse said, but it didn't. It felt like a jackhammer into my bone. I squeezed the nurse's hand and howled in pain and learned the exact place on my body called the posterior ileac crest.

Every night I watched the three lights on the East River kneel toward the one light that had no apparent source. My father brought me a set of oil paints that he got off a woman he met at the OTB. I began to paint a picture of the Queensboro Bridge on my pillow. I didn't know if it was a sunrise or a sunset. I painted the sky pink rising to orange. The bridge ended midair.

People came out of the woodwork from every part of my life to visit me and bring gifts. Johnny Denaro, I hadn't seen in five years. We only bunked into each other once since fifth grade, and that was one Saturday when Enza took Mom and me to the Castle Hill Beach Club. We were thirteen. Johnny's voice had changed, he had grown tall and had a little fuzz moustache. Now, at eighteen, he was literally "tall, dark and handsome," and when he walked into 621 carrying a big blow-up rainbow on which he wrote: "Kindergarten Sweethearts Are Forever," I was all smiles inside. Uncle Frank came and gave me his safari hat. "For every journey you need a hat." Uncle Frank said he got the hat in World War II, in Africa. Sloan-Kettering was my safari. The game we were hunting, was deep, and all over, inside me.

They had to come with carts to move me from 621, which had become a teenager's dorm room. Get well cards covered walls. Plants and flowers covered the windowsills and floor. I began to carry them to other patients. My bandanas and hats hung all over the room, off every pole and wire. The nurses explained how I needed to be moved to a surgical floor, after the laparotomy.

"I want to just stay where I belong," and right now that was in room 621 with Connie Robinson.

I walked around the hospital night and day, and talked with other patients. I knocked on a social worker's door. The door was open. She wasn't there but her white coat was. I put it on and slid my patient wristband up under the sleeve. I got in the elevator and went down. A cleaning woman name Uletha hummed a gospel spiritual that filled the elevator. She got off, pushing a big cleaning cart. I thanked her for her healing song. I walked into the doctor's medical library and found books on Hodgkin's disease and surgery. When I saw pictures of how they were going to cut and splay me open, I couldn't believe it. I carried a tall stack of books to the librarian's desk to check out. She noticed my patient wristband.

"This library is for staff only."

"I need to know this stuff," I said, "call Dr. Kempin, he'll sign the books out for me." I felt like I was five years old again when the librarian told me, "Maximum limit." Now, I had no patience for hassles. My favorite nurse Veronica came down and bailed me out, took the books out for me and I lay down and studied.

I walked to the hospital chapel and stood at the altar, which faced York Avenue. The side walls were parallel and carved with scripture, each letter filled in with gold paint. On the right wall: *"Come unto me all ye that labor and are heavy laden, and I will give you rest."* The left wall read: *"They that wait upon the Lord shall renew their strength."* The third wall was stained glass. Perpendicular to the first two walls, it separated and joined them. I faced this third wall that grew between me and the only world I had ever known. Behind the glass was York Avenue. The American flag there curled out of sight, caught within itself, holding the slanted post that secured it to the building's facade. Filled with the wind off the East River, the flag beveled into my field of view, and we waved at tinted images of one another. I lived in a young country. We shared youth, and knowledge of the struggle for existence. I got on my knees and prayed. Cancer reduced my life to being alive. I gave thanks, and started to hum. When I die I will hum. Your life you hum.

Back in 621, a nurse I didn't know came in, called out my first name, and asked if I was ready to be shaved and scrubbed. I followed her instructions, stripped everything off, lay down and opened my legs. I looked down at my feet. Each foot had a cross on it, scarred from the lymphangiogram cuts. They looked like stigmata. As she shaved me, I felt like a sacrificial lamb. I watched the man doing a handstand in the canoe. She scrubbed my belly and pelvis with Betadine. There was no algae on the rocks. I never saw rocks along the water's edge without algae. The man is barefoot on the slippery rocks.

I look out across the East River, to a solid strip of unlit buildings on Roosevelt Island, the tops of which are not yet distinguishable from the sky. In front are three smokestacks silhouetted against the darker black of the buildings. I stare at these smokestacks for hours. There is no smoke at this hour. Below the smokestacks are three light-posts, yet there are four streaks of light across the water. It's not evident what the source of light was for this fourth streak; as if it is its own source. It is much smaller yet more concentrated than the rest. The way the light bends across the water, I imagine the three wise men kneeling to the infant Jesus. I call the smokestacks the three wise men. I watch them for hours. A strip of red bleeds across the sky along the tops of the buildings. The rooftops cut into the rim of the horizon like teeth atop a castle wall. The sky is cutting teeth. The black slowly gives way to a deep purple, almost black itself. The sunrise is slow to happen. While the sky lightens, the things closest to me darken. The plants, the telephone, the IV pole, the schoolbooks I am too tired to read, the get well cards taped to the wall, all lose their definition. The sky is ribbed like the waters. I try to pick the spot where the sun itself will appear. I looked for the lightest point on the horizon.

My father walked into the room. His eyes were shiny, his hair freshly combed back. I asked my father where he thought the sun would come up. He studied the sky, not looking at anything between my bed and the horizon. He looked past the bedside table, the plants on the windowsill, the river, the row of buildings, to the thin strip of red below the purple-black.

"Over there," he said, "right over that peak, to the left of the smokestacks, that there steeple, must be a church."

"I'll bet you it'll be over that flattop, you see those two flattop buildings with all the antennae?" He nodded. The longer we looked, the more we changed our minds. Then, when we weren't looking, the circle of sun appeared. Caught between the two flattop buildings; like between two teeth. The whole sky cracked as if it were a flat side of glass hiding something behind it. The ribs trailed with pink.

"What a you worried about? Lanzillottos are survivors. Those doctors know what they're doin'. Don't worry about nothin'. You're a survivor, like me. "

The Fastigium

1. The period of maximum severity or intensity of a disease or fever. [Latin *fastigium*, apex, height.] *American Heritage Dictionary* 2. In architecture, a pediment . . . the triangle which surmounts each end of a rectangular building . . . the gable end of the roof. Smith's Dictionary 1875.

Anurse came in to make sure I was ready for the OR.

"Take off your hat," she said in a bossy tone.

"No. I want to wear it."

"You can't wear a baseball hat in the operating room."

Lanzi chimed in. "Hey, what's the commotion. What's all this racket about?"

"She won't let me wear the hat."

"Whatsamatta'with you, upsetting a kid like that?"

"I'll call the doctor," the nurse said.

"You don't upset somebody before they undergo a major operation. Whatsamatta' with that nurse?"

"Call the doctor," she said, "see if he don't tell you the same thing!"

"I will call the doctor," Lanzi said.

"Tell him the OR nurse refuses to give the patient pre op with a filthy hat on. I have other patients to prep. I cannot wait around here for you."

"I'll call the doctor. I'll call the president of the hospital! I'll call Mr. Sloan and Mr. Kettering. What's your name, nurse? You should've been in the army."

"That's not a compliment," I added, "he's a Marine."

"I'm going right to the nurse's station. I'm paging the doctor."

My father and the nurse walked out of the room.

Chief woke up. "Angel, don't pay no mind to her. It's her problem clear as day, not yours."

She sat up and noticed the painting that I'd turned upside down. The man in a handstand on the canoe at the edge of the water. She held a finger in the air, pointed to the painting and held her belly with her other hand. "I can't laugh. It hurts too much, Angel. You sure are something. That's one way to get the canoe into the water."

"You know what the best part is about it, Chief? No one else noticed."

"Something about that painting I love."

"Me too. Water's not easy to paint. I've tried to paint water. When I paint the ocean it looks like a blue curtain. There's no depth to it. Nothing underneath it. You can't paint the ocean by painting its surface, and the only way you can paint it is by painting its surface. Surface is illusion."

"So is depth. Call your Mama now. You know she can't get through the switchboard at this hour. She's probably worried sick about you."

"Okay."

"Hi Mom."

"Oh, thank God you called. We'll be there within an hour."

"My father's here."

"So! If you think we're not coming down just because your father is there, now that's not fair; Rosemarie's on her way up from Jersey. If I could have been there already I would have, you know that. I didn't have a ride."

"Everybody's coming? The family hasn't been together like this since I've been diagnosed! Too bad I won't be around."

"How you feeling today, a little better?"

"Wonderful."

"Really? Annie? What's the matter! Are you there? Are you crying? Annie? Oh Tootsie, don't worry! Everything is going to be okay. Is Connie there with you? She always makes you feel better. Sometimes I think I just make you more nervous. Remember I love you. Everything will be okay. Okay? Are you okay?"

"Yeah."

"You feel a little better? I feel better just hearing your voice. I said a prayer to Saint Anthony that everything will be okay. He's never failed me yet. We'll go through this together."

"Ma, I want to wear this hat my father gave me into the operation. It says Be All You Can Be, but the nurse won't let me."

"Did you call the doctor?"

"They're going to."

"Annie, you know the doctors will do anything for you. You were supposed to be put on a surgical floor. Remember how you asked to stay with Connie, then all the flowers kept coming? Who was gonna move all that to another floor? And what did he say to you?"

"I know, Ma."

"What did he say?"

"Ma!"

"Okay then, do you really think he won't let you wear your hat? Do you?"

"No."

"Oh. I thought so. You ask him and don't worry about anything. Okay? Give me a smile. Okay, and give Connie my love. Okay. I love you."

"I love you too, Ma, so much."

"Thumbs-up. Oh, Aunt Patty and everybody sends their love. They're all praying for you."

"Yea."

"Bye."

Dope and Demerol

Dr. Turnbull cut my belly from sternum to pubis, took out what I call my spare parts: spleen and appendix, and took biopsies of lymph nodes, liver and kidneys, and stapled my ovaries off to the side, out of the field of radiation. I was wheeled, in bed, back to room 621. Everyone stood up. Dad. Ant'ny. Enza. Rosemarie. CarKey. Mom. Chief stayed in bed. Everything was a blur. A procession of faces came close to me one by one, on the left side of the bed. Rosemarie stayed next to me on my right. Mom's blue eyes came close as she kissed my forehead. She looked so sad, so worried, but said, "Everything is going to be alright." I could feel my hand being gently held. Enza was there. I couldn't speak. I squeezed my hand to indicate I needed another dose of Demerol. I prayed to Christ. Christ didn't have Demerol while he hung on the cross with a crown of thorns pushed into his skull. Rosemarie held a yellow legal pad of paper and handed me a pen. I scrawled "ice." She lifted an ice chip to my lips. All I wanted was ice and more Demerol.

Ant'ny's face came close. "How's the Demerol?" he asked. There was a glint in his eye. Many years later he told me, "That was the first time we were ever high together." At some point it hit me, my brother had been high my whole life, from around the time I was born.

CarKey leaned over and said, "I love you."

Somehow that made being ripped open all worthwhile.

"It's only skin," my father said. "Lanzillottos are survivors."

This echoed inside me.

GranmaRose still didn't know. No one had told her.

My parents are in the same room together. This is what I've always wanted. To get them back together and heal the marriage. Peaceful, for one night. Over my sick girl body, this is accomplished, like when I had high fevers as a kid.

A few days after the surgery, two priests marched into 621 as if they were moving against a great wind, arms and knees pumping to get them through the door. They talked to each other saying Father this and Father that, it didn't matter who was saying exactly what to who, only that they talked to each other to the exclusion of Connie and me. They sidestepped into our bathroom, one after the other, flashed the faucet on and off, and came out seconds later with their sleeves pushed up, and their faces flushed. Connie and I shot glances at one another, our eyes locked.

"Glory!" one priest said, "The only place I've seen this many flowers is at a funeral!"

"They're mostly Miss Annie's," Connie said, "and at least three visitors came with every arrangement."

The priests touched the cards taped to the wall. "This one's from a whole team," one said to the other, "marvelous." The priest stepped back a bit to get the whole sight in at once. "It's unbelievable," he said. In the short time I had cancer, I'd become intolerant of phrases like *unbelievable, unreal, incredible*. Everything was believable to me now.

"Nothing is, Father," I mouthed the words. My voice was breathy, dry, weak.

"Hmm?"

"Believe it. It's believable."

He flipped open cards, one card had the face of a pig wearing sunglasses, saying, "In for repair?" Next to the pig hung a card of the Virgin Mary, in her long blue robe, the palms of her hands open and raised, the clouds parting above her, the robe unclosed to show her heart, the golden glow around the heart with spikes driven into it.

One priest had his nose in a rose. "Do you know what tomorrow is?" he asked. I hated people talking of tomorrows. Here we were, in bed, alive, in this moment. Nothing else was real for me. "The New York Marathon! I bet from here you can see them swarming over the Queensboro Bridge! What a view! A king's view!"

"God's view!" the other priest corrected him, "We'll have to come back by eleven tomorrow!"

I hated chitchat.

"This pot must be made of solid copper! I've never seen anything quite like it!"

Chief and I looked at one another. It hurt to laugh. Her with her new shunt and me stapled together. Our scars pulled with any laugh or sneeze. Holding a laugh in, was even worse. Chief's eyes widened, her neck stretched toward me. She mouthed out the words, "Heckel and Jeckel," then she said, "two old crows." She squeezed her eyes, begging me with her expression not to look at her, not to make her laugh. My laugh turned into a cough, which turned into the feeling of wanting to puke. Neither of the priests noticed us as tears filled our eyes. Laughter pulled at our scars. Excruciating. To laugh takes stomach muscles. My belly was cut clear up the center line like a trout. Before my belly was sexy. Now the femme was cut out of me. I pointed to the little blue plastic dish without being able to ask for it. My stomach heaved. A dark green slime rose out of me. The priests washed their hands and left.

The Pipeline

JANUARY 1982

I had to wait on line for chemo. Dozens of us sat in a hallway and waited our turn. I recognized one other teen from the recreation room on the fifteenth floor. Luis had leukemia. I'd beat him at pool.

"Hey Kimosabe," I said

He laughed, "Yeah Chemo-sabe. I been here all morning."

Thiotepa, my first chemo, tasted metallic, like a dull aluminum. The butterfly in my vein went in smooth. The clear liquid made its way down the tube and into my vein. The inner side of my elbows had beautiful blue veins beneath the surface. In the middle of my left elbow I had a strong vein that I called, the "Pipeline." After the first chemo, I needed help taking my coat on and off. We went to Throggs Neck to CarKey and Enza's for dinner. I couldn't move my arm. Everyone was glad to see me. At the table with all the cacophony, I felt alone. I missed my father at the table. He never was invited anymore. There in Enza's basement kitchen, the ground beneath me shifted. Enza cooked her magnificent holiday spread, but I couldn't care less: *antipast'*, the lasagna, turkey with a sausage stuffing, fruit, nuts, pastries. The taste of chemo sewage in my mouth ruined everything. After the lasagna, CarKey fell asleep on the couch. The family talked and played around him.

I called Dr. Kempin the next day, and he told me the arm thing wasn't right. "The vein must have been infiltrated."

That nice smiley Italian nurse, I thought, how'd she miss my good vein? She used the Pipeline. She went right through it. Dr. Kempin told me to get back to school. He said I could inject some of the chemo on my own, and get the rest at Rhode Island Hospital.

Truckstop Paranoia

FEBRUARY 1982

Lanzi drove me back to Brown in his royal blue Chevy Malibu, with its half black vinyl top. On our way to Providence, we stopped in a truck stop on I-95 for hot open roast beef sandwiches and cups of black coffee. He was on a rant about Ant'ny. "My son better watch his step. He's a wise guy. Thinks he knows everything. They got the eye on him too, cause he got mixed up with drugs and runs with a tough crew. He dresses like a racketeer, all in black. Thinks who he is. So they got a tag on him, thinking he'll lead them to the right dealer, and they could get a hook into a syndicate and bust up some big operation. But it don't work that way. We all ran with a tough crowd. So, one day he comes to see me and we go out for coffee. I'm talkin' to my boy over a cup of coffee in the diner, real peaceful like, and I put my hand over his hand. A man's allowed to put his hand over his own son's hand, that's the freedom we fought for, right? So next thing I know there's this meatball sittin' at the counter, staring at our hands, hoping to see some transaction. My son says I'm imagining things. But look at me. All these years of keepin' outta trouble, and ever since Meathook Mickey got indicted the FBI's on my tail. Half a' the time, these goons are takin' a shot in the dark. They don't even know who they're followin'. Just wastin' their time and the taxpayers money. Chasin' up dead ends. Gettin' nowhere fast. Another time I'm sittin' peaceful at the raceway mindin' my own business, tryin' to concentrate. So this guy's gotta' start axing me questions. He sits next to me. He says, 'You Joseph Lanzillotto.' I says, 'What's it to you.' He shows me his badge. He says, 'How well do you know Meathook Mickey?' I say, "Look I knew Meathook as a kid. We came from the same neighborhood. Me and Meathook was altar boys together. I don't know nothin'.'"

"Let's get outta here."

"Dad, I'm relaxin'."

"Now."

We got in the Chevy. He didn't warm up the engine, just threw the shaft into drive and took off. He adjusted his rearview mirror and looked more into it than the road ahead, as he drove up the dark stretch of I-95.

"Do you remember any of the guys' faces in that diner?"

"Sure. You taught me to notice everything."

"Well, forget them all."

"What?"

"You'll read about it tomorrow in the papers."

"What are you talkin' about."

Just then a tractor-trailer passed us on the left and swerved at us, to run us off the shoulder of the highway.

"What the *fhuck*?"

Lanzi pulled over on the shoulder and stopped the car. He eyed the truck as it passed out of sight. We were alone on a dark stretch of I-95, except for a pair of white lights on the other side of the highway. He began to drive again. He surveilled the road behind and ahead.

"Forget you ever saw them. Forget all their faces. Do not talk to anybody about this, not to anyone. I don't want any trouble."

The next day I picked up a *Pro Jo*—*Providence Journal*—and read about a truck hijacking that took place at that very truck stop. I knew then, that my father was the most sane person in the world. Nothing got past my father. Nothing.

The neutral and peaceful old campus grounds at Brown, afforded my father and me safe pathways on which to walk and talk, and a creative array of students and professors to bunk into and talk to for a bit, and hang out, in peace. One

night while we stood on Thayer Street with paper cups of coffee, an orange
Volkswagen Bus came toward us and beeped. The driver yelled, "Hey Lanz!"

"Who's that?" my father says.

"That's my professor. Dr. Head. He teaches about the planets."

"That guy's a professor?"

"Yeah. What!"

Dr. Head got out and shook my father's hand. "Nice to meet you, Mr.
Lanzillotto. You've got a great daughter. Annie teaches me a lot, too."

Brown gave my father a way to communicate with me without having to go
through my mother. Every day he bought the *Daily News*, cut out articles, and
wrote to me, for the five years I was in and out of school. His letters were
thick like a book, pages long loose-leaf with articles taped to them. When he
came up, I brought him to the mailroom to meet Charlie the manager, who
held the stacks of manila envelopes for me every couple of days. My father's
letters and packages were legendary at the Brown post office.

> *Dear Annie, Hi Baby—How you doing!*
> *February 23rd., Saturday, 12pm, Cool.*
> *Read Carefully. When you buy a chicken from the Butcher—you*
> *bring it home—and before cooking—"You wash the chicken parts or whole*
> *in lukewarm "Salty" water—to remove all the flem and dirt from the*
> *chicken—Salt water does that. And when you have flem in your body—you*
> *must do the same—constantly—until you get AHEAD of the flem—This*
> *means two or three times Daily + medications—and you must spit and*
> *spit and spit—Even throwing up is good—Keep plenty of paper napkins*
> *available for yourself—*
> *I love you—*
> *Take care of Your Self—*
> *Always Daddy—*

Chemistry

I studied standing up. I went to the upper floors of the Sci Li, the Science
Library, to the map division, where the cabinets were the perfect height
to lay my books across, and read standing. I thought it better than sitting
for seven hours. When my brain needed a break, I'd slide open the drawers
of maps and slide my finger over the charts of my fantasy journeys. There

were topographical maps, interplanetary maps, and nautical maps of the ocean floor. On the nights I had to draw molecular translations, I'd sit at a table in the common area where I could find a chem major or a grad student if I needed help. We called our organic chemistry textbooks, our orgo books. I carried my orgo book around with me all the time, waiting for the moment it would unlock its secrets to me, and I would *capishe* the structural relationships of the universe. I studied whole evenings away, taking quick breaks for air and to stretch. I raised my eyes from my orgo book and stared out as I memorized molecular formulas, esters, and *OH* endings. There was one grad student named Andy who indulged me in long explanations of chemical reactions. It excited me to talk to someone who really understood this stuff. I sharpened my pencil with a pocket knife and drew structures by looking at the names of compounds in a reaction. *Draw the oxidation of cyclohexanol with potassium dichromate.* A girl pulled two orange chairs together, lay down to take a study break, and fell asleep. All of us students compassionately acknowledged each other's fatigue and need for snacks for endurance during our long study sessions. We guarded each other while we napped and shared chocolate and coffee. *Draw the structural formula for 3-Methyl-3-phenylbutanal.* A Japanese guy sat twenty feet away from me, intent in his books. He had long, thick black hair, a relaxed look about him, he wore soft cottons and flip-flops. I was impressed by men who wore flip-flops. I thought how different my life would have been had my father taken off his work boots and walked around in flip-flops. No. Lanzi wore steel-toe boots, armor and weapon, or polished black dress shoes, but nothing casual. I thought about his mixture of utmost respect and bitter hatred for his sworn enemy, the Japanese. Hatred of the enemy is necessary to survive in battle, otherwise how can one participate in war? If I were a Marine in a foxhole in Okinawa, I'd cling to my hatred as tight as I clung to my rifle. My father needed to heal. I wished I could help him. A part of him had been destroyed with every man he killed. Maybe I could. Maybe someone at Brown could help me return the Japanese flag that belonged to Toshiharu Kotani, to his family. Maybe I could find his family. The Japanese boy made eye contact with me. I guess I was staring at him. There was something feminine about him, soft. He didn't look away and neither did I. We didn't smile, just looked at each other, then looked back down into our books. I wondered what Toshiharu Kotani looked like. I wondered if my father could ever look a Japanese man in the face ever again. *Draw as many structures as you can for C3H6C12 and write the compound names.* For some reason I like long carbon chains. I loved how everything was connected. How at the core we were all made of the same atoms. Carbon. Hydrogen. Oxygen. Nitrogen. If we could only look at one another like that. I looked up from my book. The Japanese boy was one step away from me. He sat on my table, leaned over, and kissed me. My mouth opened without me thinking about it and we kissed deeply. His long hair fell around my face, like a girl. I dropped my pencil and looked him in the eyes. I saw my father's enemy and a beautiful boy at the same time. We kissed again. He picked up my pencil and jotted his first name and his number into my notebook and walked away.

The next time my father came up to Providence to surprise me, I decided to surprise him and take him out to a Japanese restaurant. The war was over for just shy of forty years. We walked in, and my father walked right past the maître d', not looking in his face. We sat down. Ordered tea. He stared into the menu. He looked up at the waiter. I kept the conversation light, telling him about school and how I wanted him to meet my professors. My father stared into his cup stirring, stirring, the spoon clinked the cup, it felt like a hundred times. He was gone. I waited for my father to come back to the present moment. Finally, he got up and walked out. I got up and followed him outside. He had his hands cupped around a match to light his cigarette.

"I can't trust that face. How could I eat with those faces?"

"Okay, Pop, I am sorry." Weak half sentences came out of my mouth, "I just tried—" and, "I thought—" I realized fagetaboutit, you can't push healing on anybody.

I never tried to take my father to a Japanese restaurant ever again.

We drove up to Federal Hill and ate at Angelo's. The menu was up on a column in the center of the room. I got the ravioli and a side of 'scharole sauté. Dad ate chicken parmigiana and a salad. We put away a lot of bread, and took a peaceful walk on Atwells Avenue down past the statue of the Blessed Mother.

Amara

CANOPY was the word the creative writing teacher at Brown University put on the blackboard, instructing us, "You have fifteen minutes to write." This was our audition to get into a class. Fifty of us sat in a corner classroom in the eighteenth century building Sayles Hall off the main green. The breeze came in from the windows of the bucolic campus grounds. The old window glass turned the yellows, purples, and greens of the leaves outside into a liquid collage. The teacher handed out little blue writing booklets. I wrote about my first maple tree in the Bronx, how I lay in the dirt and looked up through the branches and leaves to the sky. How the light played on my face. Canopy. I didn't get into the class.

I walked to Rhode Island Hospital to pick up my chemo-to-go. Down Brown Street, down Wickenden Street, over the Point Street Bridge, I kept my eye open for off-campus apartments. I wrote down phone numbers that were written on For Rent signs up in windows. Maloney, her friend Littlepage and I were moving in together. Littlepage was going to drop by sometime and meet me. I walked over the bridge. The hospital gave me a bag of vials of bleomycin and hypodermic needles thick as cigars. "Keep it refrigerated," the nurse strictly instructed. Then she handed me a paper license to keep in my wallet that said I could legally carry hypodermic needles and medicinal marijuana.

My dorm room had a tiny box-refrigerator where I could store my chemo. As I assembled the needle onto the syringe with a twist, I thought about Ant'ny. Odds were he was somewhere shooting heroin at this same minute. I wiped the vial of bleomycin with an alcohol swab, turned it upside down, plunged the syringe into the vial, and drew back to ten cubic centimeters. There was a gentle knock on my door. There stood Littlepage. She looked at the needle.

"Don't worry, it's not heroin. I'm on chemo. You must be Littlepage."

Littlepage cracked into exuberant laughter and held her heart with her hand. "Oh my sweet Lord."

We both laughed.

"Don't make me laugh, I have to do this."

I pulled some fat on my thigh, and plunged the needle into the skin. The fluid golf-balled up under the skin. I rubbed it until it dissipated. From these injections, over the months, I got black and blues and patches of scarred tissue all over my belly and thighs.

Littlepage and I walked around town, and met with a few landlords. The landlords of Providence were notorious for ripping off tenants. Littlepage was a surgeon's daughter from Richmond, Virginia. Between her southern charm and my Yankee street smarts, we found a beautiful apartment with hardwood floors at a decent price on Wickenden Street, across from the only health food restaurant in town, Amara's. We went right over there to eat dinner. The waitress, Mindy, had a Brown University keychain hanging off her belt loop. We struck up an easy conversation. She was a dancer. Mindy had a warm voice and sweet brown eyes. She told me all about Amara, who was a community organizer and attracted all the spirit seekers in town. At night she had meetings for spiritual teachings. Amara opened the restaurant in this old clapboard house in Fox Point, painted it purple, and got candlelight and the fireplace going. She used all natural foods and made everything from scratch. As I left, Mindy kissed me fully on the lips. She was liberated, beautiful, alive.

"What's *amara* mean?" I asked her.

"*Amara* is Italian for bitter. You're Italian. You should know."

Brazil Upside Down

For my three-month checkup at Charlie & Al's, Dr. Kempin felt the black and blues on my thighs and belly. "That shouldn't be happening," he said, "you actually have chemo burns in the fat and muscle tissue. Are you pointing the needle straight in?"

"No. I do it the way the nurse taught me. I lift the fat and inject under the skin on a forty-five degree angle. The fluid golf-balls up under the skin."

"How big are these needles?"

I showed him with my fingers. "This big. This wide."

"That's not right."

He called Rhode Island Hospital and figured out the problem.

"Bleomycin is supposed to be mixed to 0.1 cc's of fluid, but Rhode Island Hospital mixed it to 10.0 cc's by mistake."

And so, I learned the lesson of decimal points, viscerally, in stiff black-and-blue chemo burn patches under my skin. He rechecked the doses of thiotepa and vinblastine and checked the X-rays. The mediastinal mass, it seemed, was shrinking.

"Now go down the hall and see Dr. Lourdes Niece. I want to know what she thinks about the radiation protocol. Okay, Kiddo, get outta here. You'll die of something else."

Dr. Lourdes Niece slid my chest X-rays up onto the light board and flicked the light on. By now I'd come to recognize as my own, the white shadow that filled my rib cage. Dr. Niece slowly passed her hand over my chest X-ray. I wished she could wipe it all away. Her hand paused in a spot and went back over it, as if reading a Braille. Then she turned to me. "What are you studying in school?"

"Pre-med. I'm taking cellular biology, electron microscopy. I want to be a doctor."

"The whole life," she said, and she opened her two hands like a book and bowed her face into it.

The whole life—in a book. I understood, by her one gesture, volumes. She let me know that to become a doctor took years of focused study, and at the same time, I felt that she urged me to do something else, to go out and live life. Outside of books. Live a life.

That summer I went back home to Yonkers. One day, I could not breathe at all. I looked down at my arms, all my veins had popped to the surface of my skin. I looked in the bathroom mirror: my neck, chest, and arms were bulging with veins. I panicked. What the fhuck was happening to me? I looked like the Hulk. My skin turned blue. I called Dr. Kempin and rushed to the ER.

Usually they gave me a shot of Adrenalin and a Bronkosol treatment and banged on my back. This was different, and I knew it.

"SVC syndrome," Dr. Kempin said. "The tumor is squashing your superior vena cava. We have to give you an emergency dose of radiation." They lay me down and blasted me with cobalt radiation to push the tumor back. Once they got me breathing, Dr. Kempin decided to amp up the chemo protocol from TBV to MOPP: nitrogen mustard, vincristine, prednisone, and procarbazine.

I started the nitrogen mustard while I was in the hospital. I hung my head over a silver bucket of ice with a towel over my head. I didn't want to talk to anybody. If my mother tried to talk to me, I rebuked her with harsh staccato words and a flip of the hand. All I wanted was ice. The only words I offered were, "Ice. More ice." We took the elevator up to the fifteenth floor, where Charlie & Al's had a fenced-in deck out behind the recreation room. That cage served to remind us patients that there was an outside, fresh air, birds, whistles, buildings, bridges, the distant high-pitched sound of a hundred kids running in a school yard far below. I kept my Be All You Can Be baseball hat on at all times.

Rosemarie and Peter drove up with their beautiful daughter Melissa, my five year old goddaughter. Rosemarie was thirteen years older than me, and I was thirteen years older than Melissa. I walked down to the first floor hallway to see her. Melissa looked up at me, so concerned. Her face could not hide how she felt. She had the most honest and beautiful face. Emotions registered on her lips and eyes immediately. She was the first person in our family to have an American name, but she still was one hundred percent southern Italian, and had her father's Sicilian bottom lip that puffed out at the slightest hint of her sadness or indignation. I hated being the "sick" Aunt. I wanted to inspire her, not worry her. I hoped Melissa would grow up free of everything that strangled me.

Radiation treatments came in the heat of August. A nurse took a needle of blue tattoo dye and injected small amounts under my skin around my chest. She made a series of dots outlining the boundary of the tumor, for the mantle field of radiation. Then with indelible purple ink on my chest, she drew an X, inside a box, exactly how I chalked the X on the side of the house on Saint Raymonds Avenue and threw my Spaldeen at it. Now the X was on me.

Every morning I saw the same people for six weeks straight for radiation. We developed a camaraderie. One by one we went in for the treatment. I lay down, and the radiation technician strapped my chin to the table with my head tilted up. She strapped my waist down, and told me how important it was that I didn't fidget, budge, itch, flinch. She put small lead blocks on a tray under the beam of radiation to protect my lungs and heart. The door was over a foot thick and heavy. She slowly pushed it closed. I was alone in a silent vault. Then came the strange long beeps emitting from the machine and the green beam of light, like a machine gun of high-pitched beeps instead of bullets. I kept my eyes open into the light and tried to focus my brain by humming strands of melodies. One day the small lead blocks that shielded my heart and lungs fell out of place, and I knew my heart was taking direct hits. I yelled for help, but the machine finished its course.

Three weeks in, all our hair began to fall out at once. A young boy Diego who I thumb-wrestled with as an inpatient, both had hair in our hands. We scratched our heads and more came out. We began to laugh. I pulled out a fistful of hair and threw it up in the air. "Weeee!" I said. We laughed at each other. He pulled a handful of his hair out. I pulled mine out with two hands. We tossed it in the air. My mother cried. She told me to stop. She bent down and picked up the hair. I laughed. I was mad at her for crying at something so superficial. I had no room for her feelings. My skull felt hot and churning with energy. I was relieved the hair let go of the burning bones of my head. She was hurt by my laughter. I could see that, but I laughed harder. I threw a handful of hair at her. Hair she could see. She never saw the giant tumor, but hair she could see.

"After all I've been through, you're crying about hair? What's wrong with you! You're a hairdresser. All you care about is hair. Who cares about hair?"

After the radiation, Dr. Kempin was pleased. My white shadow shrunk. He showed me on the light board. It was now precisely the shape of Brazil—upside down.

Belly Up

BROWN UNIVERSITY, PROVIDENCE, RHODE ISLAND, 1982

My salivary glands were burnt out from the radiation treatments. I ran around the track in the gym with a plastic bottle of fake saliva, squirting it into my mouth and spitting off to the side.

"What's that?" jocks would ask.

"Fake spit," I answered as I ran.

I had chemo brain. My short-term memory was shot. I needed to empty out, not fill up. Why was "education" about faraway peoples doing faraway things in faraway times? My brain needed to cool. I needed to pour out my soul onto clear blank sheets of paper. I decided to start my own class. I went to Dean Karen Romer, a wise soul. We had many long discussions over my years at Brown. She guided me through the arduous process of creating my own class and eventually, my own major. I called the class, Everything You Always Wanted to Know About Cancer but Were Afraid to Ask. I recruited my hematologist Dr. James Crowley, and psychologist Dr. Stephanie LaFarge from Rhode Island Hospital as co-teachers. Dr. LaFarge ran the support group, "Teenagers with Terminal Illness." Dr. LaFarge was extraordinarily compassionate; she'd even raised and breastfed a chimpanzee. Together, we created a semester's worth of panels with guest speakers. I loved instigating arguments between guests who had wildly different points of view. We put one woman who cured herself without medical intervention on a panel with a teenager with an incurable cancer and an old-school oncologist. The three of them went at it. I stirred up arguments. I looked for truth in the spaces between people's thoughts. The juxtapositions created fruitful conflict. I am a pluralist by nature with a penchant for debate. Psychoneuroimmunology fascinated me, how an individual's mind and nervous system responded to stress and created disease. The class helped me cope with all the stupid advice I was getting from healthy people, family members who drove me crazy with magazine cures like coffee enemas, and a professor who offered me bottles of syrup from Peruvian tree bark. The healthy thought they were experts on how to stay healthy. The sick knew better. I got better communication from the clouds. Like Lanzi, I believed in luck. Lucky Strikes were his cigarettes. They had a red bull's-eye on the shiny white pack. I thought about what "a lucky strike" meant for Lanzi. His voice spun in my head. A lucky strike is a "bull's-eye." A lucky strike is, "Hit your target." A lucky strike is, "It don't hit you." A lucky strike is "Dead Japs." A lucky strike is "The only good Jap is a dead Jap." A lucky strike is, "You walk away from battle."

I had my own battle. The enemy was deep within and made of my own flesh, and would never die. Cancer cells never died. I wish I could have talked with Alfred Sloan and Charles Kettering and asked them about their careers at General Motors, their views on "planned obsolescence" in industry, and what they thought about cancer cells which effectively shut off "senescence," the mechanism by which all things age and die.

Teenagers with Terminal Illness began with a dozen of us. I was the only New Yorker in the group. My best two friends were Peter Findlay and Melody Stappas. Peter was a student at Brown from Peacedale, Rhode Island, and Melody taught music outside Providence. Peter had leukemia and Melody had Hodgkin's disease. We sat in a circle, talked about our chemotherapies and dating, planned the music for our funerals and laughed with abandon. I told the group about the time a guy from Brown I had dated took me home to meet his mother and I asked her if I could put my chemotherapy in her refrigerator. The way she looked at me, like I wasn't a good breeder prospect for her son, was colder than the temperature I needed to keep my bleomycin for the weekend. Peter and I talked about sex all the time. We were adamant we would not die virgins. We expounded on this conversation back at the Blue Room at Brown, amidst the other students fretting about deadlines and tests. Peter talked of gearing up for his bone marrow transplant. He yanked his wig off, extending his arm straight up over his head. It was a Charlie Chaplinesque move, and a shocking public act in the days of blown-dry feather haircuts. I laughed 'til I choked. I felt in that moment, that everyone not only in the Blue Room but in the world, turned to see Peter Findlay, wig in hand way above his head, laughing with insouciance at death. Everyone in the support group died, all eleven of them; even the fish in the doctor's tank, one day were all belly-up.

Overheating

BROWN UNIVERSITY, PROVIDENCE, RHODE ISLAND

My father and Uncle Frank picked me up at the end of the school year from Brown in Uncle Frank's pickup truck. We sat three across on the bench seat and had to keep the heat on the whole bumpy ride down so the truck wouldn't overheat.

"I'm in a battle with my phlegm," Dad said. He kept a little notebook in his breast pocket where he wrote down a log of his ailments, phlegm, what he ate, and his bowel movements. I coughed from the heat hitting me in the face.

Uncle Frank said, "Spend a couple of weeks with me, I'll clear your lungs right up."

"Unc, Pop, I want to tell you about this guy I studied. His name is Søren Kierkegaard."

"Hah?"

"Kierkegaard."

"Kieka who? What kind of name is that."

"He's a Dane, Unc."

"A what?"

"A Dane."

"What a Great Dane?"

"You know, Daddy, the Dutch built New York. That's how we got stoops."

"Not Dutch, Pop, he's from Denmark. Just listen. He said a lot of cool things. Listen to this. He says, 'It is true, that a mirror has the quality of enabling a man to see his image in it, but for this he must stand still. If he rushes hastily by it, then he sees nothing.'"

"That's not true, you see a blur."

"Great point, Unc, but that's not what he was saying."

"This is what they're teaching you in school, Daddy?"

"Fagetaboutit."

"Wait a while, give her a chance. Ga'head Mary I mean Annie, you explain it, Ga'head."

"I was just gonna say that Kierkegaard says most people 'rush headlong into life.'"

"And . . ."

"And, you gotta stop sometimes."

"Stop? Fagetaboutit. You can't stop. How can you stop? Joey d'you ever stop?"

"You stop you get a whack you know where. I had a Sargeant once . . ."

"You stop you're lost. You're done. *eh finud.* You know what I mean?"

"*Capishe. Capishe.*"

"Daddy, remember, you can get knocked down your whole life as long as you don't get knocked out. Remember that."

"Wait a while. You ever hear, 'Ours is not to question why, ours is just to do and die?'"

"I like to question why."

"Hah? You ever hear that? I got eight kids. I never stopped not once. You know what I wish for you? Hah? That you should live a life as good as I."

"You two should sit in class with me. You got all the answers."

"If you walk by a mirror, you see a blur. I rest my case."

"A blur. You're right, Unc. There goes a semester's worth of existentialism out the hot truck window."

"Look at that, we're passing New London. That's the sub base. Daddy, when I was in the service, we stayed in New London. You should stay up here. It's good country. I walked every inch of this ground. My first guard duty post outta boot camp was up here. Four of us came up here from Parris Island. Hayward Preston, Alex Straub, Al Kopenig. We had to keep an eye out for German saboteurs. Starboard. Portside. The watch was four hours on, eight hours off. There was no room for mistakes. Main gate you were busy checking identification of the personnel going through, and the traffic going through, and you were forever saluting. Dry dock was the loneliest post. No one came there except the OD, Officer of the Day, and the sargent of the guard. The officer of the day was always a navy man. He would come up to you out of nowhere, and if he could remove your weapon from you, he would, if you gave him the chance. I got to know every inch of the ground, where all the cargo was, and all the places to sit and rest. I knew all the corners, and the best spots to observe. There was one path where the OD could come through, and the lights in the distance, from where I sat, would show me a form coming through the path. A few nights I challenged the form, "Halt or I shoot," and since then the navy OD would come through with his flashlight shining. No one liked the dry dock post because it was the loneliest post. I loved it. It kept me out of trouble."

"The truck needs to rest. Who's hungry?"

Triple Boiling Point

MEMORIAL SLOAN-KETTERING CANCER CENTER, NEW YORK CITY, 1982

D r. Kempin showed me my white shadow of upside down Brazil.
"It plateaued," he said.

He tried different chemo: CCNU, vinblastine, Alkeran, and scheduled me for adriamycin: Red Death. I mentally prepared for it, researched its side effects and efficacy, convinced myself that despite its cardiotoxicity in the long term, it was "good" for me in the short term, that I had to survive "now" and not worry about "later." We had to get rid of Brazil. I stared at the molecular structure of adriamycin and vinblastine. Vinblastine, $C_{46}H_{58}N_4O_9$, blew my mind, the nitrogen oxygen bonds astounded me. I couldn't wrap my head around them. Adriamycin, $C_{27}H_{29}N_4O_{11}$, looked simpler in structure, but wreaked havoc on the heart. I surrendered. I went down to Charlie & Al's with my mother, waited on the long chemo line, and that's where my memory ends. I don't remember the needle in my arm or the red drip entering my bloodstream.

A few months later, I saw Dr. Kempin again. He used the word again: plateau. "The tumor shrunk then seemed to hit a plateau."

We had to do something.

"What do you suggest, Doc?"

Then Dr. Kempin said words that I never heard him say before: "I don't know what to do."

I was jarred. I never thought I'd hear those words from him. I never thought he'd be at a loss. The floor yanked up from under me, and the walls folded. It could all completely collapse so easily. "I don't know what to do" echoed in my head. I didn't say anything. The world spins imperceptibly fast, but in that moment I could feel the spin, I was in it, held in place, back slammed up against a wall.

"In two weeks I'm presenting your case at the Tumor Board."

"What's the Tumor Board?"

"It's a gathering of doctors to discuss difficult cases."

"Can I attend?"

"No."

"Why not?"

"Well, it's against the grain of medical etiquette."

"But if you don't know what to do, how will I make a decision what to do? This is my life."

"Don't worry. I will tell you everything that is said."

I drove up to Brown. As I drove up I-95 North, the flashing red light on top of the Sci Li was the first sign I was near campus. The next landmark on the highway was a giant blue termite with wings, bigger than a single-engine Cessna, on top of New England Pest Control. After I passed the blue bug, I knew I was almost there. I got off the highway, cut through the back streets of Fox Point, and up to College Hill.

I climbed up to the roof of my old dorm to be alone with the sky. Providence has swirling moody skies, and I had the urge to get as close to clouds as possible. "Death comes when no one's looking," my father had told me. I looked at the clouds for an indication. I saw shapes and faces in the clouds like my father showed me how to envision faces and crowns and eyes in the circles he inked on loose-leaf when I was a child. In the clouds I saw the face of Jesus clearly, his beard took shape, then pulled away and became a herd of antelopes running across the sky. The clouds thickened to a deep gray, merged and broke apart again with the wind. Streaks of light shot through them. Three clouds wrestled like puppies one on top of the other without any restraint. I wanted their freedom. I thought of Penny's puppies in their cardboard box under the window, six puppies, one shifting mass of fur. One thick cloud sat right between me and the sun. Charcoal shades melted across the roof. I felt three distinct forces within me pulling in different directions. My body, my mind, and my soul were at war. They ran at different speeds and in opposite directions. I was being yanked apart, quartered as it were. I stared at the cloud that came down to me. My spirit leaped. I wanted to unleash my soul. I wanted to jump into the cloud. I felt my body lift and become part of the clouds and absorb the swirling grays and whites of the sky. I bent my neck back and spread my arms and felt my ribs open like sails to the wind. I didn't have to jump, I could be lifted. I fell to my knees crying. The voluptuous rolls of the cloud covered me. I wanted freedom from my body. I felt the peace of death. I wanted to shed life, this body, this agony, this echo of my doctor's voice "I don't know what to do." I yelled at the cloud a point-blank question:

"Am I going to die?"

"No," came the answer from the cloud, "you will live. You will live and you will suffer."

I drove away from Brown alone, blasting "Tempted" by Squeeze. Down College Hill, I looked at the buildings and street signs as if it were the last time in my life I would ever see them. My eyes swallowed the landscape whole; clock tower, locked iron Van Wickle Gates topped by Brown's seal: the sun's spikes through three clouds, *In Deo Speramus*. I cried the whole three-hour drive from Providence to Yonkers.

Eat 'Til You Sweat

"Stay with me a coupla a days, I'll fix you right up," Uncle Frank said after he listened to the phlegm in my chest. Uncle Frank ate hot cherry peppers in one hand, and clutched a handkerchief in the other. He ate 'til his forehead and neck was full of sweat. We stood next to his refrigerator.

"The tumor ain't goin' nowhere," I told him, "no matter what they blast me with." Uncle Frank took out a giant jar of hot cherry peppers, a bulb of garlic, and some fresh Italian bread. He peeled the cloves with his fingers and handed them to me raw, looked me in the eye, and delivered his wisdom:

"*L'aglio è essenziale. L'aglio è l'essenza della vita.*" Garlic is essential. Garlic is the essence of life.

Photos of four generations covered Uncle Frank and Aunt Laura's colossal refrigerator. They had eight kids, and most of their kids had three, four, five kids. Hundreds of big brown eyes looked out at me as I swallowed the garlic raw. I didn't know these new young cousins of mine, but I recognized the expression in their faces, in their eyes and noses, a familiarity. We were blood. There were so many of them. Uncle Frank handed me a hunk of bread to chase the raw garlic down. We did this standing. I coughed, and my phlegm came up knotty, white, cloudy.

"Good," he said. "Bite into it. It opens you right up."

"Okay Unc." I broke clove after clove open. I rubbed some on my chest. I stuck pieces in my ears. I wrapped slices around my neck. With the witness of four generations of faces on the refrigerator looking through me.

I began to carry garlic wherever I went, and to say things like, "Garlic can push an ocean through your aorta." I surrendered to the idea that a "*sangwich*" is a raw garlic folded in Italian bread. I began to sweat.

To find out what was going on inside me, I needed a white coat. Social workers at Sloan-Kettering left their white coats in their offices overnight. I took a white labcoat whenever I needed to sneak into Charlie & Al's medical library to find out what was happening to me. I walked into an unlocked office on the sixth floor and took a coat off the hook on the back of the door. Information was hard to come by. Inquiring about my case didn't always work. Sometimes I got Mickey Mouse answers. Once a respiratory therapist told me, "The oxygen treatment is to help you breathe." I didn't know what to do when someone talked to me like a jackass. It made me nuts. I wanted to shred them to pieces or throw chairs through the hospital windows. One neurologist tested me for the side effects of chemo. She put me through a series of exercises where I touched my fingers together and she tested my numbness and strength. Then she repeatedly commanded, "*Cross ayour eyes! Cross ayour eyes!*"

"What? I can't cross my eyes," I yelled back at her. She wanted me to cross my eyes and walk across the room. I didn't know what the hell she was talking about. She demonstrated. She closed her eyes and walked in a straight line across the room. Now I understood. I closed my eyes. Exasperated.

The white coat held power. To find out what's going on in a hospital, a patient needs a white coat and stethoscope, a medical interpreter, and a pocket medical dictionary. "I will design this kit when I am well," I thought to myself. *When I'm well, when I'm well . . .* These words held an incantatory power, as if some deity had hit the pause button on my life. I coughed and flung my phlegm into the corner of the hall. I could discern by now five shades of green phlegm. I thought of Uncle Frank. In everything he ever said to me over the course of my whole life, I heard one message loud and clear: *You must learn to desire to live more than to die.*

My body was the enemy. I had wrestled death since before birth, born with the umbilicus double-wrapped around my neck. "Boy, is your doctor quick," the attending nurse told my mother, after the life-saving maneuver of Dr. Ricciardi who wedged his pinkie between my neck and the chord, averting a potential *garotte* as I rushed headlong out of Rachel's birth canal. My father told me about the night I was born. "I was changing the channels back and forth between the fight and the Mother Goose Stakes at Aqueduct. Even Dr. Ricciardi wanted to watch the fight. The Pope was in a coma. Willy Pastrano took Johnson in a split decision for the title, and a horse called Spicy Living came in. Just before you were born the Pope came out of his coma, sat up in bed, and took a coffee down. His last words were, 'Souls. Souls. That all may be one.'"

The Tumor Board

MEMORIAL SLOAN-KETTERING, NEW YORK CITY, OCTOBER 1982

Iarrived early. I was the first one there. I stood in the hallway in my newly acquired white coat, stethoscope casually slung around my neck. I had a clipboard and a pair of clear glass eyeglasses. I was shapeshifting again, gaining entrance by any means necessary. The staff had not yet arrived. The room was on the right. I walked by, studied the door. No one came in or out. I walked a lap around the hallway until a pack of doctors arrived. I mixed in with them and entered the room. One doctor propped the door open. I listened to what they said to make sure I was in the right place. The white coat was a skin of invulnerability, the opposite of donning a hospital gown with its wide open flimsy cotton that never closed or covered the body. The white coat was stiff, structured, defined shoulders, pockets, buttons. It was useful. I felt powerful, immune. Smart. Daring. I could walk and touch the sick and not get sick. I could be around contagion and not catch it. Other doctors nodded to me as they walked by. They didn't see me, they saw the coat, their equal. I took a seat in the back. My nurse Veronica came in and took a seat right behind me. She didn't recognize me. I absorbed myself in papers on my clipboard I pretended to read. I knew that when Dr. Kempin stepped onto the platform to speak, he wouldn't even spot me. If he did spot me and ask me to leave, I had a speech prepared. The room quickly filled up, like a movie theater, a classroom, a church. There was much chatter, pats on the back, the chewing of bagels and the sipping of coffee. Did they look forward to these meetings? People were smiling. This was the most grave day of my life, and they were all socializing. Where was my doctor? I started to feel guilty. My relationship with Dr. Kempin was so blessed and based on mutual respect. I loved and trusted him more than anyone I'd ever met in my life. He was more than a doctor, he was a mentor, by far the smartest and most compassionate person I'd ever met. I didn't want to hide in the room without him knowing. I had nothing to hide. I took the eyeglasses off, and stepped out of the room into the hallway. I wanted Dr. Kempin to know I was there. If he insisted I leave on the grounds of "medical etiquette," then I would address the whole assembly. I wouldn't absent myself under any circumstances. I was the daughter of Rachele. I knew how to bounce back. I was Joey Lanz's daughter. I could summon all my powers of public speaking. I was Sister Raymond Aloysius's protégé, and she was tougher than any doctor. My life might count on this speech. I had a shelf full of trophies for public speaking, now I was prepared to speak for my life itself. My speech went like this: "Linked to this mediastinal mass is a

mind. A mind which needs to understand. Since being thrown into this world
of cancer, I've realized many physical limitations. By not allowing me to stay
here today, you also limit my mind. My doctor told me that it is against the
grain of medical etiquette for me to be here today; that when debating my
prognosis, you may withhold comments in my presence. like the mother who
spells out words in fear her child may understand. . . ."

I looked down the hall. Finally, I saw him; he walked steady and fast,
with his eyes at the floor. He was carrying my X-ray films. I tapped him as
he turned to enter the door. He turned and I looked him in the eye, his
piercing compassionate beautiful eyes. I had clearly disrupted whatever he
was thinking about. He looked at me in the white coat and smiled, then he
shook his head, laughed, and patted me on the shoulder. "Sit in the back,"
he said. His arm in his big white coat pointed into the room. "You remind
me of me when I was young."

I loved him for that. I crumpled the speech in my coat pocket and
returned to my seat. He would have done the same thing if he'd had cancer
while he was in college. He could see the doctor in me. I walked to the
back, winked at Veronica, and sat back down in front of her. A few minutes
later she put her hand on my shoulder, and with her face next to mine, said,
"What are you doing here? Does he know you're here?"

"He said it's okay."

"Wow."

Dr. Kempin stepped up onto the platform and hung my chest X-rays
on the light board. Front. Side. Lung. My chest X-ray is my mug shot. He
turned the light board on, the light flickered on then off then on at one end,
and the light shot to the other end and went out. Finally, it stayed on, and
you could clearly see the X-ray. Doctors in the crowd "oohed" and "aahed"
when they saw the size of Brazil. They were unruly. "Fagetaboutit, this one's
a goner," one shouted. I didn't know if he was kidding or not, but now I
understood why patients weren't allowed at these meetings. It was the medical
community who, behind closed doors, had no etiquette.

Dr. Kempin began his presentation. "This is the third admission for
this nineteen-year-old Caucasian female who has undergone . . ." His words
echoed in my head, *has undergone has undergone has undergone* . . . I knew all
I'd undergone.

". . . has laterally transposed ovaries, has joined the fertility study," he
continued.

I sat up straight in the cold metal chair. This was me they were talking
about in such strange language. Their coats were open. Their shoulders were
back. One woman rubbed her eyes and returned her glasses to her head. I
did the same. It was like sitting in a huge lecture hall. Suddenly I felt very
far away. Like I was back at Brown, where my friends were, sitting in classes.

I didn't know if I'd ever get back there or not. Death again was double-wrapped around my neck and I needed someone's pinkie finger fast.

Dr. Kempin continued. "Out of one hundred fifty patients status Hodgkin's disease on MOPP/TBV trials, there have been one hundred forty-nine remissions. This is the one hundred and fiftieth."

"Nobody bats a thousand!" one doctor yelled out. I refused to turn to look to see which guy said that. I concentrated on the white shadow of upside-down Brazil that nested in my rib cage.

"She presents with persistent mediastinal mass resistant to chemotherapy and external RT. She developed sudden onset of shortness of breath and right neck swelling. Superior vena cava syndrome was diagnosed and patient was significantly improved on regimen of prednisone and eight hundred rads to left lung and anterior and posterior mediastinum."

I stared into the heart of the white shadow. Veronica leaned forward to see if I was okay; she offered me help with the terms. I thanked her, but I had already done my homework the first two times I snuck into the medical library. For two days I stared at surgical textbooks and imagined the detailed drawings of ribs being retracted actually happening on my ribs. Already I ached.

"Systemic chemotherapy was subsequently reinstituted as per MOPP protocol and additional mantle RT to three thousand rads was delivered with minimal complications. Chest X-ray revealed no decrease in mediastinal mass." Dr. Kempin laid down the options as he saw them. After the facts were presented, the room was soon divided. I let their words go through me.

"Is she a suitable risk for additional surgery?"

"How many blood transfusions has she had already?"

"Does she have a suitable bone marrow donor?"

"Why put her through it? She's got a history of lung complications, asthma, pneumonia her lungs are already scarred."

"I say operate, and if there's residual disease, then put radioactive implants appropriate to the degree of metastasis," a deep voice called out.

"That's last resort," a softer voice replied.

"I had a patient like that, I tried more chemotherapy and it worked. Give her Adriamycin first," another man called out.

"She's reached the limit of RT."

"The problem is she's already had adjunct therapy and is immunosuppressed. The bone marrow had to suffer loss. If you stuck to one modality there wouldn't be this danger," a woman added.

"Forget the Adriamycin. If you give that to her and there is cardiotoxicity, you can say good-bye to further surgery. Operate now while you can. The patient is young enough to tolerate it. If she were sixty-five, I'd say don't do anything. Let the tumor make its move. If it's metastatic, you'll know soon enough, and if it's just scar tissue, then let her live with it. Put her on steroids to get the swelling down. Keep her breathing as easy as possible," one man said decisively.

"Leave the kid alone," another shouted, "let the tumor make its move."

They took a vote. The house was divided. Some said go for broke. Go through with the surgery. It was worth the risks. Others said, do nothing. I couldn't do that. Just wait, not knowing what was inside me. Sit and wait. Wait it out. Let the cancer make a move. Wait for an indication. It'll make its move. Time will tell. Others said, try a harsher chemo. I rubbed my chest. What the hell was inside me? Like a jellyfish, this tumor moved when I moved, pushed on my superior vena cava, pushed on my lungs. I couldn't live with the ambiguity. I couldn't wait. It was clear to me. I made up my mind. It had to come out. I wanted surgery. Surgery was definitive. I scribbled a one word note: Thoracotomy, and waited for Dr. Kempin at the elevator bank, where I handed him my decision on a paper folded into a square. He nodded and said, "I'll talk with a couple of surgeons."

On the way out, I ran into a cluster of nurses who had taken care of me. We said our hello's and I told them I was getting a thoracotomy; the word landed like a bomb. Tears welled in their eyes. I consoled them. "It's only skin."

I stepped out into the cold on York Avenue, pushed past the cigarette smokers that lined the doorway, walked by the hot dog vendor, and turned on Sixty-Seventh Street, heading west, as the sun turned the corner. I stopped at a phone booth and called my mother. She answered on one ring.

"Hi, Ma."

"What'd the doctors say?"

"It's not what they said. I decided. Surgery."

"Surgery? Oh God."

"Don't worry Ma. I gotta know one way or the other. I can't play a guessing game. I'm gonna take a walk and clear my head. I'll see you in a couple of hours. I don't know exactly what time."

"Don't worry about the time. Just relax will ya' please? As Granma says, 'when you get here, you're here.'"

The Radioactive Man Says, "Don't Give Up the Ship!"

SLOAN-KETTERING CANCER CENTER, NEW YORK CITY

Back to the hospital for blood work. I tire easily and look around for a seat. For one seat. My mother is with me. My left hand holds the gold and pink and blue slips to give to the phlebotomist. The colored slips are proof that I am here for me, not for a relative. I do not care where my mother sits. The only empty chairs in the room are clustered around an old man sleeping upright in a wheelchair in the corner near the glare of the window. I walk toward him. There is a dime-sized hole under his Adam's apple; his voice has been taken out. I sit down next to him. My mother follows. Old men are safe, looking straight ahead, not sideways at me. He has red tags all over him. When we sit, he grunts, lifts a wrist and swings it at my mother as if it is the arm on a Victrola. The tag reads: RADIOACTIVE. We jump up as if we are one and back away. He waves us over to the other side of him. He slaps the seat for me to come over. He quickly scribbles a note and puts it in the palm of my hand:

"You're OK on the right side of me."

The red tags read: KEEP AWAY: RADIOACTIVE.

I nod. His handwriting is shaky.

I say, "Hello," and I touch his arm. My mother tugs at my arm. I pull away. She folds her coat over her arm. She tells me to let her hold the slips. I say, "No." My man with no voice writes one line on a small white pad, rips out the page, and hands me the paper, "Nine times here since 1971."

I nod at him. "I've only been here a year," I say.

"Fight. Fight. You're young!!!" he writes.

I nod and hold up a strong fist. He smiles. He is already writing his next line, "Rad. on the left neck."

I nod.

"Stay away 3 feet left side."

"Okay," I say.

My mother's face silently urges me to move away from the man. I turn my back to her.

The man points to the cover story on the newspaper: "Queens Father Slays Two Children." He writes: "He should shot himself."

I look at the article. "Yes," I say, "I've heard of that guy."

"To hurt your own blood you are an animal," he writes.

I nod. I become as if I do not have a voice either. I scrawl a note back to him that says: "Where are you from?" Because even on paper, this man's voice has an accent, a certain syntax, an order that isn't American English, and is familiar to my ear.

"Italy." Then he writes, "Mom." Finally, "Mom she came from Italy."

I nod. "Me too," I write. Then I watch him write his next line.

"She always said, 'I *kill* anyone who will hurt my *children*.' That's parents." Then he underlines the words *parents* and the word *children*, and the word *kill* twice.

Then this radioactive man without a voice box writes words on a piece of paper that will echo inside me through all the toughest times in my life.

"John Paul Jones said don't give up the ship."

So impressed was I by the radioactive man that the next day in the library I looked up the history behind this quote. I was spooked to find it was said on my birthday, June 1st, in 1813, not by John Paul Jones, but by Captain James Lawrence aboard the USS *Chesapeake*, whose dying cry was his final command, "Don't give up the ship!"

Thoracotomy

MEMORIAL SLOAN-KETTERING CANCER CENTER, OCTOBER 1982

I was playing pool with my father in the fifteenth-floor recreation room when Dr. Nael Martini, chief of the Thoracic Service, came in to find me. Dr. Martini had a calm, warm style and soft brown eyes. I chose him, out of all the surgeons at Charlie & Al's, to perform the thoracotomy. His reputation was legendary as a pioneer in the OR. If I was gonna trust anyone to cut all around my lungs and get this thing out of there, it was him.

"You weren't in your room. They told me you were here."

"Hi Doc," I shook his hand. "This is my father, Joseph."

"Mr. Lanzillotto."

"Hiya Doctor."

"I want you to do the thoracotomy."

"It's up to you," he said, "there are a lot of surgeons here."

"I want you. And I want Dr. Carolyn Reed with you."

"You got it."

I remember my father being so impressed that Dr. Martini searched us out, all the way to the pool table on the fifteenth floor. "What a man," he kept saying, "what a man."

The night before the surgery, I sat with my father until they gave me a tranquilizer to get some sleep. I told my mother to go home early. I could only take one parent at a time. I didn't want any aggravation. My father was good at letting go. My mother clung. I couldn't afford to cling to life. 'If it doesn't stick keep it,' my father had taught me all those years ago in our basement on Saint Raymonds Avenue. Now, I had to be like gold and not stick to anything. I needed to be with someone who knew about death and could accept the possibility. My father was the one who taught me how to ride a bike. I can still feel my father's hands on the back of my first two-wheeler when I was a kid. He ran behind me as I pedaled, and let go of the seat without me knowing. I only fell down on the ground when I realized his hands were not there to support me, and I got scared and lost my balance. Now he sat beside me in the hospital. I contemplated the long cut Dr. Martini would make under my sixth rib, all around my left side, from angel wing to under the breast. "No nerves run on the underside of the ribs," he'd told me. He'd open my rib cage up with a steel rib retractor. My father read the worry on my face.

"Daddy, don't worry about nuttin'," he said.

"You never know, Pop. You gotta face the possibility."

"Daddy, that's one thing, you're right. You never do know. You think you're gonna die tomorrow? You may be around another hundred years! Who knows? Take like me. When you think you're gonna die, you don't. When you don't expect to, you do. You think Railhead thought he was gonna go when he got hit? No way! He was thinking he was gonna get pinned a hero. I'll never forget, out of nowhere he comes goddamn grenade happy. Son of a bitch jumps outta the cave. I thought I got him first. Baby, there's things I'd like to forget but can't. Then there's things I'd want to remember but don't. With Railhead, by rights, it shoulda been me, right Daddy? When it's your time, there's nothing you can do about it. Take like hoodycall, that kid around the block who ran on the draft, you were probably too little, ah whaddyacallit's kid brother. Anyway hoodycall, now what'd he do? He flees the number, and while your brother went to Vietnam, he gets himself killed in a car wreck up in Canada, and your brother came home after his tour. So, who's to say, baby? Even war you can run away from, but not death. You can fear it, yes, but not avoid it."

To try to get to sleep, I counted two hundred and fourteen ceiling tiles.

If it weren't for the waking up, I never would have known that I had ever fallen asleep. My eye opened and in that very instant of seeing, the dream was snatched away from me. There was someone standing over me, not dressed in white—my father—his dark eyes peered into my left eye, where his hand was gently on my face, not his hand but his thumb, not my face but my eyebrow, pressing it. He waited to make sure I was able to keep the eyelid up on my own before he let go, lifting his thumb off slowly as if peeling it off, carefully as if not wanting to smear a thumbprint left behind on the skin of the eyelid. His hand paused in the air just above my head with fingers splayed as if he had just released a basketball and was waiting for the effect of the touch to register. And it did. Score. I was awake, without remembering the dream or the waking or even ever being put to sleep. It all occurred in the cleft of a second. I blinked and felt a tingle where the blood came back into where he'd been pressing. There was no yawning, no gradual stretch. My voice came out strong from the first *d* sound in "Dad?"

"I wasn't going to wake you, Daddy, but I figured they wake you early anyway, throw on the lights, take early blood and what-have-you. So, I never left," he said, leaning over my bed, "If I could sleep, I'd sleep, but who could sleep? I stayed on a chair in the lobby. You know me, Daddy. Where there's a bathroom and a cup of coffee every couple of hours, there I'm comf'table."

He leaned forward then halted. He strained to pull the reins on his gaze back. This has happened ever since I can remember; my father's gaze locked directly into my eyes then shifted; I was sure he saw a bit of his own resemblance there. I was never sure it was me he was looking at. "Daddy," he said, beginning again, but his gaze strode off behind me. It didn't stop where my eyes began, but rode farther and farther as if my eyes drilled through to the back of my head, as if my eyes were tunnels his gaze could ride into. It had a will of its own, his gaze. It strode with the great speed of familiarity; destination, not in question, the way there, known; every bump and turn, the well-worn path of memory to trauma. Trauma becomes an abstract painting on the walls of your cells. The details are in motion, and they blur. You can slow it down or let it roll fast and repeat. My father looked through my eyes as if they were the wrong end of binoculars aimed at his own past he had to squint when looking at; careful not to let it all in at once or it might pierce his own eyes surely, like looking at direct sun unprotected.

I followed his gaze through my head and out the window, out across the black river. The sun had not yet taken its place in the sky. The hour was not clear. The tops of the buildings were not yet distinguishable from the rim of the sky. There was a shine upon the water. His gaze entered it. In the blackness the lights appeared molten, steaming from the three smokestacks silhouetted against the darker black sky. The sky was black translucent glass, as ribbed as the waters. There was something behind it all, I was convinced. I focused on my image in the glass. I looked like an item from a yellow tag sale. Bright tags were tied to my wrists and ankles. Tags were tied to the bed railing. I closed one eye then the other. I tried to see myself with my eyes closed. I wondered what I would look like dead.

"Hah!" he said, as if he heard my thought. He snapped back into lucidity, into the here and now.

"Daddy at least you got a shot. You cross the street you could get hit by a truck, then what shot do you got? It's all luck. Take Jimmy Ostermeyer. Jimmy O. took up photography after boot camp. He says Lanzi, let's take photography, get outta this thing alive. I tell him, if I'm goin' to battle Jimmy, I'm going with a weapon. You can carry a camera if you want to, Jimmy, I'm carryin' a rifle. I signed up for Weapons Company. Jimmy O. took up photography.

I heard Jimmy O. took a bullet in the head in Guam. It's all luck. Who's to figure? So you just give your body over to your doctors. They're professionals. Let them do what they gotta do. Don't worry 'bout nothin'. You're a survivor. Who's to say? You're lucky you got a good brain. You got the best brains in all the family. You got doctors. If you're lucky you'll walk away."

One Mis·sip·pi

I was happy it was Ugo Majori who came into my room to wheel me down for surgery. Ugo was the best patient escort at Sloan-Kettering. It would be a smooth ride, he never bumped into things. Ugo pressed a notch on the wall and the doors opened at once and automatically closed behind us. There were two rows of stretchers, one lining each wall of the corridor. Ugo parked me on the back of the line to the right, and brought my papers up front. I didn't see him after that. The beds were lined up feet to head, feet to head, head to feet, feet to head, it seemed random positioning, however they could be fit in. We were all facing in either of two directions. I was put behind an old man, feet to feet, and directly across from an old woman who moaned. The two lines were separated by an aisle big enough for the largest nurse to pass through, her unbuttoned jacket just brushing the sidebars of our beds. I heard someone cry in Italian, "*Mama, madon, madon, madonnami!*" breaking the tranquilized and sterile atmosphere. Moaning is contagious. Other patients started to call out. The nurse asked if any of us spoke Italian. "She's inconsolable," the nurse said, "and upsetting everyone."

"I'm Italian," I said. I didn't speak Italian, but I am Italian, something should come through me. The nurse wheeled my stretcher nearer to the moaning Italian. I understood the music of her words and the gist of her heart's plea. She called her mother. She called Mary the mother of God. She called the sweet heart of Jesus. She called Saint Anthony and asked him not to leave her. I put a few words together, mostly in the Spanish I studied in high school with an Italian accent. "*No te preoccupare.*" I was searching for the right words in a language I didn't speak, my grandmother's tongue. Trying to speak Italian was like picking a lock to break into my own house where I'd left the keys inside, each word and phrase a click of the right combination. I kept trying my hybrid tongue until something opened. This was no time to search for words. I tried to comfort her. I held her hand. I told her not to worry. I looked into her eyes. I tried to tell her, "We're together," and "The doctors are the best in the world," all the true crap everyone had been telling me to assuage my fears. Finally, I said, "*Pregha, Signora.*" Pray lady. The two of us together. And I started singing the *"Ave Maria"* quietly, and I realized I didn't know the words to that either, so I hummed and held her two hands in mine. I didn't know crap. She nodded and started breathing with calm. The nurse wheeled me back to my position, gave me a pre-anesthetic, and it kicked in immediately. Bliss. I stared into the ceiling, the vast white squares with thousands of dots. I counted the dots, up to two hundred fifty-two, then my eyes blurred. One day I would create a "Healing Ceiling," I thought, I would take drop-ceiling squares and paint them with calming words and images for the horizontal people.

The doors opened into a windowless room. Where was this room within the hospital? What street did it face in the world? There was no reference point to where we were in relation to anywhere else. How far from Mom and Dad and my brothers and sister in the waiting room lobby like a hotel, palm trees in pots, brothers, sister, waterfall, escalator? The instruments gleamed; still silver after all they cut, reflecting pieces of the room. My stretcher passed from hand to hand to hand until it lined up parallel with a table that was fixed in the center of the room like an altar. I was asked to slide over to the table. First sliding my buttocks then my back then my legs one by one over with their hands on various parts of me. I got a chill.

"Hi Kiddo, just relax," Dr. Martini said. "Let me do all the work."

"I'm all yours, Doc," I said. To myself, I prayed: Doctor do a good job. Find out what is inside me. Go where no one ever goes. They tell me you can tell me, you can name what it is that's wrong.

Dr. Martini tapped the words on my hat that read: Be All You Can Be. "I'll try," he said. His eyes changed shape behind the glasses and his mask creased. I could tell he was smiling. He winked. "What radio station would you like on?"

"Whatever," I said, "whatever you like to work to."

"Now count down from thirty."

The anesthesia was pushed into my vein. I counted the way I'd learned on Saint Raymonds Avenue, "Thir-ty Mis-sip-pi, Twen-ty nine Mis-sip-pi, Twen-ty eight Mis-sip-pi."

I woke up to my father's voice yelling in the post-op recovery room. Voices were muffled. Surreal. The lights were bright. There was beeping, beeping. I passed my hand over my chest. I did not feel any radioactive implants. There was a piece of paper. I held it up to see. It was my mother's handwriting: "We heard the good news. We are all waiting for you. Love, Mom." Could it be? I was cured? No more cancer? Martini got it all? A wave of freedom washed over me. I tried to sit up in bed. I was hazy. My ribs ached. A nurse looked down on me. I held up the paper, and gave her a thumbs-up. I don't remember an answer but a smile, a comforting word. And the sound of my father yelling became clearer.

CarKey and my father had a blow-out fight while I was in the recovery room. My father tried to get in to see me. Someone told him not to go in. He threw a fit. The hospital asked my brother to intervene. My father said, "I'm the father not you. What do you think you're the father?" CarKey responded with something like, "You're damn right you're the father. Then be a father. Now you want to be a father? You're some father!" This fight in Sloan-Kettering, on the day of my "cure" would be the last time CarKey would see my father for the next eighteen years, until my father lay on his deathbed, and I telephone CarKey urging him to see his father one last time. I knew my recovery would not be peaceful with the family around. I told my Mother to come Monday, Wednesday, Friday, and I told my Dad, Tuesday, Thursday, Saturday. I couldn't take the constant fighting and tension. I was done. It's all over. I told myself. I am cured. But it will be a long recovery.

On Halloween, I insisted I get outta there. My cousin Annette picked me up from the hospital. I had a lot of cousins with versions of the name "Anna." We were all named after our Grandma Anna Lanzillotto. Annette and I were going to a costume party at my favorite cousin Annie's house. My nurse Veronica took the time to wheel me downstairs. I saw a giant sign near the entrance to the hospital: First International A.I.D.S. Conference.

"What's that?" I asked my nurse.

"It's what happens when men stick their weenies where they're not supposed to."

The automatic doors slid open and just as my first blast of fresh air in weeks hit my face and chest, so did a wave of homophobia that would last for decades to come. The nineteen-eighties was rife with isolation with its Sony Walkmans and A.I.D.S., the capping of ears with headphones and the threat that sacred life-giving blood was now fatal as venom. I got lucky. No one on earth knew it then, but my unscreened blood transfusions from the New York City blood supply were free of HIV. I walked out of Sloan-Kettering feeling free, not knowing just how free I really was.

I was stunned, confused, disappointed, and ready to get the hell outta there. I wanted nothing but to get away from Sloan-Kettering, and family. I wanted out. Cecil Rowe, my beloved doorman bear hugged me on the way out, and helped me from the wheelchair into Annette's powder blue Mazda.

My reintroduction back into the land of the living, was to see all my cousins in getups. There was: James Dean, Raggedy Ann, an Oreo, a family of cavemen, a court jester. Enza came as a witch. Rosemarie put on my softball uniform. I dressed as a surgeon, in green scrubs and a white labcoat, stethoscope, and face mask. I was skinny, weak, on pain meds, didn't drink or talk much, but I was there, and that was enough.

Magnetic Lace

BROWN UNIVERSITY, PROVIDENCE, RHODE ISLAND

I propped my bicycle up against the base of the Marcus Aurelius statue in Lincoln Field, climbed up from the pedal to the crossbar to the pedestal, and grabbed the bronze horse's hind leg to pull myself up. The horse had big bronze balls. I sat there, underneath him, and watched the birds landing on the green, and the wind trembling the trees. I leaned back to watch the clouds overhead. I watched the sky until sunset. I knew death served at least one purpose: God needed painters to paint the sunset. I watched the sunset and guessed what colors my friends would paint with, bold orange and stripes of pink, or gentle pastels. I imagined the sunset I would paint when I died. Orange, definitely orange. Stabs of hot pink. One burning red sun. White stripes of clouds. A purple and blue afterglow. I will use a million colors crazily, colors you don't think you can see in a sky, colors you're used to seeing at your feet. I went through colors in my mind. Blue is everywhere. We are surrounded by blue. What a blessed color is blue: the sky, the oceans, my mother's eyes. I wanted to climb the bronze horse and see Marcus Aurelius eye to eye, but I couldn't get up that high. I hung by my fingertips off the pedestal, jumped down to the green, and rode down the hill to the bottom of Lincoln Field. There was Dr. James Head's office, a first-floor corner room with lots of windows. I walked behind the bushes to peer in the windows to see if Dr. Head was in. I knocked on the window. He looked up from his computer and smiled, "Lanz," he said, and waved me in.

Dr. Head's office was filled with maps and globes of Venus, the moon, Mars, and hundreds of beer bottles from all over the world. Just sitting in his office was a learning experience. He told me his job as a professor was like this: "You students are all sharks, and my job is to bloody the waters." He'd pull something off a shelf and hand it to me, like an iconic blue and white New York City coffee cup with the Greek key design, but this particular cup had been shrunken to an inch high. When I couldn't guess what happened to it, he told me with a sense of amazement, "Its state is due to the pressure at the bottom of the ocean, it was outside a submarine." Dr. Head made grand gifts to me, like that cup, introduced me to astronauts, and visiting Russian scientists. I told him how my father drove me to the Armed Forces recruiter in Providence, and how convinced I was that the military was a place where I could reach my potential, you know "Be All You Can Be" and fly planes. I wanted to be in the sky. I pictured myself waking up and doing push-ups. That sounded like ambition. "Plus they'll pay for medical school," I told Dr. Head. The attending sargeant already weighed me in and took my health history, and I was waiting to hear. Dr. Head was not pleased. He tried to tell me that I could reach my potential elsewhere. "I think you'll be disappointed in the military." But my father's voice was the loudest voice in my head: "Civilian life sucks. Civilians sue one another left and right. You can't trust nobody. It's every man for himself. Your best friend's your worst enemy 'cause he's the guy you trust. A stranger can't hurt you cause you won't trust him."

The military rejected me because of my cancer history. I argued that I was in remission, but they didn't want to hear it. I would never be a soldier. I had to find another way to fly, and to push myself to excel. I walked around campus and knocked on professors' doors. I introduced myself. I said, "I am here. You're here. I don't want to miss out on anything. What do you do?"

Most of these meetings were congenial but uneventful, until I knocked on Dr. Michael Scala's door. He said words that seemed so cool to me. "I CAT-scan mummies for tumors." Dr. Scala was Italian American, born in the Bronx, and knew for a fact that cancers were not strictly a post-industrial phenomenon. He gave me a book titled, *Diseases in Antiquity*. I continued to meet with Dr. Scala independently.

The pre-med dean at Brown told me not to apply to med school, "Not until you are five years cured," he said. "An applicant in remission is not a good four-year investment."

In between classes I went to funerals.

It was the fall of 1983. The one-year remission mark was upon me. One by one, my friends in the support group died. I thought of that macabre song "Ten Little Indians" that I'd heard as a child.

I sat under Marcus Aurelius and watched the sunsets as one by one my friends lay dying. Melody Stappas had an open casket and mass at a Greek Orthodox church in Pawtucket. She had thirty-five rounds of Shake 'n Bake. Too much for any one person. I drove so fast to her funeral, thoughts raced in my brain. Why do I have to speed on a highway to see you and be on time, when you're already here, with me, everywhere? Where am I driving to, to look at your empty body? I thought of all the cars from all directions racing to her funeral. I took a breath and slowed down. Where was I speeding to?

Melody lay in her coffin on pure white silk. The last time I saw her alive, she lay on rough white cotton hospital sheets connected to tubes. I couldn't get this thought out of my mind, that she would have enjoyed the feel of silk against her skin while she was alive. Juxtapositions were all I could see. I stared at the rusty fire extinguisher to the side of the crystal altar.

Peter Franklin Findlay had a closed casket. He died at home, on Halloween, 1983. I drove to Kingston, Rhode Island, to the Kingston Congregational Church. I could see its single white steeple from down the road. The year

1695 was on the outside of the building. These Rhode Island churches were the oldest places I'd ever been in, but burying teenage friends was one hell of a way to see them. There were lots of doctors at his funeral, but no beepers went off. Time stood still. Everyone stopped being in motion. I stood on the balcony watching a white butterfly circle the crystal and brass chandelier. Just a few days before, I'd stood next to Pete while he lay in a coma in the hospital, stroking his hand, and thinking about our conversations; sex, music, and mystical experiences. We didn't want to die virgins. To die teenagers didn't bother us as much as to die virgins. Pete and I talked and laughed about losing our virginity before we died. Not with each other, just on our own. We were buddies, cancer buddies. Sometimes it felt like he was the only person who knew what I was feeling. Pete had a bone marrow transplant, and played tennis later that year, which filled me with awe and hope. Then he lay in a coma. Now it was too late. Pete was gone. The preacher spoke of the dash between life and death, for Pete the dash was between 1963 and 1983. The Quaker ceremony made room for everyone to speak. I stared at the white butterfly circling freely in the atrium. I opened my mouth, not knowing what would come out.

"He's not in there," I said, looking down at the closed casket, "he's everywhere."

We buried him in a field of fallen orange, gold, and red leaves. I cried profusely and Dr. LaFarge held me to her breast. The sun was strong on my face and the hot stream of tears stung my cheeks as the October wind blew. Dr. LaFarge and I had been to funeral after funeral after funeral, she more than I, but Pete's was the hardest for me. We were close friends, and I loved him. October was the most beautiful time of year to die. Orange and red and gold, the colors of fire swirled in the sky down to carpet the graveyard. I was in a daze. There was a luncheon with music selected by Pete, beginning with Elvis's intro, moving through jazz, and ending with the Beatles' "Golden Slumbers/Carry That Weight/The End," crescendoing with McCartney's lyrics, which we both believed were the truest essence of life, that life was not measured in years but in love made.

I came home from the funeral and bunked into a schoolmate coming home from class. The exchange of pleasantries rang hollow. When I was sick, we shared deep moments, but now there was nothing to say. I went to Saint Stephen's church just off campus and lay down on the cool marble altar, for hours, alone. The air was sweet with frankincense and gave me a slightly delicious headache.

The next day I woke up at ten to seven in the morning with an intense amount of pressure, thinking, I got one more day than you, Pete, what can I make of it?

My father drove up and took a walk with me around campus for hours that night. "Daddy," he said, "you gotta keep going. Anderson was gunned down to the side of me. I bent over by his side, and the Sarge comes by and whacks me with the butt of his rifle. C'mon Lanzi or you'll be next."

I walked up and down Thayer Street and into The Penguin Café. Elias, a Rasta street poet sat there at a little square table filled with colorful papers wild with handwriting, and a cup of peppermint tea. I sat down at my own table, and began to write on a napkin with a ballpoint pen. Elias hung out on Thayer Street collecting money. I thought it was smart for a vagabond to hang out near an Ivy League campus. That must be an easy place to score cash and meals, even pot. He didn't seem to have a place to live but had places to hang out. He penned long intriguing poems at The Penguin Café. Elias decoded words phonetically and metaphorically. He penned word equations. "Mascara = Mask+Error. Surface = Sir + Face. Snow = See + No. Because when it snows you see-no." I introduced him to my friend David, and he said, "Ah, Day of Vision, David." We fell into deep philosophical conversation easily. He was quixotic, spoke in parables. I took to buying him food and giving him a twenty here and there, along with a set of my Pembroke dorm keys so he could store some stuff in my room. I had one room on campus I used as a writing cave, and one room off campus with Littlepage and Maloney where I slept.

I wrote wildly for hours. Not since I sat with my father with his wild pages of circles did I have a mentor. Elias dressed in green and wore a brass horn, and bells. He had a gray dreadlock beard. He had color Xeroxes of his wordplay that he would hand out. When I had bronchitis, he gave me a paper bag of fresh rosemary and told me to chew on it. Elias ate by color. "I need green." "I need some orange." He talked about "Magnetic Lace," a healing power of the cells of the body. I was studying cellular biology, cancer pharmacology, ancient plagues and diseases, and studying with Elias. Magnetic lace is the energy within cells and between cells. In cellular biology we called this the matrix, endoplasm, ectoplasm, interstitial fluid.

Lesbianism, Suicide, or the Nunnery

I telephoned my mother late rainy Providence nights from a phone booth on Thayer Street outside the 7-Eleven, with intermittently either of two proclamations. The first set of calls was: "I'm ready to kill myself. I feel

trapped in a body. I want to rid myself of 'this mortal coil'" I was out of
my mind standing in the rain shouting Hamlet's words to my mother. "What
the hell are you talking about!" she'd say. She'd insist on talking with one of
my housemates who pledged to see me through the night and call her first
thing in the morning. Then she'd call Dr. LaFarge to get her take on my
level of crisis. The second set of calls was: "Mom, I am ready to become a
nun." To which she'd reply, "I always knew." By junior year, I allowed myself
to be a lesbian and both of these types of midnight calls to my mother
promptly stopped.

The first girl that kissed me deeply was a star jock, aptly named Gale,
which matched the maelstrom I felt inside me. After that kiss, I went to
confession and prayed for nine hours straight. "Bless me Father, for I have
sinned . . . I kissed another woman. I am giving in to the desire in my heart,
even though I know my actions insult God. I don't want to dishonor God."

"Don't be so hard on yourself," the priest said, "pray ten Hail Marys."

"That's it? Father. I'm so confused. I don't know that I can control my
desire."

"Keep praying. An answer will come."

I knelt on the altar, cried, and prayed. Maloney and Littlepage were very
patient. After three hours, they said, "Let's go home."

"Just leave me here."

I knew once I left the church, I'd run back to kiss another girl. I lay
down on the marble altar with my green pocket Bible. When I got cold,
I did push-ups to pump up my blood, then I went back to prayer. I felt I
betrayed Jesus who delivered me through all my pain and suffering. Is this
the thanks I give my God? As soon as I'm in remission, I go out and give in
to all my desire? The words of Leviticus ran circles in my head: "The earth
shall spit you up." "The land will vomit out those who are defiled." I read
the word *spue*, which sounded like the violent vomiting I did on chemo. I
didn't want the earth to *spue* me.

I read Saint Paul: "Wherefore God also gave them up to uncleanness
through the lusts of their own hearts, to dishonour their own bodies between
themselves." I thought of my softball buddies. When I went home for check-
ups, I tried to save one's soul, by talking her out of being a dyke. I quoted
Bishop Sheen. I quoted Saint Paul. She invited me out to the bars that night.

I was in a tug of war. I felt an immense pull in my gut toward women.
Women contained the creative suction force of the universe. Women had
secret compartments. Women were like enchanted eggs. As a little girl, I loved
licking the sparkly outside of enchanted Easter eggs, with dioramas inside. I
would lick the large sugar crystals, close one eye and peek inside the clear
plastic window with the other eye. Women were like that, they could keep

you out, but you know there's a whole amazing world going on, inside them. And once they open and let you in, you never want to leave.

The church locked the doors. I had to leave.

Six months out of Sloan-Kettering, I found myself in Gale's heated water bed in Fox Point. I slept over her house, bought Portuguese sweet bread in the morning, and took the long walk back to campus while I chewed the doughy bread by the handful. This became my newest pleasure in Providence. Gale reminded me of my early nuns, if the nuns had worn sexy ripped denim and let me see them sweat. She quoted Thoreau with ease and was independent in her thoughts. She didn't look away from me when we talked. When we drove in her MG on back country roads, I felt that was exactly where I belonged. Her eyes were light blue like her denim, bright with thoughts. Making out in a water bed for the first time posed its own challenges, making out with a girl for the first time and feeling how a female body moves differently than a guy's without one protruding focus, together with the rocking motion of the water, was too much for me all at once. Gale got on top of me. I punched her. She said, "Feisty" and "Whoa, Nelly." I'd wrestled and roughhoused with girls for years. Punches, shoves, chokeholds, wrestling, that's what I did, that was an acceptable way I could touch girls on the softballs teams, and that's how I was used to being touched. Zing and I wrestled all through high school, but this was different. Gale opened. I didn't know what to do. I always had the Catholic emergency brake on, when it came to sex. Finally, when a woman was on top of me, ready to open up and kiss, my first natural reflex was to punch. One punch, turned to grabbing and grabbing turned to hugging and hugging to kissing. I surrendered. We made out intensely, full body, on top of, as it were, a giant hot-water bottle. The water moved, churned, and shaped around us, approximating what was going on inside me. I felt enveloped, overcome. I stopped fighting. The water shaped around us like a third lover. We drank vodka. Her tongue felt so soft in my mouth. I opened up, settled in, flipped. And that was it. Throughout my life, my father pulled magnets out of his pockets and showed me reverse magnetism. Lanzi always had magnets in his pockets. When you flip one polarity, two magnets, that at first hold each other at a distance, now lurch together; flip again and the force field stops you—you push and push, but the magnets will resist at that invisible thick wall and one will flip. This is what I felt, for the first time in my life with a woman on top of me, the magnet had flipped, and that repellent barrier I was accustomed to feeling with boys, was gone. Gale's sheets pulled off the edge of the water bed, and my legs felt the rubber of the warm water-bladder against my skin. The bed with her in it, was a charged magnetic field. I was sucked in. The world was a giant vagina sucking in the galaxy and me along with it. Suction, not protrusion, was the life force of creation of the universe. Pulling, not pushing. Opening, not protruding. Opening.

Gale stopped me short of making love with her. She was a senior. A psych major. A veteran dyke with an array of lovers. "Whoa there, take it slow," she said. She grew up with horses. She could feel my unbridled spirit. She held me. My heart was pounding. I wasn't broken in.

One weekend, we drove to Maine and went skiing. I didn't have "ski clothes." What I did have was Lanzi's wool Marine uniform from World War II. I heard wool was warm, so I wore his uniform down the slopes, until it fell off me, literally ripped apart at the seams as I zoomed down the mountain. Forty-year-old thread was done holding the seams together. I came down the slope in my long johns with Marine pant-flaps sailing in front of and behind me.

Dean Donovan called me into his office. "I've gotten complaints that there are men in the hallways wearing bells and taking showers in the dorm."

"Just one man wears bells," I reasoned with him. "He's got nowhere to go, *no*where to go."

What were these Ivy League kids so pent up about? What was their problem? Don't they all read and enjoy Elias' poetry on Thayer Street? How can I call myself a Christian and not give my dorm keys to the local homeless guy?

How to Wake Up a Marine in a Foxhole

Out of Brown University's whole library system, the Science Library had the strictest bag checker, Tom O'Neill, an old man, hunched over with thick eyeglasses and eyes wide open like two bright blue marbles. He checked every bag thoroughly of every student who ever left the Sci Li. No one dared ever take a book or map or any library holding. Period. On nights when he worked, there was always a line to get out. Time was precious, and transitions determined success. I hustled from class to softball practice to dinner to the library. I didn't have an extra twenty minutes to wait on line just to get out. While Tom looked through everything in my backpack and athletic bag, I got into conversations with him. He was eighty-two, read the Bible in Greek, and was well versed in the local history of the Narragansett Indians. When he spoke, he was as animated as a little kid, and lost his breath laughing, threw his head back, with his mouth wide open. He sang me a local chant, *"I am*

Rhode Island born and Rhode Island bred. When I die I'll be Rhode Island dead."
One night, Tom invited me over to his house, which felt sweet to me, but
his next words stunned me:

"Come meet my mother."

"Your mother?"

"My mother. I told her about you. She'd like to meet you. Her name's
Mary."

I told my schoolmates about it. Nobody believed Tom's mother could
still be alive. I walked home with him one day. Tom was short and bent
over, but walked fast and without a cane. I didn't know what to expect. We
walked down Brown Street, to Wickenden, took a left and walked to Fox
Point Manor, a retirement community at the bottom of the hill. We took
the elevator up. Tom opened the door with his key and yelled, "Hiya Ma!"

There she was, in her cushioned plaid chair, a hundred years old, Mary
O'Neill, under a crocheted blanket. She was beautiful.

"Ineffable, huh?" Tom said.

I hugged and kissed her and sat next to her. I told her what a phenomenal
son she had. "Tom talks to all the students," I said, "he gives us quite an
education." Tom cooked us Cornish hens as I talked with Mary. She told me
about her life. She'd had Tom when she was an eighteen year old immigrant
from County Cork. She was proud that she'd voted in every election since
women's suffrage passed in 1920 when Warren G. Harding was elected
president. I fell asleep on the couch and Tom covered me with a blanket
Mary had crocheted. Even though I was in remission, all the chemo, radiation,
surgeries and the cancer itself, had taken its toll. I needed naps, and I learned to
give into them. I fell asleep thinking of GranmaRose and my mother Rachel.

When I woke up, it was instant and peaceful. Tom stood over me, his
eyes peered into my eyes.

"Tom," I said, "how'd you wake me?" I had had this experience before
with my father.

"An old army trick. That's how you wake up a soldier in a foxhole."

"What?" I was stunned, "that's how my father wakes me up."

Tom gave me a piece of shrapnel from World War I, and an Army Air
Corps pin of a propeller over a brass circle. I walked back to campus, and
called my father.

"Pop, I gotta ask you something. You know when you wake me up
with the thumb under the eyebrow? Is that how you wake up a marine in
a foxhole?"

"Yeah, I guess so," he said nonchalantly, "it's the gentlest way of waking
up. Light, gradual light. You take the thumb, and press it under the middle of
the guy's eyebrow. You want him to see you. You want him to know it's you.

If you nudge him awake he might think you're the enemy. It's your detail to wake him. You take the thumb. You press under the middle of the eyebrow. You let some light seep into the eye."

Red Death

MEMORIAL SLOAN-KETTERING CANCER CENTER, NEW YORK CITY

Iwalked in through the front door at 1275 York Avenue, where I gave Cecil Rowe a bear hug under the American flag. We chatted about human nature. Cecil told me that one day he dreamed of retiring back in Jamaica where he was born. He told me a Jamaican saying, "*Bak a dog a dog, before a dog a mista dog.*" He laughed and helped people to their rides in the ubiquitous traffic as I tried to figure it out. I taught him the southern Italian phrase, "*acasi acasa*," where you flip your hand over, palm up, backhand up. "It's no good without the hand gesture," I told him. These peasant wisdoms expressed different slants on the same thing; people treat you one way in front of you, and another way behind you. Character flip-flops.

Dr. Kempin looked me in the eye and we had a good long talk. He told me everything with me was stable. I told him,"You wouldn't believe how many people come up to me now with lumps in their necks. I feel the lumps and ask them questions. One student read an article about me in the local paper, the *Pro Jo*, and he found me on campus. I think he's got swollen glands, he's had phlegm and neck pain. Another is this beautiful soul, a waitress named Mindy, and I'm a little more worried about her because she's been tired for months and her lump doesn't hurt her. I told her to get a biopsy, but I might have to send her to you." We laughed about me becoming a street diagnostician. I felt blessed to have him as my doctor. I had one year of remission under my belt.

As I walked out of the office I ran into Connie's nurse practitioner in the hall. We talked for a few minutes, then as I left she said, "I'll tell Connie you say hi."

"You've seen her?"

"You didn't know? She's relapsed."

"What? You mean she's back in?"

"Room 610."

I ran for the elevator as it swallowed the conversation of two men inside and rammed my sneaker in the gap against the door's black rubber tongue. "And I don't have to tell you to wash up before you go see her!" She called out after me. The door bit my foot twice and choked on it. The men stopped talking. I felt their noses at my back. I was always ready for a silent energy fight. I bulk up, look bigger and tougher than I am. The tension courses up my bones. A nurse came into the elevator casually complaining about "Mondays." People who are healthy do these things. I contemplate preaching to her. Instead I breathe heavily. My eyes bounce from my shoelaces to the light hopping the number line above the door. I walk toward 610 and sidestepped into the bathroom off the hallway and milk the liquid soap dispenser. Connie Robinson was as fanatical about ridding herself of germs as she was about sin. When it came to Connie's health, I was fanatical about ridding myself of germs. I didn't know about sin anymore. The liquid soap plopped into the palm of my hand like a pigeon dropping. I rubbed my two hands together and watched the black city air wash off my hands and swirl around the sink until the drain gulped it down. I wet my lips but lips don't come clean. C. Robinson was written on a temporary card above the numbers 610, which were screwed into the door more permanently. I wedged my face between the cold doorframe and the door. Connie lay inside the same eggshell-white robe cracked with whiter embroidery as the first time I saw her in room 621 down the hall. A stack of blue-and-white striped pillows with yellow tags like tails propped her up in bed. She had two corners of a square of paper pinched and held it up to the light coming in from behind her. The free corners curled at the edges. Her head stayed in line with her body, as she moved the paper back and forth and up and down in front of her face. The outline of a house the size of a dollhouse was sketched on the paper. The house was hollow, as in a coloring book, a skeleton to be fleshed out. I stood in the doorframe, staring at the slope of her neck and how her head looked too heavy for it, and the calico bouquet that sat on the windowsill behind her, with the East River in the distance. I felt as if I had never left the halls and rooms of Sloan-Kettering. Connie's head bucked back as she held in a sneeze and the intravenous line in her neck pulled at the skin around her vein. The paper she held of the house drawing crinkled.

I sent my voice into 610 without knocking, "God bless you Chief."

"Thank-you," she answered naturally, as if I still lay in the bed next to her. The intravenous line in her neck pulled at the skin around her vein. I said bless you again, as she held back a quick chain of sneezes, while supporting her neck brace with two hands. The paper coiled into a scroll and landed in the plastic tray of food on her bedside table. Her hands and eyes opened, and she steadily rotated her whole body toward my voice coming in through the door. As she inhaled, she squealed with as much breath as she had, "Annie? Is that you?"

"Hey Chief!" I cradled her with a tamed hug and caged a kiss inside my mouth by rolling my polluted lips around my teeth. "How you feeling?" I touched her arm's skin with my clean warm hands.

"Ahh," she said, "now now, look at you Miss! Turn around girl! My, my, it sure is good to see you looking so fine."

I asked her if there was room in there for me. She glanced at the scroll, and told me she had just bought a plot of land. I packed my eyes full, 'til they bulged and I couldn't close them, with the details of her body, hoping I could see clearly for the rest of my life: her maple face tuck under her whipped-cream turban and the white teeth she got to match by buffing them with Q-tips, and the timber suede shades of her skin, and the fact that it was black inside the caves of her dimples.

Chief looked like she was sucking on something delicious when she told me, "Didn't I tell you about the plot me and the Reverend were buying?" Her eyes lowered without moving her head, and scanned the tabletop that stretched over her lap and hid beneath her bosom. The only things Chief kept within reach were the little white New Testament the Reverend had given her, the scroll, and the push button to call the nurse's station. Her hand lowered down to the scroll, and snapped closed around it like a crane. "This here's the blueprint." She pushed the New Testament aside to make room for the blueprint, which was as see-through a piece of paper as the pages out of a Holy Book. She laid her arms across either side of the blueprint to hold it down. The black points of her eyeballs retraced the lines of this place that she said was being prepared for her, and stopped at the snail the architect had drawn. "This here's the spiral staircase and above it's the stained glass skylight. In the morning the light will come through and pour light down the staircase. Mmm-mm, child, now just wait 'til you see it. Can you picture it?" Her nose aimed at the center of the blueprint. "The best part about it is there is no front gate! There is no gate. All the rooms are being done in white and all the doorways topped in arches." She pointed out the garden and a sitting pond. "I was just setting down which seeds get planted where." The blueprints lay flat, pinned down by her hands. A nurse came in pointing her toes in front of each long step as if she was about to receive the crown, sash, and roses, and said at Chief, "How are you feeling? Good!" Chief didn't need to answer since the nurse answered herself. She just showed the upper row of her teeth in a kind white smile and pulled the turban down over her ears with one hand like a woman trying to conceal her hips by smoothing her blouse over them. The nurse announced that she was giving Chief some Compazine to reduce the nausea of the Adriamycin she was about to get, and handed her a tiny fluted paper cup with two white pills inside. The blueprint tumble-saulted up to the Bible as Chief used her hands to tilt the cup to her mouth. The nurse watched her throat pulse to make sure she swallowed, and told me Chief would be asleep in fifteen minutes, so our visit would have to end.

I asked the nurse, "What's the name of that chemo again?" as she stood on her toes to hang the plastic pouch full of redness next to the clear, sugar water-bag.

"Red Death," Chief answered. Her eyelids fluttered and a teardrop spilled over the edge, cascading down to the pillow. She unrolled the blueprint and rested her arm on it.

" 'Scuse me," she said. Her arms seemed anchored, one on the floor of the bed and the other on the table; a hand was too heavy for either arm to lift to cover her yawn.

"You just rest, Chief. We'll talk later." Her head tilted backward over a pillow and she blinked widely like a doll. The finger jacked the Bible up, freeing the blueprint, which coiled into her hand. The brown yolks of her eyes slipped to the side and drifted out the square of sky on the wall, floating far away over the smokestacks and the river and the bridge, as if they had been inflated with helium and let go. She blinked less and less wide, her hand wilted and the blueprint rolled forward and backward, settling itself on the table. The nurse pressed a button on a panel on the side of the bed. There was a loud buzz as Chief's feet were raised, then the nurse pressed the button above it to bring her feet back down and another that made the bed sink in the middle as if it were folding up in half. The buzz was the kind of buzz that tells you time is up. "Left," she said, "the one on the left," and her head was lowered, and the nurse yanked out the top pillow from under her head. Her head nested in the one pillow remaining. "You take special care now, Annie." I nodded. She opened one eyelid by bending up the iron brow above it, looked at me and said faintly, "Me 'n you got to take special care with ourselves." Chief's eyes closed and she said, "Don't feel 'shamed, to wear hat and scarf, even when the others don't. You hear?" I watched the redness drop from the bag into the long plastic tube. "Ah'll be seeing you soon, Annie." The red tributary was diluted in the mainstream just before the solution entered Chief's neck, and the metal taste seeped up her throat to her tongue; the tongue came out of the mouth for air. The breath smelled like sewer water.

"Sure Chief. Sooner than you think," I mouthed over her. Nothing in the room moved except the red drip in the IV line and me. I never wanted anyone to tell me, "See you soon," ever again. I closed the door and just sat there 'til the red dripping stopped.

Interventions

BROWN UNIVERSITY, PROVIDENCE, RHODE ISLAND, 1984

I climbed the statue of Augustus Caesar, but there was nowhere to sit and meditate with Caesar. I made an appointment with Dean Donovan. "I never once have seen my brother Ant'ny not on drugs," I told him. "He started taking heroin around the time I was born. I want to quit school and go help him. Somebody has to do something to save him."

"What do you see yourself doing to save him?"

"He's on crack and he disappears for days at a time gambling. He's gonna end up dead one day, and what did I do to help him? So many of his friends have OD'ed over the years. Ever since I was a kid, his friends that he had over the house disappeared one by one. I gotta do something, or he'll be next. I don't know. All I know is, I've been saved. Now I gotta do something. Something must be done. We gotta stop our lives for one another, not just go about the day to day. I gotta help him. He's my brother. School can wait."

"The best thing you can do for your brother is to stay in school."

"How's that gonna help him? God sent Jesus to the cross for us, the least I can do is quit school and go help my brother."

"I understand your urge," he said, "it's commendable to want to live a useful life. That's the heart of the Brown Charter: 'for discharging the offices of life with usefulness,' but I urge you to stay. In the long run, that's how you'll do the most good."

My mother hopped a train to Providence, and the three of us sat together in the Dean's office. She adamantly made me promise not to quit school. I loved when my mother was fierce, determinate, strong. I obeyed her.

I went and sat under Marcus Aurelius and wrote letters to Ant'ny and my father, proposing that we all move West, go live in the sun where other people seemed to enjoy life. If my brother OD'ed while I was in college, I'd never forgive myself. He'd been getting high since I was born. Maybe it was partly my fault. All the attention a new baby gets. I pictured him at eleven, with his big dark eyes, being ignored by everyone around him in that crazy violent house.

I received a letter in the mail from a Reverend Petty saying, "Connie died as peacefully as she had lived."

I bicycled to Marcus Aurelius and sat there for a long time watching the pink feathery sky. I wondered what kind of sunset the Chief had painted.

Mindy walked by, twirling to a stop to say hello. She was always dancing. The lump in her neck was hard and hadn't gone down. I urged her to get a biopsy. She said she was looking for a room to rent for the summer and she'd deal with it then. I gave her Dr. Kempin's phone number and told her she could rent my room.

200 Angell Street was prime housing off the main drag, Thayer Street. Maloney, Littlepage, and me traveled to church on Sundays to hear a fiery Pentecostal preacher speak in tongues. At night, I kissed girls.

One was a softball player named Rachel, and I trusted her implicitly because she had my mother's name. Rachel was from Memphis. She was the most honest and fair person I knew, and I was sure that one day she would become a judge. She called me "baby," in three syllables, *buh'aybee*. I wanted to hear her say it over and over again, *buh'aybee, buh'aybee, buh'aybee*. Whenever I wheezed she gave me strong back rubs. A back rub was where it all began. I leaned back into the rub. I loved kissing her. She had husky shoulders and strong biceps, with a pronounced chin, and the softest lips that were sweet to nest in. We were good friends and amorous softball buddies. We made out in my room on Angell Street, underneath a ten-foot stick-figure rendition of the Last Supper I painted right on the wall in thick black strokes. You could tell Judas, by the tilt of his head. I put the restriction on us that we kiss silently, lest my roommates hear what was going on. Breathing, or even the rustling of our clothes was too loud for me. Being in the closet is the worst feeling in the world. I felt like Judas every step of the way. Judas to myself, Judas to Jesus, Judas to Rachel, Judas Judas Judas. I didn't take into account how much suffering I caused her. I still could pass as straight, and I was going to, as long as I could.

One night I brought Rachel into a room on campus I had keys to, locked the door, pulled the shades down, sat her in a chair in the middle of the room, sat on top of her, wrapped my legs around her, and began kissing her.

"What are you doing, Annie?"

"You know."

"What."

"Kissing you."

"No, I mean, locking the door, and pulling the shades down."

"I don't want anyone coming in."

"What are you afraid of?"

Rachel didn't want to kiss in the shadows. I knew my double life caved in, when Rachel woke up all of Angell Street, yelling, "Hypocrite!" She hollered in a Southern drawl and drunken anguish, "Hypocrite! Annie, tell them what you are!" I was inside studying biology, rewinding cassettes of lectures I had taped. I heard Rachel yell my name. My housemates got up and we all went outside on the porch. We all loved and knew Rachel well. She stood on the street with a beer bottle and swayed. There was a fire burning in her eyes.

"What are you doing Rach—."

"Tell them what you are. You're a lesbian. That's right."

"Rachel, look at me. Stop it."

"No you stop it. Tell them what you are. Tell them."

A couple of us walked her home and made sure she got to bed alright. I was out. To my housemates, and a little more to myself.

Falling and Flying

I drove out to T. F. Green Airport in Warwick, Rhode Island, to watch the planes take off, and saw they had a civilian flight school. I walked in to inquire. The instructors were war veterans, an Italian guy named Joseph who was a fighter pilot in World War II, and an Irish guy Brian who fought in Vietnam. I was at home. These were "guys you can trust." I felt safe there because my father's name was Joseph. For my first flying lesson, Joseph took me up in a Cessna Single Engine two-seater. We talked about war and I told him about my father as we climbed to a thousand feet. I felt elated. Joseph said, "This plane can fly itself," and at eleven hundred feet, he shut off the engine and pulled the yoke all the way back. The nose of the plane rose straight up in the air. I could feel the air under the plane's wings, and for the first time in my life sensed how solid air was. You could stand on air. For a few seconds I felt the plane stand still as if the wings were feet. Air was buoyant, like water. Air had body. The Cessna bobbed on the waves of air. Joseph pulled farther back on the yoke, and a shrill deafening alarm went off. Then the plane fell out of the sky, the wings were at such an angle that they sliced the air backward like knives. I laughed loud, exhilarated that we had toyed with death. We could die if we wanted to, and that gave me a sense of power. Joseph pushed the nose of the plane down, and we did a dive bomb toward the land. The land came up fast. Joseph pulled back on the yoke to pull up out of the dive, and turned the engine back on. He pulled and then let go of the plane. It bobbled in steady waves up and down until it reached steady flight. "See?" he said. I laughed and breathed deeply, amazed at the plane's relationship with air. "I see you have the stomach for this," Joseph said, and we scheduled our next lesson. "You just passed your first test in flight training. Pure guts."

I drove back to Brown in my pushbutton transmission, slant-six engine '64 Dodge Dart with the top down, blasting the Steve Miller Band, got eggs over easy and a bran muffin for breakfast at Louie's Diner on Brook Street, underneath a classic photo of Louie and his brother Dom in their World War II army uniforms. By my second flying lesson, I realized it was the clouds and not the clear sky I wanted to be with. Joseph told me, "You never know what's on the other side of a cloud. We're not authorized to fly through clouds, since we're navigating visually." But I knew that as soon as I soloed, I would aim for a big fat cloud and take my chances. I wanted to be inside the clouds. I wished I could feel in my body, what I felt in a two-seater airplane, my stomach drop and the pitch, roll, yaw elation. Before every flight we had to register a flight plan. There was a blue mailbox near the hangar. I got into the habit of mailing someone a copy of our flight plan with a note before I left the ground. Usually I wrote to my father.

Life took on the feeling of being in a perpetual bank turn. Joseph taught me how to hold a bank turn by flying in circles around a fixed point. Lighthouses were our fixed points. I trained over Newport around a white-and-black lighthouse Joseph told me to circle six times, maintaining speed and distance. Every time I circled back toward the shore, I saw the long shadows the mansions cast into the shallow light-green water. In a perpetual bank turn, you end up going in circles, and circles make you dizzy. You must fall or come out of it, level off, regain the horizon in line with your wingspan. In a steep bank turn, gravity reverses itself. The simple act of lifting your arms up off your lap feels like lifting a great weight. Lean over, lean into the turn and roll at the same time increasing the yaw angle. Grip the yoke, give in to gravity just enough to keep you in motion. I would have to learn. At the time I was signing the maximum amount of student loans, ripping up hospital bills, and living as hard as I could, pulling back on the yoke just enough to know I was alive.

Civilian Life Sucks

WEST HEMPSTEAD, LONG ISLAND

Lanzi got himself a furnished apartment between Belmont Raceway and his mother and two of his sisters, Archangela and Tessie, who lived across the street from her. Whenever I went out to see him, he sat at his round kitchen table, cutting out newspaper articles and listening to talk radio late into the night. A thin layer of Formica that looked like wood, pulled up all around the edges of the table. His *Galaxy* radio's shell was cracked and broken in places. I could see its insides where the yellowed plastic had broken off: multicolored wires, copper-headed cylinders, coils, screws, a red light indicating the radio was *on*. Next to the radio stood a collage of old photographs taped to the ornamental top of a maple bedpost. I can only describe my father's creation as a photo-pole. At the apex of the photo-pole was a color picture of my sister Rosemarie holding her baby girl Melissa, which my father surrounded with silver tinsel so it took on the appearance of a religious icon of mother and child. Below it was a black and white shot of my father's parents with a strong, stoic and timeless look into the camera, a color photo of me holding my puppy when I was a child, a shot of my brothers as young boys dressed up in suits, standing in the sun, their hands folded in front of them. My brothers looked like Starsky and Hutch, Ant'ny was dark haired and olive skinned with big brown eyes and full lips, a Southern Italian look about him, and CarKey with his platinum hair and sapphire eyes had the *Barese*-Greek look that could have passed for a Swede. Their looks expressed our true *Barese* mix of DNA representing centuries of migrations and invasions. Next to this was a button from the feast of *San Gennaro* with me and my father, arms around each other's shoulders, smiling. The photo-pole leaned up against an old wooden hat rack which opened across the table accordion style and held stacks of greeting cards that had been sent to my father. The cards were mostly from Rosemarie and my father's four sisters who he called "The Four Roses," Apollonia, Archangela, Laura, and Tessie. I glanced at notes written inside the card: "Here's a picture from the Communion. Hope you liked the sweater I sent you." "Thought maybe you could use a shower curtain, I had an extra." Next to this card rack was a bowl of water with two raw peeled onions, a bite taken out of one; my father's version of an air purifier, and home remedy in the battle against phlegm and headaches. Two composition notebooks were on the table, a dish of blue BIC pens, *The Disabled American War Veteran's Journal,* and a copy of The Presidential Unit Citation:

> "The President of the United States takes pleasure in presenting the Presidential Unit Citation for extraordinary heroism in action against enemy Japanese forces during the invasion and capture of Okinawa Shima, Ryukyu Islands, from April 1 to June 21, 1945. Securing its assigned area in the north of Okinawa by a series of lightning advances against stiffening resistance, the First Marine Division, Reinforced, turned southward to drive steadily forward through a formidable system of natural and man-made defenses protecting the main enemy bastion at Shuri Castle. Laying bitter siege to the enemy until the defending garrison was reduced and the elaborate fortifications at Shuri destroyed, these intrepid Marines continued to wage fierce battle as they advanced relentlessly, cutting off the Japanese on Oruku Peninsula and smashing through a series of heavily fortified, mutually supporting ridges extending to the southernmost tip of the island to split the remaining hostile forces into two pockets where they annihilated the trapped and savagely resisting enemy. By their valor and tenacity, the officers and men of the First Marine Division, Reinforced, contributed materially to the conquest of Okinawa, and their gallantry in overcoming a fanatic enemy in the face of extraordinary danger and difficulty adds new

luster to Marine Corps History and to the traditions of the United States Naval Service."

    For the President

    John L. Sullivan

    Secretary of the Navy

The three windows behind his table were always shut tight. The window shades had a manila color from years of being soaked with cigarette smoke. In the late afternoon light, the window shades glowed, giving his whole room a smoked golden-manila glow. Each shade was cut jagged along the bottom edge and pulled down so it curled up across the window ledge. The windows had four panes of glass, their wooden frames and cross beams cast shadows into the room in the shape of three large crosses, one on each shade, giving the room an eerie Calvary decor. Under the windows, one radiator.

His room had gold walls and ceiling; an old gold born of misery and tarnished dreams, a sunset gold paint saturated with years of tobacco stains, coffee, and time. The room gave the stale feeling of browned teeth. Brittle strips of Scotch tape clung to the walls, having lost the newspaper clippings they once held. One by one they lost their grip to the walls themselves, leaving startling brighter rectangles in their places. The floor was red. The ceiling was level at the start, then slanted downward to the wall. Dead flies, I remember the outline of their wings, clung to the underside of the square of glass that covered two lightbulbs.

My father could never keep warm, complained of poor circulation, dressed in layers, and advised me repeatedly, "If you ever trip over a broken piece of sidewalk, just lay there 'til an ambulance comes, and sue. Sue the city. Sue the landlord. Sue." I could see the archaeology of the layers of clothing he wore as they stuck out along the neckline, sleeves, and pant cuffs. A royal blue pullover V-neck sweater, very soft, with worn-out transparencies at the elbows was his top layer. Under this he wore the same sweater in red. Under the red sweater I could see the zip-up neckline of the thick black sweater with a red zigzag design across the chest that my sister bought him. Under this was the blue wool vest his mother knitted for him, square across the neck. The under layer next to his skin was a white t-shirt over a white tank shirt. His red and green striped knit hat folded low over his eyebrows fit his head like a helmet. He wore two pair of pants, one on top of the other: one pair black, one pair brown, both creased straight down the middle of the leg. On his feet were maroon velour sleeves, each sleeve tied with knots at both ends to make the sleeve fit the foot, becoming in effect, customized velour slippers. I kept repeating to myself, "This is your father, this is your father. This is your father." I walked around the two rooms, like an investigator, trying to understand the man.

He drank his coffee with his right hand and smoked with his left.

As he talked on and on, I contemplated his refrigerator, on top of which was a bottle of cough syrup, a tin of black shoe polish, and rows of medicine vials. Somehow this summed my father up for me. As long as you could get rid of your phlegm, keep a shine on your shoes and take your medicine, you're okay. His refrigerator was a still-life portrait of his brain. A yellowed newspaper clipping, "Salt, the Silent Killer" was held to the outside of the refrigerator door by a magnet in the shape of a copper dustpan. Two other magnets in the shape of a copper teapot and a copper frying pan held phone numbers: one for his old buddy Nicky DiSilvio, and one for Annie, a woman he dated from the OTB, *Off-Track Betting.* According to my father, the day her grandkids called him 'Grandpa,' he announced he was going out "for cigarettes" and never went back. My father pressed hard on paper with his pens, I could feel the imprint of these phone numbers through the back of the notepaper. I opened the fridge door. Inside, everything was in strict order. On the upper shelf was a glass coffee jar filled with cigarette butts and ashes, the top screwed on tight, the label removed, no lipstick prints on any of the butts; my father spent his hours and nights alone. On the second shelf, a plate with alternating slices of whole wheat and raisin bread, the slices overlapped evenly around the dish. Two halves of Hershey bars, duct-taped shut. One package Stella D'oro S cookies, duct-taped shut. Potatoes and oranges lined up in an alternating pattern along the door, potato orange potato orange. The cold had hardened the wax, whitening the pores of the oranges. Two orange skins had been peeled in one long strip then reshaped into spheres and taped shut with clear tape. One box white rice, duct-taped shut, the print around the spout had peeled off after many openings and tapings. One coffee jar, filled with coffee. In the refrigerator drawer, my father kept his trash wrapped in clear plastic and sealed with thick transparent packing tape wound in a tourniquet: cans without labels, bread crusts, broken pasta, scraps of beans, potato skins, cheese wrappers, bits of rice, chocolate bar wrappers.

Lanzi, thinking I opened the refrigerator because I might be hungry, brought the plate of bread to the table as an offering, along with a stack of individually wrapped orange cheese slices. I took a slice of raisin bread and a slice of orange cheese, folded it over and bit into it. The raisins and cheese tasted good together, soft and sweet. When my father ranted on and on, he took long pauses. Age and smoke had stripped his voice and breath. I didn't interrupt him, I just listened and allowed myself to get drenched with his reminiscences. He lost his breath, coughed, spit, spoke with inflection, and at times his voice shattered to a raspy shadow.

"You take fear. We had this here Corporal Callahan. A corporal in our outfit. He went through Guadalcanal. He was in four, five invasions. Now, Callahan wasn't scared no more but he was just a drunk. Actually he became a psycho. We used to call it 'Asiatic.' He just went along with the times."

He lit a cigarette and coughed into a hanky, looked closely at his phlegm, and stuffed the handkerchief back into his pants' pocket.

"But you, you follow like here, take this cancer. Now, one thing I'm glad about it, is you'll be up on everything. So who knows Annie? All it can be is a plus, right? Who knows? You think you're gonna be here a lifetime, you may be outta here tomorrow."

The freezer was a metal compartment with nothing in it except the build-up of ice. As I looked inside, my brain made a sentence of what I saw: "The building up of ice over the years, the lessening of space."

"Me and three guys, we all had quadruple bypass together in the V.A. Now, take like, they come around with the menu. Hank loved milkshakes. He always said, 'Lanzi, you're shrinking. Have a milkshake! Fatten you up. You're disappearing.' He'd pinch his fingers like this, see, and look at me through them. He'd say, 'You're only this big.' So I looked in the mirror. I told him, 'You're losing your mind. Stop that, talking like that. One day you'll believe yourself.' Sal loved fried foods and calamari, and everything he had to have butter on, vegetables, butter on bread, white soft or toast. I told him, 'You wonder why you got phlegm?' I told him, 'Take a lemon.' He said, 'Lanzi, you smoke.' I said, 'You gotta die of something. If the war didn't get you, tobacco will.' The third guy, Vinny was a *soppressata* man. Whaddyagonna do? They were all dead in six months. Me? I'm not really here. I'm on borrowed time. I boil everything."

Lanzi talked on and on, his monologues swirled around me. I never diluted my father's rants and musings with chit-chat or normalcy. I went with it, went with him, rode the contour of his mind.

"I wrote you a little whaddyacall, a little thing. Do you know, Annie, even a squirrel that's blind eventually will find his nuts. With patience. Right? So what is this blind squirrel gonna do? Is he gonna go sit and die? He'll have to go hunting and with patience he'll find his food. Same thing, take yourself. Find something hard? Patience. You get enough mileage, you become financially independent. You take at school. You're around these here rich kids. Kennedy, Mondale, the Prince of Jordan, what-have-you. You know how to express yourself, you know what you're talking about. If you don't know, you listen. That's it baby. Now you take John Kennedy, Jr. It's easy for him to get the job, he'll buy the place. One thing is, relax. One thing is being relaxed. If you find yourself all confused, you walk away from it. Then you go back. You have to be relaxed in anything you do. Relax. Study. Relax. Everything is, relax. And you have the guts, that's important. Sure, things bother you, but that's the world. Sometimes I think these oceans were made of tears."

In the bedroom, under a row of windows that faced Nassau Boulevard, was an improvised construction that served as a clothesline: two metal crutches with arm clasps laid horizontally across the tops of two chairs. This is where my father hung his clothes to dry, and once dry, this is where he hung his clothes. Black Banlon socks, stiff white tank shirts, light blue boxer shorts, all dried stiff on wire hangers. In the pocket of the raincoat were thirty-eight racing stubs in a silver money clip engraved: Belmont Raceway Where You're a Winner! The money clip itself was a silver replica of a winning raceway stub; seventh horse to win in the seventh race on 7/7/1977. A tower of books was stacked on the floor: *Old Breed: A History of the First Marine Division, The Importance of Living, Victory and Occupation: History of U.S. Marine Corps Operations in World War II, Famous Quotations.*

"Years ago they wanted me to get involved, but all these years I kept my nose clean, always doin' business honest. Now half of them are behind bars and they're the survivors! They told me, 'Joe, you'll have it made. You got one truck. We'll make you part of the business. You'll have seventeen trucks.' *Ba beep ba bop ba boop.* I told them I had enough headaches."

In the bathroom were two mirrors, one on the door of the medicine cabinet and the other on the back wall. I opened the medicine cabinet mirror and I could see myself reflected endlessly back and forth between the two mirrors. There were a thousand of me receding deep into a tunnel. That could drive you crazy, I thought. Inside the medicine cabinet, one bottle of Vaseline hair tonic, one black pocket comb with lint between the teeth, one silver razor, a short stack of blades. Under the sink, a can of shaving cream, a plastic bucket with the ends of old soap bars. My father threw nothing away. He used every dreg and scrap of society, soap ends melded together into one lumpy mass and were smoothed over by his hand's use. The shower curtain was clear with a pattern of blue and green waves. The window over the tub was covered with black plastic trash bags duct-taped to the tile to keep out the draft. Toilet paper was in its proper holder built into the wall. An extra roll was under the pink crocheted dress of a doll on top of the toilet tank. I recognized his mother's handiwork in the doll's dress. On the back of the bathroom door hung two white towels stiff, rough, stained with rust. On the floor, serving as a rug to keep the chill off his feet was a pullover maroon velour shirt, the sleeves and buttons and the collar cut off.

My father's landlady lived on the first floor of the building. She'd open her door when he entered and invite him in for a cup of coffee. This aroused his suspicions. When she gave him plenty of heat, his suspicions grew worse. He'd listen to the hissing of the radiators and say, "Always sending up heat. What's she trying to axphyxiate me?" After months of her solicitations, he gave in. "First she sneezed," he reported, "then she cut the cake with the hand. Who even wanted cake? It's Russian roulette. I've had green phlegm ever since."

I catalogued in my brain the arrangement of his apartment as if I could take inventory of his soul. Against the wall was an improvised filing system, a chintzy gold metal stand, turned upside down like road kill, its four wheeled legs stuck straight up in the air. Empty boxes of Brillo pads were lined up as a filing system. In one box, napkins, then paper bags, loose leaf paper, plastic bags. I remembered a particular photo of my father when he was three years old. He looked just like me. You couldn't tell if he was a boy or a girl. He wore some kind of white dress. His lips were full and his eyes looked sad as if they predicted his boyhood labor as an iceman, his teenage years fighting the Japanese in Okinawa and Guadalcanal, his prime rife with violence that bubbled up inside him in his marriage, and the eventual breakdown of everything he built in life, including his mind. His stream of consciousness monologues and cigarette smoke had a narcotic effect on me. I got overtired and drank his drink, black coffee, until I couldn't hold my eyes open any longer. I propped myself up on the bedding he kept on the kitchen floor, sofa pillows covered in green and maroon velour shirts, buttoned up the back, sleeves cut off, the pillows looked like decapitated torsos. On the floor underneath the table he had stacks of newspaper articles and *Ching Chow* cartoons cut-out from the *Daily News* and taped to loose leaf pages. I reached over and grabbed a stack of the *Ching Chow* to read: "A peasant on his legs is taller than a king on his knees." "Many a good sword is dressed in a poor scabbard." "A nation's strongest wall is the courage of its people." "A man cannot say how long he will live but only how nobly." "Bright armor doesn't make a knight, and an ape wearing diamonds is still an ape." "The father opens the road upon which the son travels." "The sages agree, all empires die of indigestion."

Above my head, taped to the wall were calendar months: September, October, November, December, January. All the days on all the months were heavily X-ed out in indigo ink. Above the calendar was a topographical map of the world. Okinawa was circled and circled and circled. I put my coffee cup on the floor next to me, and pulled the pea-green wool army blanket up around my legs. I felt I was in a Marine camp on the edge of a jungle. The war had been over for forty years. I fell asleep knowing my Dad would be up before me, coffee ready, change jingling in his pants pocket, ready to go get the newspaper.

Deep Bell

BROWN UNIVERSITY, PROVIDENCE, RHODE ISLAND

Iknocked on Dr. Alfred Senft's laboratory door. He opened the door himself.
"Hi, how are ya?" I said quickly. "I'm Annie Lanzillotto. I'm a
sophomore."

"Dr. Senft. What can I do for you?"

He shook my hand. Dr. Senft was a man my father's age. He had a
kind and intelligent face with thick and unkempt eyebrows, wore a sweater
softened with age, and stood bent over with knowledge. He looked at me
over the top of his eyeglasses.

"I'm lookin' to work in a lab on campus. I'd love to know about your
research."

"C'mon in. Take a look around."

"What do you teach?"

"Tropical medicine and parasitology. I'm working to isolate schistosomal
hemoglobinase to find new protocols. Schistosomiasis, left untreated, leads to
bladder cancer."

"You know where cancer comes from?"

"In this case, yes. Outside of lung cancer from asbestos exposure, bladder
cancer from untreated schistosomiasis has the clearest etiology of all."

I was amazed. None of the brilliant minds around me at Brown or
Sloan-Kettering had any idea where the cancers my friends and I had, came
from. I wanted to study a cancer with a clear etiology. No mystery, like the
cancers my friends and I had.

"Dr. Senft, can I study with you? Work with you in your lab?"

"I can't pay you."

"Pay me? I'm not lookin' to get paid, I'm lookin' to learn."

Soon I had the keys to every biology building on campus from the
laboratories to the one that housed the electron microscope. I drove Dr.
Senft's mice up to Harvard where we worked with a sister lab, and visited
him at Woods Hole in the summer. Dr. Senft had served as an army doctor
in World War II. He asked me what my father did.

"My father's into oil and horses," I said, pretending for a moment to
live up to the Ivy League, then added, "he fixes oil burners, and gambles at
the track." I pronounced *oil* the way my father would say it: *earl*. Dr. Senft
didn't think this was as funny as I did. Dr. Senft was in the market for a
new furnace, so we wrote my father a letter to ask his advice. That's how my
father and Dr. Senft started a written correspondence. Now I had three World
War II vets in my life, my father, my pilot instructor, and my science mentor.

When I saw the letters my father wrote to Dr. Senft, it struck me that both men were of equal intelligence, but their stations in life were vastly different. I was sad when I thought of my father, living alone, on disability, gambling on the races, and writing me letters every day. Dr. Senft was an accomplished research scientist at an Ivy League university, he sculpted bronze fountains, and was an avid listener of classical music. Somehow I straddled both worlds. In Dr. Senft I saw what my father could have been, had his intellect been cultured, and his psyche not destroyed in combat, had he received adequate psychological care and medication. I studied for the next three years in Dr. Senft's lab night and day. Sometimes I slept there to wake up in time to take the next enzyme assay and add more substrate to the next batch of test tubes.

I wanted to see schistosomiasis for real, in the clinic. I decided to awaken my childhood passion for Egypt, and finally go. I applied to study and do fieldwork in Egypt. At first, the American University of Cairo rejected my application. I knew it was because I had cancer. Why else would they reject me? I was pulling good grades. Cancer was a stigma, and I couldn't get used to it. I was so mad, I got on my bicycle and headed down Route 1 out of Rhode Island toward New York. I rode the surge of survivor's duty, fueled by the constant witness of the souls of my peers who I buried. I hopped with my bike on the ferry from New London, Connecticut to Orient Point, and continued to ride westward through Long Island on Route 25. I spent the night at a friend's house in Long Island, then hopped Amtrak into the city, and biked to the United Nations in the morning, where the American University of Cairo had an office. I banged on the door and stormed in with brio. My thighs were pumped. My biceps were pumped. I was sweaty. "I want to know why my application was rejected." The ladies in the office were very nice, not at all prepared for my lack of polish and Bronx Italian rage. I bashed into the office like water out a johnnypump.

It couldn't be my grades, so, I asked them, "Is it my grades?"

"No."

I had excellent recommendations, so I asked them, "Is it my recommendations?"

"No."

It wasn't the money, because it cost more to stay at Brown than go to Egypt, so I asked, "Is it my financial aid package?"

"No."

I knew it was because I had no spleen, and I was a health risk, and they couldn't come right out and say that, because that would be an act of discrimination. I was sick of this stigma. First the military rejected me, then the pre-med deal told me not to bother applying to med school, now this? "Is it because I don't have a spleen?"

"No."

"Then what is it! I demand an explanation."

"Tell you what. We'll review your application again, and get back to you."

A week later I got an acceptance letter in the mail.

I'd never been outside the northeast except for that train ride to boot camp to see my brother CarKey. Now I was going to Egypt. What the hell would I need over there? I had no idea. Asthma inhaler, that's for sure. Cash, yes. Clothes? What would I wear? Could a woman just walk around anywhere she wanted to go? I didn't know what to bring, so I didn't bring anything. I went with the clothes on my back: navy sweatpants with two white stripes down the sides of the legs and my dungaree jacket. In my red backpack I put an asthma inhaler, underwear, socks, an Arabic dictionary, a blank notebook and pen, cash in a money belt, and Mom threw in a clean sheet and a bottle of Tylenol, which almost killed me. She bought it off the shelf in the Bronxville A&P where Tylenol had been laced with cyanide. By the time investigators linked the local death of a young woman to the Tylenol, I was long gone and hard to reach and my Mom was in a panic. Luckily she had grabbed a box that hadn't been tampered with. My roommates and I, in Cairo, had already swallowed every pill.

As I packed to go to Egypt, I had a stroke of intuition. I decided I needed a moustache. It was August 2, 1985, the sixth anniversary of the death of Thurmon Munson, the Yankee catcher I'd idolized. His photo was in the newspapers. I clipped it and stuck it in my back pocket. Munson died piloting his own plane. Being a pilot required the same level of attentiveness as being a catcher. Catchers control the game. It's the only position that faces the whole team. The catcher communicates with the team from out to out, keeps the infield tight and alert, calms and focuses the pitcher, sets the strike zone, reads each batter, and razzles them. A catcher's eyes are everywhere, see everything. A great catcher can anticipate what's going to happen next. I stared at the picture of Thurmon Munson for nine days and then it hit me: I needed a moustache.

I walked in off the street to a *parrucchiere* on Atwells Avenue in the Federal Hill section of Providence. The barber Francesco flashed a big grin when I handed him the newspaper photo of Thurman Munson and pointed at Munson's signature moustache.

"This is exactly what I want. Can you make this for me?"

"Yes I can."

"How much?"

"Seventy-five."

"Okay. Let's do it."

Francesco had a thick moustache himself. He moved like a disco roller skater. He had blown dry hair like Barry Manilow and wore soft faded designer jeans that fit tight around the outline of his cock. I felt lucky. Think about it. A Bronx Italian dyke who identifies as Thurmon Munson walks into a hair salon off the street in a Mafia-infested neighborhood because she wants a moustache, and happens to sit in the chair of a gay Italian Barry Manilow disco queen. Oh, what a beautiful world.

I told Francesco that I was going to the Arab world, and he nodded in agreement that a moustache might be just the thing. He measured my mouth with precision, gave me a short haircut, saved the clippings and told me, "Come back in one week."

In the meantime I drove around Providence looking for a mosque. I figured I'd better learn a couple of things about Islam. I found a mosque that was an old house, painted white on the outside. I saw a woman, in full Muslim dress, on her knees in the garden. I walked up to her and said hello.

"*Assalaamu alaikum.*"

"Your garden is beautiful."

"*Shokran.*"

"My name's Annie."

"Khadija."

"Kadya?"

"Khadija."

"Khadeejah."

"*Aiwa.*"

"You think you can help me? I want to learn about Islam. I'm going to Egypt to study."

She looked up at me, trowel in hand, and said words that would resonate with me the rest of my life. "I cannot help you. Only Allah can." It struck me as brave of her to say she couldn't help me. Most people think they can help, then just waste my time, like someone you ask directions of, and they don't know, but they give you directions anyway. No thanks. Then, with a blast of inspiration, Khadija looked up at me again and added words that stabbed me with the prescient truth that only a complete stranger can hit on:

"Be like the tree, my love, be like the tree."

I drove to my friend's house. Caroline was a pre-med student, a lesbian studying anatomy. "What are you gonna stick in your pants?" she asked.

"I hadn't thought of that. You really think I need something?"

"Yeah, if you're gonna pass. *Helloooo.* The soft cotton *galabeya* in the wind will hug your body."

"What?"

"Don't worry, I'll sew you something."

"Sew me something?"

"Yeah a little doll."

"A doll?"

"Shaped like a penis."

"A penis-doll?"

"Okay, a penis-doll."

"That'll be my first doll."

The week passed and I went back to Francesco. He presented me with a small plastic case: a custom moustache made from my own hair. I looked at it and pictured Thurmon behind the plate.

Francesco said, "First you wipe the frenulum with alcohol," and he carefully wiped the skin between my lip and nose.

"That's a frenulum?"

"Yes. A very special little place."

I touched my frenulum with my pinkie. "That is a secret little place."

"Now I must clean it again. It must be free of skin oils to adhere properly."

He brushed spirit gum onto the skin around my mouth, carefully lifted the moustache out of its case with the thumb and forefinger of both hands, and fitted it over my lip and around the sides of my mouth. He patted it onto me with his fingertips.

"That's it. Fits perfect."

The moustache felt like a caterpillar asleep on my lip. I looked in his wall mirror with a huge smile. I lifted my lips this way and that, opened my mouth wide and side to side to feel the pull of the skin.

"It won't come off?"

"It won't come off. You can even stand in the rain."

"I'm going to the desert."

"You're all set."

He gave me a whole moustache kit: a pocket bottle of spirit gum, a comb with tiny teeth, and a case.

"Just peel it off and put it back in the case. When you need to, gently shampoo it with a toothbrush. Gently. Not too much water, not too much shampoo. Just to keep it clean. Remember, it's hair. You take care of it like any other hair. *Buona fortuna,* eh? Don't get into too much trouble out there."

I peeled seventy-five bucks out of my wallet and thanked him profusely. I felt like he just saved my life. Without knowing it, he gave me freedom. I walked out onto Atwells Avenue. Now I could be an asshole Italian American man just like the rest of them. Even the giant iron pine cone hanging under the arch over the avenue looked smaller to me now. The moustache felt about as comfortable as a bra, it had the same gender-signifying tug. But I was pleased. I had to try it out. I crossed the street, got into my car and drove slowly. At the red light, I stared at a man in the car next to me. He looked away. Is that all men had to do? Just stare you down? This was powerful. I looked in the rearview mirror. Even in the rearview mirror I could exude power to the driver behind me. The moustache looked like I was born with it. It was me.

I drove to Caroline's house and she gave me the penis-doll she had sewn out of flowered cotton fabric and stuffed like a little animal. We laughed. I pushed it into my underwear, and made some adjustments with my hand.

"Okay I gotta take off. Gotta try it out on the public. I'll see you later."

I walked into the largest supermarket in all of Rhode Island, Dave's Marketplace, twenty minutes outside of Providence. Over a stack of red peppers, I asked a woman the best way to pick peppers. It was harder, being Italian, to fake not knowing how to pick peppers, *papparule*, than it was to act like a man. My maleness went unquestioned. This was the first time in a store, that I felt in sync with how the world perceived me. Straight women made eye contact with my blue eyes. The penis-doll led me up and down the aisles. I felt my center of power change. I felt powerful, threatening even. I walked with a prowl. It was as if I was armed. I took on the postures of my brothers, I leaned against walls and pillars with one arm up. I crossed my arms over my chest. Pulled my wallet out of my back pocket. I handed over cash for my peppers. I didn't feel any discrepancy with the cashier. She could call me "Sir" like cashiers normally did when they heard my voice. I scratched my balls and left.

Back at Caroline's, I practiced how to eat and drink. She had pizza. I bit into a slice, and stroked the lines of my moustache with my hand for stray bits of *mozzarell'*. I tried yogurt and granola with a spoon. My lower lip came up over the moustache to clean it. I bit into an apple. I did pretty good. Now I had to increase my level of skill to be ready for any situation. I had to kiss somebody. Caroline had a couple of lesbian friends over, hanging out. They were disinterested in me when I walked in 'cause they thought I was a guy, then they all laughed in amazement when Caroline told them who I was. They knew me from around campus.

Jade was hot. Over six feet tall, almond skin, plush lips, toned biceps. She played rugby. I'd seen her around, she jogged the streets. In Providence the steepest hills of College Hill were painted with words of inspiration for the athletes who ran. I couldn't make it up those hills more than once or twice. Jade could. I never would have approached her on campus, never would have come on to her. She was sexually experienced. I knew she'd been in relationships. I looked at her. My eyes lingered on her. A woman knows when your eyes linger on her beauty.

"Would you help me with something?" I said.

"Maybe." She giggled. "What with?" Her eyes were open. Curious.

"I need to practice kissing."

"Sure," she laughed, "okay."

Only with the moustache, would I ever have come on to her. I leaned over her and came in close. It's all in the approach, I told myself. Her lips met my lips, then they opened. I was caught off-guard. I didn't expect her mouth to open. A reverberation spilled down to my clitoris. Somewhere inside me a deep bell rang.

"Mmm. It works fine," she said.

I stepped back. Who knew the moustache would lead to adventures so immediately, and on this side of the Atlantic? My clitoris pulsed. I felt more like myself than ever. For some reason, I'd assumed the moustache would make me feel incognito. I leaned in and kissed her again. Again the deep bell rang.

"Yeah, that works real good," Jade said.

I gently pulled back, feeling the moustache tickle her lips. The moustache stayed on perfectly. That kiss was real. I stepped into the bathroom and looked in the mirror. My eyes were bursting bright and in this moment were as blue as my mother's. I dropped my dungarees and tore off my shirt. I looked at myself naked with the moustache. The scar down my belly, the scar around my ribs, the moustache, none of it made much sense. I peeled off the moustache. I pulled at my long scars as if I could peel them off as easily. I combed the 'stache and put it away in its case. I stepped into Caroline's shower. It was summer. I was hot. The shower was small like a corner phone booth.

A few minutes later Jade came and stood outside the shower curtain and said something.

"I can't hear you," I said. "C'mon in."

And she did. She stepped into the shower naked. Her face came into the pulse of water. The water beat down. I took a breath and we kissed deeply, water rushing into our mouths and eyes.

"Mmmm. Good without the moustache too," she said.

The water slicked down her curls over her shoulder—her hair was longer than I'd imagined. Her knee pushed between my legs. I leaned back against the plastic walls. For the first time in my adult life I felt small. She bit my neck. Her lips found my first scar where the lump used to be. My head fell back as she sucked. The curve of my neck was my caving place; my knees buckled. I grabbed onto her shoulders as her knee lifted me. We could topple this whole thing over. She kissed down around my breast, licked in circles down my belly scar, where the thirty-two staples once held my split belly. She didn't ask what happened to me, she just kissed each place. I pushed back against the two walls. I sucked on her breast, imitating what she had done, the tip of my tongue pushed into the ridge of her nipple. She moaned. I could hardly take it. She parted my labia with her fingers, then she bent down. I held onto the sides of the shower stall as her tongue went inside me. The heat of her mouth sucking my cunt made me melt. I couldn't stand up any longer. And so she did, and lifted my body with the strength of her thumb inside me. She found my rhythm. Her hand pumped in and out of me, sliding up the roof of my cunt with the force of her knee behind her hand. She breathed in my ears a soft cry under the force of the water. I held onto her as if she were the side of a mountain. The friction of our rubbing together started a fire that would never get put out. I wanted to stay inside my skin—for the first time in a long time. Skin had many purposes, and as I was learning, this one was ecstasy. Our eyes connected through the water as she pushed into me, her chest on my chest, her belly against my belly, her neck around my neck, our breath merged. I shut off the water. We just leaned there, our breathing filling the space of the four plastic walls.

I learned to orgasm the same time I learned to fly. Once I flew at night, there was no turning back. It excited me to have to navigate over dark water and find the blue lights that demarcated the runway. Joseph and I flew to New Haven during the new moon. The runway was just at the water's edge. Out over the Long Island Sound, I couldn't tell the difference between stars and points of lights on boats. Without a moon or horizon line, the only way I could tell the black sky from the water was to make sure I flew right side up. I checked my instrument panel and kept my wings level with the horizon line on the gauge. Landing was all about the approach. I could start a gradual descent three miles out or I could maintain altitude and slip down at the last moment. That was my favorite. Joseph said it was a good skill for short-field landings, or if I had to clear a mountain or tall obstacle and then land. I loved skidding in air, using rudder, flap control, and wing angle in a crosswind to slide out of the sky.

The tip of my tongue had the knack to coax a clitoris out of its hood. I applied to Jade, what I had learned all those years ago as a child; to lick the cathode of a battery to test for the charge. For that I had my father to thank. Inadvertently, he trained me to be a lesbian lover of the most sensitive caliber. My tongue was sensitized to the salty sting of energy. I could taste voltage. Find the pulse. Love women. The world was one great battery charged by the saltwater oceans. Women were the keepers of the saltwater charge. To cum was another matter. I felt like I was ascending a cliff but I could never get to the top, never fall off, never let go. I had to learn.

One day I flew touch-and-goes with Joseph, practice for takeoffs and landings. I flew a rectangular pattern at a thousand feet around the airport, called in for clearance to land, approached the runway, landed, and instead of stopping, accelerated again into a takeoff. I had done this six times in a row when

Joseph said, "This time land the plane and taxi off." I did. The engine was still running. He opened his door, stepped out of the plane and said, "Now you go. You're ready to solo."

"What are you talking about, ready?

"You never think you're ready. You just are."

"Alone?"

"Do three touch-and-goes. Go."

He closed his door, patted the plane twice and walked away. I watched him saunter off in his bomber jacket. He didn't turn back.

I called into the tower and headed back to the runway.

I lined up the nose of the plane with the centerline of the runway. This would be my first time in the sky alone. I yelled as loud as I could and gave her full throttle. I pulled the nose of the plane up and lifted into the sky. I loved takeoffs; the world got small quick. All I could do was laugh and sing in the sky. I felt silly up in the sky all alone. I shouted. There was freedom in the fact that there was no one to hear me.

As I came in for a touch-and-go, I saw Joseph give me a thumbs-up. After two more rounds I landed and we set up a date for my solo flight test.

I started sleeping over at Jade's apartment. She lived with a couple of pre-med lesbians. There was a lot of lovemaking going on in their room and ours. Jade had endurance. She was ambitious and eager to teach me to orgasm. She'd lick me for hours. I had no idea that people actually spent time this way. I tried to relax, which was almost impossible for me to do. I didn't know what to do with my brain.

For my solo flight test, Joseph mapped out a few airstrips for me to find hidden in the hills of Vermont. The test was for me to navigate visually to the airstrips, land, run in and get a signature from the ground manager, and take off again to the next airstrip. It was like an Easter egg hunt in the sky. I had to find the landing strips. When the day came, I walked around the plane and tapped the body all over, which I loved to do; I felt like a doctor tapping the body in a checkup. I did my pre-flight checklist, got in the plane, turned on the ignition, and took off my sneakers and socks. I flew barefoot. This was about freedom and feeling the sky. Somewhere over Vermont, I busted through the fattest cloud I could find. To fly through a cloud in a Cessna is like going through a tunnel, a momentary darkness. I busted back out into the baby blue sky. On the way back to Providence I got lost. I was having too good a time. I saw an immense body of choppy dark-blue water in front of me. It didn't end. It had to be the ocean but I wasn't supposed to be anywhere near the ocean. If I had enough gas I could fly straight to

Italy. The ocean appeared frighteningly endless. I veered right. A tidal wave of gray buildings came upon me. My altimeter read 1,100 feet. What city could that be? Where the hell was Providence? My aeronautical maps were open beside me. I called into a nearby tower, gave them my plane's code numbers and said, "I'm a student pilot and I am lost."

"What do you see over your left wing?"

"The ocean."

"Your right wing?"

"Houses."

"Lower your left wing. Do you see a water tower and a railway?"

"No. Oh yes, there it is. I see a water tower to the left of a railroad."

"Okay, we have you on our radar. You must elevate to fifteen hundred feet immediately. You are in the jet-landing pattern for Logan Airport."

"Logan Airport? That's Boston?"

"Attain fifteen hundred feet. Adjust your heading to . . ."

They gave me a new heading and I got the hell outta there.

"Do me a favor. Call Joseph my flight instructor at T. F. Green. Tell him I'm a little late but I'm on my way."

"Roger that."

I learned to lick Jade at the same time she licked me. We tried to cum together. I felt the tension in her body mount until she fell apart and all her muscles let go. I tensed my body and held onto her until all my muscles were taut and my cunt reached up to the sky. Finally I fell. It was a release like I never knew existed. I breathed deep. Deeper than I'd ever known.

I left for Cairo with one red backpack and a thousand and one questions.

My oratorical coach, Sister Raymond Aloysius, and me. Memorial Day Parade, Yonkers, 1977. *Photo: Rachel Lanzillotto.*

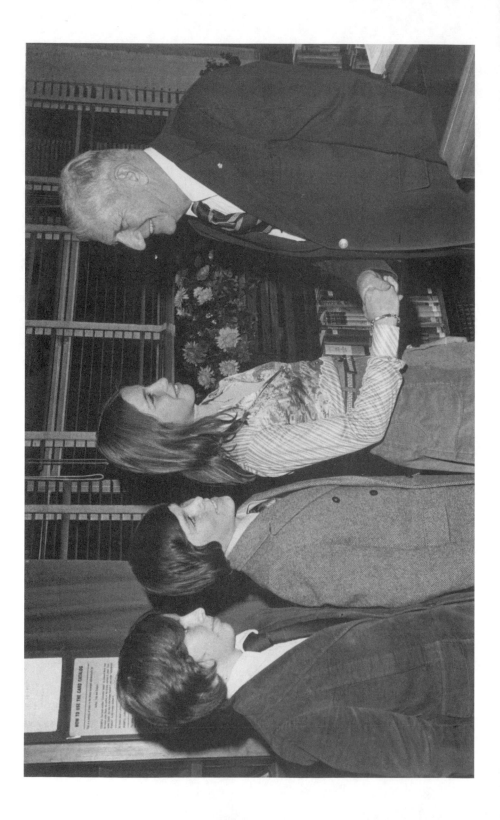

Above: Cecil Rowe, the doorman, *aka* spiritual gatekeeper of the front entrance of Memorial Sloan-Kettering Cancer Center, 1275 York Avenue, New York City. *Photo: Annie Lanzillotto, 1982.*

Left: Me, beating the boys. I win first place at the Catholic Youth Organization Oratorical Contest. Stepinac High School, November 23, 1976. *Photo: Larry McBrearty.*

Self-portrait of the author. *X* marks the spot of the tumor for radiation therapy. Memorial Sloan-Kettering Cancer Center, New York City. 1982.

Me and my hospital roommate, Connie Robinson, Memorial Sloan-Kettering Cancer Center, New York City. *Photo: Anthony Caliendo, 1981.*

More Demerol please. Nurse Arlene and me. Memorial Sloan-Kettering Cancer Center, New York City. *Photo: Anthony Caliendo, 1981.*

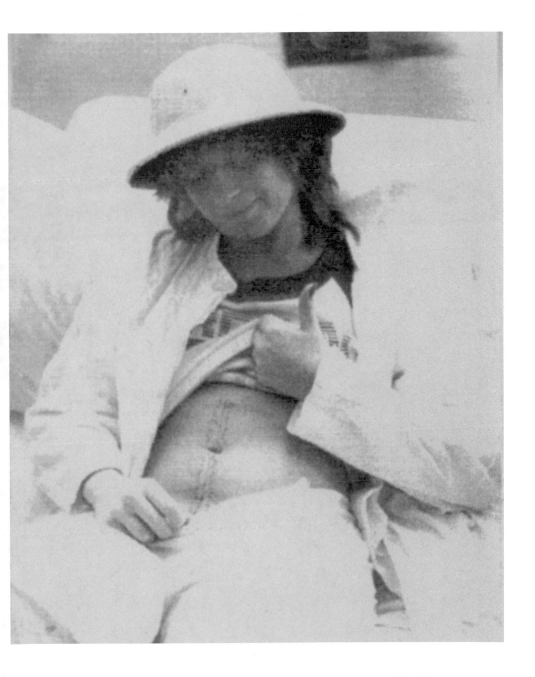

Me, gutted. Recovering from a laparotomy, Memorial Sloan-Kettering Cancer Center, New York City. *Photo: Anthony Caliendo, 1981.*

Above: Me as Abdul, in Cairo, Egypt. 1986. Photo taken in a passport photo shop near Tahrir Square.

Left: Me, atop the Great Pyramid, Giza, Egypt. I climbed with my friend David Basilico, and his girlfriend Kate. *Photo: Kate Fielder Vickery, 1986.*

Me as Abdul. Abdul was popular with the ladies. Zamalek, Cairo, Egypt. *Photo: David Basilico, 1986.*

part four

How to Cook a Heart

Wallid Walla Bint

I walked into a dress shop in Cairo and bought myself a traditional woman's Egyptian gown; floor-length emerald-green cotton with red beading in a pattern of tall feathers. I pulled it on over my head and hailed a cab, one of the many navy-blue Peugeot taxis constantly beeping around Cairo. The driver spoke a couple of words of English and introduced himself as Yusef. Then he said 'Amerrreek?' and I said 'yes' and he said 'Joseph, Joseph' with his hand on his heart until I understood that Yusef was Arabic for Joseph. This made me happy. I felt that everywhere I went there would be a Joseph to guide me. I told him, *'mi Papa esta Joseph,'* and he understood and said, *'Babba,* Joseph. *Alhamdulillah.'* He asked me what I did, and I told him I was a student of schistosomiasis. He asked me what that was. I tried different words and combinations until he understood what I was struggling to communicate across language. I told Yusef I was trying to understand why people were getting reinfected throughout their lives with a disease that there was good medicine for. I talked about how babies were getting infected in canals where their mothers gave them baths.

"Ah *bilharzia,"* he said, *"bilharzia* like Abdel Halim." Then he clarified, "The Egyptian Elvis," and to make me understand, he played a cassette tape.

"You like?"

"Aiwa." Yes.

"El Helwa Hayati," The Beautiful is My Life, Abdel Halim, good."

"Abdel Halim," I repeated.

"Die. *Bilharzia.* Before eight years." Yusef showed me Abdel Halim's photo on the cassette box; striking brown eyes and the drawn-in cheekbones of a cigarette smoker. Then through a mix of radiant facial expression, verbal phrases and hand cues, Yusef communicated to me something that changed the course of my studies, *"Allah* has brought you to Islam through your fascination with *bilharzia.* I drive you to my shaykh." He refused money for the ride, as long as I let him take me where he wanted. When we drove up to a pale brick building, I saw the sign: First International Conference on Islam and Medicine. I knew I was right where I needed to be. I felt so lucky, and in place. Yusef walked me into the building, found his shaykh and registered me for the weekend conference. He said he'd drive me there the next morning.

The conference was attended by Muslim doctors from Egypt, The Sudan, North America, Iran, Iraq, Kuwait, and Saudi Arabia. Their common purpose was written in the program as: "We come to respond to the challenge of the Qur'an to contemplate the universe and its marvels, for to examine scientifically and to appreciate aesthetically is to lead the human heart to Allah. If scientific inferences in the Qur'an, transcribed fourteen hundred years ago, appear compatible with modern fact, then the miracle of the Qur'an is upheld, and science reconciled."

I sat back and listened. The headphones had many languages to dial into. I set mine to English. One shaykh had an illuminated presence, Shaykh Abdul Majeed Ben Aziz al-Zindani. His gaze caught me from across the room. He had a white turban, a long beard, and a luminous smile. Shaykh al-Zindani quoted inferences about genetics in the Qur'an and *Sunnah*, the words and acts of the prophet Muhammad as a prescription for life, and then said, "Since Muhammad, peace be upon him, was illiterate and since science in the seventh century knew nothing of genetics, therefore, this upholds the miracle of the Qur'an." I tried to follow his logic. The shaykh compared the word translated on my headset as *clot* in English, into the scientific word for embryo, zygote. Shaykh al-Zindani founded the "Commission on Scientific Signs in the Qur'an and Sunnah." He encouraged modernization in Muslim society by saying that technology was not in conflict with *sharia*, Qur'anic law. He helped ease Muslim communities into development. I spoke with one western doctor near me who explained that al-Zindani helped Saudi Arabia accept new technologies by convincing the people that technology was pre-ordained by the Qur'an. Al-Zindani advocated for technological advancement where technology was thought to be in conflict with beliefs and traditions. This interested me. I knew he could help the *fellahin,* Nile floodplain farmers get better medical care. I wanted to talk with him directly. The man had power, faith, conviction, political prowess and spiritual presence.

I walked up to Shaykh al-Zindani and extended my arm to shake his hand. This was a big mistake. He withdrew his palm to his chest and lowered his gaze. He wouldn't talk to me, or look at me when I stood in front of him, or acknowledge my presence in any way. Being a woman was in the way of my interactions. I said "*Ma'salaama*," peace, and retreated. I wasn't used to being so invisible. I hated having to remember that I was a woman. I bought a white headscarf, and wore it to the banquet that night. One of the Western doctors, a Caucasian man named Dr. Allison (Pete) Palmer, embraced Islam, and declared the *Shahadah*: "*La ilaha illa'allah, Muhammad Ur Rasulullah!*"

There is no God but God and Muhammad is his prophet. The crowd burst into "*Allahu Akbar! Allahu Akbar! Allahu Akbar!*" God is great, three times.

Shaykh al-Zindani made an announcement, that was translated as, "Dr. Palmer was already a Muslim unknowingly, for this follows the natural order of the universe and the Islamic concept of *ayah*, where every creation inherently honors its divine author."

One of the Western male scientists asked me to continue our talk over dinner the next night. I wanted to stay on topic but he had other more intimate ideas. Two things became clear. I had to get a sense of Islam if I were to understand how people interacted with medical systems, and being a woman would get in my way. Islam had to enter my cells as a man and as a woman. The cabby Yusef was right; *bilharzia* was leading me to Allah.

When I walked in the streets of Cairo as a woman, I had to ward off men. It was common for a man to hide behind two parked cars and ejaculate at me as I walked down the street. Some mornings, men leaned on the *Kasr El Aini* bridge as I crossed over the Nile on my way to school. One guy showed me his erect penis. I joined the *tae kwon do* team on campus. When I saw his hand display his penis for me, my natural reflex was to shove him, with the force of my two arms. He fell down the concrete flight of stairs down to the riverbank. He got up and shook it off. I was sick of men. Some followed me for blocks as I walked to school, saying, "*Ishta*," sweet cream. This was an everyday occurrence. Most of the foreign female students had similar stories. My father trained me from an early age in the Bronx to be aware of everything around me. I was hypervigilant; I could spot guys across the street who were even thinking about following me. Most of the ejaculators wore *galabeya*, the traditional long loose dress for Arab men.

My first three days I walked in Cairo with friends and listened intently to the way men talked in Tahrir Square, and the souk the *Khan el Khalili*, a maze of alleyways packed with vendors of spices, bronze, alabaster, and a myriad of goods. We sat in the oldest café in Cairo, *El Fishawy*, whose mirrors on the walls were so old they held their own visions. *El Fishawy* was a place where a woman could get a coffee. Most cafés were filled with men only. I closed my eyes and listened. One thing was clear to me. Men grunt. I listened to the pitch and intonation of their grunts. I was surprised by how much a man can get away in public with just vowel sounds and moving his eyebrows to communicate. Women worked so hard at public interactions. Men could just recede into the background and grunt, relax. There was less pressure on them in public, it seemed to me. I was a quick study. Eyebrow movement meant the opposite in Cairo as it did in the United States, where lifting eyebrows meant "no." I practiced the deep vocal guttural patterns men uttered and moved my head and eyebrows up to answer "yes," and bleated the sound "*la-aa*" for no. Sounds and facial gestures for yes, "*aiwa*," basic numbers and money, how to order coffee, tea, and a *shisha* pipe at a café, and the words: *Alhamdulillah*, and *Salaam Wa'ahleekum*. That was my arsenal. About twenty words. My register was a natural alto. I was the kind of woman people said 'Sir' to over the phone or when I approached their cash register. I chalked it up to my energy, my directness, my vocal pattern, my spirit. I walked into a tailor and ordered two custom *galabeya*, "for my father," I said, "who is about my size." When the tailor gave me the *galabeya*, it fit comfortably, like pajamas but with a long open V-neck. I needed *sederi*, the button-up cotton and silk vests men wore on their chests. *Sederi* had pockets under each armpit, and some had a secret diagonal pocket under the balled cloth buttons in front of the chest. A great place to carry a wallet. I attained *sederi* in unorthodox ways. I couldn't find exactly what I was looking for in the souk, but I would see them on men passing in the street. So, twice, when I was with a friend, I stopped a man and traded or paid American cash for what they were wearing. American dollars made a man strip right in the street. A pair of men's sandals, and I was ready to go. I slipped the *galabeya* over my head, and I was surprised to learn that it had a built-in false pocket, an open slit posing as a side pocket. I stuck my hand inside. I called it the masturbation pocket. I thought about the men who squatted by the roadside, one hand in this slit, masturbating under the tent of their *galabeya* as it fell open around their knees. I wrapped a *keffiyeh*, the traditional red and white headdress for men, around my head like I'd been doing it for lifetimes. Wrapping turbans felt natural to me. I wrapped in the style of young men, with the tail hanging from the side over the ear. Out came the moustache. After one look in the mirror, I took the name Abdul. I shoved my penis-doll in my underwear, walked down the marble staircase where I was living in *Mohandessin*, and walked out onto my street, *Sharia Abdel Moneim Riyad*. I walked right by Hamdi who sold gum and cigarettes on my street. I walked over the *Qasr El Nil* Bridge, into Tahrir Square. I was finally left alone to think, and to experience Cairo. Abdul walked in *galabeya* without interruption, sat in cafés where only men sat for fenugreek tea and *shisha* pipe, watched the people go by through hours of sweet honey tobacco and strong coffee sipped through a sugar cube held in my white front teeth. The caffeine and tobacco kept me slightly high all day. This is what men did. I felt happy. With the moustache, men left me alone, even if I didn't totally look masculine, it didn't matter. No man ejaculated at me again. What a relief. Women walked by me and averted eye contact. A couple of times over the months, in the market crowds of the *Khan el Khalili*, I would hear people around me look at me and say, "*Wallid walla bint?*" Since this happened more than once, I asked a teacher what that phrase meant and she told me, "Boy or girl?" I knew nothing about the kind of trouble I could get into if I was caught cross-dressing. I knew nothing of Egyptian law. I could rip Abdul off on a five-count and toss *galabeya*, *kaffiyeh*, moustache and penis–doll into the bushes, and on several occasions, I did. There was a policy in Cairo at the time, aimed to protect women tourists and students from harassment; Egyptian men had to have identification if they were walking with foreign women. This policy never helped me as a woman, but almost got me into trouble as a man. Once, as Abdul, I walked home with two friends from the university, David Basilico, my best friend in Egypt, an Italian Rhode Islander Brown student and his girlfriend Kate who was visiting. A cop car drove by the three of us once, then twice, then it circled to come back a third time. Suddenly I realized that I was the "Egyptian man" the cops were looking at and coming after. I ripped off Abdul, tossed his getup into the bushes, walked ahead alone in the dungaree jacket and pants I had underneath, and turned the corner. The cops pulled a fast U-turn, drove straight up to David and Kate and demanded to know, "Where'd the Egyptian man go?" My friends were smart, and played stupid. After that I was more cautious and walked the streets alone, or fifteen feet in front of my friends.

The call to prayer echoed in the alleys and in my soul. Overlapping voices of *muezzin*, those who call the faithful to prayer, ricocheted from the minarets erect in the sky to my bones. Abdul followed the men into mosques for ablution and prayer. For Friday night *zhikr* at *Al Azhar*, the oldest mosque in Cairo, I entered through the revered green door, took off my sandals, and panted the name of Allah hour after hour. I had prayed with a Muslim girl named Gheda from school who brought me home for dinner and prayer. What I didn't know is that men and women prayed with a different choreography. My movement was out of synch with the men. I was sunk. I didn't know how to pray like a man. Sheer naïveté saved me from panic. I moved into the thick part of the pack of men and mimicked their movement.

The *zhikr* began. We stood shoulder to shoulder, panting "Allah," and undulating. The crowd got larger. We squeezed in, chest to chest. *Zhikr* was easier than prayer, simpler choreography. We panted "Allah" for three hours. I felt my heart and whole soul vibrating with the "ah" sounds in "Allah," and for me "Allah" became short for "Alleluia" as I chanted in the *zhikr*. It was the most high I'd ever been in a religious ceremony. There was something quite animal about hundreds of men thrusting in synchronicity and a deep guttural prayer coming from the deepest part of ourselves. The mosque rang with our energy and collective sweat. Being Abdul, I felt freedom. I had confidence in the moustache Francesco made me, he was a pro, the thing didn't fall off or tilt with all my sweat at *Al Azhar*. After a few hours, I let go of who I was and where I was and joined the mystical spirit of the prayer. Abdul got to experience things Annie never would. I was on a high.

With the spiritual encouragement of a shaykh on campus, in time, I declared the *Shahadah* and was given the name Rabia, after a Sufi saint and mystic poet. Like me, Rabia was the fourth child born in her family, and the name Rabia means the fourth. The shaykh asked for my passport so it could be stamped: Muslim. My mother hit the roof when she heard this.

"That's ridiculous. Nobody's stamping your passport with anything let alone Muslim. I never heard of such a thing."

"It's necessary," I said, "so I can go to Mecca for a Hadj."

"Mecca-shmecka. I thought you're going to Jerusalem for Christmas. You really want to cross the Israeli border with Muslim stamped on your passport? What a ya' crazy!"

I focused on my studies. Students evacuated Cairo after the ship, *Achille Lauro*, was hijacked in the Mediterranean by the Palestinian Liberation Front. All over Cairo, and even on campus, there were burnings of the U.S. flag. I listened to the P.L.O. youth on campus, talk of their views of history and politics. The Middle East, it seemed to me, is a seat of collision. If I waited for peace, I'd wait a lifetime. I stood at the crossroads of three continents, three religions, and two tectonic plates up the Red Sea. I felt I was in the center of the world. Everything collided.

To further my fieldwork, I went to the Egyptian Ministry of Health where Dr. Mustafa received me. We sat and were served *shei*, black tea, poured by a male tea servant who refilled our cups every so often. We spoke for hours. He mapped out rural health clinics in the Nile floodplain that I could visit to see the Ministry's fecal smear collection and analysis program. One thing he said to me, I will never forget. He quoted a colleague as saying in an address to the International Conference on Schistosomiasis in Cairo in 1979:

"If you, Mr. Scientist, came to Sadat with the immunity pill for *bilharzia*, he'd cut off your head."

I drank the sweet glass of tea as I listened to this sour news. I had assumed governments wanted the good robust health of their people. I learned otherwise. The Egyptian economy could not absorb the peasant-class majority to have energy, health, and desire, because that was a direct path to dreams, freedom, and revolution. Schistosomiasis kept peasants lethargic for decades with abdominal pain, bloody urine, and fatigue, keeping the peasant class down for generations. Now I saw the shadow side to Egypt's legendary patience. Somebody had to get the peasant class out of its chokehold. Access to effective medical care would give millions of *fellahin* an increase in vitality, which would disrupt the status quo, and the Egyptian government couldn't handle the influx of productivity. My mind was blown. I thanked him for the conversation and set up our site visit.

Dr. Mustafa accompanied me to a rural medical clinic in Kunberra, and steadied a few microscopes for me to eye the signature razor-edge triangle on the tail of a *bilharzial* egg that up until then I'd seen only in books and slides back at Brown in Dr. Senft's lab and at the Sci Li. Here was the culprit that cut into the bladder wall, the infestation of which caused irritation and calcification turning into granulomas, rendering the organ useless, and led to cancer. We talked to villagers waiting to be seen, and two clinic workers who showed me education pamphlets and medicine vials that had instructions written in symbols of the sun and moon, for the illiterate. Crates of medical supplies stamped with the words "From your friends in the United States of America" were stacked inertly, unpacked. What good was I to anybody? As useless as medicine in an unopened crate. GranmaRose's words echoed in my head: "What good a' you!" The next months I set out on my own up the Nile and down into the delta, visiting villages, rural clinics, city hospitals, and farms, frequenting the oasis town El Fayoum and venturing through Kafr El Sheik, Damietta, Beheira, Gharbiya, Daqahliya, Sharquiya, Minufita, and Qalubia. Sometimes I'd take an Egyptian friend with me from school to help translate. Most times I went alone and walked up to peasants in the fields and along the canals and handed them a pen and paper. Thanks to Yusef, I knew the magic words to tell *fellahin,* "I am studying *bilharzia,* like Abdel Halim."

Women were affectionate in Egypt, and unassuming. One Muslim friend Aziza took me home from school often, where she always insisted we immediately change out of our street clothes and into pajamas; she took off her *hijab* and we got into bed to read, talk, and rest. Her mother taught me how to peel mangos and make stuffed grape leaves. Another girl on our *tae kwon do* team scrubbed my back in the showers after our practices, while the coach made us *sheii.* The team had a long warm-down, unlike any teams I'd been on back in the States. My sparring partner was a red belt, an Egyptian guy named Koolib. We got some *kushari* together in Tahrir Square, and he said to me, "Annie make luff to me efvery Tuesday night, under ze Sphinx." It was the most unique proposition I'd ever gotten. But I didn't take him up on it. Instead I started seeing a Muslim woman on campus named Jamilla, who looked me right in the eye. One afternoon she sat on a low cement wall and stared at me. As we talked, I got closer to her, and squared off my hips in front of her. She didn't turn away. Her irises opened. I brought my lips to hers and we kissed softly. There's levels to a woman. There's what you see, then there's this other place when she opens and lets you in, behind what you see. We had to kiss indoors. This was the Muslim world. I visited her room, we made out and made each other wet. She was an Egyptology major, and I invited her to join me on a *felucca,* a sailboat into Upper Egypt. She said yes. Many years later, she would become an expert Egyptologist with a forté for being able to smell the dynasty of a mummy. Different dynasties used different embalming chemicals, and she developed the sensitivity to smell the difference.

All along the Nile, our *felucca* stopped in ports, and I ran into fields of hibiscus and cotton, sugar cane, and palms. I talked with women cleaning their bowls, clothes, rugs, grain, and children in the canals. Women expressed that they did not have enough hours in their day to take for themselves to seek medical attention from the local clinics. When they could not bear their symptoms anymore, they'd give in, and go to the *mustashfa*, the city hospital, with progressed diseases.

Nadia wore a bright lime-green dress and stood knee deep in a canal in the Tropic of Cancer sun. She lifted her baby Ali out of the water. Woman, river, baby, an ancient trinity in the act of washing in the Nile. This canal was clearly contaminated with parasites. The water was thick and green and still. There were snails in the reeds along the banks. I understood from Nadia that her mother and grandmother and great grandmother and on and on, were all *fellahin* whose destiny had been linked to the Nile. She was told to stay out of the water by, as she said, the "one-who-wears-shoes male doctor." I held out my notebook and gave Nadia a BIC pen. I prompted her to draw the life cycle of the schistosome as she knew it. "*Bilharzia. Bilharzia.* Abdel Halim." Nadia smiled, raised her head, and took in a deep quick breath in assent. Nadia quickly sketched two worms linked together in copulation, then a standing human stick figure cut off at the knees by a squiggly line indicating water. She drew the spiral shell of a snail and the worm coming from the snail toward the foot of the stick figure. Health education efforts had worked. Nadia understood transmission and the life cycle of the parasite, yet all the while, she stood calmly in still waters, Ali balanced on a shoulder—waters she had been warned to stay out of by health officials. I looked at the women washing clothes in the canal. They washed with their ancestors as well as their neighbors. I thought about the schistosome eggs I saw under the microscope in the clinics, and how they can cause infertility, complications with pregnancy, and lesions in the vulva, vagina, cervix, and uterus. Nadia said, "*Ahamdulilllah*," thanks be to Allah, acceptance of life and fate, and above all else a belief in divine will over her knowledge of *bilharzial* transmission. Health information was nowhere as powerful as faith. She proudly took my arm and walked me to her home for dinner, quoting popular *hadith*, deeds and words of Muhammad, and *sura*, quotes from the Qur'an, which reinforced for her the belief that infection doesn't exist in and of itself, but only through the will of Allah. "*For where did the first infection come from?*" and "*If Allah will thee with infliction, none can remove it but He.*" This is an old story, I thought, as we walked through fields of sugarcane—the collision of belief and knowledge, religion and science. Like anywhere on earth, the control and regulation of water is power over life itself, and the understanding of women's lives key to creating collective healing. Nadia broke off a stalk of sugarcane, and we chewed the sweet, raw power of the earth.

At her house, eleven of us ate *kushari*. We sat on mats around a cool mud-brick room. She lived in the west bank of Luxor. I thought of Nahkte, whom I had learned about through Dr. Scala. At Brown, Dr. Scala had shown me images of Nahkte's CAT scans. Nahkte was a weaver who lived in roughly the same area as Nadia, only in 12 B.C., in the village Deir el Bahri. Nahkte's sarcophagus showed calcified schistosoma ova in the liver, kidney, and intestinal mucosa, and red blood cells in his bladder epithelium, histologic proof that schistosomiasis existed in the times of the pharoahs. Nadia's mother placed a one-inch cube of meat on top of the bowl she handed me. I was given the meat the father would have been given. Women need the iron most, but in the gender rules of eating, this is not a consideration. I tried to pass the meat cube to the mother and got rebuked with her hand waving in the air at my face. After we ate, Nadia decided to teach me about *bilharzia*. Her brother Hadjaj, who made money from tourists and spoke a little of eleven languages interjected translations. I recorded the syntax exactly as I heard it, and intentionally did not correct grammar with respect to Hadjaj's lingual facility. This is what Nadia said in Hadjaj's English:

"When I was young I going to school. On the way home from school it's hot. There was small canal. Brother would jumping in canal. In school they warned us, "Take care of the water. Don't jumping in canal. Don't drinking dangerous water!" I have seen *bilharzi* in the Nile and in the canal. There are people here bigger than us who know this is *bilharzi*. Also in school they show us a picture. They told us, "If you swim, if you drink, *bilharzi* come to you like Abdel Halim." But we young. We don't care. I washing things, bowls, things allways all girls. We laughing, washing in canal. If the water has current she's good. If the water stop, she's no good. When I was seventeen-years-old, all way I making blood. Pains all my body was tired like having baby. Inside my stomach. *Bilharzi* he take allway he eat my body. I was like this. [She pulls a cigarette from Hadjaj's ear and holds it straight up]. And one day when I be thirty or forty, *Halas!* My mother my father taking me to clinic. No doctors come here to village. Never. The doctors come from Cairo. If I walk with Baba in Cairo with his *galabeya* and stick they clear the street. They say this man has no mind, take care, he'll hit you with stick. No *fellahin* are doctors but there is one, but he's special. If you have much money you go. I going to clinic. I say I have *bilharzi*. I making blood. The doctor just looked to me like you.

[She passed her eyes from down to up.] He said okay. He write pen and paper to going to buy medicine. Okay I buy medicine in pharmacy three pounds. *Filoos kitir.* [Very expensive.]. A lot of people can't afford this. I eat six or five or ten. It don't make me nice. I making blood blue red black very dirty rocky. Then finish. I sleep in bed ten days. I drink *karkade* [hibiscus]. I drink anise or sometimes *sheii* [tea] or chocolate. I eat not so much. Bread cheese or meat or something rice cabbage. I feel good. Each morning I drink one bottle mineral water. Once a year I making blood. Now it's clean. I don't go doctor. I just drink mineral water. I don't going back to doctor 'cause he's very bad doctor. He don't understand. Just allway wanting money. Shoe Guy! [Colloquial curse for one who wears shoes, a literate white-collar punk.] I don't have *bilharzi* now. Thanks to my God, Allah."

I joined a *felucca* leaving Luxor. I stared into the morning, gazing at the gas flame blue colored Nile. I contemplated my own blessed cure. Why had I accessed medical care? Why had medicines worked in my body and not in the bodies of my friends? I looked out over the skin of the river. I reflected on how different my life seemed from my ancestors, but we shared some of the same diseases. I knew the *fellahin* would continue as they have for thousands of years, washing in the Nile, and the canals. The Nile is the life of Egypt, without the Nile there is no Egypt. The floodplain runs on either side of the river, and the delta. The rest is desert, and oasis villages. The construction of the Aswan Dam made everything worse in terms of schistosomiasis, bringing the snails inland and spreading the parasite. The word had to get out through the mosques. Shaykh al-Zindani, or someone of that magnitude, would have to reconcile medicine and doctors with the *fellahin's* faith in God and *la vita quotidiana* with the Nile.

I bent over the side of the *felucca*, breaking the skin of the river with my hand. I had a lot to think about. The river streamed coolly through my fingers. Easy now, you don't have a spleen, I reminded myself. The sailor told me, "Who drinks from the Nile returns to the Nile." I had to return. Without a spleen complications from parasites could be fatal, despite medicine. I had to return. I cupped my hand, overcoming thoughts of schistosomes, and lifted the water to my open mouth. As my hand passed the river to my lips, I thought *Alhamdulillah.* I swallowed. The *felucca* picked up speed with the wind. Women washed their children along the riverbanks. That is the image of the Nile that stayed with me, the river, the mother, the child, an eternal trinity. A sip of the Nile flowed down inside me. My pact with the river was sealed.

Equator Crossings

Lanzi picked me up at JFK airport. All my baskets rolled down the luggage ramp and came apart. My papers and clothing were all over the place, so all the passengers pitched in to help retrieve my stuff. I wore a white *galabeya* and *keffiyeh, sans* moustache. I gave Lanzi the blue striped *galabeya* I had made for him, but he gave it right back to me.

Before I went back to Brown, I got a devastating call from Mindy. I thought back about our brief but impactful time together: I walk into a restaurant in Providence, the ebullient waitress kisses me on the lips, I run into her once or twice around campus, she develops a lump on her neck, she rents my room for the summer, I hand her a piece of paper with Dr. Kempin's phone number. The nightmare begins. Mindy went to see Dr. Kempin. She was diagnosed with Hodgkin's Disease, but had serious complications which changed her diagnosis. She had been admitted to Sloan-Kettering and I ran down to see her. She seemed so little in that big white bed. She had been such a strong dancer, now her skull was too heavy for her to align on top of her spine. Weeks later, I sat *shiva* with her family.

At my graduation from Brown, Dr. Seuss received an honorary degree. We gave him a standing ovation, thousands of us. I cried and felt my whole class cry, under a glorious Providence three-day rain. Dr. Seuss entered all our imaginations, a whole generation from all over the world. Jade and I got on our bicycles and took off cross-country.

My father told me, "Wherever you settle, I'll come move down the block." As a parting gift, he handed me the national directory of U. S. Marines: "If you're ever in trouble, look up a Marine. You're bound to get a flat tire. Tell him your father fought in the First Division, Fifth Regiment. They will help you. Marines you can trust."

No better friend. No worse enemy. That's a motto of the 1st Marine Division I found to be true. When my father and brother were for me, I felt protected. When they were against me, I feared for my life. I was petrified to tell them I was a dyke and that I was on a mission with nineteen other fags and dykes to bike through the Bible belt and make our presence known as a consciousness raiser for A.I.D.S. The U.S. Marine Directory, I left behind. Big like a telephone book, it was too heavy, and I had to carry all my gear on two wheels in front and rear axle panniers. Three months, twenty-two hundred miles, and sixteen flat tires later, we made it from Philadelphia to San Francisco. Jade and I picked up a friend of ours from Brown, and biked down the California coast. It was five hundred

miles down US 101 to Camp Pendleton. I wanted to reach the base where
Lanzi had shipped out in 1944 on the USS *Grant*. At that time he was
with the First Marine Division, A-Company, Second Platoon, Thirty-Second
Replacement Battalion, Fleet Marine Force. The Pacific Ocean was just
over my right shoulder the whole way down the coast. I thought about my
father. He crossed the equator on that old ship. He told me about getting
initiated into King Neptune's Kingdom. They blindfolded the Marines who
never crossed the equator before, made them climb ladders up and down,
whacked and belted them, covered them in Vaseline and shaving cream, hosed
them down, then said, "King Neptune always meets new members of his
kingdom. Throw him overboard." Four guys grabbed my father and tossed
him into the air. He hit the water, panicked, took his blindfold off, and was
relieved to find he wasn't in the Pacific Ocean. He was in a pool two decks
below.

At Camp Pendleton, the three of us dykes biked onto the base. We laid
our bikes down, rested on the grass, and massaged each other's sore calves.
We were involved in a *menage a trois*, and very unconscious about our public
displays of affection. A Marine on guard duty approached us. We got promptly
escorted off the base.

"My father's a Marine," I said to the young Marine.

"We have a behavior code on base," he said, and watched us past the
base perimeter. I felt "spued." The Marines and I would never mix; it was a
fait accompli.

I wrote a postcard to Lanzi and told him Camp Pendleton looked
beautiful.

Jade and I rented a room in San Francisco on the corner of Eighteenth and
Douglass Streets, and for six months we worked as bike messengers on the
San Francisco hills for Western Messenger. I biked with abandon, racing down
the San Francisco hills and parting traffic like Moses did the Red Sea. Once
I clipped a pedestrian's tie, zooming within a shave's distance of him. He
followed me to my drop-off, grabbed my bike and yelled that he was going
to sue me. I shouted, *"Ahamdulilllah!* No one got hurt!" That's what they
would have shouted in Egypt. I missed the Egyptian sense of a moment to
moment gratitude to God. Now I was in the U.S., and had to engage in a
verbal street fight.

One afternoon I was on the phone with my mother. I pulled the phone
out the window where I climbed onto a ledge to sit in the sun. "Ma, the
California sun. It's so strong and life-giving. Our block is immaculate. I have
an Egyptian guy across the street who owns the deli. We talk Arabic. And
the houses, *madonn'*, the moldings on the facades are painted in three tones.
Pink, blue, purple, like seashells. It's gorgeous. When are you coming out?"

"Well, your brother's getting out of rehab in Minnesota in three weeks. His apartment is a fiasco. I don't even know if I can push his front door open, with all the crap in there. How am I gonna clean it, God knows."

I hung up the phone, closed my eyes and breathed in the sun. I'd wanted my whole life to see Ant'ny clean. The vortex to come home was overpowering. I decided I needed to clean my brother's apartment. My family had a hold on me. A chokehold.

Back to Yonkers. Jade and I stayed with my mother. We pushed the door open to my brother's apartment, shoveled the foot of trash that covered the floors, dumped the dishes that had made an ecosystem in the sink into the trash, emptied the crack vials, bullets, and pennies that filled his daughter's bronze baby shoes, and for two weeks solid, cleaned and painted his three rooms in pastel San Franciscan colors. When Ant'ny walked in the door, I had a pot of wakame miso soup for him on the stove. The whites of his eyes were so clean, clear, and bright; so clean, I thought, this is what clean looks like, this is why they call it clean.

Bronx Italian Butch Freedom

On Saturday nights we danced. The Paradise Garage was our refuge. Walking to Varick and King Streets, the whole sidewalk thumped as the bass beat summoned us up a long inclined ramp with lights against the concrete. What was an old parking garage became a runway to paradise. Walking up the ramp, we began to unbutton ourselves from all the homophobic crap we dealt with all week. We stripped off our outer layers, down to something skimpy to sweat in. I wore my spandex bike clothes. I never knew how to dance, but I followed Jade's hips, which found beats between the beat. She said, "It's a black thing." I didn't know. I listened to the words of every song. They were stories of liberation and love and sex and life lived hard with operatic vocal riffs. One song told of the life of a kid in the Bronx with crooked teeth. I could listen to this over and over. Everyone at the Garage took their dance expression seriously. No one just watched. Everyone moved 'til the mob lost all self-consciousness. It wasn't just a club, it was a tribal gathering on a ritual freedom ground. The beats came from deep within, as if the DJs read our bone marrow. The dance floor was a centrifuge spinning us into freedom land. Gays from uptown, crosstown, and God knows where stripped off their passing layers, the clothes that kept them from getting gay-bashed in their home neighborhoods. Nowhere did it feel safe to be gay except here. The bass pulse laid out path. People got busy, moved all night long. Legendary DJ Larry Levan spun us higher and higher, and he never let a moment drop until eleven on Sunday morning, when we'd walk back out on Varick Street, sweaty with a sweet exhaustion, and never wanting to towel it off. Downtown was empty. We walked north searching for a breakfast we knew we earned. We emboldened each other to survive. We celebrated being alive in our gay bodies in a decade of the decimation of our community, when governments and homophobes were convinced gay blood was the new poison. At the Garage, my butch body was soothed, in the mass of gay bodies all moving to the same beat. As a butch I got spit on in the street by passing cars of boys with yellow Jersey plates who drove into town for this purpose only. Once I got spit at right on Greenwich Street, in front of the library that used to be a courthouse and the New York Women's House of Detention, where Mae West was imprisoned for obscenity after her play, *Sex* in which she danced the shimmy. Mae West might have inhabited me as I yelled at the car of boys, "Yo! This is the West Village. I'm not supposed to get spit on here. Spit on me anywhere but here, assholes!"

The night the Paradise Garage closed, we were there. It was Saturday September 26th, 1987. Five years of remission equals a cure. I was cured. I took to the floor of the one mass of breathing, moving freedom seekers; the night spun on forever, masterfully mixed. The air was sweet. Baby powder, and drugs I never saw, but smelled. All I drank was cups of water. I traveled to a place inside myself and that place was called freedom. My butch body, for those ten hours, was healed. Up in the booth, the DJ was God, and it wasn't over until his last spin.

Never Come Out in a Lincoln Continental

One afternoon the telephone rang. It was CarKey. He said, "I want to take you for a ride. I'll be right over." My big brother never wanted to spend time with me. Pick me up. Go for a ride. Those words sounded so promising. No one understands CarKey. I've tried to imagine war, tried to see how hurt and fragile he is underneath his gruff, monstrous exterior, but I never learned how to approach him. Reflecting on my airplane landing drills, it's all in the approach, I reminded myself. When I saw him, I'd kiss him hello. That didn't seem to work. He turned his cheek and I landed a kiss. Then I tried not kissing him hello, I did what he did, offered a cheek. We both bunked cheeks. That didn't work. I tried a pat on the side of the arm. I tried no touch, just a verbal "Hey Bro." The most affection I got was when I was sick. But vertical, the best hello I got was when I completely ignored him. Then he would initiate, "Hiya Annie, haaya doin'?" I hoped that one day we could have a good conversation. Maybe this was our chance. Maybe he was finally ready to know me, hang out with me, take me for a ride.

I had a dream that my father had died, and we all got one chance to visit him in Heaven—an all white room with a dark wooden piano. My Dad told us to each sit at the piano and play him a happy song. One by one, CarKey, Rosemarie, Ant'ny, my mother, my father, and I sat at the piano and played solos; upbeat tunes, singing happily, laughing. In the dream we were together in a way that we had never been able to be in life, not one time, not even once in a lifetime.

I skipped down the hill and got into CarKey's dark blue Lincoln Continental. The cream leather interior was soft and cushy. He didn't say a thing, he just looked directly ahead like he was going over something in his mind. He flicked a small silver switch, and the windows zipped up around me. He fingered another switch and the doors locked; the clicks went all around me: *tch, tch, tch, tch.* The Lincoln felt like some kind of fortress. His leg pressed down on the gas pedal and we charged up the hill. He swerved around the streets.

"Where we goin'? What are we doin'?"

"I know what you are," he said. "I don't want you bringing anybody over. I don't want your friends near my kids. Stay away from my kids. I know what you are, and I don't like it. Keep your friends away from my kids."

I felt like I was mugged, ambushed, bashed in the back of my head. All I wanted was to get out of the car, get back on my own two feet. Get away from family.

The Paradise Garage was closed. Where the hell was I going to go?

A Nightclub Named Devotion
"Roma o Morte!"

ITALIA 1987

In New York City, the Paradise Garage was closed, and in Rome, a new club was opening, called Devotion, the first house music club in Rome. Jade met the club promoter when he came to New York to buy records at Vinylmania. We got on a plane. I got the job as Devotion's *guardaroba*, coat check. I guarded hundreds of *Fatto in Italia* leather jackets, the finest stitchery

I'd ever see in my life. Walking the *Via Appia* in Rome, I knew one thing, my mother had to come to Italy, and I would make this happen. I stood in the *Piazza della Signoria* in Florence, and wept as the cobblestones and marble statues spun around me. I was struck with the one question that any traveler in Italy comes to ask: What can my hands make? What can I make all by myself? *Cosa possono fare le mie mani? Cosa posso fare da sola? Faccio io!*

There are only three places in the world that I have sensed the curvature of the earth. The Red Sea. *Il Campidoglio.* The Cape of Good Hope. I climbed the steps to *il Campidoglio* at night. Michelangelo's lines on the *piazza* emphasized the meniscus of the earth. I will never accept that *il Campidoglio* is level, even when I lay down on its stone with my eyes closed. The lines led me to the center of the *piazza*, where there was an empty marble pedestal. I leaned against it, and looked out over the Capitoline Hill, I felt I could lift off into the sky.

"*Marco Aurelio sul cavallo!*" A man yelled to me, pointing to the empty pedestal, "*dove è?*"

"*Boh.*"

"*Quando ritorna?*"

"*Boh.*"

Where was he? My buddy from Brown? I found him serendipitously. I met a girl named Lucia at Devotion who studied art restoration. She invited me to visit her school's studio. I walked into the room and there he was, the giant bronze Marcus Aurelius on his big-chested horse, shockingly at eye level. This was the original. Eighteen-hundred-year-old bronze. The statue I'd climbed at Brown was a replica. *Ciao Marco, finalmente, ci vediamo a faccia a faccia.* I felt his hair and the mane of his horse, and touched my hand to his hand. His right arm extended right to me through almost two thousand years. I went to a library and took out his *Meditations.* When in Rome, read Marcus Aurelius.

Another girl I met at Devotion did me a favor. Giuliana telephoned *Acquaviva*, got my cousin Nino on the phone, and arranged a date for me to take the train to Bari. As a Roman, she teased me for being *Barese.* This was my first taste of the north looking down on peasants from the south. In America I was a northerner. In Italy I was a southerner. Living in Rome, I was *Barese.* *Sì sono Barese.* In Rome, whenever anyone learned I was *Barese*, their voices took on a twang, their syllables twisted, and they yelled, "*Uè! Annarell!*"

At the Bari train station, Nino and an entourage of cousins and friends awaited us. I stepped off the train and they cheered and hugged us. I arrived at a long-lost home. In every face I saw sweetness and a potent love. All heart. I was overwhelmed with the reception. I felt like a hometown hero, a representative of GranmaRose. By stepping foot on the old stone streets where GranmaRose was born, I was completing the circle of life. We were brought on a whirlwind tour from house to house, town to town. I was the first American-born person in our family to make it back to *Acquaviva* since the great immigration. I had to represent all that my grandparents had accomplished since they left their families seventy years ago. I was the bridge. I wanted to know them. I wanted a relationship with them for the rest of my life. I wanted to reunite our family. I wanted my nieces and nephews to know the next generation of cousins. One century of separation was one hundred years too long.

GranmaRose's sister Maria looked just like her and was gorgeous. I sat with her and held her hand and caressed her white hair. She came out of her afternoon slumber to sit up and sing for me. I tape recorded her singing and sat with her in the cool shadows of their stone house in the hot hours of the *Mezzogiorno* sun. I was overjoyed but at the same time sad that no one else in my family would ever meet GranmaRose's sister. I met all my mother's first cousins, *Rosa*, and *Isabella*, and *i tre Michele*—three cousins with the same name. I wished Mom could have grown up with them. Up until seeing them face to face, I didn't quite realize that my mother's cousins and aunts and uncles actually had lives in modern times. It was as if GranmaRose had come from the mist, like the *Duca degli Abruzzi* had sailed from some long lost place and time. I couldn't help but wonder what if Maria had gotten on that boat instead of Rose? It's conceivable my grandparents would have met anyway, and even my parents, since they all came from within four miles of each other. I jogged to the periphery of town with my cousin Tonino and stared at the single road that connected *Acquaviva delle Fonti* to *Cassano delle Murge*, where Grandpa Giuseppe Petruzzelli came from. The dirt road, *Strada Provinciale 48*, dipped through olive trees patterned in perfect symmetries like one of GranmaRose's giant crocheted quilts. There was a pattern to these fields, an order, a *sistemazione*, a perfection. The growth of the trees was guided by careful hands. *Le mani del aria fresca, le mani del cavallo, le mani della terra.* Yes, it was conceivable that little Rosina and little Giuseppe might have met here, on this road, in these fields, tending these olives.

Jade was a foot taller than every single one of my relatives. We didn't broadcast our relationship. She stayed for four days then headed back to Rome where she was working at Devotion. I stayed in *Acquaviva* to get to know my family. I met many cousins and aunts and uncles and neighbors, some for short minutes, others for long ventures and conversations. A combination of mime, charades, and a mixture of words in *Acquavivese, Cassanese, Bitettese,* Italian, and my English, filled our attempts to talk to each other, but the only time I was absolutely sure we were all on topic was when a young cousin of mine said, "Michael Jackson," and I said, "Ahh. *Sì*, Michael Jackson." *Thriller* we had in common. Many of my cousins from different towns came to see me. My generation had spread out all over Italy. These cousins were descendants of my grandparents' siblings who'd stayed in Italy when my grandparents left on boats for New York Harbor. The bulk of their siblings stayed in these *piccolo paese*, small towns, around Bari. The ocean separated our blood for a century. I tasted each of their homemade wines and olive oils. I heard stories of how GranmaRose, as a child, was known not to like farm work. I was shown a tree that Grandpa Giuseppe climbed when he was a child. This was the first time I'd ever heard anything about GranmaRose's restless traits as a child. How she didn't write enough letters when she was in her twenties. But she always sent money, they all said. One elder cousin brought out a five dollar bill that GranmaRose had sent him fifty years ago.

"I could never spend it."

The date on the bill was 1931. Another couple brought out a bedspread. It looked brand-new. Granma sent it to them for their wedding, just after World War II. One cousin, a woman named Cristina, walked into the white room and we both broke into tears. She sat next to me. I wept. We could not speak to one another. It wasn't just a lack of common words, it was a feeling I had never felt before, like a color I had never seen, like the first time I saw a green sky, it tumbles your sense of the world. I was at a total loss. Same with my cousin. I wish I could have told her who I was. But all I had were my eyes. There was nothing to say and nothing that could be said except: *You are my cousin. I have dreamt of you all my life.*

In the *piazza* were red signs with yellow lettering: *Acquaviva Svegliati*! I wondered what this small town had to wake up about and wished I could get involved in its modern politics.

Zia Isabella, the daughter of GranmaRose's older sister Maria, took me out back behind her kitchen where she had a small sun-bleached white yard. She handed me a washboard, a tub, and a bar of soap.

"*Spinge. Spinge,*" she said, with an up-and-down pushing motion. I scrubbed my clothes and hung them on her clothesline.

"*Stai zzit? Stai zzit? Perche no maritt'?*"

I didn't know what she asked me, so I grabbed her hands, which flew as she spoke, and danced around her courtyard. I laughed, and repeated, "*Stai zzit!*" though I didn't know what the hell it meant. I turned the flight of her hands into a dance with her.

"*Mannaggia,*" she said, and reached up and grabbed my cheek.

I asked my cousins what "*stai zzit*" meant, and then I understood all the implications. This was the conversation I dreaded. *Are you engaged? Are you engaged? Why aren't you married? Are you married? Are you married? Why no husband! Why are you traveling around the world without a man by your side? A woman alone is no good.*

Zio Michele took me out to the *campagna*. I walked under his grape vines, pulled *i couloumb*, dark black figs with pink-and-gold insides, off the trees. I pulled a pear to eat.

"*Non quell'*," my *Zio* said, "*questa*." He picked a pear that already had little bites taken out of it. He pointed at the naked spots on the fruit. I understood him to say, "The birds know the sweetest fruit. In America, fruits are big, overgrown, full of water, bloated, skin waxed to a shine. On the outside they look beautiful, but when you bite into them, there is no flavor. Here it is the opposite. It may not look so good to you on the outside, but the inside explodes with sweetness."

I sat with an older cousin, Beppe, the last of the great *contadini* in the family, at his dining room table for a late night homemade *fettuccine* made by his wife Adalina. His hands were so muscular, the fingers stayed open like a starfish. I turned his hands over in mine. I could hardly recognize them as hands. These hands were tools, thick hard tools, paws, claws, vice grips. As we ate and drank his homemade wine, potent as blood, mixed with Fanta, he wept. He salted his pasta with his own tears like *Pasta Lacrime*, Pasta and Tears, the *Commedia Delle Arte lazzo* I call, *Mangia Piangia*, "Eat, Cry." Pulcinello takes to the stage with a plate of spaghetti, and as he eats, he weeps profusely.

"*Perche piange, cugino mio?*" Why do you cry my cousin?

The more *fettucine e vino* he put into his mouth, the more his heart opened. He made the wine and oil on the table. He cultivated the fields that grew the grapes and olives. He opened the earth to make the foods. And the foods opened our souls.

He talked to me about his children: one stayed away after the army, one doesn't call or visit, one will never leave the house, one refuses to talk to another, one has been heartbroken and is sure to become an old maid, a role the town still despised. *Cugino* Beppe ate and drank and cried and plowed the air with his hands. Then he paused and made deep soulful eye contact with me and repeated phrases, as if repetition would hammer comprehension into my brain. I came to understand that none of his children wanted to tend the fields. He was confused by their values. He felt his children were lost. The daughter cut her hair and moved far away in the north and bought lots of shoes.

I can't remember the *Barese* expressions my cousin used. I repeated to him, what I understood in Italian, and he nodded. "*Qualcosa è cambiato nel profondo del cuore dei miei figli. Sempre ridono.*" Something changed deep within the hearts of my children. They always laugh. Always laughter.

I had a compulsion to buy lace. An inner urge to set the table, make the bed, let the curtains blow into rooms filled with wind. Lace was made by hand in *Acquaviva* by the women who crocheted endless circles and webbing with tiny metal hooks and connected the circles into large patterns that dazzled me. The message was clear: life itself had some grand design. I knew I'd never have the patience or presence of mind or dexterity of fingers to create what they did. The place in my brain to hook white cotton had deteriorated, I was sure of it. Lace called to me. I stood at the outdoor market, pictured the maple table. I needed one large oval lace. The maple table needed to be dressed in white lace. I closed my eyes and counted how many people could fit around the table with the leaves inserted to approximate the size of lace I needed. The vendor opened many lace tablecloths under the Saturday morning sun. I couldn't tell the difference between the handmade and machine-made lace, but *Zia* Isabella quickly separated the handmade from machine-made lace and sternly haggled the prices. She threw some aside with a rejecting swipe of the hand. *Zia* Isabella brought lace closer to my eye, turned it upside down, and showed me the difference. I was afraid that if she knew I was a lesbian, I too would be swept to the side. *Zia* Isabella was a quick talker. I couldn't keep up with her commentary. She wanted me to make up my mind and not buy too much. When I reached into my flesh-colored money belt for my greenback dollars, she told me to put them away. She wanted me to pay in *lira*, and get a better price. For myself, I found a round lace. I had no table, but found comfort in round. One day I would have a table, and the lace from my grandmother's town would hold us, whoever us would be. The lace from Granma's town would weave all our tables into one big web. The pattern I chose for myself began with one central eight-petaled rosette, and built out concentrically, eight petals surrounding the rosette, then twenty-one rosettes forming a perimeter of the circle, and variations on and on, with thousands of interstitial stitches. I could see that this work could have been built in an infinite radial pattern outward, but it was in a human proportion, finished in a scalloped edge to fall over the thighs around the table.

I was sent off with a procession of food. Days before my departure, *Zia* Isabella and *Zia* Rosa began to cook presents for me to bring back to GranmaRose in America. My aunts worked too hard. *Zia* Rosa cooked and cleaned all day and all night. She made everything from scratch, *fettuccine* and *cavateel* and *orecchiette*, and *melanzane*. She handed me whole *mozzarell'* like apples on a fork. The last meal was at ten p.m. *Zia* Rosa was the first one awake and the last one to sleep. She was on her feet all day every day in an endless cycle of shopping at the market, cooking, and cleaning and caring for everyone in the family. I didn't know what I could do for her. Before I left town, I got on my knees and soaked and rubbed her feet, and gave her the shoes off my feet, my Birkenstocks.

Zia Isabella made *biscotti di mandorle*, almond biscotti. I followed her from her house through the streets and alleyways, each of us carrying a tray wider than a sewer cap full of raw *biscotti,* which she'd been making for days, from her own almonds. Where were we walking to in this procession of *biscotti* through the old town square? We communicated with mime, laughter sprinkled with *Acquavivese,* hands in the air, no English, and my limited grasp of Roman Italian, which didn't translate to *Barese* so well.

"TENZione!" Attention! *Zia* Isabella instructed me to follow her, putting the trays on the stone ground in line behind other large trays in what felt like a cave, guarded by a huge sweating man with a hairy chest holding a twenty-foot wooden pole on the end of which was a flat head that pushed the trays into a stone oven. I looked inside and the heat hit me. The oven was big enough to cremate a Cadillac. The man adeptly shuffled the many trays around, and ate a bit from each for payment, or tips. I never saw my aunt hand him money. This was *la stufa communitá,* the community oven.

When I left for the train, my aunts filled my backpacks with a five liter container of their homemade olive oil, a five liter of my uncle's vino, figs and almonds from their trees, a *focaccia* made by a neighbor, and a wheel of sheep's cheese requested by GranmaRose. *Zia* Rosa and *Zia* Isabella sent me off to America with their blessings, foods they had grown, prepared, and alchemically transformed through the miracle of their hands and fire. Granma must have left this way, I thought, not so abundantly or she wouldn't have had to leave in the first place, but with some of these valuables.

Zia Isabella's neighbor came out onto the street with a strong purposeful stride and walked hurriedly toward me, carrying at gut level, a giant thick round of *focaccia.* I remember her smile. I remember her warm dough, her warm eyes, and strong hug. I remember her eyes and her hands as she brought it toward me. Neighbors waved at me from three levels, on the street, on the balconies, and up on the rooftops. Preciosa Abbondanza, in her mid-nineties, stood at her doorway of lace, meekly pushing it aside, waving me inside, offering me hard candy for my journey.

Thirty-six hands, like a flock of birds on the train platform—the wind from their hands sent my train on its way. One cousin I couldn't find to say goodbye to, my handsome cousin Tonino who I had jogged with on the outskirts of town, on the one road that led from *Acquaviva delle Fonti* to *Cassano delle Murge.* When he heard I left, he raced to Bari to catch me. I was already on the train. I heard his yell and saw him on the platform. The train slowly pulled away. He ran and waved with his whole arm. Waved and waved and waved goodbye as the train backed out of the station. I hung my head and arm out the window. I felt the force of his arm as it waved. Tonino was about to go off into the military. I was starting grad school. We knew we were saying goodbye for the bulk of our lifetime, the way our grandfathers, who were brothers, did, eighty years before. He waved with all his might, as did I, as the train pulled away.

Vrrooooom!

NEW YORK CITY, 1987

My mother and Jade threw me a cure party at the Essex Hotel on Central Park South where our friend Kass was the concierge. That night I found out that one of my cousins was gay. On my father's side I have twenty-eight first cousins. Three of us, all around the same age, are gay. I knew about Lucia. We recognized each other's dyke jock friends immediately and even hung out a bit. But Nico I wasn't sure about. I remember that night at the party asking my friend Ira, "Do you think my cousin Nico is gay?" and Ira said, "Does Jimmy Carter have teeth?" I stayed with Jade a couple of months after that. I thought we'd be together forever, but we ended in a particularly explosive break-up in the Bellevue Psych ER when I found out that she and Ant'ny had had an affair back when we were painting his apartment. I went ballistic. There were six cops at the bottleneck doorway of the emergency room. I grabbed one of their guns and got locked up for the weekend and kept under observation, which is the best place, as a writer, to observe others. I saw something there that night that stamped itself on my brain as the wildest human behavior I'd ever seen. Amidst the ER chaos of genitalia hanging out of those flimsy hospital gowns and patients and inmates diving for baloney sandwiches and milk cartons when they came out, there was one guy who was handcuffed to a wheelchair. After his rage built to an untenable pitch, he stood up and spun the wheelchair over his head in circles, rodeo style. It took five cops and a needle of Thorazine to subdue him.

It was the 80's. A.I.D.S. was rampant. Sloan-Kettering had more young gay people than I'd ever seen before. Emergency rooms were filled with young gay couples and teams of friends. It was a striking new demographic from just five years before. I was twenty-three, heartbroken, and on top of that filled with survivor's guilt. I buried so many of my friends to cancer and I thought about them every single day. I was particularly pissed off that so many young people with H.I.V. and A.I.D.S. were not getting the medicines they needed. I went to the only place I could have gone in that condition and state of mind. Downtown.

I joined ACT-UP, the AIDS Coalition to Unleash Power. Meetings were held on Monday nights at the Center on Thirteenth Street (now The Lesbian, Gay, Bisexual, and Transgender Community Center). I marched, went to meetings, met girls. We stopped traffic for our marches by kissing in the intersections. A bunch of us would run ahead and kiss in pairs along the middle of the street to block the crosstown flow of cars. The queer kiss to stop traffic was powerful. I needed a dyke signifier. A leather jacket was a way to begin. I walked down Orchard Street, where merchants stood at the edges of their shops calling to me, "Lady! Lady!" They held up leather jackets with epaulets and waistbands. I got the hell out of there. That was the opposite of what I wanted. I walked north to Saint Mark's Place. I didn't see the jacket for me. I stepped off the curb at Third Avenue to cross, and there, in the middle of the crosswalk, was a guy holding open a brand-new black leather motorcycle jacket with thick silver zippers. He stood off to the side like a matador luring a bull. The jacket was classic, simple, old school, Brando. I slipped my right arm into it, turned, and my left arm went up and in. This jacket, right there in the middle of Third Avenue, was mine. Test ride it: the zipper came up with the heavy-duty roar. I gave him all the cash in my pocket less five bucks to take the train home. In this new skin, I felt protected. Now all I needed was a motorcycle. I called my trusted softball coach from high school, Cal. His family had sold old cars in Astoria since the horse and wagon days of New York. Cal took me out there and I found my motorcycle, an old Honda 500 with a black tank and lots of chrome. Butch. No frills. I walked into the Queens Harley dealer to pick up a couple of helmets.

"You got a hundred dollar head or a two hundred dollar head?"

I learned to ride in one shot by getting the bike home from Queens to Yonkers. As the bike shivered beneath me on the grating of the Triborough Bridge, I held on tight. Cal drove in front of me and paid my toll. This was as good as flying a Cessna.

Walking into the Clit Club with two motorcycle helmets was a guaranteed pick-up. Some femme always wanted a ride. I was scared walking into that club. A few Friday nights I had my friend Mark meet me on the outside and literally push me across the threshold. I never appeared scared. I wore my silver snake chain around my chest like a round of ammunition. I rode my motorcycle up on the cobblestones of West Fourteenth Street in the meatpacking district where asphalt didn't cover the cobblestones of the old city streets. The bumpy ride mirrored my nerves. I locked my back wheel with the silver snake and stepped into the club. Then there was the moment of dyke recognition. Julie Tolentino and Lola Flash, in my memory, sitting at the door whenever I entered, were the vanguard. They set the fashion and tone for what it was to be a dyke and A.I.D.S. activist in New York City in the '80s. Walking into the Clit Club, there was a moment at the door that was as quick as blowing out a birthday candle. I handed over a fi' dollar bill, and Julie and Lola smiled me a hello. That was it. I was inside, wind in my sails and set on course to be free, to be myself. I set my own heading, and charted my own bearings. Girls danced on platforms in nets and cages. I checked my leather jacket downstairs but kept my helmets and knapsack with me. My freshest manuscript was always in my knapsack so I never let it out of my sight. I drank a cold beer and watched the dance floor. At some point I had to dance. Getting onto the dance floor was a prerequisite to sex. I didn't know how to dance. I knew how to box a speedbag so I threw soft punches into the air to the beat and backed my body onto the dance floor. Soon I'd find a hot body next to me riding the same rhythms. I'd focus my dance energy on one woman, see if anything was there, perhaps she'd focus her hips on me, perhaps not. This was the dance. One night I gave a ride home to an NYU student. The way she danced at the club made her look older than she later seemed, with her awkward moves in her loft bed of the condo her father bought her on Lafayette Street. I remember two things about that night. One, she had her period, and I impressed her when I rip-corded her tampon out by yanking the string with my teeth, and with how candidly I asked her if she'd been tested for HIV. Most impressive to me were her empty bookshelves. Her father had bought her bookshelves for college, more than what she needed for her scattered texts. That was Heaven to me, like open fields, to have enough space for all my books and notebooks, to not be crowded, to be able to grow intellectually. Someday, I thought, I'm gonna have plenty of bookshelves.

"Cosa Mangia Oggi!"

NEW YORK CITY, 1989

Rich girls loved my crooked teeth and thick as polenta Bronx accent. My cunt was an eggplant parmigiana hero in their mouths, fried light, luscious mozzarella, and tart tomato on bread soaked with all life's vital juices. Eggplant parmigiana is the most delicious thing you will ever put your mouth around. You melt around it as it melts inside you. One night at a party of Brown alums, I picked up a straight girl studying to be a social worker. I drove her down to the piers in my convertible and parked at the edge of the water. We made out to that old Earth, Wind & Fire cassette: "Shining Star" and "September" and "Reasons." Nothing beat parking by the river in an old American car with good springs, making love to a straight girl across an upholstered bench seat.

The frayed edges of the city marked the start of our journeys. The Christopher Street piers were a gay sanctuary. Strut the pier. Breathe the sunset. Flex your muscles in the wind next to the mighty river wave. Let it take you. Quiet, Gays Mating.

New York City ended in broken hunks of concrete that dipped down into the waves made in the wakes of speedboats. We all, at one time or another, sat on the broken and crumbled concrete edge, and touched water.

I taught poetry in Brooklyn and Harlem for an outreach program of the New York City Ballet. My students' poems started with descriptions of princesses spinning, then turned sharply to broken brick skies, crack vials with colorful caps in stench-filled hallways, the yellowed eyeballs of A.I.D.S. monsters. One little girl wrote of getting beaten by a belt that felt "like an apartment building falling on top of you." I tried to forget that line, but decades later it is still a hangnail in the back-left side of my brain. I twitch when I think about it, but can't shake it off.

Between classes, I stopped downtown for lunch. Downtown, amid the denizens of Bohemia, I always felt safe. My first trip to the Village was when I was seven and Rosemarie was twenty. Peter and Roe each held one of my hands, and gave me my first gift of night with all its possibilities, as we looked into frosted shop windows opening into glittering dioramas. When I was sixteen, a pack of us sought out Bleecker Bob's to look for punk accoutrements. We raided our mother's cabinets for safety pins, ripped our shirts and pinned them back together.

I got out of the F train on Second Avenue. Hungry, I was. In search of an honorable lunch. Where O where can an Italian girl find a lunch in the city she can admit to her ancestors? Houston Street was my home plate on the grid from where I could pivot in any direction, north for falafel or borscht, south for mozzarella and chicken cutlet on focaccia, east for knish, west for over a hundred soups at Shopsin's on Bedford. If all else failed, I could get another bowl of hot borscht at Veselka; Ukrainian for rainbow, on Second Avenue and Ninth Street, the blessed corner that I bet has fed more artists more soup than any corner in the world. And you always met the best people to talk to there, avant-garde souls who just stepped out of a time and land all their own. Carlos for example, sat there for over a dozen years that I can remember, always at the front table whether it was two a.m. or two p.m., making his sterling silver creations on his black hat which got heavier year by year. Gritty attitude I was promised in any direction, but nowhere could I get what I was really looking for, GranmaRose's roadside *cicorria*, boiled with hunks of garlic in an aluminum pot, so that all I had to do was breathe in the steam from the food, not even eat it, to be healed. To swallow her hot green broth with the little rocks at the bottom of the pot was the cure for ills I didn't even know I had. I was hungry for the old New York described by my mother: "The boys would start a fire in the lot, we'd each steal a potato and get a stick, and we'd be there for hours." My mother's days of the "Hot Mickey" were long gone by the time I walked the streets of the Lower East Side. One thing remained the same: ancestral accountability. Everything that passed my lips, entered my gut, and became my soul had to pass GranmaRose's daily unforgiving: *"Eh COsa MANgia eeOGGE!"* *Thing you eat today! What d'you eat today!* Worded in the imperative, *il imperativo*, the conjugation of orders, a whole verb tense for issuing commands, the only tense in which GranmaRose spoke. I had to answer. Did I feed sweet tooth or soul? My friends' families asked them: Where you been? Who with? What d'you do? D'you finish all your homework? All GranmaRose, ever wanted to know was what I ate and if I made any money. *Cosa mangia oggi!*

Broccoli rabe sauté—$4.95, an endless procession of Italian bread with a good crust brought to the table, *zuppa di lenticchie, past'n'fazool, 'scharole*; La Focacceria on First Avenue, just below Saint Mark's Place, had many of the foods of my youth in syllabic lingo I understood and prices that didn't give a young artist *agida*. I walked into the restaurant and got smacked in the face by the indifferent deadpan stares from the men who worked there. Two walls of white board scrawled with names and prices of foods in black marker served as a giant contract for the hunger of who I was, the hunger of my soul to be connected with family and with *Italia*. In this regard, I was famished. Sign right here. Buy a piece of your own soul. Cash only. I stared at the giant menu vacantly, as if it was skywriting. *Vesteddi* stood out at a buck ninety-five but I didn't know what the hell it was. Sides of vegetables were $2.95; perfect. A side of *macheroni*—only a buck extra with an entrée. A lanky guy in a crisp white apron up to his neck shuffled back and forth between the kitchen, the tables, and the front door, barely lifting his feet off the floor, like a penitent. *Braciole*, rice balls, *mozzarella in corozza*, mussels *marinara*; I will have to bring my mother here. She loves a heaping plate of mussels over linguini to remember her mother Rose pulling mussels off the rocks at Golden Beach in Throggs Neck. Fish was above my price range. Veal I didn't even consider. No meatballs matched my mother's, so what's the use. Lentils are always good. A glass of house red wine—$3.50, excellent. Me and the penitent sized each other up with quick darting eyes and instant disdain. I put up with my discomfort, all for some hole inside me that only bitter greens in quick hot *aglio'olio* could fill, and that is exactly what *La Focacceria* sold, gustatory soul spackle.

"What's *vesteddi*?" I hollered, overlooking a tray of stuffed artichokes.

"Spleen," the Penitent answered from the back.

"Spleen," I muttered to myself. Hell, I didn't grow up eating spleen, I don't even have a spleen, what am I gonna eat spleen for? If I ate it, could it give me something I was lacking? Could I grow one back? In my medical chart, one line out of a thousand pages sticks with me: "It was passed off the table." My spleen, "with a smooth, grayish purple capsule, a small amount of normal hilar fat, and a homogenously dark maroon parenchyma." Ah, *fagetit*, I ain't eatin' that. I'm not Italian Italian like my grandmother Italian. I never boiled a goat's head. I never saw eels in my bathtub, never spread bone marrow on toast, or marinated a head of any kind. Never saw the goat's eyes cry. Never saw goats' eyes. Never saw goats. Never saw boiling eyes cry. My Bronx was the flat earth, paved by my concrete thoughts. I pirate myself. I play myself. I chop the ends offa words. Back the fhuck off! If you come too close to me I'll put a scapular around your neck. My hands filled with blood do all the talking.

A short older man with a penguin strut attended the cash register. This clearly was the boss, who had a virtuosic vacancy of expression. "*Pigghia pi fess'*," my mother would say—smart enough to act stupid. A cut-out serving window showed two Mexican men with bandanas on their heads sweating over the cooking fire. The boss had freshly scrubbed hands, short gray hair combed back neatly; a look in his eye that told me he had no interest in conversation with me. No music. No coffee. The message was clear: you could eat here but you had to digest somewhere else. These Sicilians knew they were doing me a favor by letting me eat there; you couldn't get this stuff anywhere in those days. The boss would soon retire to Florida, his quick short step and a sturdy one-finger punch on the cash register told me he didn't need my five-dollar lunches. The Penitent stood outside the glass doors blowing smoke slowly out onto First Avenue, and added quarters to a meter where a pink Cadillac was parked. The color reminded me of the glossy inside of a clam. Definitely the boss's car. The Penitent had to be the boss's son-in-law, I thought, who he wanted to keep productive, and keep an eye on. The boss was probably doing his daughter a favor. I pictured the woman who had brought these two men together. She looked just like the father but with hair. She walked like her father, swift and stout with a slight swivel as she made her way forward.

I concentrated on the smell of garlic sautéing in olive oil. This is what I came for. If I could close my eyes, eat, and breathe, and have no conversation, I'd be fine, if I could behave and blend in. I sat down at an empty table in the middle of the room with my back to the street, pleased to find the table level. My father had me place a level on everything in our house to keep it all straight. The Penitent was cutting open stems of broccoli rabe at a table in the back. He got up, cut a fresh Italian bread and brought it to my table in a basket with inch squares of butter wrapped in cold gold foil. I opened one, rubbed it on the inside of a piece of bread and stuck it in my mouth, butter down tongue side. Out of the corner of my mouth I said, "Gimme a bowl of lentils and a side of 'scarole." Four mob-esque customers sat at two tables pushed together in the back near the restrooms, two women with bleached blonde hair teased high into sweet cotton candy, with their thick-fingered gold-ornamented men who orchestrated the meal. Their eyes sized me up in a quick character summary. New York Italians are masters at making vigilant and immediate studies of our surroundings. I don't like getting sized up by thick-fingered men, but I respect how quickly it's done. We allow each other quick introductory glances, a quick casing of the joint, for mutual protection, and to satisfy our survival instincts. I gave off a few tell-tale signs of a working-class butch, lesbian, artist, teacher, hair shaved up my neck, sneakers always sneakers in case I had to run, oaktag sticking out of my thick leather shoulder bag that looked like something a postman of a century ago would carry while riding a horse. I was in the habit of carrying oaktag, so I would get pegged as a teacher. I felt safer on the subway being identified as a teacher; too often I was perceived as an undercover cop, pushers would leave the corner phone booths whenever I walked by.

"Ay, why's the 'rabe two bucks more than 'scharole, huh?" Maybe it was the way I said *Ay*, rather than the content of my question. The Penitent looked down over my glass of water and basket of bread. He dished me the fact slowly, as if he were reciting the number of soldiers killed in combat that day: "It's a labor-intensive vegetable."

I stuck a hunk of soft bread in my mouth—*il centro del pane piena di aria*—the center of bread filled with air. With just a crust in my mouth, I can still talk and chew on the side, but with a hunk of white inner bread filling the roof and tongue, I can't talk at all, and don't. I've learned to choose when to shut up instead of mouthing off, especially to men. I stuck another piece of soft bread in my mouth; at *La Focacceria* I could finally eat and talk with GranmaRose about it afterward. I wasn't gonna blow it. I already wanted to come back for the dollar side of *maccheroni*. I wanted to eat everything written on the wall. I breathed through my nose and kept chewing. I kneaded my words and spit into the dough so the words wouldn't come flying out of my mouth. The Penitent walked to the back table nearest the kitchen and picked up his short knife. I swallowed, thinking of GranmaRose cutting crosses in the bottom of each broccoli rabe stem with her shoemaker's knife. The Penitent sat to snap tails off a heap of string beans. The thick-fingered men's eyes turned from me to the oncoming plates of a mound of mussels, linguini and veal, brought by two-good looking Mexican brothers, the elder nodding directions to the other. My heart beat hard. The Penitent sat mute at the back table, then after a while got up and filled my amber water glass and cut me another whole loaf of Italian bread.

Eat. Shut up. Get up. Pay the man. Get out. That's what I told myself. Focus on the steamy greens and how proud I would be to tell GranmaRose what I ate today.

The handsome Mexican brother-waiters had obviously been trained by the boss over the years to treat his customers with New York Italianate mannerisms. "Sweetheart" and "Hon" they called me, sharp pencil stubs tucked behind their ears, black hair parted on the sides and slicked back and down. They wore starched white shirts, black pants and shoes that held a shine. I started to feel nervous in there. I breathed in the steam of my hot greens, ate the stalks to suck the energy right up from the earth, lifted the plate up to my mouth and slurped the juices, shaking my head with gratitude. I could stay alive if I could eat like this in the city. I could live a useful life.

I ate efficiently and stood up to wait for the boss who took my cash. Now I could call my grandmother. There was a phone booth on the corner outside *La Focacceria* just for this purpose: to report everything you ate. I imagined GranmaRose sitting alone in the dark.

GranmaRose lived in an apartment that faced an interior courtyard full of echoes and kids playing with blue Hi-Bounce balls. Granma had amassed a collection of Hi-Bounce, the faux Spaldeens that had come in through her windows. She sat in her dark apartment. Granma lived in the dark with beings, curtain beings, fire escape beings, lampshade shapely beings, gas flame rings on the stove beings, squeaky floor beings, heat knocks in the pipe beings, beings in thick coats of paint that clogged the sockets on the walls, beings in the couch that exhaled when she lifted her body off it. There were beings living in the dark. The more hours I experienced there in her apartment, the more I dreaded the light of day, where ordinary objects came back into focus and the world turned inanimate again. "Hey, where'd everybody go?"

I dropped two quarters into the payphone and punched TA 2-7487 onto the keypad. TA was for Talmadge, her Bronx phone exchange. I thought over GranmaRose's and my family's codes for eating.

(1) Never pay for garlic or parsley. Some things in life you should not pay for.

(2) Breakfast is to coat the stomach.

(3) Lunch is to clean the blood.

(4) Eat 'til you sweat.

(5) Carry food wherever you go. The law of "Rachele's Pocketbook Frittata."

(6) Cook in crisis.

(7) Let water run. Water is meant to run.

(8) There's a *sistemazione*, an order in which things can be eaten, and a *sfragganizze*, peasant wisdom saying, for each.

(9) If you were born in America, you must learn how to eat.

(10) Hunger beats *agida*.

(11) Being overweight is God's way of protecting you in case you get sick.

(12) Focaccia is cut with fabric scissors, never with a knife.

(13) Cook. You don't have to know who for.

(14) Visiting each other's homes is akin to food shopping. Don't arrive empty handed. Don't leave empty handed.

(15) Savor the end of the meal. Perform *a'schapett*.

(16) Be open to new foods and spices.

(17) No matter how you fight with your family, return to the table for the lasagna at least once a year; it is the family glue that keeps you together.

I braced myself, as the phone rang in her apartment, happy and relieved when she answered.

"Hello."

"Hi Granma, it's Annie."

"Annie!" she replied, with an elongated *e*, then came the reinforcement of the Italian greeting with the southern Italian Bronx lilt: "*GOOma sta?*"

"*BEHnay*," I sang proudly from the time I was two, "*BEHnay!*"

"*Brrrava*," she would say.

And I would repeat her inquiry, "*GOOma sta?*"

"*Menza menz.* No complain, honey. I'm acooking stringabeans and lambachop." Then came the zing: "*Cosa mangia oggi!*" Boom. Never in English. Foods we confessed in Italian.

"*Scarol'agli'olio!*"

"*Brrrava! Brrrava!* Smarta gherl." Escarole aced her test every time.

"*Un poco di vino.*"

"That's okay."

"I'm thinking of when I could get up to see you."

"That's okay, Honey. Stay where you are, make-a da money."

"Make the money? But I want to visit you Granma!"

"*Ehhh! Back ena forth, back ena forth. Stai tranquillo. Make-a da money.*"
Boom. She hangs up.

My Mother's Aorta

YONKERS, 1992

"**H**ey Ma, I'm home." I kicked off my sneakers and rolled down my pant leg that I had cuffed so it wouldn't get caught in my bicycle chain. The chain made a grease print on my ankle. I was staying with my mother for a couple of days. I'd just gotten home from a softball game, just ahead of the rain. I had the best arm on the team. I wore cut-off sleeves. My throwing arm was the strongest part of my body. I threw my glove down. I heard paper, tape, and scissors going in the other room. My mother had the louver door shut. Here she worked on her feet all day at the beauty parlor and now she was wrapping presents for my birthday. That's how my mother loves. We planned to have dinner together, then I was going downtown to a gay club to meet my cousin Nico.

My mother walks out of the bedroom with a big box behind her back. She can't keep her eyes from sparkling. She stands in front of me smiling. She hands me the box. I rip it open. It's a pink short set.

I yell, "Pink?"

"It's not pink."

"What do you mean it's not pink."

"It's shrimp."

"Shrimp? It's pink." I pulled out the shoulder pads. Shoulder pads enrage me. "You don't know me, you don't understand. You're a sexist." She's pushing for me to dress as a girl even now when I'm an adamant twenty-nine year old butch. I toss the box aside and go into the kitchen for a glass of water.

"It's one hundred percent cotton," she says. "What's the difference between this and your orange shirt?"

I sat down on the milk pail behind her. She threw *rigatoni* into the boiling water and began to stir with her long wooden spoon. There was a pounding on the door like an elephant hoof. That could only be one of my brothers. No one else bangs at the door like that. Instinctively my mother rips open a second bag of *rigatoni*, for whoever it was will surely stay and eat. In that moment, *rigatoni* midair, the door opened and my brother Ant'ny walked in. He carried suits in dry-cleaning plastic over his back, his two thick forefingers in the crook of a hanger over his shoulder. A girl was with him. "Hi Ma. I just came up to get my pinkie rings. You still got them in the teacup on top of the fridge, right? I got an audition for De Niro tomorrow. This is my friend. She's a dress designer for Michael Jackson."

"Annie!" My mother calls my name and falls back into my arms. The sound of my own name terrified me, the way she yanked my name like a rope when she fell. As she fell, my name losing ground for her. My name, not enough to hold onto. She called it like a question. Like confusion. And a strange calm panic. I was right behind her. I felt placed. Like a chess piece. A pawn. She was soaking wet. She wilted into my arms. Her arms had no power, no movement, they just hung there.

"Breathe Mom, breathe." I expanded my chest to support her.

"I'm okay," she said. "I just need to lay down on the sofa."

Ant'ny pulled the telephone on the wall. "Heart," he said, "my Mother doesn't go down like that. My mother doesn't go down."

The EMT's came in nine minutes. One of the EMTs was a kid I went to high school with. I hoped I was good to him; my mother's life was in his hands.

At the ER of Lawrence Hospital, a doctor came out and said, "This is definitely not a heart attack. Whatever it is, this hospital cannot handle it. She has to go elsewhere. I'll give you three minutes to decide."

Elsewhere. Elsewhere. I stroked her hand and cried.

The doctor tells me I am acting weird. He addresses Ant'ny for the decision.

"My mother would prefer to die back in the Bronx, where she was born," he says decisively. Michael Jackson's dress designer is trying to figure out the Metro North schedule back to Manhattan.

"Valhalla," the ER doctor recommends, "There is a Dr. Fleisher there. He is a surgeon."

To Valhalla! I ride in the ambulance. Ant'ny drives behind. So, is this how it ends then? Red lights flashing over the familiar terrain? Trees black at night. The signs on the side of the highway alighting: Central Avenue, Tuckahoe Road, Jackson Avenue.

In Valhalla, Dr. Fleisher arrives in a baseball cap. Ant'ny looked him up and down and mouths to me, "He looks like some kid on a corner."

CarKey arrives.

Westchester Medical Center was under renovation. After Dr. Fleisher examined her and looked at the films, he stood with my brothers and I in a hallway full of cardboard boxes. He took a pencil and drew two arcs on the side of a box. "She has an ascending arch aortic dissection. This is the aorta. This is the heart. Here is where the split occurred, close to the heart. The blood has formed a tunnel in the wall of the aorta."

"What are her chances without the surgery?"

"Zero."

"What are her chances with the surgery?"

"Fifty-fifty."

Fifty-fifty. Fifty-fifty echoes in my mind. I don't look at my two brothers. We all nod in unison: "Do it."

A nurse hands me my mother's gold jewelry, panties, and false teeth.

Dr. Fleisher wheels her past us, toward the OR. Her eyes emanate blue light and love like the hottest point of candle flames. She says, "I hope I hold up for you, Doc."

I write her a note. I hold it to her face. Her eyes pass across it.

CarKey grunts, "Take the note away." I want my words with her. He goes outside in the parking lot to sleep in his Lincoln Continental. Ant'ny asks me if I want anything. He buys hot dogs from the silver truck outside the ER, and brings me back one. We sit and watch this other family whose father is dying. The mother looks like she'd been dropped from a great height into the chair. She slumps back, the chair holds the full weight of her head. She has loquacious daughters. Two are dressed pretty, with well-brushed black hair, legs crossed ladylike, the way GranmaRose always wants me to sit, and the third with gold holy medals dipping into her cleavage and big brown wild eyes that look like she could make love to you one minute and murder you the next. She strangles a black purse in her lap, the strap double-wrapped around her wrist. One of their husbands arrives with a tray of teas and cookies.

"I was gonna cure my meat, but I thought, why cure it if you can freeze it?"

"Why'd you take the lid off my coffee?"

"Why don't you just sit down?"

"Vito, you know I hate it when you crumble the cookies."

"You put lemon in my tea?"

"That must be mine."

"Here take it out. I didn't even squeeze it."

"Why don't you just sit down?"

"You know what? I love Cajun food. I ate a lot of it when I was down south. Once I knew what it was."

"Let me tell you, the crock-pot is fantastic; before you go to bed, put the meat in the crock-pot with potatoes and carrots and onions and you're done. Eight hours later it's all ready."

Dr. Fleisher came out of the operating room and I saw my mother's blood on his paper shoes. He nodded at us: "We still got a long way to go."

I kneeled with my forehead on the floor of the waiting room, chanting, "Live Mom, Live Mom, Live Mom Live." I wanted my voice to have the power of my throwing arm. I didn't know where to go or what to do. I felt crazed. I stopped a priest in the hallway I said, "Father, I need a word. I need to practice the Lazarus call. You know. Walk. Walk. Rise. I want to pull her back. Call her name."

He pet my head and told me where the hospital chapel was. I walked down and around hallway after hallway. The door was open but heavy to pull. I pulled with two hands. The chapel felt immense. The space inside. The silence. I closed the door behind me, shutting out the din of the hallway. The altar was in darkness. I chanted, "Mom Mom Mom heart beat like a drum Mommmmm. Live Mom live Mom live Mom live. Mom you Mom Mom, Mom Mom Mommmm." The birthday candles, her eyes, she was hiding a terrible surprise. All I could think of doing was throwing a chair through the stained glass window. Something's gotta break. Walls aren't walls. Walls are tunnels. From the moment I was born I mourned the day I would lose her. It's not possible that I will never see her again, face to face. *Non è posso che mai piu ci vedremo faccia a faccia.*

I hadn't slept in three days I telephone Uncle Frank.

"Whaddya need?"

"Sleep."

He drives down and sits next to me under a tree on the hospital campus.

"See that bend in the tree? That must have been a tough winter. You can tell the life a tree had by its shape. Look at that wire that one grew right around."

I lay down and closed my eyes. The bike chain grease still circles my ankle.

Three days later, the pasta is still on the stove and I cannot not bring myself to straighten out her shoes. They are as she left them, one on top of the other as if trying to climb out. Her gold earring, on the floor. The clearing where the table was pushed back to make room for the stretcher. The rug folding over itself. Empty dishes in place waiting. Every object with the trace of her touch. These objects have taken years to find their places and now, silence. From the candy dish, silence. I can't touch anything. The objects are a map of her presence, how she turned over the parts of the aluminum coffeepot in the draining board, how she hung up her shirts to dry over the tub, how she folded napkins into neat and purposeful triangles.

My mother had an open chest wound the size and heft of a banana along her sternum. I had to keep it open for the pus to drain, and twice a day, I had to rinse the blood, dab it clean, pour sterile water over it, and gauze it up again. She never even saw her wound. I'd look at the wound and she'd look at me. My face was the mirror of her wound. She would judge by my expression how it looked, so I had to believe it was healing. Beneath all the blood and pus and open tissue I had to see—healing.

I was convinced that she would make it back home. I threw out the *rigatoni* on the stove. Once I touched one thing, I had to change everything. I redid her whole apartment. I polished the floor where she fell. I spackled, I painted, I hammered. I got her neighbor, George, to help me do the heavy lifting. Light blue cabinets. Wallpaper in the bathroom. Ceiling fans, white, thirty-five inches. One gallon of "Balmy Day" Pittsburgh Paint. Blue Onion cabinets. Shelf, eleven and a half inches. Get brackets. Hang plants.

My mother's neighbors around the courtyard saved me during this period. Al drove me to the hospital, and talked with me. Diane across the way gave me spiritual support and rides to the hospital. "Your mother is already healed," she told me. George in the corner building helped me paint. At night I visited two elderly shut-ins, Erica upstairs, and Amelia around the corner. Erica drank and smoked, and doted on me, bringing me sandwiches and shots of whiskey. Amelia came with me to pick out a La-Z-Boy rocker recliner for my mother's return. My mother couldn't sit up on her own.

Aunt Patty told me I was being ridiculous. "It's so much money and you don't even know if your mother will ever come home."

I stopped talking to her.

Ant'ny was clean and sober but smoked cigarettes in his car and talked incessantly, so I couldn't ride with him without feeling trapped and getting sick. Rosemarie lived hours away. I was on my own.

I stopped talking to CarKey after a comment he made in the Intensive Care Unit. ICU visiting time was brief. I tried to heal my mother in any way I could, efficiently. I brought peppermint oil and a special healing brew of immune boosting tea I'd concocted. I drew a label on the bottle, "Rachel's Super Healing Tea." Two visitors were allowed in at a time. A bunch of us were in the waiting room: CarKey, Enza, Ant'ny, Al and me. When they unlock the doors to ICU, me and CarKey go in first. He was the oldest and I was the primary caregiver, the only one who did healing work instead of "visiting." The others stood around and asked questions. I gave our mother sips of tea and administered peppermint oil onto her feet.

CarKey stood against the wall with his arms folded. "You *skeeve* me," he said.

He knew just how to say it so only I would hear him. I could tell that my brother saw everything I did as a lesbian act. I'd had enough. I was done with my family. They were of no use to me. I hired a private nurse named Bobby. Bobby saved me. I didn't listen to the protests. Everyone had a problem. Aunt Patty insisted, "Your mother don't need a private nurse. It's too expensive. How could you hire a male nurse? How could you hire an Indian?" Bobby and I each did twelve-hour shifts. Finally, I could get some sleep. Only I wiped my mother's chest wound. Only I knew the effort healing took. Bobby was phenomenal. We split the day and night, and he lent me his car so I could go sleep. Finally, I had a way back and forth to the hospital, and I could force myself to rest, knowing she had everything she needed.

Al visited her in the hospital all the time, and coached her with these words, "*Fa na caca, e get outta here*." Take a good crap and leave. Al spoke the truth. My mother had to get out of there. I believed she'd make it home, even when the surgeons talked about staph infections, and reopening her chest up. At home, I dusted off her ceramic angels. I hung her coleus plants at different heights. Put a stone angel in the garden. This kitchen. This is where she fell. One gallon of white semigloss. Three roller pads. She will live past this moment. Another set of coordinates will claim her. This is the spot where she stood and washed dishes for twenty years, never knowing death would come right here to try to kidnap her. I found a cross of Holy Palm under her mattress over a photograph of Frank Sinatra, and old papers in the blue suitcase under the bed. All our kindergarten diplomas. The 1969 newspaper from when the men landed on the moon.

My friend German Pete was over the apartment to support me while my Mom was in the hospital. I told German Pete how upset I was over how my brother treated me in the hospital. My body buzzed with hostility over CarKey's homophobia. Swirls of heat took root in my gut. I picked up the telephone and called CarKey. He answered. I looked at German Pete as I told my brother off for being so rancid and homophobic in the hospital toward me. I breathed hard and fast. I could have destroyed something. We got into a tense conversation. He hated me, I could feel it. He hated who I became. Cancer saved me from becoming a Republican hard-ass money-maker prosecutor with a big bank book, someone CarKey would have respected. Cancer ripped me open, destroyed my factual recall, stripped me of surface accoutrements and with it, altered the course of my life irrevocably.

CarKey was free to be gruff. Everyone tiptoed around his disrespectful behavior because of—the war, the war, the war. But it was more than that. He was the firstborn son, a prince in that regard. He was tall, handsome, charming, had an alpha quality everyone bowed down to. I had more empathy for him being a Marine than anybody. I knew how the war destroyed my father, and I could see that it destroyed CarKey. He became a *miseratz*. I was sick of it. He could tiptoe around me, for once. As a lesbian, I have my own frontline. I've been spit at, cursed at, disrespected, even had rocks thrown at me. Our mother lay there in the hospital half-dead. Who knew if she'd ever come home? I detonated. I knew what would trigger him most of all. I was done. In that moment I remembered the time I was seven when his chokeholds made me lose my breath in terror, and I reached up into the freezer and grabbed a can of frozen orange juice and slugged him in the jaw. This time I slugged him with a homoerotic comment. I called him a cocksucker. I let the words fly out of my mouth. It felt liberating. Then he said in the most simple, clear, direct language four words that sent me fleeing for safety: "I'm gonna kill you." He hung up the phone.

I said to German Pete. "We gotta get outta here. My brother's coming over here to kill me."

"When?" he said. He wasn't Italian. An Italian wouldn't ask this.

"Right now. Let's go."

"Where to?"

"I don't know. I'm not kiddin', let's go."

"Is he serious?"

I grabbed my asthma inhaler and some money and ran out of the house. I had exploded, and it felt great. What a release! My gasket finally blew.

The family mute had finally spoken. We ran down the hill. I ducked on the floorboards of the backseat of German Pete's car as we sped up the hill.

Downtown.

I grabbed the outside brick wall of the Gay and Lesbian Center on 13th Street and held onto the hull of that building like the life raft it was to me.

After six long weeks, I got my mother home.

A cigar-smoking lung surgeon told us, "We want to do a bronchoscopy on her."

"No," I said, "Enough's enough. She's not strong enough, she just got out of heart surgery."

"There are spots on the lungs. We don't know what they are."

"She's a smoker," I said. "Gimme six weeks."

We had to clear her lungs. I fed her infusions of nettle tea, hung her head over eucalyptus steam, and taught her to sing Puccini arias. We listened to Kiri te Kanawa sing *"O Mio Babbino Caro"* ("Oh Dear Papa"), which my mother sang as *"O Mia Bambina Cara"* ("Oh My Dear Little Baby"). Pavarotti's rendition of *"Nessun Dorma"* ("No One Sleeps") was useful, so by the time we sang the last words of the aria: *"Vincero! Vincero! Vincero!"* she hacked up knots of thick phlegm and the atelectasis of her alveoli began to unglue. Clearing my mother's lungs was not something that could be done in English. We needed the raw life-and-death drama of Puccini arias, blessed words that end in vowels. To open up her lungs, we needed Italian.

I wheeled her out to my old baseball field on Central Avenue, where I'd hit so many line drives up the middle over the years. She had come to every game. My father never came to one. I wheeled her out onto center field and I ran the bases.

"Cheer for me, Mom."

"Go, Annie, go!" She yelled and the blessed phlegm came up.

And that's how my mother escaped lung surgery. She spit and coughed and yelled on the outfield. A woman's gotta open her lungs.

We got home, and I helped her into the bath. I sat on the toilet, and we talked. Her scar was healing. Both our bodies were filled with scars. We were Raggedy Anns. She opened up, and finally I heard her full story.

"The neighbor saw me and thought it was a doll tumbling out the window. I credit my parents for being forward thinking enough to have the good leg operated on to slow its growth. This way my legs are the same size. They brought me to a private doctor. The appointment was fifty cents. I thought like what kind of money my father had to pay to take care of me? Do you know what fifty cents was in those days? Who even saw a fifty-cent piece? After his consultation they took me to Bellevue. That's where the first surgery was, they operated on the damaged leg. The second surgery, they operated on both legs, was at Orthopedic Hospital, I think it was Fifty-Ninth Street. The first one I wasn't in school yet. The second I was in third grade. Second or third grade. They asked my father the height of everyone, they tried to estimate how tall I would be, they kept measuring and measuring. They tried to slow the growth of the good leg, and increased the growth of the damaged leg. I think there was three quarters of an inch difference between the legs. I remember they left me in a room all by myself on a table waiting for the doctor. God forbid they let your parents in with you. No, you had to be all alone up on the table. The train kept coming by the window. I felt like the whole world could see me. I felt so alone. After the surgery and therapy, I remember feeling so guilty walking out of the hospital, holding Papa's hand, leaving the other children behind. There was a lot of kids. Crippled. I don't remember faces. I saw kids that couldn't walk. None of us could walk. My father would bring me to Orchard Beach and bury my legs in the sand. And he'd carry me into the salt water, and let the ocean beat against them. It was curative. Little by little, I learned to walk again. They wanted other doctors to see my legs to prove the surgery worked. Every year I went in front of doctors, with nothing on. They had to see my legs. I did that until I was eighteen. Then I'd had enough. I learned to dance. I could never roller skate or do anything. The once or twice I went to the roller rink I knocked everybody down. I was so happy I could dance. I became really good at it, the Lindy, the Peabody. I was so happy."

a'Schapett

Six months later, I folded her wheelchair and put it in the trunk of the car. "Let's go," I said, "wherever you want."

"Where do you wanna go?"

"It's up to you. It's time you leave the house for something other than a doctor."

"I'm not up to it."

"Trust me. You are. C'mon Ma, wherever you want. You gotta make a decision."

"I don't know."

"Look. If it was a doctor's appointment, we'd go. So, let's go. Put on your lipstick."

"You wanna go sit by the water, the river, the duck pond, window shopping, whatever you want. You wanna go up the Hudson?"

She put her magnifying mirror by the kitchen window, and began to apply lipstick. That was a great sign. I asked her what color it was.

"Coral Rose," she said, "Pink Lightning went out after World War II." I saw her magnified reflection, when she said, "Arthur Avenue. Let's go to the market."

"To the Bronx?"

To the Bronx, where we all grew up, the Bronx where all our relatives this side of the Atlantic were buried in Saint Raymond's Cemetery, the Bronx which held the trauma of our youths, the Bronx, our collective hearts' home.

We parked on Hughes Avenue. I went to get the wheelchair out of the trunk. She stepped away and said: "Leave it behind."

I pulled open the doors to the Arthur Avenue Retail Market. It was big, like walking into a cathedral of fruits and vegetables. The market took up the width of a whole city block. It was brick and cinderblock with a central skylight running the distance up the middle. Rachel walked down the right aisle between a pot and pan stall, where the man was in a black military beret with a red star. Her eyes opened as she looked at the artichokes and peppers, the green and dazzling purple bouquets of *broccofiore Romanesco*. Her eyes began to blossom with character; sarcasm, wit, mischief, love—my mother's eyes beamed with intention. For the first time in a year, my mother was in a store on her own two feet again. She ambled among stacks of peppers, tasted from the grapes, folded a sprig of parsley into her pocketbook. She walked down passed the butchers, one who looked sleepy or bored. The vegetables brought her to life. One merchant had a ceiling of hanging hot red peppers. Bold red and green awnings. A perpetual feast. Italian pop music blasted from the back. It could have been nineteen forty-three, she could have been sixteen again, she reached into an open barrel of black olives, and took a small hunk of *Parmigiano Reggiano*, from a tasting tray. She whispered to me that the man behind the counter had been in the market since she was a young girl. "I remember his blue eyes." Enter Rachele Petruzzelli Lanzillotto, back in her own skin; a Bronx Italian babe who though just getting on her feet, unearthed the power of how to interact, bargain, flirt, argue, sparkle, steal. He leaned over the counter, a military portrait of *El Duce* on the back wall between the hanging salamis, and as if no time had passed he handed her a slice of *sopressata*, singing *"Ciao bella,"* with very elongated *l* sounds. For my mother, his slice of *sopressata* had the memory prodding magic of Proust's madeleine. *Sopressata* was definitely not part of her strict keep-the-blood-pressure-low to stay alive, no salt diet, yet she accepted the slice, put it on her tongue, and a rush of stories followed:

"I remember when my mother brought me to the market as a little girl. She'd pick out her own chickens. She'd feel their breasts. There were soup

chickens, and then there were baking chickens. I remember the first time
I baked a chicken after I was married. It came out like rubber. What did I
know? You know, my father sold vegetables on this street when I was a kid. I
used to bring him his pepper sandwich for lunch. It wasn't like now. Nobody
locked their doors. We walked all over the place and never thought about it.
The iceman used to come, the milkman, the vegetable man with his wagon.
He'd shout in the streets and we'd go to the window to see what he had.
The fish man yelled the loudest. He had to get rid of what he had, or it'd all
go bad. They had horses and the horses would walk over the cobblestones."

Here was a woman who had lived through the trauma of a near-death
whammo vascular catastrophe, had quit cigarettes and fatty meats in the matter
of a day, and *boom!*—the moment she steps foot on Arthur Avenue she is
sucking on a slice of fat-speckled salami. It had taken us months to clear her
lungs, weeks on a respirator.

"Ma, are you gonna go back to eating salami and smoking cigarettes?"

"I can't. Only here, I assure you. They got the best stuff. I'd never eat
it anywhere else."

She chatted with other shoppers. Another guy had the same paper tape
crosshatched on his sternum, peeking out of his V-neck shirt, gripping the
scar from his recent surgery. Then I noticed another. They all came back to
the Bronx to do their walking, their *passeggiata*, and to feel alive, to sample
life with childlike smiles.

I went to get us a couple of *cappuccini* in the market *caffè*.

I ordered, "One regular and one decaf," and the man's reply was rife
with Bronx attitude, "What a you ahandicappa'?"

"*Sì*, handicapped," I said and stared into his eyes, "*uno decaffeinato per
favore.*" I sat and sipped the creamy cappuccino. Old dusty wooden models
of the *Nina*, *Pinta*, and *Santa Maria* adorned the *caffè*, the framed portraits
of Pacino's and Brando's Corleone, and Stallone's Rocky. What was I doing
here? A butch-dyke escort for her mother. I stared into my cappuccino and
blew on the foam. I was surrounded by green bottles of imported olive oil,
pyramids of watermelons, honeydews, cantaloupe, hot trays behind glass filled
with *gnocchi*, eggplant, string beans in tomato, sausage, ravioli, square pizza,
manicott', broccoli rabe, *past-n-fazool*. I wondered what this place was like when
my mother was a kid, when the pushcart peddlers yelled in the streets up to
the windows, when laundry crisscrossed the alleys on clothing lines, when
people slept on their fire escapes to get some good Bronx air.

My father carried ice. His father carried ice. My mother's father carried
ice. My grandfathers and father carried ice up and down the tenement stairs,
knocked on doors, went in and out of apartments. My father's parents had
lived in a part of the Bronx known as the "Alley," and despite the squalor,
I imagined the voices of the peddlers bouncing off the brick walls, filling

the alleyways with song. These voices were gone in New York City, but I imagined I could still hear them. The icemen didn't have to cry, "Ice, ice, ice," because they had a route with customers. Still, I imagined my father as a boy with the blocks of ice double and triple his weight, then as a young man just back from the war, back carrying ice. I fantasized about ice, blocks of ice spinning in white light. Ice heals wounds. Ice is crystalline. A 300-pound block coming down the wooden chute, moved with his tongs, scored by his pick, ice bigger than his sore soldier's body. I saw my father pausing before he carried the ice up the stairs, and stare into the spinning cold sun, through the giant prism of ice he shouldered. Joey, the Smiling Iceman.

My mother finally took a break from gallivanting around the market and came and sat down with me at the *caffé*. I asked the *barista* to blow some steam into her *cappuccino* to warm it up.

"*Euuee!*" he yelled, dumped it, made it from scratch, then waved me and my dollars away. I bought two corners of pizza. I ordered some broccoli rabe and bread. We were eating out of *sistemazione*, but we were home in the Bronx and happy. We had performed *a'Schapett!* We'd taken the heel of the bread and wiped the plate clean. We savored the juices, the end of the meal. The market had brought my mother back to life.

Shave My Head

"Yes, yes, yes."

My mother was cornered, on the telephone.

"Yes yes right right right."

"Oh yeah, she lost a second breast."

I went into the bathroom, pushed the door as tightly closed as it would go, and began to cut my hair. I went out to get something. My mother was still on the phone. Her eyes widened, in a way that told me she loved the haircut. I went back in the bathroom. I took the electric razor. I buzzed up the back of the neck. The less hair I had on my head, the less I wanted. There was only one thing left to do, go all the way. I left one long strand of hair to the front, then I took a new plastic razor, and shaved my head down to the scalp. I had a smooth head. A beautiful head. I was happy to see my head. Chemo didn't do it. I did it. Fhuck chemo. I couldn't stop petting my head.

"Do not come out of there without your head covered. I know what you did."

"You don't want to see it?"

"No."

"Why not?"

"It upsets me. That's how they punished women in World War II."

I put a towel over my head, walked out of the apartment, down the grassy hill, and caught the bus downtown.

I needed my own life. I walked the New York City sidewalks 'til I got one.

I called my cousin Nico and slept on his couch.

A couple of days later, I went home, and my mother said, "Lift up the mattress." Under the photo of Frank Sinatra and stalks of Holy Palm, my mother had stashed a bank envelope. She opened the envelope and handed me a bunch of cash.

"What's this for?"

"It was for my burial. Get yourself a shrink."

And that's what I did. I found a Southern gentleman named Clark Sugg. With my smooth head and black leather motorcycle jacket, I walked up five floors of a marble spiral staircase on West Seventy-Fourth Street, and sat down and stared at him.

"I'm tired," I said.

"You want a cup of coffee?"

"No, really tired. Tired in my bones."

"A cup of coffee can help."

"I don't drink coffee. It's bad for you."

"Well, if you're tired . . ."

"Is life really so simple?"

"We'll do a blood test. In the meantime, I'll make you a cup of coffee. I'm going to make one for myself."

I walked. I walked downtown with my résumé in my red knapsack. In CBGB one night I met a woman who was recruiting for Housing Works. I got a job. Boom. I kept walking. I walked down Eighth Avenue between Fourteenth and Fifteenth Streets with my friend Mark. Two guys walked by. Something in me turned around. One of the guys yells "Annie?" in a Bronx accent, with thick *nn*'s and a long *eee* almost like *aaay*. I remember thinking, no one says my name like that anymore. This voice called me from my deep past. This voice tugged my soul. In this man's face, I saw his boyhood features. Johnny Denaro. "Johnny!" We jumped into each other's arms and spun around. It had been a dozen years since I'd seen him, when I was first in Sloan-Kettering and he gave me the blow-up rainbow on which he'd written in blue marker, "Kindergarten Sweethearts Forever."

"My father died," he said.

We held each other as Eighth Avenue pedestrians streamed around us. Now that we were in each other's arms again, we would never let go.

Johnny Denaro was my heart's destiny, the Italian boy around the corner I was fated to marry and have kids with. All my siblings found their Bronx Italian spouses, and it was clear from kindergarten that Denaro was mine. There on Eighth Avenue, I held his warm hands and looked into his deep brown eyes. We parted, but promised to talk at once. We walked in opposite directions, each with the friend we'd spent the day with. It struck me, Johnny Denaro is gay. Scenes from our childhood flipped through my mind. He was so good at jumping rope, playing hopscotch, and he was so ebullient and expressive. Of course he's gay. All the princes in all the storybooks were gay. I looked at Mark who said, "Of course he's gay." We're both gay. He's gay. His friend is gay. My friend is gay. I'm gay. We're in Chelsea. We're all gay. Our destiny was even stronger now, but in an opposite way than I had imagined as a young girl. The magnetic fields were both flipped; Johnny and I had a double repellent field. Our bodies could never push together. We would never make love and procreate, and yet, I would never love anybody as much as I loved him. I felt doomed. I knew I was meant to be with him in that Catholic idea of "forever." He was the only soul on earth I would ever consent to walking down an aisle with. I had to bend my mind around all this. One part of me was relieved. It would have been horrible if one of us was gay and the other, God forbid, homophobic. Another part of me was gravely disappointed. Could our childhood love simply resume? Was the stationary bike in my basement all we would ever have, a stationary love that would never go anywhere? I felt a deep loss, and it felt impossible to explain it to myself or anyone. I still wanted Johnny to "call for me" in that longing way he did as a child on my front stoop. I was haunted by The Partridge Family's "I Think I Love You" lyrics, "a love there is no cure for."

I sat down and wrote him a postcard saying, "Shall we march together at gay pride? I Hold a sign: "Catholic School Kindergarten Sweethearts Turned Queer."

He telephoned me, "Are you coming out for me, or for you?"

"For both of us."

He laughed his louder than anyone in the room Johnny Denaro laugh. And we planned to drive down together to DC for the March on Washington for Gay Liberation.

Enter Audrey Lauren Kindred

The New York City street currents threw me up against some of the same characters every three to five years. Oftentimes we'd acknowledge each other. "I know her from the city streets," was something I found myself saying from time to time. It was April 16, 1993. I walked up Avenue A, just off Seventh Street. There was a woman in the crosswalk heading toward Tompkins Square Park who I recognized. The city had thrown me together with her just three years before at a poetry reading at the Ear Inn. And before that, I remembered her from Brown. We had a talk once outside the Rock. I didn't know her name. She had long straight brown hair, wore a blue Gore-Tex jacket, and appeared so straightforward to the point of being out of place in the East Village. Tompkins Square Park was a tent city full of people. I'd hang out there and talk to runaways who left their Midwestern families for New York and now slept in the park. As soon as I saw this long haired beauty in the crosswalk I changed the direction of my step, and walked out into traffic to say hi to her. A yellow cab careened by me. I stepped back, pulled the bottom of my leather jacket down as if to pull the reins on my inner horse. "Slow down Lanz. Leave the woman alone," I said to myself. Do her a favor. Walk on. So I did. I walked back up Avenue A toward Eighth Street with my head down. I looked at the shadows on the sidewalk of bicycle wheels, from bikes chained to posts outside the restaurants. Just as I forgot about her, she magically appeared right in front of me. She looked at me like she saw something beautiful. She opened her arms and I walked into her hug. There we were on Avenue A hugging, when we realized we didn't really know one another at all. She got polite.

"I was just going to have lunch," she said, "wanna join me?"

"What's your name?"

"Audrey."

"Audrey. I'm Annie."

"Shall we go right here to Odessa?"

"Sure."

"Where were you off to?"

"I was just walking."

"You?"

"I just walked through the park to say hi to my friends' kids at the playground, and I came back around to have lunch.

We sat down in a booth and looked intensely at each other's faces.

"Wanna share some fried eggplant?"

"Yes. And some *tzatsiki*."

We talked about how we both thought we knew each other. As it turned out, she had a twin sister who went to Brown. Audrey and I had never talked to each other before, but somehow we fit together. She told me she was also going down to DC with her friends to join the march. I told her I'd find her down there. I didn't know if she was straight or not, but I knew she unabashedly was flirting with me, looking at the details of my shaved head.

"Do you know you have a beauty mark behind your ear?"

"Don't flirt with me unless you mean it."

"Wow. Okay. Umm . . . You have a beauty mark behind your ear."

Our first kiss was a few days later on Houston Street. She carried a shopping bag of blue glass bottles. There was something about the blue glass. Our lips met, and I felt a jolt zigzag through my whole being. Deep bell rang.

I ran down Houston Street to a telephone booth and called Johnny Denaro. I hollered, "Johnny, I just kissed a girl. Her name is Audrey! This is a big one! I can feel it."

The ride down I 95 was a queer caravan. Johnny drove. People flirted out the windows of cars, in the rest stops, all along the eastern seaboard. Some hot chick with freckles yelled out a car window to me, "Hey, want some sushi?" and we slowed down so she could stick some in my mouth. Good times. In DC, I walked all over to find Audrey Kindred. I walked for three hours through hundreds of thousands of happy gay people from DuPont Circle to the Washington Monument. There she was at the Dyke Kiss-In under the Washington Monument. I jumped into her arms. She caught me and spun me around. We kissed deeply as we spun. Kissing and spinning made me wild with excitement. Hundreds of girls were kissing in pairs and trios. The obelisk turned into a tall white blur.

A shrink, a job, and a lover. That constituted a life in New York City. A sublet and I was all set. Mayor David Dinkins had the glass recycling program going. The asphalt streets were paved with crushed glass mixed in, and at night the whole city glittered. The recycling truck passed my window on Bedford and Barrow at five a.m. I lived over the old speakeasy, Chumley's, which put out bags and bags of bottles. The men hurled the bags of bottles into the truck, and the truck would eat it. The sound of broken glass made my body turn. Audrey held me as my body jackknifed in my sleep.

"What's up with you? Audrey said.

"What are you talking about?"

"You and the glass? It's like you're being punched in the stomach. It happens every time the glass recycling truck comes up the street."

"That's funny," I said, "because images about glass have been coming up in my writing. Look at here in my notebook. It says, 'Glass like rain suddenly all over me. The terror so beautiful, the sound so bright. Glass there like laughter breaking. Glass tripping down fire escapes like rain, like bells lingering, dropping, sparking. I see the glitter of it all. Somehow it is spectacular.'"

I said to Audrey, "I better call my mother. Maybe she remembers something."

I called my mother. "Ma, I gotta axe ya' something." I tell her about the truck. "What is it with the glass? Did anything ever happen to me with glass when I was little? Something I don't know about?"

"Yes," she said, "you had your own whatchyamacallit. Crystal whaddycall. You know the night of glass breaking."

"Kristallnacht?"

"Kristallnacht. Yes. The crib was in the kitchen. I was always cooking. Your father came home all hours. I never knew when he was liable to walk in the door and want to eat. When he wanted to be alone, he moved the refrigerator, you remember how massive it was? He moved it like it was light as a towel, he'd just slide it over, move it aside, and block me out of the kitchen. When he came home he'd say, 'Where's my dinner?' If there were no pots on the stove he'd start yelling. If there were pots on the stove he'd say, 'I'm going out to eat.' I couldn't win. So I got wise to him. I set out empty pots on the stove. A whole bunch of them. He never got wise.

One night he went berserk out of the blue. You were in there with him. He pushes me out of the kitchen and blocks the door frame with the refrigerator. I was on the other side screaming, and pushing. It wouldn't budge. He broke every dish, every cup. You were screaming. He was very cunning your father. I yelled upstairs to call the cops. By the time the cops got there he had all the glass swept up and hidden. I opened the cupboards. I said to the cops, 'I have four children! Don't you see the cupboards are empty?' But they always sided with him. 'My wife, she's going through her changes,' he told them. The cops backed off. It was after all, 1966. What was a woman's word against a man's? Your father was a hard-working war hero. Everybody knew it."

"Thanks Ma, I appreciate you're telling me."

"What," she said, "you think I don't see you suffering? You think I don't know my children suffer? If I knew now what I didn't know then, I would have killed him and saved all my children the suffering. You stay for the children. You damage them for life. He robbed me of everything, even my children's egos."

"Ma, it's not that bad. I don't want you feeling bad for anything. It's just, Dr. Sugg asks me questions, and things don't make sense. My nightmares and panic attacks. This makes sense. This helps. Mom, you're the best. Please don't start feeling bad."

"Goddamn priests and cops were no help. They always sided with your father. The judge was a jackass. One priest showed up for me in court, as a parishioner. He knew what kind of mother I was. The judge was so arrogant, he says to the priest, 'What are you doing here?' I almost got help for your father. He was a brilliant man. He was sick. He needed help. We had one social worker that was an angel. Mr. Wilcox. He was with the Salvation Army.

I loved that man. He saw your father in therapy. He used reverse psychology. I remember your father came home after a session and he says, 'Boy, that guy's got more troubles than me. I really helped him out. He's in the same situation as me. His in-laws want to come over all the time. I told him, Keep a baseball bat by the door. That'll fix that. I don't know what he'd do without me that guy.'

"Then Mr. Wilcox had a death in the family. He had to go down south. He missed an appearance or didn't file a letter on time, I don't remember. The judge said, 'You're Catholic. You belong with Catholic Charities.' That was the end of that. He said we couldn't see Mr. Wilcox anymore. The case would have turned out altogether different. A couple of more sessions with Mr. Wilcox and he could have required that your father go for psychiatric evaluation. Your father would have gotten help. It would have been a whole different story. It breaks my heart to this day. At Catholic Charities there was a young girl. Your father sweet talked her. She believed everything he said, and that was the end of that. I was so close to getting your father help and to keeping the family together.

I went to the rectory. I asked the monsignor to come to the house, but he wouldn't come. He feared your father. What was his name, whaddycall, Monsignor Calda-something. The whole neighborhood knew he was a hard-working man, your father. He never drank. He was a veteran of war. No cop, no priest would dare differ with him. The monsignor told me, 'Leave him.' I said, 'Isn't there anything you can do? I want to keep my family together.' Caldarola, that was his name, Monsignor Caldarola. He grabbed the vestment he was wearing. I'll never forget. He said to me, 'You see this? This is only cloth.' Not even the priest would take your father on. Everybody feared him. But there was one woman from the court system who saw what was going on. She was a worker in the Bronx County Courthouse. I'll never forget, she said to me: 'In your case, the wheels of justice, are going backwards.'"

Rachele's Pocketbook Fritatta

My mother had me paranoid about eating out. She said, "Never buy anything out you can make at home." The only place where she condoned eating out was the cafeteria at Sloan-Kettering. She trusted the food there as she trusted everything there. Our trips to Sloan-Kettering were the only trips where she didn't pack a lunch, and it was the only place where she would order pecan-crusted trout. I tried to get my mother out of the kitchen and into the city as often as I could. The kitchen where we summon life and take up swords with death. The kitchen, where my crib was kept. The kitchen, where my mother was posted over the hot stove, where our ancestors enter in the dark hours, where the faucet calls me to our fountains of *Acquaviva delle Fonti*, yes, where the running water makes me feel at home and calms my soul. The kitchen, I try to get my mother out of, as often as I can. And so, she will leave, but not without a frittata. The frittata inside her pocketbook.

This all began after a trip one day to the Met. It was me, my mother, Audrey, and my niece Lina, Ant'ny's daughter, a tall beauty with eyelashes that my mother said, "danced." We exhausted ourselves looking at knights and mummies and a chessboard of slaves versus musicians. We walked up Madison Avenue looking for someplace to eat. We were, as my Mother said, "famished." We saw French names on awnings; French looked expensive, we looked for English. On one window was printed: E A T. Couldn't get plainer sounding than that. Plain sounded affordable. We went in, sat down, drank fresh, tall clear glasses of the best New York City tap water, which refreshes like no other, looked down at the menu, and looked up at each other with wide eyes. We were appalled. The cheapest sandwich on the menu was $18.95. A cup of coffee was $6.95. So, what does an Italian family of four do? We ordered one sandwich and one cup of coffee and passed it around. The sandwich was lamb. My mother cut it into four neat triangles. The coffee arrived in a single-serving-size silver carafe. We asked for four empty cups. My mother vowed to never leave the apartment without food again. And as we know, Rachel's food vows are serious.

"Rachele's Pocketbook Frittata" became our favorite meal. We've eaten them uptown, downtown, midtown, Trump Tower, Battery Park, Ellis Island, at the base of the Statue of Liberty, on a bench outside the Met, in Central Park, on the hood of our parked car on countless streets, so that I started to carry a purple tablecloth that fit the hood of my car. There isn't a place my mother won't sneak a frittata out of her pocketbook. She loves filling the whole express bus down from Yonkers with the smell of parsley, potatoes, peppers, eggs. She lays asparagus crossways to hold it all together like steel rods in cement. I call her and say, "Ma, how bout meetin' us downtown?" and before she looks up the express bus schedule, she opens the fridge to see what's there. A *tarantella* beats inside her. In her words:

"I open up the fridge. I see asparagus! Onion! Parsley! Cheese! Swiss! Pecorino! How many eggs? I get out the big frying pan. On goes the gas. In goes the oil. I start the onion. I beat up as many eggs as I have. I add a splash of water. The onions caramelize. I drop in the asparagus. I throw in the parsley, cheese, if there's a little *mozzarell'* I throw it in. Depending on the bus schedule I eliminate potatoes. If I cut potatoes, thin! If a few mushrooms, throw them in. Add eggs. Add cheese. Go around the edge of the pan with the spatula. Tip the frying pan side to side. I get a plate a little larger than the pan, take the pan off the stove, cover the pan with the plate. Flip it over. Make sure it's firm enough, otherwise I'll have eggs dripping down my legs. Slide the frittata back into the pan from the plate. Let it cool while I get dressed for downtown. Put on my lipstick. Wrap it in a dish towel. Of course, you gotta have the right pocketbook. Run for the bus. Somebody's out there waiting for the frittata! Every time I see them, they're always hungry. They always ask, Ma you got anything to eat?"

How to Poke a Guy's Eyes Out

Audrey and I moved in together in Park Slope, Brooklyn. It was just before Audrey's birthday when I walked by a red truck parked outside the old Reformed Dutch Church on Seventh Avenue. A man was selling a litter of collie-shepherd puppies. All the little girls from the neighborhood circled the truck, cooing. I reached into the flatbed to pick up one of the puppies and he stepped back. I grabbed him and lifted him to my heart. He had that fresh puppy smell that had made me feel so safe as a child. I zipped him up in my jacket with his head sticking out, and borrowed the ten bucks off a friend of mine, and that's how Audrey got Scaramooch for a birthday present. Scaramooch means skirmisher from *Scaramouche*, *Scaramuccia*, *Scaramuzza*, the Neopolitan *Commedia dell'Arte* swashbuckling sword-carrying long-nosed lover of women and wine. Scaramooch had a hyena's howl for my mother's meatballs. He'd sit in her kitchen, at attention, by her side, and howl. He was trying to speak.

She'd offer him her empty hand, and say, "What. What do you want? You're not getting any more meatballs."

"*Awwooooooohhh!*" he licked and licked her hand with faith, like rubbing Aladdin's lamp, the licks magically procured more meatballs. She always gave in, opened the 'fridge and got the pot of meatballs out. After a meatball, his long spotted tongue cleaned all around his nose and mouth, and my mother would say, "He's licking his whole head," proud of her meatball prowess. It was Scaramooch who found Cherub. Scaramooch found his littermates in Prospect Park and they'd play together. One day he ran off into the woods with his brothers Kismet and Samson and his sister Tricky, and all of us people ran after our dogs. Scaramooch circled an abandonded puppy who sat still and looked up, "Yipe, yipe, yipe, yipe, yipe!"

The puppy followed Scaramooch home, prancing behind him. He looked like his son, they both had dirty blonde widows' peaks. The puppy's name was revealed to me a few days later when I watched him run. His ears flapped like wings over his stout body. I ran home to Audrey. "I know his name! I know his name! Cherub!"

I thought of cherubs as fat angels that witness all human endeavors, and push us to do things we otherwise wouldn't do. I pictured them as I'd seen in Italian Renaissance paintings all around the human characters in life scenarios, but as Cherub grew he taught me the true etiology of his name. He got into a lot of fights in the park. I was always diving into packs of dogs to pull him out. That's when I learned the etymology of the word cherub, "fierce avenger of the Lord," a fitting sobriquet for our little snarling dog with an abandonment complex.

One night Uncle Frank drove Audrey and me home from a family gathering. We lived a couple of blocks away from where he was born and raised, and delivered ice. The three of us sat up front on the bench seat of his car. Audrey sat in the middle. We talked and joked around as he pointed out buildings where he delivered ice and coal. Uncle Frank put his arm over the seat, grabbed the cuff of Audrey's coat sleeve, pulled it up over her hand and in one swoop brought his thumb to her eye socket. "Hah?" he said laughing, "How's that? If anyone ever comes up to you in a car, this is how you poke his eyes out.

Audrey looked horrified at me and Uncle Frank as if she was watching a movie and we were the characters. It bothered me but I couldn't put words to it. Except for Johnny Denaro, I had no Bronx Italian friends and worse, I never thought about it. I hadn't dated an Italian since college, and worse, I never thought about that either. I didn't have an Italian hangout, and it never even occurred to me. I didn't have a *cappuccino* place, or a *passeggiata* street, or a *primacolazione* buns-n-rolls Sunday to look forward to. I didn't know who was baking my daily bread, and there's nothing like a Bronx roll lathered with butter, dunked in your morning coffee and stuck into ya' mout'. Even two-year-old Bronx Italians love that. I avoided Bronx Italians like the plague, and I never questioned what that meant. Fifteen years after that night in Uncle Frank's car, Audrey and I took a self-defense class together at Brooklyn Women's Martial Arts. A woman taught us how to poke an attacker's eyes out, using our hands like claws. Audrey went at the exercise full force like an animal. What seemed violent and irrational to her in an Italian-American car was utterly palatable and acceptable to her in the context of a feminist studio. I realized I was more confident learning fighting lessons from my Uncle on the bench seat of his American car. That was true ground school.

I was tired at how entrenched I was in white educated culture. "Educationa Girl" boomeranged back at me and clocked me in the head. I was exhausted on deep levels. Something inside me was uneasy. Being a cancer survivor when I was young meant I was treated like a sage. Inspiring people was hard work. Being a Bronx Italian was to be a thrill ride for the uninitiated; meanwhile Educationa Girl was estranged from Bronx Italians. I was tired of being sage and joy ride, some combo of a nun and The Fonz. Ever since I left the Bronx in the backseat of that gold Mustang, people gathered around to hear my accent. Seriously, I thought, I should have charged admission. And that's exactly what I began to do. I wrote poems, monologues, and stories, and got on stage, and people paid at the door. My first poem was about growing up with two brothers, a junkie and a Marine. The title was "Come Home or Die." Then I wrote a story that began the first line "CAW-FEE!" and I hollered it in the basement of the Pyramid Club the way my father yelled up at my mother's clothesline window. Then I bought fifty pink faux Spaldeens and threw them on stage at an X on a brick wall at Manhattan Class Company and Under One Roof Theater while telling the story of my mother's miracle aorta. Then I carried a fifty pound bag of cement up a flight of stairs into Dixon Place and mixed it on stage, making cement raviolis while talking about having cancer. Then I carried a case of garlic into The Knitting Factory where Franklin Furnace Inc. commissioned my play about GranmaRose *Pocketing Garlic*. Then I bought ice-tongs and a three-hundred-pound block of ice and wheeled it on stage at The Kitchen in an old chrome frame of a baby carriage with big white wheels and strong springs exactly like I had as a baby. Ice in spotlight became my obsession; it shone brilliantly as it melted. And I began to spin ice, and sing of icemen. After a lot of trial and error I finally got a three-hundred-pound block of ice spinning fast. I added hot white side light that spun through the spinning prism of ice. I told Okinawa stories I'd heard from my father. The spinning ice whipped the light around the audience. I created characters out of the crises in my life and out of my psyche, even the guy in Bellevue who spun a wheelchair over his head, eventually I portrayed him too, but in full body paint as a zebra in Salley May's show at Dixon Place. My mind put things together in strange juxtapositions, and on stage I let my mind fly. I did everything Sister Raymond Aloysius taught me. I was slow, loud and clear. And Audrey Kindred was there every single step of the way, even painting the zebra stripes on my ass. I visited all my relatives at all the cemeteries and I prayed. I prayed at the graves of my icemen grandfathers. I prayed at the graves of Enza's four Uncles who died in that explosion so many years before I was even born. I went back to Bari and prayed at the graves of my grandparents and great grandparents. I thought of Toshiharu Kotani and I performed with my father's Japanese flag projected onto my naked chest. And people bought tickets to these shows. They were paying to hear my Bronx accent and my words. *Dancing In the Streets* commissioned me to go back to the Arthur Avenue Retail Market and perform the history of the pushcart peddler singing in the streets and alleyways up to the women at the windows. When I walked back into the market the *barista* said, "Oh you the *andicappa',*" and I said, "No, *due regolari.*" I told him I wanted to rent a stall in the market. "Talk to the butcher," he said, "the one with the moustache."

How to Cook a Heart

ARTHUR AVENUE RETAIL MARKET, BRONX, NEW YORK, 1996

"I'm a writer interested in the history of the market," I told the butcher. "My family's from Bari. We've shopped here three generations. My grandfather used to deliver ice here. I'm wondering about renting a stall in the market, maybe bring a piano up, bring some artists up."

We talked across the counter full of meat. He stopped to tell a customer how to cook a crown roast.

"Where are your people from?"

"Bari. *Acquaviva delle Fonti, Bitetto,* and *Cassano delle Murge.*"

"I know exactly where that is. I was born over there," he said smiling, "call me after the holidays. I'll talk to the merchants and see what we could do, on a trial basis."

That was the first time in America I didn't have to point at the heel of my shoe to tell the guy where Bari was. Mike the butcher was a *paesan'*. I was elated.

The merchants voted to rent me a stall, and I trucked up a piano, hooked up a microphone, and the Opera Stand was born, a two-year open mic I hosted where all the neighborhood old ladies and wannabe tenors could sing.

To learn all I could about the history of pushcart peddling, I took rides with some of the merchants on their daily rounds and talked with them about their lives. I went with one of the butchers named Saverio, at five a.m. to the Hunts Point Terminal Market to see his daily rounds. As we drove into Hunts Point, with the sun ripening the sky over the water, the Bronx is as gorgeous as anywhere else on earth. Saint Francis and Saint Anthony stood on Saverio's dashboard. He pulled over to the side of the water and we watched the sunrise.

"I love it," he says of being up this early, and he smoothed his hand over his shaved head.

"You're a *signorina*?"

"Si."

"You're not married?"

"No."

"You got a boyfriend?"

"Yeah." I hated this line of questioning.

"Steady?"

"Eh."

He leaned in to kiss me the way I've done to so many girls. I was afraid to tell him I was a lesbian. Petrified actually.

"Can I kiss you?"

"Don't you got a wife?"

"Yeah. But I got trouble. She lives upstairs. I live down. I can't divorce because it'll kill my mother. You know, the old fashioned. I love you so much. You are just like a *Barese* girl. No all this." And he puts his hands up to his face so I know he means makeup and doodads. I laughed. I couldn't believe I was in this situation. I think of myself as a butch dyke, but he sees an old-fashioned girl. I don't wear makeup. I don't wear brassieres. I wear my hair in a ponytail. I can imagine how dykes can be perceived as old-fashioned girls. Some of my softball buddies looked just like their grandmothers.

We walked into the building of meats, and he said to the guy, "I brought my girl up to see the freezer." Then he turned to me and said, "Not everybody comes in the freezer, I get to go in alone because when this was a slaughterhouse, I worked for the boss." The freezer shelves of the Hunts Point Meat Market are eerie when they are empty, they take on a light purple glow. We walked through a series of rooms that were giant freezers big as malls. Frozen malls of meats. Saverio told me, "Now, all the meat comes in boxes. We buy buckets of blood and mix it in the chop meat so it looks fresh'a-kill. Ten years ago all the organs came hot, in barrels, straight from the animals. Today everything is frozen."

GranmaRose and Audrey performed with me at the market. Granma made *cavateel* as a demonstration. She sang, *"O Sole Mio."* I videotaped her cracking eggs and put a cathedral bell soundtrack to it. I put this on a monitor at the entrance to the market and called it, *Eggs and Bells*. Audrey made tribal masks out of garlic and onion skins, choreographed dances where watermelons were passed clear across the market, and took care of Granma. They became best friends. Granma was ninety-six and called Audrey *"Oggi"* because she couldn't pronounce the *drr* in Audrey. *Oggi* suited Audrey perfectly. It means "today," and Audrey had a true spirit of being in the here and now. We should have ceremonies when peoples' nicknames find them. Something simple like tapping them on the head with a sprig of hot pepper. It's a magnificent blessing, to earn a nickname. I started calling her *Oggi* too. I once asked Granma Rose what she thought of homosexuals. She got angry and indignant and said "watch'a you mouth." When I moved in with *Oggi*, Granma said astutely: *"Bah!* Two hens. No rooster."

Another show I called *How to Cook a Heart*, based on the story of the one butcher in the market who only sold offal: heart, liver, lung, tail, feet, head, brain, stomach, tongue, penis, testicles. His name was Mario. Mario made specialties for the feasts. He filled spleens with parsley and spices and wrapped them with intestines. His was a disappearing art, and not one he passed on to his daughters. Mario told me, "You got the same heart like the animals. The only thing the animals' are bigger. Ours a little smaller. But it works the same way." I talked to Mario all the time about hearts, and how to cook them.

"So you slice the heart this way?"

"Yeah, about a quarter of an inch, and you put them in the oven, like a steak."

"You slice 'em diagonal?"

"No. Across the top. Like a slice. And heat in the oven. Or you barbecue. Broiled and you put some lemon on the top and you eat it like that. Like a steak."

"How do you know when it's done?"

"You turn it a few times, you know. Or you can chop in small pieces and fry with a lot of onions. That's the best way, more tastier."

"What kind of onions?"

"Onions. Lot of onions. Hot pepper, olive oil, salt, and onions."

"Now, when you chop it, you go through the whole heart?"

"You get a knife. You go through the whole hearts. Take off a little fat, and you know you make it in small chunks, and you fry together, with a lot of onions."

"And you put oil."

"You put the oil, a little olive oil, a little hot pepper, a little salt, and that's it. And you turn them, you know. Fry 'em, fry 'em good."

"The veal?"

"You fry 'em together, the lambs—"

"The lamb?"

"Yeah, those the small ones. Then there's another way you can make 'em. You make a hole in the heart."

"A hole in the heart? How do you make the hole?"

"What you do is you cut the bottom of the heart. You cut. Then you take the hole. And you chop it very small. First you cut the bottom. That's the nerves, the fat. You throw that away. Then you turn the heart over. Like a circle and you—"

"You scoop it."

"Yeah. And that you chop. You save it. You put it aside. Get parsley. Get *Romano* cheese. And garlic. And chop it. You mix it all together. And you stuff it that way. You put it back in the heart."

"Like you bury it in the heart?"

"Yes. Put them in. Let them cook. About three-fifty."

"How do you know when it's done?"

"You know."

"How long does it take?"

"It depends on the heart. It gets brown. Very tasty."

The night I directed and performed *"a'Schapett"* at the Guggenheim Museum, December 2nd, 1996. The program was *Dancing In the Streets'* "Insight into On/Site," hosted by Elise Bernhardt. The evening was part of the "Works and Process" series curated by Mary Sharp Cronson. I had twenty cast members in this show including my mother and GranmaRose who was ninety-six and got a standing ovation. The DVD of the night is at the New York Public Library. The prop I am holding was donated by Dave Greco of Mike's Deli. *Photo: Andrew Perret.*

My grandmother Rosa Marsico Petruzzelli, *passaporto*, 1919.

Duca degli Abruzzi, on which my grandmother Rose rode steerage
class to America in 1919 with her sister Lucia. The boat weighed
7793 gross tons, measured 475.8 feet x 53.4 feet, had two funnels,
two masts, twin screw, speed of 16 knots, held 80 first-class
passengers, 16 second-class passengers, and 1,740 in steerage. Built
by Cantieri Navale Riuniti, Spezia (with engines by N. Odero &
Co, Sestri Ponente). *Photo of a drawing: Courtesy of the Ellis Island
Immigration Museum.*

Above: Petruzzelli family. Two sisters marry two brothers and each have two daughters with the same names. *Left to right*: Rachele (Mom), Rosa (GranmaRose), Lucia (Aunt Patty), Rachele, Lucia, and Lucia (GranmaRose's sister). *Standing*: Giuseppe (Granpa) and Franco (Granpa's brother).

Left: GranmaRose and me performing at the Arthur Avenue Retail Market in the Bronx. *Photo: Andrew Perret, 1996.*

Dad and me in the basement of the mental home where he lived. He had a poster of the white horse he had told me about in stories when I was a kid. *Photo: Audrey Kindred, 1996.*

I went to the National Archives at 201 Varick Street in New York City to find my grandmother's naturalization papers. When the clerk handed this to me and I saw her original signature, I cried.

Zia Isabella in bicicleta, Acquaviva delle Fonti, Bari, Italia. Photo: Annie Lanzillotto, 1987.

Audrey Kindred and me, after my first solo show. "Confessions of a Bronx Tomboy: My Throwing Arm—This Useless Expertise." Under One Roof Theater, New York City. *Photo: Carolina Kroon, 1993.*

Thursday   December - 8 -1983
                                8 PM
                            Weather - Warm -

Dear Annie -
        Hi Baby - How are you! I'm
sitting here drinking coffee black - which
I shouldn't be - The doctor sez
(No - coffee - tea - cigarettes. Brocoli -
cabbage - cauliflour - salt sugar etc)
        I stopped listening - the
next time I go back I'll discuss
my body with him _____
        ___ Annie I didn't write because
I thought you would be home for
3 weeks and my letter too you
    would be sitting up there,
I thought you would be home
    the early part of December ___
Anyway ___
        This morning when I talked
to you. you were saying you
wanted to do missionary work.
Baby only you know what you have
to do - and if you can do it ___
    it is your life - and you can
always change directions. And in
life you change directions anyway.
    Up to the present, at 20 yrs
old you can look back and see

Dad wrote me hundreds of letters when I was at Brown. Here's a page from a letter dated December 8, 1983, where he says, "It is your life—and you can always change directions."

Dad's jars line the walls of the boiler room workshop in the basement of the mental home. The mental home was once the site of Guglielmo Marconi's workshop, where he sent the first radio signals in this country to ships at sea. Fire Island Avenue, Babylon, NY. *Photo: Audrey Kindred, 1997.*

Rogele dei cartellato,
1 bottiglia di pruno giuse.
1 bottiglia di grepepe giuse.
1 ponte di zucchero brown
e dopo lo fai bollire
2 ponte di farina
2 uova ecc.

Date
dic 18, 1979

GranmaRose's recipe.

Regole dei biscotti
Ginn Corusso,
6 uova
1 bichiere di d'olio
1 coppa di zucchero
6 cuchiarini beghe
polvere
farina quando
se, me prende
un po di burro.
nella pendola.

21 novembre
1979.

GranmaRose's recipe.

Above: GranmaRose, Mom, and me. Bear Mountain. Mom's birthday 1993. *Photo: Jimmy DeVita.*

Left: Johnny Denaro and me at the March on Washington for Gay Liberation. holding our banner *Catholic School Kindergarten Sweethearts Turned Queer.* Washington, DC, 1993.

GranmaRose rolling dough and teaching the crowd how to make *cavateel* at The Arthur Avenue Retail Market, during my show, "Mammamia You'll Never Get a Straight Answer Again!" 1997, The Bronx. *Photo: Andrew Perret.*

part five

Annie's Parts

Mr. Fixit

It was the fiftieth anniversary of the First Marine Division, the oldest and most decorated unit in the Corps. Lanzi told me he felt bad he didn't have the health or the money to go to the Marine Corps reunion. "If you can't treat people to dinner," he said, "what's the use?"

My father suffered a complete breakdown, broke all the windows of his apartment, and threw everything out onto the sidewalk. He wasn't arrested. Cops understood. "Joey's a decorated U. S. Marine, don't charge him with anything." He was placed in the violent ward of the VA hospital, diagnosed with paranoid schizophrenia, depression, and anxiety, prescribed antipsychotic meds, and released. One of his sisters told me they found a book in my father's sidewalk rubble, with highlighted passages which delineated the difference between what was considered criminal behavior versus psychotic behavior. She told me this as if his breakdown was part of a master plan to secure himself government services. I didn't know what to make of this, although at the time it soothed me. Anything to prove my father was sane soothed me. He moved in with Aunt Laura and Uncle Frank. One morning when they drove Aunt Laura to work, my father jumped out of the car, wielding two heavy crystal ashtrays that he had grabbed from their house, and smashed car windshields in the parking lot.

Cops understood. "Joey's a decorated Marine . . ."

Next stop. Babylon. A four-story mansion converted into a residential mental home with accommodations for sixty, on the exact spot where Guglielmo Marconi sent the first American ship to shore radio signals one century before. Lanzi settled into the boiler room. He decorated the boiler with a white picket fence and chicken wire. He earned the privilege of caretaking the basement workshop full of tools, in exchange for fixing the plumbing and the boiler. He scavenged the neighborhood trash, and carted machines and computers back to the basement, to take them apart into their distillate components.

To visit him, I'd walk down a short set of exterior cracked cement steps and take a sharp left through the red door into the subterranean basement. I bumped my head on the low doorframe. I remembered our house in the

Bronx and the curved steps that led down to his basement workshop, and his sign that read: Watch Your Head. If my father was to be found, he was to be found in the boiler room. I walked in and called, "Dad!" and heard a muffled response from the back. Lanzi climbed out of a crawl space set into the wall behind the boiler. He crawled inside walls.

I gave him a huge hug and kiss.

We put a piece of plywood over the pool table stashed in the basement. This was our table now. I rolled down my sleeves so I would not get splinters in my elbows.

I admired my father's solitariness. He didn't value Cadillacs or haircuts. He devoutly rejected participation in the gossip and crap of life. At the same time I pitied him. He was doing penance, all alone, a broken man, next to the giant furnace of a mental home, taking apart other people's garbage. The walls were lined with jars covered in white or red lids, labeled in Lanzi's distinct handwriting, thick block letters in black marker, with the name and size of the part. ½" U-Bolts. Nozzles. 1³/₈" Flat Head Screws. Plastic Washers. Hasp. Faucet Handles. Wire Nuts. Assorted Sink Parts. Nails T 3½". T nails 4". 3" Nails with Threads. Small Chains. Elec Coffeepot. Computer Keyboard. Assorted Bolts Thread End to End. Screws to Stop Leaks in Hot Water Tanks. Lock Plates. Male-Female Connectors.

He handed me oversize mental home coffee containers filled with obscure parts. Padlocks he dismantled into slices. Padlock plates had odd cut-outs to accommodate keys. He gave me a jar of these. I kept the jars along the edges of my bookshelves, shined the padlock plates with Brillo, strung them on leather string and wore them around my neck. No one ever guessed what they were. No one I ran into ever saw a padlock plate before. To hammer the shackles off a padlock and pop the riveting pins out, Lanzi customized the tools himself and used his bare hands and brute force. He got cash for buckets of scrap metal at the junkyard. A penny a pound for steel frames, two cents a pound for PVC vinyl, thirty cents a pound for cast aluminum. For copper wire, ninety cents for dirty, a dollar for clean. Nickel-coated aluminum, twenty-five cents a pound. Contaminants he put in jars. Computers were just beginning to be found in sidewalk trash. My father separated each computer into hundreds of component parts, each in a jar, down to tiny gold-plated pins and titanium bits that he put in glass vials with cork tops, and offered to me as gifts. He mapped out what countries all the parts were manufactured in, and told me, "Daddy, do you know one computer has parts from seven, eight countries?"

A bell rang.

"What's that?"

"Medication hour. Let's go upstairs. C'mon. They think I'm a paranoid schizo."

We walked through the television smoking room where residents sat on couches like automatons, elbows mindless as hinges, bringing cigarettes back and forth to their mouths. They all yelled, "Mr. Fixit!" when they saw my father.

"Joseph can fix anything," the attendant told me smiling. She handed my father a tiny plastic cup with a blue pill inside and a paper fluted cup half-filled with water. He tossed the pill into his mouth, downed the shot of tap water, and swallowed exaggeratedly. Then he turned around, spit the pill into his hand, put his hand in his pocket, winked at me and went back down to the basement. On the staircase, he showed me what was in his pocket, hundreds of light blue pills.

"You're not taking your medicine?"

"Fa'what. They're crazy."

"C'mere," he said, "I wanna show you something. Look at the mouths of the pipes. What do you see?"

"I dunno. Pipes."

"There's one that's covered."

He lifted one pipe out of the stack of pipes. He took black electric tape off the mouth and pulled out an amber medicine vial. He opened the cap and showed me a roll of money.

"When I die, don't forget. Look in this pipe."

I never wanted to go out to Babylon alone. Once I was there I was fine, but I'd always fall apart on the long drive home. I clung to friends who would take the ride. Mostly Audrey, who entered Lanzi's world with ease, imagination, and endless patience. When he saw the instant necklace and earrings she made out of the spare parts he gave us, he looked us both dead in the eyes and said, "When I'm dead, don't go decorating my gravestone. I know you two. Leave it alone like all the rest of the soldiers. I don't want no distinction from the rest."

He made us promise.

Lanzi decorated the boiler room more and more, and he made his own art. He hung a 1970s toilet seat on the wall that was silk-screened with a silhouette of two lovers holding each other. He had a poster of a white horse, just like the one in the bedtime stories he used to tell me. He nailed a Cinderella mask to a wooden board over a magazine cut out of the ocean, so you could see the ocean through the holes in her eyes. Nailed to each side of her head, like earrings, were a pair of tan high heels.

"Pop, you're an assemblage artist," I told him. "You could sell this in SoHo. People get big money for stuff like this."

He found someone's lifetime collection of ceramic owls in the trash on a street. He cut up a stack of Depends geriatric diapers from the home, and wrapped each owl up in a strip of diaper. Anytime any of us visited, he'd unwrap owls and hand them out. Everyone always left the boiler room with a present. Me and Audrey got owls. Rosemarie and her kids Melissa, Jonathan and Catherine got owls. Ant'ny and his daughter Lina got owls. I loved to think of my father's owls on all our shelves watching over us. I had owls in my bathroom, on my table, on my bookshelves; a papa owl and a baby owl on one branch next to my soap dish. An owl with plastic green eyes that glowed with candlelight, on my table. There will always be a tiny cement owl overlooking my bookshelf. These owls would look out over each of us for the rest of our lives.

One day Audrey and our friend Hope came with me. My father had maps of Okinawa spread across his lap. He was re-envisioning the Japanese defensive on the island, fifty years later. One map detailed the seize of Kunishi Ridge in topographical detail, with markings for each division and regiment and the progress they made day by day, yard by yard. My father had the First Division circled.

"Here. Have a seat," he said. He overturned buckets inside the picket fence around the boiler. The three of us sat down. It felt like a cozy clubhouse.

"You want coffee?" he asked.

He handed each of us a Styrofoam cup and a plastic drink stirrer. He spooned in Nescafé. Then with his forefinger and thumb, he unscrewed a nut on the side of the furnace and the hot water came from the copper tubing off the side of the furnace directly into the cup. He stirred the bubbling coffee nonchalantly. The girls laughed. He said, "What! Where do you think the hot water upstairs comes from?"

To me, my father's furnace was the most giant cappuccino maker in the world.

This particular day, he gave me my own custom jar of an assortment of nuts, bolts, washers, screws, wingnuts and all kinds of rusted things he knew I'd need one day. He'd put a lot of thought into this. This jar he labeled "Annie's Parts."

I put it in the car and drove off, feeling that I was carting around my own remains. He walked behind the car to the end of the driveway, stood by the road, and flapped his whole hand good-bye hinging at the wrist. All the way down the block, I saw him in my rearview mirror, his whole hand flapping. That's where I see him still.

I said to Audrey and Hope, "I need to clear my head. Let's go to the ocean."

We drove to Robert Moses State Park. I ran straight for the ocean. I needed ablution, renewal. The water enveloped me. I swallowed water, waved my arms. A riptide held me in place, its freezing cold fingers grabbed me by the spine. The lifeguard watched me calmly. There was a wall in the ocean I could not climb over. Any moment now the ocean could yank me back into itself. Pull me all the way back into the depths.

Six Places to Buy Milk

Aunt Patty honked and honked in her Cutlass Supreme down by our johnnypump. Mom waved from the kitchen window, muttering, "Alright already, she's gotta honk like that? Whatsammata wit' her." We hustled down the staircase in the hill. I slid into the backseat. They lit Tareyton cigarettes and blew the smoke out the windows. I yelled that smoke was coming in the backseat and they said it wasn't. "Once we get on the highway you'll be fine," Aunt Patty said. The mission for the day was to go to GranmaRose's apartment in the Bronx, and break the news that they were moving her up to Yonkers. We swerved around the hairpin curve onto the Bronx River Parkway. Aunt Patty ranted, my mother appeased her, and I transformed into The Mute.

"Mamma thinks I can keep running back and forth. What does she want to wait until something really happens? One day she falls down, I get a call from the neighbor. Another day, somebody climbs in her window and takes her television set."

"Sis, you're all worked up. Just do me one favor. Calm yourself. It's no good, even for you."

"Aay! She's ninety-three years old. And I'm the only driver. It's different if you say your sister drives or you got a brother and you take turns. Hey that's a whole different story. I don't blame you. No one's asking you to do highway driving. But c'mon."

"Sister, no one's disputing you."

"People are living too long these days. It's no good to die young, it's no good to grow old. Today they cut you open then they sew you all up. They don't even let you die today."

1233 White Plains Road had a marble hallway like an echo chamber, that smelled like bread baking. Our voices and steps echoed. I slid my finger up the brass banister and down the list of names to the Petruzzelli buzzer. No answer. Aunt Patty used her key. I ran my finger across the wall of shiny brass

mailboxes in the hall. The names used to be all Italian on the mailboxes, now
they were mostly Spanish. The wall of brass mailboxes ran to her steel plated
black door at the end of the hall. We knocked on the door. No answer.

"Sis, I told her two o'clock."

"Knock again. You think something's wrong?"

"No. Ninety-three years old and with her you still gotta make an
appointment."

"Butch, go ask the shoemaker where she is."

I walked two doors down to the shoemaker. I remembered that when
I was a kid, my Granpa Giuseppe used to sit out here on the sidewalk and
play a card game called *Brisch*.

The shoemaker hadn't seen Granma that day. I walked down the block.
There was no sign of Granma.

Aunt Patty opened the bureau drawers and pulled out Granma's underwear.
"Look at this. She must have this from the year one. She sewed her bloomers.
Look at this elastic! It must stretch from here to eternity. Sis will you look
at this?"

"Sister, stop, you're gonna rip it. Sewing gives her something to do.
Mamma always sewed her bloomers even when we was kids. If Mamma wants
to sew her bloomers let her sew them. Look how precious, she even sewed
her name inside, Rosa Petruzzelli."

"Nothin' doin'. They don't buy nothin'. Before they'd buy anything,
they'd rather choke on it. They don't go for spit! Ga'forbid you buy one
thing new. All their lives they save, save, don't spend a nickel, then they have
these elaborate funerals. All roses. Roses! You'd think they was in opera houses.
This is our one chance to get rid of things. She ain't moving into my house
with all kinds of crap. How many times over how many years can you sew
a pair of bloomers?"

Two hours later, we heard the key in the door. There stood GranmaRose,
two plastic bags heavy with food digging into her arms.

"It's time Mamma. I left you here as long as possible. You're coming to live
with me. And you can stay at Lilly's whenever you want."

"What? I gotta go where there's a no place to buy a the milk?"

"Again with the milk. Milk and bread, milk and bread. Sister, if I hear
this one more time."

"How many times we gonna have this discussion?"

"Here there's six corners to buy milk. *Un', due', tre, quattro, cinque, sei!*"

"And tomorrow there'll be seven. I know. In the Bronx they have
everything. Milk on every corner."

"It's true Sis."

"Up a there what am I gonna do? The car you take even to the milk to get."

I looked at these three women, Rose, Patty, Lilly. I couldn't imagine them ever living without each other. I wondered who would be the first to die and who would be the last. My mother was so vulnerable after her aneurysm. Granma was strong. She still shopped for her housebound neighbors Concetta and Paulina. She carried groceries across four lanes of traffic on White Plains Road, and even though she was four foot eight, she insisted, "The cars, they see me."

Granma walked away into the kitchen. She had a disgusted look on her face. Patty and Lilly followed her.

"Look at this broiler. Will you look at this?"

"Don't touch'a that, The door it falls off. That's a my favorite. It cooks a the meat a good."

"Where'd you find this? Sis, what a we from hunger? This is not going on my clean counter!"

"Sister, calm down."

"No, Mamma. We'll buy a new one."

"Yeah, tomorrow. Bah! Everyting'a new. *Sembra* buy, buy, throw everyting'a outta, buy new, new, new, but it don't cook as good as this one. The meat comes good, in ten minutes it browns, tender onna in'aside, nice a brown on the out'aside. Sure, big oven'a she turns onna even for a small'a piece a meat, big oven. Eeeee! The big oven you have to turn on and it creates all'a this'a heat. The meat never comes like it comes over here."

"It looks like a charcoal pit. Sister, God knows where this is from."

"Do you want to give Mamma a heart attack?"

"That's why she's ninety-three, cause of all the heart attacks I'm giving her."

"Sis be a little smarter than that. Control yourself. Don't say nothing. Just get rid of it later. Tell her you lost it, will you please!"

"She's gonna have to learn to use the microwave."

Patty yelled in a frenzy and ripped and ripped. I sat mute as the dolls on the couch that GranmaRose crocheted bustier dresses for. This was a horror show. I got up, walked to the window, and pushed aside the lace curtain. Two floors down in an interior courtyard, kids ran and played with their blue Hi-Bounce balls, the closest you could come to a Spaldeen. The courtyard was a concrete canyon in the back of six attached apartment buildings. The bounce of the balls and the shouts of the kids echoed up to the windows.

My Father, Marconi, and Me

I was living with Audrey in Brooklyn, equidistant from my father in Babylon and my mother in Yonkers. I still felt very much pulled apart by the both of them. Every day off I had from work I drove the hour in either direction to visit one of them. I was still so angry at my father for never admitting the simple truth that he beat my mother up and terrorized her daily. One day I stepped out of the shower, grabbed a towel, and stood in front of the mirror naked. I had a jolt of clarity, I am bigger than my father. The tables had turned. I could kill him. I saw the power of my biceps, and the height I had attained. I was almost as tall as my height chart; my father had planned well when he cut that piece of wood. I was strong. Years of playing ball had toned my muscles. I am no longer the little girl who hid teaspoons behind the heat pipes and bit my father's kneecaps as he shook my mother by her scalp. Lanzi was now a skinny old man and I was a big tough athlete. I could knock him over with one punch in the gut. I decided to go see my father alone. I could knock him flat out cold. This was my chance. Somethin' I had waited for my whole life. To club him over the head. I arranged for my friend Mark to be my getaway car, to wait for me on Fire Island Avenue an hour after I arrived at the mental home. The same Mark who pushed me over the Clit Club threshold when I needed *coraggio* in the dyke dating scene. The same Mark who walked with me in Chelsea when I reunited with Johnny Denaro. The same Mark who helped me when my mother was sick. Mark was a writer and a good friend through it all and I trusted him. I didn't tell him what I was up to, just what corner to meet me on and what time. An hour was all I needed to confront my father and then sock him over the head. I took the train to Babylon alone. I walked down Main Street up to Fire Island Avenue. I read the sign outside the house before I went in: *This is the site of the birth of the American wireless. A pioneer station here in 1901 first talked with ships at sea. —Guglielmo Marconi*

My father and Marconi shared a spot on the same earth, ninety years apart. I wrote a play for three characters in my mind, *My Father, Marconi, and Me*. My father next to the furnace, meticulously takes apart a computer, a motor, a padlock, and a pulley. Marconi, in his shack next to a tall pole extending into the sky, receives messages from ships coming into New York Harbor, and relays their messages to the city. There is an urgency to his message relays. A third character played by me, plays multiple parts and traverses both worlds and times: a mental home attendant delivers meds, a messenger brings in the mail, a daughter visits her father.

I walk in unannounced through the red basement door. I pass the storage room with its stacks of Depends, the pool table, the boiler my father had fenced off with the white picket fence and chicken wire as if it was a shrine, into his tool room where he was bending over his workbench light. His red-and-green-striped knit hat is pulled low over his brow like it was part of his skull. I stand there for a moment and look at him. My father is a broken down old man with a toilet seat hanging on the wall as a decoration.

I come at him like a bull. "Dad."

"Annie."

"I want you to admit that you hit my mother. For once. After all these years. Admit it."

"You're crazy."

"Admit it."

"Look what kind of woman you turned out to be. You're like your Aunt Bella, you know that? You're a liar. The Petruzzellis brainwashed you. Get out. Leave me alone. Why are you coming here to bother me?"

Fists were where my feelings went. My fists were heavy and needed to swing. My fists were mouths. My fists spoke for me. I pressed my fingernails into the ball of my hands and my hands into tight knots. I opened my mouth. Some loud sounds came out. I turned my back and I ran up the flight of curved stairs to the attendant's office.

"'Scuse me," I said out of breath, "but, I upset my father. You better check on him. Please. Thank you."

"Yes, they get upset after family visits sometimes," she said.

Sciamannin'

ITALIA

I had a spiritual imperative to get my mother to *Italia* while she was alive and well to meet her cousins Isabella and Rosa and *i tre* Michele in flesh and blood so they would cease to be phantasms to each other. The three of us went: Me, Audrey and Mom. We rented a car in *Roma* and I drove a whirlwind loop around *Roma*, up through *Amelia, Ferrara, Spoleto, Firenze,* to *Venezia* and down the east coast through *Ravenna* and *Acquaviva delle Fonti* then up the *la Costiera Almalfitana* back to *Roma*. In *Firenze* with my mother, I stood absolutely still in the *Piazza della Signoria* with my arms spread open like wings and let the art hit me in the chest like a tidal wave. I wept. I hadn't been able to take it all in before I stood there with my mother, holding her hand, the full beauty of *Italia,* the impact of what it means that the hand and eye and heart and soul have the capacity to create such work, such art and architecture as happened during *la Rinascimento*. I stood in the *piazza* holding my mother's hand and I wept and the cobblestones and marble statues spun around me. Again the question hit me like a lightning bolt: if humans have the capacity to sculpt and paint and write and create such beauty: *What can my hands make?*

A man in a maroon beret walked purposefully up to me as if to answer this question, *"Perché piangi bellissima?"* Why do you cry, beautiful one? But it was as if he already understood my tears, because how else can one react to *Firenze*? At a total loss for utterance, I asked him if there was a book to understand, *per capire*, a book of the story of Florence. I wanted to know what were the forces that came together, what were the conditions around which human beings lived up to their creative potential? *"C'è un libro che spiega tutta la storia di Firenze?"*

"Sì! Sì! Aspetta qui. Un attimo, un attimo." Yes, yes, wait here. One moment.

He ran out of the piazza. I stood still and continued to cry. He came back in a few minutes with a heavy hardcover book, "One Thousand Years of Florence." I opened it and saw a photo of Michelangelo Buonarroti's *Davide* in a wooden box being hoisted out of the piazza during World War II. The caption said, "David, being evacuated."

"Grazie," I said to the man, *"ma, non in Inglese! In l'Italiano! O tutto due, italiano ed inglese?"*

"Ho capito." He ran off again, and the image was nailed to my brain of this big statue of a muscular naked young man being evacuated during the war so he wouldn't get harmed. I thought of my father. I wished he had been evacuated during the war, but no, he was sent into the thick of it. He fought the worst of it, and though he came out alive, he suffered the most; for him the war never ended.

The man in the maroon beret yelled when he returned, *"Ecco!"* and handed me an even heavier bilingual edition in Italian and English. *"Mille Anni di Firenze."*

"Grazie," I said, *"Graziemille"* and I kissed the book and held it to my heart. *"Perfetto. Cuanto costa?"*

"Venti sei mille lire, bella."

I gave him cash and walked on. There was something I needed to *capishe* here. My mother asked me why I was crying and all I could say was "It's too beautiful. What the hand and the heart is capable of making." But there was so much more going on inside me. I carried the heavy book with pride. Maybe I would understand something. The line outside the *Uffizi* was around the building. I went to the front of the line and told the museum guard about my mother's heart surgery, and the guard made a fuss, insisting I bring my mother at once to the front of the line. *"Mamma Rachele! Mamma Rachele! Subito!"* We did the same at the *Galleria dell'Accademia.*

In *Acquaviva, Zia* Isabella knew we arrived of course, ten minutes before we pulled up. Word travels fast in small towns. I made out the word *"sbagliato"* in what *Zia* Isabella said to me, with her hand jutting to the side, she heard I made a wrong turn to find her street. Perhaps the same wrong turn as when I visited her a decade before. All through the north of Italy, my Mom didn't speak a word of Italian. She was confused by simple sentences in Italian like, *"un bicchiere d'acqua per favore"* or *"dov'è il bagno?"* As soon as we pulled into *Acquaviva delle Fonti*, she broke into dialect and rambled on fluently. She surprised herself. Her cousins Rosa and Isabella laughed and laughed. My mother spoke the dialect of one hundred years ago, when her mother was a little girl in *Acquaviva.* Her antiquated expressions tickled them; no one talked like this in *Acquaviva* anymore. Some phrases she said were *"Dingeel a me."* Tell me. *"Ye tutta fatt."* It's done. *"Disch a ked."* I told him. *"Ke de ditt a me."* He told me. All her cousins were amazed by this American cousin who spoke the local dialect of a hundred years ago! They took us around from house to house, so my Mom could meet *i tre* Michele. Since GranmaRose was ninety-nine, I had the forethought to videotape all her relatives singing *"Tanti Auguri"* and wishing her blessings on reaching *"cent'anni."* My mother's cousins regaled her with stories of how they dreamed of their American cousins all their life. The tallest Michele told us he was a prisoner in Egypt during the war and he kept a photo of his American cousin with him through those years. We didn't quite understand until he took out the photo. There was my Mom as a sixteen year old Bronx beauty in her bathing suit at the beach. She was astounded. Then his wife Ada took out the bedspread they showed me on my first visit, that GranmaRose had sent them as a present for their wedding. Although forty years old, it looked brand new as they unfolded it for display. And finally he took out the American five dollar bill that Granma had sent him, and that I'd seen almost a decade before. "It meant so much to me, I never could bear to spend it," he said. My cousin Nino brought us to the *Cattedrale di San Eustachio* where GranmaRose was baptized. We stared at the ornate silverwork and marble baptismal font in wonder. Imagining GranmaRose as a little *bambina* was easy. She was that to us now. Nino told us we must come back one year for *La Festa della Madonna di Constantinopile.* He told us that the Emperor Constantine founded Constantinople as a new Rome and capital of the Roman Empire. Rome fell in 476 AD and Constantinople was called the capital of the Eastern Roman Empire. The Turks assaulted what was left of the empire in 1453. The emperor fought to his death. The city was sacked and burned. They made churches into mosques. As Constantinople burned, the Greek Orthodox Christians tried to save their icons, their paintings of the Madonnas from the fire by throwing them into the sea of Marmara. The people ran to the sea *hanno portato La Madonna*. This Madonna floated into the Mediterranean Sea and all the way to Bari, and was carried to *Acquaviva delle Fonti*. And that's how she became *la patrona di Acquaviva delle Fonti*. Then still laughing about my Mom's dialect, Nino taught us this local tongue-twister, *"Se na ma sci, sciamannin, se nana ma sci, non g'n' scim scenn."* It means something like, if we're gonna go, let's go. If we're not gonna go, let's not go. It's the long Italian goodbye, filled with lingering and extended talk. Leaving one another is so hard it rips you apart. I wondered how my grandmother as a young teenager had ever gotten on that boat. All I could think is that she was young and full of the future, *giovane e piena di futuro, speranzosa.*

Horizontal People

NEW YORK

My first cancer was diagnosed by a boardwalk portrait artist on the Jersey Shore named Rhoda Shapiro. My second cancer was diagnosed by a surrealist painter named Ulek Tosher. I met Ulek in a beautiful way. One day in Sag Harbor, I walked down the main strip to buy an ice cream cone. I saw an old man in a wheelchair next to a bench. I went into the ice cream store and ordered an extra vanilla cone for the old man. And that's how our amorous friendship began. Ulek ate the cone voraciously and got all excited like a little kid and invited me up to see his paintings. His nurses aide helped him up the stairs. Inside, his apartment was a world full of paintings like Marc Chagall. I was taken by the whimsical floating juxtapositions of Ulek's dream images. Fish flew like clouds. Characters danced. Garbage pails had rococo designs. A bull smiled at a long onion stalk. Ulek and I began a correspondence that lasted for years, until his death. One day he mailed me a photograph of a portrait he painted of me. One eye was more closed, one more open, the face was blue, and in the neck was a yellow light bulb, with a man curled up asleep around the light bulb.

Ulek was right. My thyroid gland was asleep, and I didn't know it.

My neck began to grow. Fatigue and depression set in. My fingernails cracked. My hair was brittle. I went back to Sloan-Kettering on a regular basis, by now I considered it a part-time job. Fifteen years had passed since I'd had chemotherapy, surgeries, and radiation, and specialists still wanted to scan me, now more than ever, to see the long term results of the treatment. The cardiologist monitored the effects of radiation and chemotherapy on the heart, pericardial tissues, and major arteries. The pulmonologist listened to my lungs and quarterbacked the team. She'd listened to my lungs for half my lifetime, since I was eighteen. The ENT surgeon and dental surgeon argued about a mass in my maximus sinus that originated in the border between the sinus and the root of the gum. There is no doctor for this border. The hematologist reviews my Hodgkin's status and checks my glands. A gynecologist keeps an eye on an ovarian cyst and the cervix. The breast surveillance oncologist kneads my breasts once a year and sends me for scans to monitor the effect of radiation on breast tissue. The breast surveillance diagnostician I see twice a year. He invented a special machine for core biopsies and breast sonograms and keeps an eye on the schwannoma he discovered in my armpit. The physiatrist works with the effects of radiation on my musculoskeletal system. My neck muscles have atrophied from the radiation, and the innervation to my rotator cuffs, which gives me trouble pulling my sword out of my scabbard. Not a good thing for a Lancelot, and I am Lancelot, Lanzillotto, Lancillotto, Lancelot, and life is mission after mission in service to love. The physiatrist sent me for an orthotic fitting for a brace to hold up my head. The handsome colonoscopist I go to every three to five years. The urologist follows the cyst on my kidney, which has grown bigger than the kidney itself. I refuse to continue to use fruit metaphors to describe cyst and tumor size. A neurologist tests my peripheral neuropathy from the chemo. I see both a shrink and a psychologist who specialize in long-term cancer survivor issues: guilt, confusion, the inability to make long-term goals; fear of the cancer returning, panic. The endocrinologist gives me a blue pill to make sure I stay functioning with a sleepy thyroid. The national specialist in long-term survivor care looks at things no one else thinks of, like the vagus nerve, which got fried by radiation and yet regulates my heart rate and pulse. He gave me a piece of paper to stick inside my wallet in case I am found somewhere unconscious: ASPLENIC: USE BROAD SPECTRUM ANTIBIOTIC AND TAKE BLOOD CULTURES. The general practitioner I don't have any time to see, but when I bunk into her at the hospital, she says, "You can come see me you know."

The vertical people come in fast and throw on the light. Even the best of them startle you. Sloan-Kettering has become a home for me, some sanctuary. The first time I had cancer I was a virgin, though that's not what the medical chart will tell you. The medical chart will say, "This eighteen-year-old Caucasian female presents with . . ." You remember the place that gave you your soul, showed you your mettle. You remember your proving ground, yes, you remember it your whole life. The bed takes my body, adjusts to me, I adjust to it. Nowadays these beds breathe actually. I can't get used to the electric air bladder; if I shift, it breathes me back into place. Mr. Passalacqua is in the next bed. Everything comes through these curtains. His son speaks a dialect to him. What do I know if he is *Calabrese* or *Napolitan*? He's not from my town, that's all I can tell. Maybe Mr. Passalacqua is from some village I never heard of. Still, the language is my music. It's strange to hear my native language here, my language of the fields, the music my grandmother speaks. I hear Mr. Passalacqua's phrases to the doctor, and his phrases to his son. I understand him when he says he drank eight glasses of water today. We are horizontal, Mr. Passalacqua and me. I understand him even when his phrasing eludes me. I turn into the bed. The bed inflates under my thighs and back. We try to hide from the light. It's hard to stay in the game. At some point you need a big win to even catch up. The light across the room on the ceiling passes easily through the mesh of the curtain and into my eyes. I wear a baseball hat. A baseball hat gives me selfhood here and shields me from the ever-present light.

Sloan-Kettering slowly leaves the harbor and enters a world and crosses time zones all its own. Before you know it, the shore is the bright spot on the horizon and then, long gone. Manhattan is long gone. Relativity is gone. You are not on land. You are on the ocean between two lands. No point to try to get back to land. Better to float. Stare at the white foam, look up at the ceiling. Count the dots on the drop ceiling tiles. Stay horizontal. Let the waves take you into their own rhythm. Let the waves take you where they will. Once a riptide had taken hold of me. I was in the ocean at Robert Moses State Park, after a visit to my dad. It was the day that Audrey and our friend Hope accompanied me to see my father. I jumped into the ocean to cleanse my head, my sinuses, get the stale air of the mental home out of my pores. I was held in place. I waved and shouted. Just the day before I watched on the news a summer special on riptides, "It doesn't pay to fight it," the news anchor said, you'd sooner exhaust yourself trying to swim to shore. "If you get caught in a riptide, swim horizontal to the shoreline, and wave for help. Don't fight a riptide." I stroked parallel to the shore. I was sucked in place. I couldn't get my legs to the top of the water. The water felt like two strong hands, one pushing on top of my head keeping me from advancing to the shore, and the other pulling my whole spine from behind. When I was a kid my older brothers used to fight me that way, the top of my head in the palm of their hands, me swinging wildly to land a punch. My brothers would laugh at my effort, and smack my face at will. Now the ocean was like a big brother taunting me. I feared for my life. Audrey's arms swung wildly to the lifeguard, but he looked calm. I waved to expose my distress. Hope stepped waist deep into the water and reached her arms outward for me. I could easily have been sucked out to sea and vanished. A rescue wave came from way back deep in the ocean, a hand, it felt like a hand, grabbed my spine, I could feel cold fingers between my vertebrae fling me over the wall. A wave that felt like a hand. My body lunged forward and Hope grabbed me to shore. I was shaken up. I lay down on the sand and caught my breath. Ten minutes later, another woman got caught in the same spot in the ocean. This time, the lifeguard with his orange lifesaver made a dash for her. Then he put up a red flag to mark the riptide and warn the swimmers.

You hear footsteps, you get hopeful. The nurse looks at my eyes with a sympathetic smile. Touches me twice extra. The patient escort remembers me from seventeen years ago. Ha! I've been here a lifetime. I'm being pushed around in a wheelchair, going into the public spaces like a piazza; the X-ray waiting room, the hallways. Some of the escorts upset the patients. The patients wear it on their faces as they get jostled. Ugo Majori is the senior escort. He's been good to me since I was a kid. He has eleven months and eight days to go until his retirement. He's smooth. I've seen his hair turn white over the years. I've admired his gold cross and smile. I'll be here longer than him. I'll be here longer than Aletha the cleaning lady, Cecil Rowe the doorman. I'll be here longer than all the workers from the Caribbean whose smooth hands and warm bright smiles have helped to heal me. I will outlive my oncologist.

Over the decades the diseases have changed in this place and so have the paintings that hang on the walls. There used to be paintings I could relate to; a Native American man carrying a canoe over his shoulders down a rocky stream, van Gogh's skeletal The Langlois Bridge at Arles with the solitary black figure crossing with an umbrella, and best of all, the back of a naked bald man pulling a long red vein, like a rein, standing on horseback. The women who work in X-ray remember that one. I walked rectangular laps around these hallways. Now, all these paintings have disappeared. They've been replaced with cheerful tourist landscapes and designs that are horrible when you're in pain, horizontal and disoriented, and the air circulating the corridors feels like Arctic winds. Here, we know one thing: we are not on vacation. Having cancer in front of van Gogh's Arles is one thing, but with these other decorative landscapes, one of a rectangular pool with empty lounge chairs? Uh-huh. I don't want to feel sick in front of beach umbrellas and cloudless skies. Once the butterfly is in my vein, the plastic circle naming me on my wrist, and I'm in a wheelchair, I hear all the stories. Ugo, parks me behind a divider, near a horizontal man. This man, on a stretcher in front of a painting of a white lattice fence open to a blue sea and palm trees tells me: "They did this, they did that, they sent me home, said come back once

in a while for a checkup. I was like a pig in shit. Then they called. They
said you better come in. I said you gotta be kiddin' me. It grew back. They
took tests. They said we gotta do something. It's in your kidney. It's in your
liver. It's in your bone marrow. We gotta treat you through the head. Maybe
you have six weeks. Eight weeks. Ten weeks. Send me home. Gimme four
weeks. Four good weeks. I'll be a pig in shit. They're killing me. They think
they're curing me."

You lose your cockiness quick in here. I see a neck flap on a biker chick.
I see her cheeks are swollen. So incongruous to her tight jeans, biker boots,
big red hair, Confederate-flag-wearing big chest boyfriend. We hold onto the
land. Then we let go. People look at me for a sign. Here's a woman, her
hospital gown open in the front, showing her cleavage. A sexy woman is a
sexy woman in or out of a hospital gown.

This is the outpatient building. People aren't really here, really horizontal.
We walk in, we get dressed again, we walk out. We rip our paper bracelets
off on Sixty-Seventh Street by the smokers on the bench next to a small
bronze statue of a girl in pigtails doing a cartwheel. When I walk, I dodge
the smoke of one, then another. I zigzag. No one can take a walk with me
down the sidewalk. I constantly shift direction. Some patients rebel in minor
ways. Here, every little thing is a rebellion. One young girl in a red bandana
rearranges the furniture slightly; pulls a double chair forward to put her feet
up. I used to turn the paintings upside down. Who'll notice anyway? Vertical
people hardly stop at all. Now they have this shit nailed to the walls. They
used to switch paintings often, a volunteer used to come around with a cart.

I waited weeks for this appointment, but when the hour comes, they
are right on time. They've been expecting me. I've been moody all morning.
To Audrey, to my mom. Everything they say bothers me. Audrey says I am
pushing her away. I act the way I've seen cancer patients act in these waiting
rooms for two decades. My mother brings a humor book by Loretta LaRoche
and feels accomplished when I laugh before I go in for the biopsy. Laughter:
mission accomplished.

Five white coats are around me. The higher up they are, the less they
manually do. The technician offers me a gown. The latest are maroon. In fact,
there's not a blue one to be seen. Just hundreds of stiff, folded, maroon. I
wish I brought my own, saved one from the old days. The blue were so soft.
The maroon will get soft in time. Then, they'll buy new stiff ones in stripes,
different colors for different size bodies. Some women tie these gowns tight;
they seem form fitted, fancy. Like we're all at an occasion. Like we are monks.
I let mine hang open. Tie it? Fa'what? I am horizontal. I wait for the chain
of command. The technician finishes and waits for the doctor. The young
doctor waits outside, reads the paperwork, and waits for the senior doctor.
When we are all set up and ready to go, we wait for the cytologist. The

technician calls Cytology repeatedly. The senior doctor tries to make things efficient. She knows the Cytology number by heart. She knows where they might be when they do not answer their lab extension. The senior doctor is over the resident's shoulder every step of the way. She chooses the nodes from the screen, and decides where they are in the neck. With a magic marker supplied by the technician, she marks the spot on my neck. The resident today is a puppet. All except for her rapport with me, the patient. Without being told, she asks me how I am, if she is pressing too hard, am I sure, etcetera. In one sense, I am between the doctor and the resident. When I tell the resident that I felt a sensation from my neck to my ear, she informs me that there is no nerve that runs in that direction. When she checks with the doctor, the doctor smiles, nods and says, "Yes, sometimes that happens."

The thought of getting a second cancer frightens and confirms something in me, a part of myself that sometimes is a memory, a scar down my belly when I look in a mirror. I am afraid to get a second cancer, but I know I will take it head on. Lightning twice. A lot of people in my theater life don't know I ever had a cancer. It is a lifetime ago. Am I ready for a life where no one knows I ever had cancer? Perhaps I should walk away. Enough testing. Enough treatment. At some point I will have to walk away. I do not want to die in this place. I, too, can refuse to believe the tests and doctors' conclusions. I can refuse what they tell me. Do it my way. *You gottada wronga guy.* I can die my way. Or I can go along with the protocol of the day, give them all the organs they want. She has the needle in my neck and her eyes are on the screen. I am aware of our eye contact. I am aware of the roles we play. I am aware that the roles could have easily been reversed. I could be the resident. I could be the Chief of Radiology. I am her in my car, in my kitchen, on stage, in the places I give all the orders. I could be vertical.

The biopsy came back negative, just like the four before that one, but my neck kept growing. I made some phone calls and hooked into a community of opera singers who had thyroid surgeries. I figured they would be most picky about who they let cut their throats. One singer told me to wear yellow cotton or silk around my neck and I would be fine. Another gave me the tip to go to an old-timer Doc at New York University. I wore yellow. His office was full of cobalt blue glass apothecary bottles from the last century of medicine. He gave me a two-hour medical examination, the most thorough of my life, as if it was 1890, and he must write all his impressions in meticulous penmanship, because my disease hasn't been named yet. Back when I was in college, I'd read these handwritten medical observations in the basement of the Harvard Medical Library. In the 1800s, doctors wrote down everything they observed with their senses before diagnoses had any names. At the end of the exam, this doctor did not offer a firm opinion either way about whether to recommend thyroidectomy or not. I thanked him, paid my five hundred cash, put on my coat, and opened the door to leave his office. Off the cuff, he said: "If the lump keeps growing I'd get it the hell outta there."

Those last six words were spoken directly from his gut. *Get it the hell outta there.* That's all I heard, and all I repeated when my mother asked, "What did the doctor say?" *Get it the hell outta there.*

I telephoned Sloan-Kettering immediately and scheduled the operation. I had my choice of two doctors. I trusted Ant'ny's assessment: "Go with the surgeon with the Ferragamo shoes."

Radioactive Feast

MEMORIAL SLOAN-KETTERING CANCER CENTER, 1997

My thyroid was packed with cancer. "Even the isthmus," Dr. Jatin Shah said.

I was admitted to the isolation floor to swallow liquid radiation. Radioactive symbols were on the outside of my room door. I remember those yellow and black trefoil symbols from the bomb shelter signs on apartment buildings in the Bronx. I walked by those yellow-and-black signs when I walked to Santa Maria School. Now I walked into it. My room didn't have an East River view. It looked out over buildings and rooftops of medical facilities with air vents and giant curled silver pipes. I wanted to stare into water, to watch the sunrise over Roosevelt Island. I punched the room, the bed, the bedside table, the walls. I slammed my books on the windowsill. I bounced off the wall. I wanted to run through the wall. These walls were thick. I jumped onto the bed. A doctor appeared at my glass door pushing a heavy steel cart on thick rubber wheels in steel swivel casings. A brass cylinder was atop the cart. This strange altar rolled directly toward me with her slow gentle push. She unfastened the hinge with great care. She had tiny fingers. Inside was another cylindrical container.

"What's that?"

"Lead."

She handed me a cocktail straw and instructed me to place the straw into the lead cylinder when she opened it, and to drink all the contents quick. I put the straw between my lips and teeth. This liquid radiation transported in lead surrounded by brass, this dangerous liquid was about to slide down my skinny throat.

"*Salut! Cindon!*" To health. "*Cent'anni.*" A hundred years. I inhaled, exhaled, pushed the straw deep in my mouth, and in my head recited a line of Jalaluddin Rumi: "*Tonight remove whatever remains.*" I surrendered. I drank the drink. I downed the Radioactive Iodine 131 in big pulls on the straw. I tried to suck it right down my throat and not taste it, not swish it around my mouth. A cup of poison down the hatch. Let it do its work. I opened my eyes and she was already gone. I was sealed off for the next few days in isolation. I had my mantra: *Tonight remove whatever remains. Tonight remove whatever remains. Tonight remove whatever remains.*

I had the idea I could sweat the radiation out, as illogical as this may be. I wanted to get out of Sloan-Kettering before the weekend was over. Any tissue I spit in, or toilet paper I wiped myself with, got taken out of the room in bags marked with a radioactive symbol. I was toxic waste. No one could be near me. GranmaRose would never have a clue of my life experience. I imagined her youth, her immigration, her Bronx prime. I'd washed and straightened her toes with my hands as she turned eighty, ninety. But did she imagine my life? Did she have a clue? My life would be measured by her life, her strength, her values, her ability to leave her family and immigrate and survive, her aptitude for *sopravvivenza. Tonight remove whatever remains.* My tongue is thick metal, a slab of steel. I'm so contaminated. I whirl around the room, yelling. Rumi was a Sufi, tonight I am a dervish, I must whirl. *Tonight remove whatever remains.* Remove my brain if need be, remove my guts, place them in jars for some future life, my love, remove, like decay from my heart, any longing I have for another. Tonight remove, pick at whatever remains. Tonight, do not make me wait. Not another minute. Tonight remove whatever remains of the splinter in my heart. I would trade it not for another's bottle. Toxicity is a part of my life. A huge brass cylinder. I am a lesbian in a scanning machine. It is tight right over my face. Straight women hold my hand hotly. Moist hand-holding. Hours go by. The radiation engineer comes in with a Geiger counter and measures as he slowly steps toward me from the door. He steps away from me and keeps taking accurate measurements.

"I keep drinking water and twirling around," I tell him, "how soon can I get outta here?"

"I'll bring you some movies," he said.

"I will get out of here in record time. What's the I-131 record?"

"Three days."

He comes back and hands me the film, *Babette's Feast.* It is slow and takes place in simpler times. I am on fast. I wanna jump up and get outta here. What I remember of that film is the pageantry of food, women, peasants' offerings, women with breasts and potholders, carrying pans and dishes of pheasants or something with feathers, and fish. I remember something about a visitor, an occasion, how an eternity swells up into one sit-down meal, one *festa*, one giant turtle for soup, and all I want, as I watch them eat, is to expunge, to spit, to rid myself of anything inside me. To spue. I have drunk more poison and it will keep me alive some more.

Ant'ny comes and sits outside the door and talks with me through the doorway. I feel safe with this new imposed radioactive distance.

Three days later I am released.

"Do not sleep next to anyone for thirty days. Stay six feet away from anyone pregnant. Do not hug pets," the Geiger Counter Engineer says.

"What happens if I sleep next to someone?"

"They will get more radiation in that one night than they are supposed to get in one lifetime."

I walk out onto First Avenue. A man dressed like an athlete but with a fast walk like a junkie shouts at me and stares. He's got the eyes of a bull and his nostrils are flared like he can't get enough oxygen. He approaches me and I spit at him. "Stay away from me, asshole. My spit is toxic. I am radioactive. I'm not kidding." He backs off, and I feel like a superhero. I expectorate a powerful toxin. I am a snake with radioactive venom. When I get home and the phone rings, I answer the telephone, "Toxic Lesbians Unite."

Limoncello and the Black Bra

TOSCANA, ITALIA

Friday, six p.m. I duck out of the thick heat that butters my skin, and into the dark stone interior of a church on the corner of the piazza. An instant cool relief. O brilliant stone that cools air. Rows of scarved heads turn toward me, stocky old women and Filipina nuns with the orphans the convent adopted. I cover my knees by pulling my cotton shorts low. I cover my head with an Egyptian white cotton scarf I carry in my knapsack for crashing churches, and sit in a pew in the back. An old man reaches with a flame on a long torch to light the candles all around the apse. The lower walls are engraved with the names of the dead and descriptions of their attributes, deeds, and service to the community. The stones are big. Bodies are buried in these walls. Outside, electronic beats bash through the open windows high up in the cathedral vault. An Italian rap artist heaves his voice into the microphone, "Aw, Aw, AAW!" a cry that sounds distinctly American. All day I listened to rap artists rhyme and break down Italian syllables in ways that mystified me. Now, the simplest words rang in rhymes in my head: *pasta, basta, mi lascia, nella piazza. Madonna mia, compania, zio e zia abbondanza addolorata pasta decapitata zuccherata parcheggio, messaggio, oggi, dopo domani lunazione.* In Italian I heard rhymes within rhymes and meanings within meanings as it entered my bloodstream and opened my lungs. Inside the church, the women prayed in unison, fingering rosary beads. Their collective voice washed over my sweat, the murmur of their soft, repeatable prayer. I wrote down words, one by one, like beads, and deciphered each in my pocket dictionary. I had to learn Italian one word at a time. One phrase at a time. I strung words onto lines of music I already knew by heart. Even English I speak with an Italian syntax. "Ma! The car. It's here?" The women finger each bead. I write down each word. "*Ave, O Maria, piena di grazia, il Signore è con te. Tu sei benedetta fra le donne e benedetto è il frutto del tuo _____, Gesù.*" To find the word I can't make out, I go over the English in my head. "Hail Mary, Full of grace. The Lord is with you. Blessed art Thou amongst women, and blessed is the fruit of thy womb, Jesus." What word are they saying for *womb*, "*frutto del _____?*" On Jesus, we all bow our heads. I look up *womb* in my pocket dictionary. The old man finished his methodical lighting of all the tall candles in the apse and around the church. He put down his long torch and picked up an even longer pole to push the top windows closed, muffling the rappers. The amplified "Awww!" yells of the local youth freestyling into the microphone at one end of the piazza, and this deep perpetual rumbling *Ave Maria* at the other end of the piazza made a vocal sparring and deep prayer. *Ave Maria* took on the rap beat. "*Ave Maria, Piena di Grazia, Aww, Aww. Signore è con te.* Yeah. Yo that's what I'm talkin' about. *Sei benedetta fra le donne . . .*" With each round of the *Ave Maria*, I got more and more words, and joined the choral recitation. I had no rosary beads with me but could picture the crystal rosary I got when I was seven for my First Holy Communion. The crystal beads looked like frozen tears, like diamonds. The rappers unplugged their amplification, as they had agreed to, for the Novena. The *Ave Maria* continued for one hundred rounds.

This is what GranmaRose did when she arrived in America. She paid constant attention and learned new words one by one. She read words on the sides of Bronx trucks, on buildings, on food labels. Into her nineties she wrote words down. My mother laughed when Granma asked her to write down the word *swish* and teach her what it meant. Later she was proud to use it in conversation. "I'a swish it around." Words that had Latin structures she could understand. *Acquavivese* was a whole other beast. Each word was twisted and spun with a head resonance, these syllables turned corners, bent meanings, and hand signals were strewn in amongst the phrases. *Acquavivese* was a symphony each person conducted for themselves.

My dictionary said *grembo* for womb, but that sounded nothing like what the congregants were praying. It sounds like they said *petto*. I look up *petto*. Chest. That doesn't make sense. I move on. "*Santa Maria, Madre di Dio, prega per noi pecca tori,*" Let's see what the word for *sinner* is, *ah peccatore* yes that is what they are saying! What a beautiful word, *peccatori, peccatori adesso*, sinners now. Now and at the hour of our death . . . *Adesso, e nell'ora della nostra morte, Amen.*" Beautiful.

After the *Novena*, I walked back out into the heat of the *piazza*, able to pray the *Ave Maria* in Italian, all except for the word for *womb*. The rappers stood around chatting about where they'd grab dinner. My favorite rapper, Fabrizio, was sixteen, skinny, with a shaven head, and dramatic brown eyes. He was all eyes. He waved in the crowd at a man a little older than myself with a young boy on his shoulders. The man had to be his father. I introduced myself as a fan of his son. This opened his face into a broad smile. I complimented him on his son's stage personality in simple words like *un ragazzo bravo*, but told him with hand signals that I thought his son should stop smoking, to which he agreed. Paolo invited me for dinner. I got in the front seat of the white *Cinquecento* and the little brother of about eight got in the backseat. I wondered if the kid thought it was odd that his father was bringing a woman back to the house; but then again I'm not quite a woman, what am I? I'm a woman, yes, but a dyke, I put out signals that are androgynous. I think it's a soul thing; a way I walk, carry myself, you might say, for if you know me, you know I'm a woman. We got to the flat and Paolo invited me to take a shower. I didn't know if he meant with him, or alone. For a second I had to remind myself that I was a woman, in a strange man's house, in Italy. But in the same moment I was embarrassed by these fears and distinctions. The discomfort was all inside my own twisted American head. It was scorching hot out. I was sweaty. Paolo had invited me to dinner and now handed me a towel for a quick shower before we ate. Of course! He was making no advances, just treating me like family. *Madonn'* what was wrong with me? Sometimes it is as if I carry the censorship of my whole family in a piggyback ride everywhere I go; at times I can barely move. Paolo pointed to the bathroom. I was conscious to not use an American amount of water, but lavished some soap under my arms and stood gratefully under the shower head. I felt so much better and cooler, revived. I shook out my clothes before getting back into them. I sat on the couch and Paolo gave me a tall glass of *acqua minerale* with lemon. He knew the order of things. The *sistemazione*.

The front door opened. I anticipated his wife would be coming home from work. What I wasn't prepared for was how drop-dead gorgeous she was—dark hair, dark eyes, strong nose, and a serious inquiring sexy look, *Magnani-esque*. I jumped up to my feet. I had asked her name in advance.

"*Ciao! Selvaggia.*"

"*Chi sai?*" What else could be said to a stranger on your couch, wet from a shower, but, "Who are you?"

"*Anna, un'amica di Fabrizio.*"

Her smile disarmed me; any reference to her firstborn son would provoke this smile. He was her joy. I was forthright with women, immediately wanting them to know I wasn't a threat. I wasn't there for their man. I was one of the boys. The first thing she did was take off her shirt. She wore a black lace bra. I don't know if she would have done this if I were a guy. I have no idea. Italian women, I thought, *Madonn'*! She tossed her work blouse onto a chair. I sipped the *acqua minerale,* and let the fizz pop all my cells open.

"*Questo è l'Est*," she said. This is the east. Selvaggia threw open the shutters, threw off the requirements of being in public. I was in her space now. She walked to the other side of the room and threw open more shutters, "*Questo è il Sud.*" This is the south. The mountains and wind and setting sun were guests in her house. Her gods. The wind. On her terraces. At her table. Paolo handed me a glass of red wine. "*Artigianale*," he said, local. I drank the *vino.* My blood set with the sun and moved with the wind. All of Italy was just beyond Selvaggia's balconies. The wind threw the long green shutters open and shut. More *vino. Grazie.* I stepped out onto the balcony and breathed. All of Italy, all the world was just beyond Selvaggia's black bra and balconies. Selvaggia put a cigarette in her lips and bent over the stove top. Some people are so *ffhuckin* sexy when they smoke. No wonder Fabrizio smokes, his mother is a goddess united with fire. I stretched my arms on the balcony in the mountain wind. I pretended not to notice Selvaggia's body. Would it matter if she sensed I was a dyke? Would they care? They didn't probe. They didn't ask *Stai zzit'*? Northerners were different. *Toscana* was not *Bari. Montevarchi* was not *Acquaviva.*

Selvaggia sat down at the table in her black bra, as her husband, what was his name? poured *olio d'oliva* over a plate of *cicoria, agli'olio limone.* She called me in from the balcony. She didn't seem to mind me noticing her glorious *scolatura,* cleavage. *Scolatura, natura tura, faccio na mura.* Everything could rhyme with *scolatura.* The sun set over Selvaggia's *scolatura.* I sat up straight in the chair. I lifted a forkful of *cicoria* doused with *limone* into my mouth. The salty greens snapped me alert. Eating in Italy is breastfeeding straight from the earth.

The conversation came around to each of our work. He was a family counselor, she, a psychiatric nurse. A psychiatric nurse? Now we had something to talk about. My family needs a psychiatric nurse, I said. "*Necessito. Necessito.*" I talked about my father being traumatized from World War II, and the depression rampant in my family. I spoke words in Spanish and Italian and I used hand signals; we made eye contact and they understood me perfectly. I was so relieved to have two Italians to talk with who had a professional capacity to understand my father, and my family. My family experienced the inverse of the American dream, I said. I turned my sleeve inside out and showed Selvaggia the seams, to illustrate. More *vino. Grazie.* I sucked on the garlic and the olives and the bitter greens and the pasta and the good tough bread.

During all my years growing up, my father sat at the table in his boxer shorts and tank shirt and socks, but my mother never hung around the house in a bra, and certainly never in front of strangers. My sister, I thought, would never take home a stranger and take her shirt off. What happened to us after we crossed the ocean? *Vino? Sì, grazie.* Thick bread I pulled with my teeth. Fava beans. I drank the wine and stopped struggling with words. The thought crossed my mind as the *vino e olio e verdura* set into my blood—I must get Italian citizenship. This is me. I belong here. I open up here.

Paolo pulled down a pot like a silver bucket from on top of the refrigerator. With pride he introduced me to his homemade *limoncello*, from Amalfi lemons. The breeze lathered me from all angles. I breathed in deep and leaned back in the chair. Paolo told me the recipe for his *limoncello*, emphasizing the amount of time involved, and the importance of Amalfi lemons. *"Limone Amalfi,"* he emphasized.

I sipped his *limoncello* slowly. Night was upon us and here in this little shot glass was the elixir for my soul. Paolo was detailed in his instructions, especially the precision of picking the dozens of lemons, *"grande, dolce, limpido."* big sweet and clean. It mattered where they came from. Only lemons from *Amalfi,* or *Sicilia,* were good enough to do all this labor for the drink. He kept saying, *"lasciate riposare"* let it rest, *"lasciatelo respirare,"* let it breathe, so that the making of *limoncello* sounded like the cure I required. *"Lasciatelo riposare per due o tre settimane."* Let it rest for two or three weeks.

Here it was, all this work and knowledge handed down, a wisdom for life, in a tin pot on top of the refrigerator offered to a visitor from a faraway land.

On the way out of the apartment to the evening rap concert, Selvaggia showed me her son's room. A life-size photo cut-out of Che Guevara was where Mickey Mouse had been just a few years before, she said. She touched my shoulder, and we left the apartment to head back out into the *piazza*.

Garlic, the *Ave Maria*, and the Blue Leg

NEW YORK

It was Presidents' Day, when my mother telephoned me at eleven at night. I was at home in Brooklyn, Cherub had just hidden his hot chicken dinner under his pumpkin-colored velvet bed.

"What's up Ma?"

"GranmaRose hasn't gone to the bathroom. I put a suppository in. I hoped she could get a little sleep. She's been throwing up a little bit."

"What did she eat? Put her on the phone."

"Granma, *cosa mangia oggi!*"

"*Mammami, Sant'Antonee.*"

"Ma. Ma!"

"Annie. Annie!"

"Yeah. Ma."

"We were over Enza's. She ate all day long. She and Gaetano kept drinking black coffee. No one was counting how much she ate, but when I went to take a jelly donut home there were none left. She must have ate six Annie—"

"Yeah."

"Everything's okay."

"I'm getting in the car now. I'll be there in a half hour."

"That's not necessary—"

Audrey slept in the passenger seat as I drove over the Brooklyn Bridge, up the FDR, across the Willis Avenue Bridge and up the Deegan past our *colosseo* Yankee Stadium lit up at night. We walked into Mom's apartment, and immediately it hit me, "What's that smell?"

"Lysol. She's been vomiting, and I've been disinfecting."

"No, that other smell, underneath what you've been covering by cleaning. Granma, look at me. *Apre la boca.* Open the mouth! *Oh madon'.* Ma, I'm taking her to the hospital. Audrey, pull up the car. I'll carry her down. She's puking up liquid shit. Ma, what, you think it's coffee 'cause it's brown?"

"Two black coffees, and later on top of that she had brown coffee."

"Ma, her intestines are blocked. Her feces are backing up through her throat. It's not black coffee."

"Oh, the black coffee that was hours ago, who knows where it is now. But the proximity of the brown to black coffee."

"Granma, I'm gonna lift you up, okay?"

"Okay. God'a bless you."

Her head was heaving and the liquid spewed out of her. I lifted her up in my arms, carried her down to the car and drove to the ER, where the doctor confirmed that she vomited half-digested fecal matter, calling it copremesis; Granma's intestines were twisted.

"I can go in with a tiny bit of anesthesia," he said, "and see what I can do. At ninety-nine, I can't give her too much anesthesia."

Audrey and I stood vigil outside the OR, and prayed the *Ave Maria.* We held hands and sang softly and cried.

"No, it doesn't go like that."

"What are the words?" Audrey asked.

"It's like the Hail Mary. *Ave Maria,* is Hail Mary, it's like Hello Mary."

"Ahh, hello Mary. Did the nuns teach you this?"

"No. All those years in Catholic school, the least they could have taught us was the *Ave Maria* in Italian and Latin. The best gift in all of Catholicism, the most beautiful song in the world. And they leave that out. I hadda teach myself. I mean the Hail Mary I learned in school. They had the third graders teach the second graders. They paired us up in twos and sat us in the stairwell. We went over it and over it and over it and over it. Then they tested us. It was terrifying. I couldn't remember the second stanza."

"And the Italian?"

"I sat in a church for a Friday night six o'clock novena."

"Novena?"

"Oh c'mon Audrey. Right now you want a primer on Italians and Catholicism?"

"No sorry, I don't mean to—"

"Oh look I'm sorry, it's just I'm stressed. I hope Granma makes it through surgery."

"I know."

"I mean who gets operated on at ninety-nine years old?"

"Rose is the strongest person I know."

"I know. So, the novena is when you pray together for nine days straight."

"With the beads."

"Yes, the beads."

"A prayer for every bead. We could do a prayer your way. You lead a prayer. I don't have to lead the prayer."

"Dear Molecules, help all the cells of Rose's body—"

"*Ave Maria. Grazie Plena.* Just sing the Ahh's 'til you get it. *Maria Grazie plena. Maria grazie plena.* That means Mary full of grace. *Ave Ave Dominus tecum. Benedicta tu i mulieribus. Mulieribus* means amongst women. It's a great word. *et Benedictus Benedictus fructus ventris tui, tui Gesu. Ave Maria.*"

I pushed open the doors into the post-op recovery unit before GranmaRose was awake. I touched her hand to make the connection, as if I could ground GranmaRose's spirit back into the body even before she was conscious. Granma wasn't yet conscious. I held her hand until she smiled. As soon as her eyelids opened, there were her sky blue eyes full of character and vitality and sharpness. She said to me, "Everyting's okay Dolly, God'a bless you."

GranmaRose is stable, I repeated in my head, and in phone calls to my siblings, GranmaRose is stable.

Ant'ny and I agreed that Aunt Patty ought not to feed Granma any more heavy bowls of *pasta'riguth'*, shells and *ricotta*, which "turns to cement," Ant'ny said. A week later, Aunt Patty made *past'n'peas*. Granma screamed to Saint Anthony and the Virgin Mary that her leg felt like a stone. "My leg! My leg!

E come 'na pietro! It's like a stone! *Madonna mia! Madonna mia! Sant'AntoNEE Sant'AntoNEE, la gamba e come 'na pietro. Sant'AntoNEE! Sant'AntoNEE!"*

I called the doctor.

"Give her Advil," he said.

"Advil? Doc, it seems like a post-op blood clot. She is pointing to a spot below her knee. She's in excruciating pain."

"Impossible. If it were a clot the leg would be swollen and blue. Give her Advil."

I hung up, lifted her up in my arms, carried her to the car, and took her to the ER. I am Lancelot. *Lancialotto. Lancillotto.* Lanzillotto. Lanzi's kid. Rachele's kid. The Lanz. Lanzo. I wasn't gonna listen to no *chibobi.* Blood clots were diagnosed. Her leg became blue and ice cold. In intensive care for three weeks, she developed a bedsore on her heel. We rolled a towel underneath the ankle of her cold blue leg.

"She is too old for corrective cardiovascular surgery," the cardiovascular surgeon said. "The best option is amputation below the knee. If it was my grandmother, I'd amputate, and get her out of her misery."

CarKey and Aunt Patty's son stood in the ICU waiting room and quickly nodded in assent. "It's a piece of meat," CarKey said pragmatically, "cut it off." My cousin nodded. But what did he know. He had a hammerhead shark mounted over his living room couch. The thing was nine foot long. Its head stuck out from the wall so that the shark eye-balled everyone who walked through the front door. No way I was gonna let these guys make this decision over Baby GranmaRose. She had lived a whole century. Where was the dignity?

I stood up and pointed into the air. "Give me eight days," I said, "if nothing gets better, then you can amputate." Some voice inside me said, when all else fails, get the garlic out. Did I really believe in the power of garlic? I telephoned Al Paoletta. "Al, go get me some of that good garlic with the purple skin." The next eight nights, Audrey and I kept vigil by Granma's side. Granma stopped eating. I needed her to eat. I went to my mother's apartment and cooked two lamb chops in a cast iron pan, wrapped the whole thing in a dishtowel, and drove back to the hospital. She sat up in bed and grabbed the lamb chop in her fist and bit into it. I crushed the garlic, smothered her leg with a fine coat of Vaseline, then a poultice of virgin cold-pressed olive oil and crushed garlic. Then I wrapped the leg in a white cotton pillowcase. The hospital put her in a private room, and nurses stopped coming in, because of the garlic stench the lesbians were causing. Audrey led Granma in visualizations: "See the blood flowing freely. Rivers of red blood flowing." Granma would concentrate and point to the spot on the leg where it hurt her, saying, "Blooda clock." Her veins were collapsed and dry as arroyos.

Aunt Patty told my mother, "I don't believe in Annie and all this voodoo. I took care of Mamma all these years and she's been fine."

With the garlic, Audrey and I could see the blood fill the veins to concavity then ebb to convexity. The infusion of blood made the leg arteries swell with another life. We held our hands' heat over the spots Granma pointed to.

At ninety-nine years old, GranmaRose began to talk, for the first time, about her childhood goat. She'd point around the room as if she were in *Acquaviva* and say, "You got a goat, she got a goat, he got a goat, I got a goat. In the mornin', we each bring'ada milk from'ada goat and put'inda pail and put'ada stick'a in. Whoever's got'ada highest on'ada stick takes'ada milk and makes'ada *formaggio*, and take'ada biggest'a piece'a home."

She repeated this story for everyone who visited, and when I was there I asked them to take a turn and add the energy of their hands two inches over Granma's leg. Ant'ny had a big powerful hand with a lot of energy. He believed in what me and Audrey were trying to do. We prayed the *Ave Maria* with our hands over GranmaRose's leg. I do believe in garlic. We are heel of the boot people.

"*Blooda clock*," Granma said as she guided our hands over the spot, "*blooda clock.*"

GranmaRose walked out of the hospital with two legs on. Her doctors didn't say a word. The nurses showed their amazement and sent her off with well wishes, and asked us what the hell we did.

Cittadinanza

"**I** need Granma and Grandpa's documents."

"What for?" Aunt Patty snapped.

"I'm getting Italian citizenship."

"What's wrong with the United States! What, this country ain't good enough for you! What's wrong with you! What are you gonna do over there. What they got over there we don't got here. Hah?" She smacked the table.

I choked on the bite of custard pie that was in my mouth. The crust was cardboard. I coughed and took a sip of tepid tea. "It's not about getting something, Aunt Patty, it's just . . ."

"People are ungrateful to the United States. I don't understand what's a matter with you people."

"Sis, she's not renouncing the U.S." My mother got up and put the green Jello back in the fridge.

"Sister, they all think alike. All of a sudden the United States isn't good enough."

"Sis, calm down. Don't get yourself all worked up."

"*Madonn'.*"

"What do you think you're gonna do over there?"

"Sis, you don't have to get rid of your U.S. citizenship, you can have both these days."

"Both?"

I gulped my spit. I became The Mute. No matter how accustomed I was to sudden bursts of abusive tirades from family members, it was still, for some reason, shocking. I could feel Lina's eyes on me to see how I would react. I wanted to be a role model for my niece, on how to not take abuse. I had no answers. I pictured myself cursing my aunt, storming out of the house, renouncing her for the rest of her life, knocking the bullfight paintings off her walls, and the Hummels of peaceful fishermen and clowns, and walking right across her champagne carpet with my dirty sneakers, slamming the front door, knocking all the tiny knickknacks off their shelves. I bit hard into the mushy center of the custard pie.

As instantly as she burst into her rant, Aunt Patty stopped, turned, and walked out of the kitchen into her bedroom, her oxygen cord sliding across her linoleum made to look like Italian *terracotta* tiles. A few minutes later she came out with a shoebox and put it on the table.

I shuffled through the documents. We stared at GranmaRose's teenage *passaporto* headshot, and her original signature. Grandpa Giuseppe's passport described his coloring as "*bruno.*" I opened Granma's birth certificate handwritten in fancy script from a fountain pen on yellowed paper. We passed the documents around the table and we all touched the words. The ocean had passed, then the century, now Granma was turning one hundred years old, and our families had been separated across the ocean for the bulk of it, and in some way I was determined to tie it all back together.

For Granma's one hundredth birthday we all gathered in a restaurant, my siblings and their children, Aunt Patty's kids and their children, and the children and grandchildren of GranmaRose's sister Lucia and her husband, Grandpa Giuseppe's brother, Franco. All my grandmother's descendants were in one room for her to behold. Audrey and I bought one hundred taper candles, and numbered them from one to a hundred. I got everyone on their feet in a circle, including the waitstaff of the restaurant, so that there were an even fifty of us. We passed the flame around the circle and called out the year we were holding. Each of us held two candles. GranmaRose held the candles representing 1900 and 2000. As the years were called out, I coached family members to call out significant dates. The year Grandma crossed the ocean, the year she got married, births, etc. With one hundred candles in a circle of all her descendants, GranmaRose truly glowed. We blew the candles out, applauded her *sopravvivenza*, and I played the video I made in *Acquaviva*, where my grandmother's nieces and nephews Isabella and Rosa and *i tre Michele* and all their kids sang *"Tanti Auguri"* in duos and trios. GranmaRose put her hand on the video screen as they sang and she cried.

Assassination Focaccia

At the Italian Consulate on Park Avenue and Sixty-Ninth Street, the bureaucrat pointed her polished fingernail tip at the vowels and consonants in my parents' and grandparents' names. The fingernail pointed out variations from document to document: dropped consonants, varied vowel endings, Americanized first names.

"You must prove all the documents represent the same persons. You have to legally change the spellings, to make it uniform throughout."

I set about the task, examining a century's worth of documents down to the letter. I found oddities. On my parents' marriage certificate, my father wrote "chauffeur" as his occupation. He was an iceman. What did he chauffeur, ice? I figured he didn't want anybody knowing his business. I'm sure my father had his reasons. On my mother's baptismal certificate, the name of the priest who baptized her was Father Focacci. I couldn't believe that. I called her right away. I said, "Ma, do you know the name of the priest who baptized you?"

"No," she said, "why?"

"You're not going to believe this. You sitting down?"

"Yeah."

"Seriously Ma, sit down."

"Okay, okay, hold on a second, I was just in the middle of something. Okay, I'm sitting."

"Focacci. Father Focacci."

"What!"

I could hear her losing her breath. I dropped to the floor and rolled on my back trying to get the words out: "You were ordained to make thousands of *focacce.*"

"I have made thousands of *focacce.*"

"I want one right now. Listen to this. Reverend Severino Focacci baptized Rachel Petruzzelli, 1926, Our Lady of Mount Carmel Church, 187th Street, the Bronx, New York."

"Would you believe it? I made *focaccia* since you were a little baby. I made *focaccia* every Friday night. I made two *focaccia* the day Kennedy got shot. That's how I know it was a Friday. You were five months old. I'll never forget, Walter Cronkite cried, you know dignified, but you could definitely see tears. I was getting dressed to walk to Tremont to get dough. On the way back, it took me two hours to get down the block. Everyone was out. We all talked. We were in shock. The dough rode home with you in the carriage. Since we took so long, the dough had already risen, and by the time we got near the house the bag was inflated and about to explode. You had the first whaddycall those things."

"Airbags?"

"Yes, even better. An airbag filled with buoyant *focaccia* for the bumpy ride home."

I picture her alone with me and the television that was a tiny bit bigger than a human head. I see Walter Cronkite's combed hair. In my vision his hair is white, so I adjust for the years backward and darken his hair. I see her lift me out of the crib that she kept in the kitchen. I actually can feel arms reaching in and hands hooking under my armpits and being lifted up in the air while I kick. I can feel the change of light. I remember the stripes of light and the bars and wanting to get out but not being able to do it on my own. I had to wait for the arms. I could call and call but the arms only came when they were ready. I feel the tension in my mother's body. I am in the carriage. The rhythm of the great white carriage wheels over the sidewalk seams put me to sleep. The pace along the cement squares of the sidewalk was regular like turning the pages of a book. Then there were jarring bumps, and also long rocking stops when my mother talks to the neighbors. She rocks the carriage on its formidable springs. Cook in crisis. When all else went to hell, cooking offered her a way to order the world. A *focaccia* imperative pushed her down the block as she pushed the stroller. The *focaccia* must go on.

Spearmint Gum Cure

BABYLON, NEW YORK 1999

Lanzi was convinced that Wrigley's Spearmint gum would cure his lung cancer. My visits to the mental home included jaunts to the supermarket where he could buy large quantities of chewing gum at discount prices. He had a rationale for his Wrigley's protocol.

"When I go to sleep," he observed, "I put the wad of gum under the bed, and in the morning it's filled with dust. So I figured it's doing the same things in my lungs. I've read about mint. It's got healing properties. I chew forty packs a day."

Lanzi's lung cancer got progressively worse. Still, he smoked. On one of my last visits to the VA Hospital, I drove out to Northport, Long Island with Ant'ny. The doctor came in with a group of interns. They stood in their white coats at the foot of my father's bed and talked among themselves about the progression of his lung cancer, and how benevolent it was of him to participate in the experimental chemotherapy program just to benefit patients in the future.

Like a good soldier, my father said, "I'm glad to be of use."

"I have one question," I said. "Why did the military issue cigarettes to the Marines in the first place?"

The crew of doctors mumbled to themselves and walked out of the room. My father went ballistic, he got up on his two feet and chased me and Ant'ny out into the hall. "Nurse! Nurse!" He ranted on and on at me. "You don't talk to the doctor like that. You don't talk to nobody. You're on government property. You don't even talk to the nurse's aides. You think they're here to change the sheets, really they are here to listen."

I walked down the halls of the hospital. I saw the nurse's aide and looked hard at her. She was smiling and humming a spiritual. Could my father be right? What would she be listening for? What would she report back to the government? My father didn't want anyone to know that he had the Rising Sun flag. This I knew. He had read in the newspaper about a soldier being tried for war crimes many years after battle. His words echoed inside me, "You're on government property." I pictured bugs recording our conversations, and spies carrying bedpans, and cute young social workers with pens poised on their pads asking, "How're you feeling today, Joe?" I thought of all the blue pills my father had not swallowed, but had spit back into his hand, thousands of antipsychotic pills he didn't swallow but didn't throw away. He saved them like he used to save old racetrack stubs when I was a kid. My head was so full every time I left my father. I walked out the lobby, full of its patriotic pride, plaques, flags, and signs honoring veterans. I telephoned CarKey and told him, "I just want you to know that your father's dying. Do yourself a favor and go see him one last time. He asks about you." CarKey hadn't seen my father in eighteen years, since they had the blow-out argument when I was under Dr. Martini's knife for my thoracotomy at Sloan-Kettering.

My last visits to my father I went alone. I'd stop in the PX and buy him slippers, magazines, and spearmint chewing gum, then I'd sit in a chair by his bed and keep my mouth shut while his television was tuned to a show on war in primitive cultures. The other soldiers in beds around him were in varying states of agony and misery, the guy next to him had no limbs. My father was content to be with soldiers. "Guys you could trust."

One Day My Horse Will Come In

NEW YORK CITY, FEBRUARY 2000

I dreamt of a dead horse the day before my father died.

It was a Thursday, February 24, 2000. I walked out into the drizzle on Lexington Avenue after a women's literature seminar on the Upper East Side, given by a professor who told firsthand stories of Franco's revolution. Lexington Avenue was shiny, ambulances and fire trucks hurtled toward me, red lights amplified on the wet black streets. I stopped at a pay phone to call my answering machine and retrieve messages. There was a message from my cousin Nico. "I'm so sorry to hear about your Dad."

I felt like I had been shot in the gut. I buckled over in tears. I opened my mouth in the rain and cried, "Daddy."

I didn't know who to call. I fumbled to get two quarters into the coin slot. I pushed the phone numbers to CarKey's house, because I knew he'd be succinct.

"It's Annie. Is it true?"

"Yes, he passed away."

"That's it?"

"That's it."

I walked down Lexington Avenue in zigzag steps. I cried aloud in the rain, giving my pain to the slick city. Passersby looked at me. I thought of my father yelling, "Hewitt!" at his buddy gunned down beside him in Okinawa. I yelled down Lexington Avenue at the top of my lungs, "No, Hewitt, No!"

The next day I did something I had never done before. I took out my father's Rising Sun flag and ironed it. For fifty years, my father kept the flag wrapped in Saran Wrap in a manila envelope. As I ironed it I began to see what was missing, the parts of the flag that were bullet ridden, shrapnel torn, knife shred. Chunks of the flag were missing. Chunks of the story were missing. By ironing the silk, I exposed missing pieces.

My father told me about his Marine buddy who kept a jar full of ears that he had cut off the enemy. My father had a photo of his buddies holding up a dead Japanese soldier, and pushing a smile onto his face. When I first looked at the photo, I was young. I knew there was a slump in the guy's body, but I didn't see death until my father explained the photo to me. Once I knew the guy was dead, then death was all I saw.

Nine U.S. Marines came to the funeral to salute my father's corpse, a corps of veterans who honored Marines as they died. They marched by him one by one, saluted him, and turned on their heels.

"He's gonna haunt us," Aunt Apollonia told me.

Ant'ny brought a pack of cards, a pack of Lucky Strikes, and one of my father's knit hats. I brought a pack of Wrigley's Spearmint Gum and a fi' dollar bill to tuck inside his pocket. My father had worn his green-and-red knit hat every day. I was resolute. The casket would not get closed without the hat on my father's head. So I waited. When it was just us kids saying good-bye to our father, I lifted my father's head and pulled his hat on him. I pulled it low to his brow, and kissed him good-bye for eternal rest. Joseph Rocco Lanzillotto: saluted, kissed, prayed for; cigarettes and cards, gum and cash, tucked inside his pocket, his red and green hat on. It was time to bless and bury him.

Everyone was in the church except my mother. She grieved privately. No one offered condolences to her because of their divorce so many years ago, but for her, it was the end of their story:

"There's no resolution," she said to me, "it's so final."

My father had been the love of her life, her Bronx knight, her soldier boy who survived vicious hell, and came home, so handsome, to marry her, and have children, her Lancelot. Now she knew how their story ended, without reconciliation. He never got the help he needed. So few do. I walked to the pulpit. The priest held three fingers up to me, signaling that I had three minutes to eulogize my father. I nodded. Then I spoke for twenty.

"He was born Giuseppe Rocco Lanzillotto at 370 E 163rd Street, the Bronx, baptized at the Church of Our Lady of Pity, 276 East 151st Street, went to PS 3 on 157th Street between Courtlandt and Melrose Avenue, where his teacher told his parents, Anna and Carmine, to change his name from Giuseppe to Joseph. He got a high school diploma from Bronx Vocational High School, in Electric Wiring. He worked the ice business from the time he was eight years old. By twelve, he'd earned the nickname, the "The Smiling Iceman." He worked the ice truck from five until eight a.m. every morning, then went to school, then worked from three to seven p.m., ate, slept, and did it all over again. He had been working for four years when he tried to run away. He bought milk and cookies and got as far as a park bench at 161st Street and the Grand Concourse where he slept the evening, returned home, and got a beating. His Father Carmine Lanzillotto started his own ice and coal business after World War I. He worked up to having his own horse and wagon. His Bronx ice route ran from 161st Street at Courtlandt and Melrose Avenue to 163rd Street. He kept his horse at 163rd and Courtlandt. He had a 1929 Ford truck and a two-ton coal truck.

In World War II, Joseph was a decorated U.S. Marine, serving from 1943-1946 and earning six service medals including a Presidential Unit Citation to the First Marine Division for heroism in Okinawa. Joseph boarded the USS *Grant* from Camp Pendleton in A Company, 2nd Platoon, 32nd Replacement Battalion, Fifth Regiment, First Marine Division, Fleet Marine Force. On

April Fool's Day 1945 he served in Weapons Company as part of Operation Iceberg on the island of Okinawa."

I called out to the congregation, "Aunt Tess, what was his dog tag number?"

"Eight Four Four Six One Four," she chimed right in without hesitation.

I left my mother's name out of the eulogy for my father. Omitting her name was the most difficult task of my adult life.

We all drove out to Calverton National Cemetery. It was a freezing rainy day. They played a recording of "Taps," folded the American flag into a triangle, and presented it to CarKey. While I have the Rising Sun flag, CarKey has the U.S. flag straight off the coffin. We had to leave my father above ground. Old soldiers were dying fast. They buried them all at the same time in the newest field. I turned to Audrey, "My father is in a box above ground, and I'm supposed to just drive away? This isn't right." And bless her soul, she looked up at me and said, "I'll wait with you, for as long as it takes."

Ant'ny chose the words "Bless Them All" from the soldier song my father sang, to get engraved on the headstone. We will all remember Lanzi walking around the house on Saint Raymonds Avenue singing, "*Bless 'em All, Bless 'em all, the long the short and the tall . . . You'll get no promotion this side of the ocean . . .*"

Two years after my father died, I read an article about the hottest new million dollar industry called "E Shred." The article profiled one family who went into business and took old computers apart, destroyed information, shredded component parts, recycled the metals, and made millions. The toil, the precision tools designed to take computer parts apart, the precious metals, the contaminate waste, the destruction of information; this was the industry of the future. If only I hadn't dismissed my father as crazy. If only I had joined him. If only I had magnified what he did, my father with his bare hands, worn tools, and time, all alone next to the furnace. The man was just doing what needed to be done. E-shred.

Madeleine and the Magic Biscotti

MOTHER CABRINI NURSING HOME
HASTINGS-ON-THE-HUDSON, NEW YORK, MARCH 2000

"This is my new post," GranmaRose said with resignation and disgust. Her sarcasm was palpable, through her century-old blue eyes. My heart shattered seeing her sitting there, all alone in the solarium of Mother Cabrini Nursing Home. GranmaRose was one hundred years old, detested old people, and stayed away from them.

"On the Hudson," my mother and Aunt Patty kept saying to add solace to an unforgivable situation, "it's on the river."

For me it was our family's collective failure. I'd been to *Acquaviva*. I'd met her older sister Maria. I saw how she was taken care of so that she could die at home, in her little bed that fit her little body. Our grandmother was our baby, but we couldn't collaborate to take care of her. I lived up three flights of stairs in a Bohemian railroad flat with Audrey and our two big unneutered German shepherd mutts. I would have carried Granma up and let her stay there, but Aunt Patty and my mother were clear, Granma wanted to be near them; she was to stay where she was. They had their own health problems and couldn't keep up with her care and her demands for a wide variety of cooked meals. And so, our conversations circled around what possibilities we might create and all ended with, "it's on the river." Some family members had pockets and others hearts and pockets and hearts never could see eye to eye.

GranmaRose's first roommate at Mother Cabrini Nursing Home was Madeleine DiDomenici. Madeleine was in a state of catatonia. She chirped like a frog, in a husky baritone, "DoodoDOOdo DOOdooDOOdoo." Every day I walked in, I handed Madeleine a single *biscott' regina,* with the sesame seeds. I entered the room, passed her bed, tucked an aromatic sesame *biscott'* into her folded hands:

"Here Madeleine. Here's a *biscott'.*" Then I sat next to GranmaRose for hours. I sang Puccini's *"Nessun Dorma."* I fancied myself a heroic tenor who would win the day, help Granma die dignified like her sister Maria in *Acquaviva*, who died *a casa*, at home, in her own bed, *la famiglia* around her. One day I pulled all our chairs into a circle. Granma was in her chair cushioned with egg crating, so she could fall over asleep whenever she wanted and the chair would catch her head. My mother, Audrey, and I were in the plastic orange room chairs. I undid the locks on the wheels of Madeleine's bed and pulled it into the circle. GranmaRose twisted her lips in annoyance,

"Bah."

"DoodooDOOdo DOOdooDOOdoo."

GranmaRose sang, "Boop! Boop!"

"What are you doing."

"I might as well learn the song. Boop! Boop! Some'tinga new."

Outside in the hallway, a nun pushed herself backwards in her wheelchair, with swinging kicks at the floor to gain momentum. Every so often she passed our open doorway yelling, "Mother! Mother!"

"Who you looking for?" I yelled back.

"The Mother of us all!"

We sang *"O' Sole Mio,"* then *"Santa Lucia."* Then I turned to Madeleine. "Madeleine, what's your favorite song? Madeleine." The sesame seed *biscott'* was gone, and there were crumbs on her lips. Madeleine burst into song, all the while staring straight ahead. Open sesame. She sang in a resonant and strong contralto, "Let Me Call You Sweetheart." When she was finished, she snapped back to catatonia. "DOOdooDOOdo. DOOdooDOOdo." My mother, Audrey, GranmaRose, and I looked at each other, all stunned. We witnessed her come to life for a song. A week later she was gone. Madeleine left her body, and her body was taken out of the room. GranmaRose got a new roommate who talked too much, claimed Granma was stealing her clothes, and threw paper cups at her from across the room.

How GranmaRose Became a Peach Tree

GranmaRose hadn't slept a whole night for years. At my mother's apartment, she'd sew in the middle of the night, make a cup of tea, meander with the spirits. I drove up a couple of late nights to Mother Cabrini, made her tea in the middle of the night, and visited with her when she couldn't sleep. Other nights she buzzed the nurses' station for a cup of tea at two a.m., so they drugged her to sleep, the next afternoons she could barely open her eyes. One night, Audrey and I and our friend Salley May drove up. Salley brought her Boston Terrier and stage partner, Phantom Louise. Salley juggled scarves for Granma, coaxing her back to being present for a while. Granma asked if it was a chicken we put on her bed. We told her it was a dog, Phantom Louise was the last animal GranmaRose saw on earth. The next day her roommate complained to the nurses that two gypsies and a man visited in the middle of the night, in wide skirts, and juggling. I guess I was the man, with my husky voice.

She ate less and less, and then nothing at all. The day GranmaRose refused to swallow, I knew it was all over. I would have given anything for her to demand to know one more time, *"Cosa mangia oggi!"* I coaxed teaspoons of Mother Cabrini nursing home hi-cal pudding into her mouth, until the day she let the vanilla pudding slide out the side of her mouth, her head hanging to the side, in the egg-crating of the chair. She stopped looking at me. I felt as if water was slowly filling up the room, as she slipped away. Her blue eyes no longer focused, they were like a baby's again, wandering with the light. The pupils got smaller and tinier. I held her limp hand, her skin as see-through as onion skin. Audrey whispered into her ear. Granma didn't respond. Audrey

Kindred talked to her soul, "I'm so sorry Rose. No one knows how to take care of you. You were their mother. You took care of everyone. But no one knows how to take care of Rose."

First, her heel had a bed sore, tender and red. We raised her feet with a rolled towel under her ankles. The sore turned into a pocket of pus. After the pus oozed out, GranmaRose was left with a hole in the heel of her foot, the size of a big green *Pugliese* olive. The same part of her heel where she used to point down on her black strap shoe when people asked her, Where are you from? The part of the heel I learned to point to as a little girl whenever anyone asked, Where in Italy you from? and I'd kick up my sneaker, and tap the back of my heel with my index finger. Right there. "*Bari*. On the heel of the boot." And so, Rosa Marsico Petruzzelli died, with a hole in her foot, marking the exact spot she was born.

"GranmaRose is in Heaven now," my mother told me over the phone. My heart sunk, and I broke down into tears as if a baby had died. For her funeral, I went shopping for artichokes and garlic and peppers so everyone in church could hold a vegetable in her honor. One of Aunt Patty's neighbors flashed me a twisted look down the pew: "I wanna trade the potato for the artichoke."

"I couldn't afford artichokes for the whole congregation. The potato's good. Somebody's gotta hold the potato."

At the funeral home, I looked at GranmaRose in the open casket. The undertaker made her breasts pert like they never were in life. That pissed me off. I hated looking at corpses. They had nothing to do with anything that resembled life. Italians carried *la bella figura* to the grave. You had to get dressed up on your way out, strike a good figure. I was thinking, I never want to be a corpse, never want to be put in a box, when my nephew Carmine barreled up to me, threw his arm around my shoulder and said about Granma, "She looks great don't she!" He said the wrong thing to the wrong woman at the wrong moment. I snapped at him in the castrating tone I had mastered, "I guess if you haven't seen her for a year." My voice was loud in the quiet room. I heard a yell, "Mom!" in the back of the room. My mother fell down on the floor in the coat closet. She didn't pass out, just got weak and nervous and fell, in response to my outburst. I told my nephew to step outside for a moment. I didn't want this to fester. I looked in his blue eyes, through the muscular hulking body and shaved head, to what I knew to be his sweet nature. I remembered him as a baby. He had been the most affectionate baby. He ran up to everyone and landed big hugs and kisses. This was Enza and CarKey's son. I noticed behind me, CarKey stepped outside to keep an eye on us, to make sure the argument didn't escalate. He eyeballed me. I was used to eyes being on me. I reconciled with my nephew, told him I love him, and stayed out in the fresh air for a while. Funerals made me itchy. I needed to shower. I hated the way we all pretended we were not next to lay down and be released by our souls.

In church I chanted Rosa Marsico Petruzzelli in *ottava rima*, eighth rhyme, the pattern in which Dante wrote *The Divine Comedy*. We buried her in Saint Raymond's Cemetery over Giuseppe, and next to Lucia and Franco. Then we went out to eat. On the wall over our table, the shadow of a giant rose appeared. Rosemarie was particularly amazed. She knew it was the soul of GranmaRose, who she was named after, and whose gold ring, so old and soft the detail had worn away, she now wore on her pinkie. The rose stayed the whole time and faded just as we stood up to leave. Rosemarie tried to figure out where the rose came from. She analyzed the angle of the sun bouncing off the mirror of a van that was parked outside, through the plate glass door that had a small appliqué of a rose, which cast the four-foot shadow on the wall. But beyond all rationale, she knew it was an apparition of our beloved powerful grandmother. A potent soul making her presence known.

Aunt Patty walked up to me and handed me an envelope. In the Italian family, an envelope is known as *la boost'*, from *la busta*, envelope. Traditionally, everyone gives you *la boost'* at your wedding, and it is filled with money. It literally gives the young couple a boost on their new life together. At a funeral, an envelope is not called a boost. It's not called anything. Traditionally, envelopes are given with money in them to those left behind, to help defray the costs of the funeral, or as tribute. When Aunt Patty handed me an envelope, my first fleeting thought was, what is this for, were all the grandchildren getting a little cash from Granma? I opened it up. It was a bill for sixty dollars. I looked up at Aunt Patty, bewildered.

"For the rosary of roses with your name on it, over the casket."

Every day, Audrey and I walked our dogs, Scaramooch and Cherub, in Prospect Park. We saw plaques all around Prospect Park at the base of trees, memorializing people. That gave me the idea to collect money in Granma's name and plant a tree in a park. I made a few phone calls to the family but no one forked up any cash. Granma died on March 20, 2001. That May a tree sprouted right outside my mother's living room window where GranmaRose tossed her peach pits out the window. The sprout was centered among my mother's three contiguous windows. Granma would always spit the pits into her hand and toss them out the window. When I saw the baby tree, I heard my grandmother's voice loud and clear:

"I'a do'a myself. Educationa Education, whattayou need'ada money to plant'ada tree for? You no need'ada money my dear. You eat'ada fruits. You take'ada pits. You put 'em in a ground. God a'does'ada rest'a my dear. He puts'ada soul into'ada soil. I no wanna be ina park a with ada dogs. I stay'a right here with'a my *bambina* Rachelina."

When my Mom and I saw two peaches on the tree we were astounded. "One for each of her daughters," I said. My mother sliced hers and gave everyone a taste. The other peach, she brought to Aunt Patty: "Here Sis, this is from Mama. She's still bringing us fruit." By the fifth year GranmaRose was over two stories high and gave thirty-three peaches. We ate them raw, sweet power from the earth. In her eighth year, the day before Easter, on Holy Saturday, GranmaRose Peach Tree burst into pink flowers right into my mother's window. My mother opened the window and the pink flowers came right into the living room over the rocking chair.

My mother held the branch, her rose-polished nails around the pink flowers. "My mother is bringing me flowers for Easter."

My grandmother peach tree produced one thousand peaches. I counted them, as I pulled them off the tree. She was more productive than those of us who still walked the earth in human form. We blanched and froze hundreds of peaches, baked pies, gave bags of peaches away to the neighbors. Every year on Granma's birthday, September 6, my mother and I eat her peach pie, homemade, not just from scratch, but from the pit.

In October, I prune her branches and clip the suckers prone to twist around branches. I remember how Granma asked me to pull her toes straight and press flat her second toe, which twisted up on top of her big toe. My mother and I save the branches. To us, they are Granma's legs. The branches hold our wet laundry over the shower and on the fire escape. One branch I carry around as a walking stick. It started because I wanted Granma with me.

Fruttificare

I was reading, *Cristo si è Fermato a Eboli* ("Christ Stopped at Eboli"). Carlo Levi quotes the relatively upper-class peasants' salutation to one another in the streets and *piazza*: *Cosa mangi oggi?* When I read this, I put the book down. I had to take a walk. I couldn't believe what I just read. There was a history to why GranmaRose greeted us this way! Carlo Levi conjugated the phrase as a question. GranmaRose conjugated in the imperative form, she ordered a response. *Cosa mangi oggi?* was a *Mezzogiornese* "Gimme five." I yelled in the apartment, "Let's go take a walk." Scaramooch and Cherub jumped to their feet, their nails slipped on the parquet floor, and they sat by the door, ears up and ready.

I wrapped one leash around each of my hands and walked down the street with my two proud lions on spiked choker collars, one on each side of me. Nobody fucked with me in Brooklyn, at any hour of the night. People crossed the street when they saw us coming. I liked it that way. I'd tell Scaramooch, "Bark," and he let the world know we were coming. This is how I always wanted to feel having two older brothers, protected. I felt like that once, when I first walked out into the street to play in the big boys' stickball game. But I never felt as protected in my whole life as when I walked with Scaramooch and Cherub on either side of me.

I contemplated Carlo Levi's words, as my lions lunged at the nightly garbage piled on the curb outside the bagel shop. Cherub bit through the Hefty bag and pulled out a bagel. They strutted down the avenue with hunky Brooklyn bagels in their jaws.

GranmaRose was not upper-class *Acquavivese*. She was more like the peasants in Ignazio Silone's *"Fontamara."* As a girl, she worked in fields owned by others. She didn't trust administrators who wore shoes and, in Silone's words, "pushed paper and made life difficult and ate well." She was from the class Silone describes as, *"gli oumini che fanno fruttificare la terra e soffrono la fame, i fellahin i coolies i peonies i mugic i cafone"* ("the peoples that make the land bear fruit and who suffer hunger, the *fellahin* [Arab landless peasants], the coolies [Chinese and Indian unskilled laborers], the peonies [impoverished Jews in China], the *mugic* [Russian peasants before 1917], the *cafone* [Italian landless peasants, such as my grandparents and great grandparents]").

It hit me. In the Bronx, Rosa Marsico Petruzzelli reinvented her life in a land and time and circumstance where she could try on this upper-class greeting, *"Cosa mangi oggi?"* A greeting for "the haves." GranmaRose was in America, where there was a multitude of food responses. Life was unpredictable but eating, as an act, wasn't. No longer was she where she needed to make jokes. I thought back to the time when I asked Granma what she ate as a kid. She answered with a *sfragganizze*, a peasant wisdom saying: *"Oggi, patate riso e fagioli. Ieri, riso patate e fagioli. Domani, fagioli patate e riso."* Today, potatoes, rice, and beans. Yesterday, rice, potatoes, and beans. And tomorrow beans, potatoes, and rice.

GranmaRose was the first in our family to try tofu. She was in her mid-eighties. She brought it home from the store, calling it *"Mozzarella Cinese"*—Chinese *mozzarell'*. To GranmaRose, *"Cosa mangia oggi!"* was a greeting of abundance, of arrival. She ushered her grandchildren into *L'America* every day, by greeting us this way, by never saying a simple but meaningless: Hello, how are you? GranmaRose insisted we realize the abundance of choices we grew up having each and every day: *Cosa mangia oggi! What* did you eat today!

Hunger had driven GiammaRose across the ocean. I didn't know hunger at all.

The Lasagna Stands Alone

September 11th, 2011 was the first day in my life that I had company in staring at the sky. From my first day of kindergarten when I embarked to walk to Santa Maria School, Lanzi warned me to keep my eye on the sky to look out for stray kamikaze. Now, almost forty years later, my city had been hit by "Divine Wind" and everyone looked skyward wondering if planes were on their paths or not. In times of war Lanzi seemed perfectly sane. One night I dreamed I breathed in the Twin Towers. Tower One whirled up into the air, a helix through the sky, through my window and up into my left nostril. All the floors piled up one back on top of one another in my left lung. Then Tower Two took off, whirling like a silver slinky of itself, through the night sky, in through my right nostril, all the floors stacking up, tall in my right lung.

It was the Christmas after 9/11 when the lasagna finally outlasted us. The holidays came with the usual pressure to get together. My mother declared "too much work," about cooking. The question hung in the air, who would make the lasagna? My brothers would not sit in each other's houses. So my mother had to choose. Ant'ny telephoned her and announced, "I will make the lasagna." I agreed to go. Ant'ny and I were on peaceful terms. He'd given me an electric guitar in acknowledgement of the one he stole from me to sell for dope when I was a kid. Things were as good as they were ever gonna get. Christmas Eve day Mom took the express bus down from Yonkers. Audrey and I picked her up on the corner of Twenty-Third Street and Fifth Avenue. As I drove down the left lane of Twenty-Third Street toward the bus stop, I honked and flashed my headlights. There was Mom, pretty and dressed in purple from head to toe. She waved her purple gloved hand, the hand that waves from her second-story kitchen window whenever I arrive or depart from her apartment. There was my mother waiting. The sight of my mother's pocketbook causes me to salivate. It's soft and deep and always contains something to eat. She gets in the car and the whole car smells like stuffed peppers.

Things were peaceful at my brother's, but as soon as we walked in, his eyes followed every little thing I did, around which chair I put my coat, and how I walked into his kitchen with the premise of helping and naturally picked a stuffed mushroom cap from the pan. This is what we do, like dipping our fingers in the holy water font upon entering a church. We step into each other's kitchens and put something tasty into our mouths. I felt like an enemy intruder, not a guest, not a sister. Tension vibrated down my arms and around my gut. Never needing anything substantial to argue about on a holy day, we just got right down to it. My brother and I snapped at each other. I didn't want to be in the same room. The past ten Christmas Eves, Ant'ny and I went to see Dad in the mental home. He'd heroically drive to a men's store and do some good shopping for my father to make him feel warm. Slippers, insulated gloves, sweaters. Ant'ny was a great shopper and generous. He was handsome like my father and knew what looked good on a man. My mom spent Christmas Eves with GranmaRose and Aunt Patty, or at CarKey and Enza's house. Now, GranmaRose and my father were gone, and there seemed less reason to put up with each other. I thought of my father's green-and-red-striped hat that I'd pulled on his head in the coffin. By now, it was just on the bones of his skull. A fight erupted. Emotional shrapnel hit all of us. I know how to yell, I know how to walk out, I know how to come back to the table for the lasagna. Tension sat between us like an uninvited houseguest. If I removed myself from the situation things would simmer down. Maybe it was me. I left the apartment alone. The city would heal me. Audrey stayed behind, she was a good buffer for our Bronx Italian rage and we all felt a little more secure with each other when she was around. She played the mild-mannered WASP girlfriend. Audrey studied "nonviolent communication." She said things that were alien to us, like, "How does that make you feel?" and "Let me reflect back to you what I hear you saying." She was Kay to my inner Michael Corleone.

The city was cold. I relished the chill, zippered up the snorkel jacket, triple wrapped my long blue Egyptian scarf around my neck. As soon as I was in the cool air, I knew the whole family should have come with me. New York City was the great healer. The chill smacked sense into me. I drove across town, the glittering Christmas lights all around me. I drove down Broadway, and walked into St. Paul's Chapel at Ground Zero for midnight mass where the Reverend John Denaro was the preacher. There he was, my kindergarten sweetheart in his vestments up on the altar. He winked and smiled at me as he said the mass. The chapel was filled with paper angels handmade by children, taped up onto the pews, signifying the souls of 9/11. I kneeled down and cried. The angels peeked up from the wooden pews and faced the altar. An arc of chandeliers hung bright like icicles in an arch over the altar, surrounded by blue walls like we were inside a giant delicate bluebird egg. And we were. The world felt like that sometimes. We were all inside a giant egg, fragile to shatter. After mass, Johnny Denaro gave me a paper angel for my mother, with a gold pipe cleaner halo, and Cecilia, "Age 5" written on the back, the age when we'd first met.

I drove back crosstown to pick up Audrey who met me downstairs, and we went home to Brooklyn and walked Scaramooch and Cherub. They lifted their legs and held their arabesques as they peed together on the million-dollar Brownstone stoops, with robust Christmas trees inside the long Brooklyn windows and red bows on their polished cherrywood doors.

That night my father came to me in a dream. His face hovered over me, his big open brown eyes, and he said four words. "*L* is for *Lion*."

The next day was Christmas morning. Audrey and I drove to Ant'ny's for the lasagna. When we entered the apartment, we walked into a massive wall of silence. My mother and my niece Lina were visibly distraught. They said nothing, but stood stiffly and widened their eyes. My brother and his daughter had fought during the night. My absence had made no difference at all, the vile tension just shifted into other bodies. Lina's eye signals bounced to my mother, then to me, then to Audrey, woman to woman to woman to woman, as if to say, "Don't ask." The red flag was up: Danger, thin ice.

I didn't take my coat off. We looked at each other and then we all looked at the closed oven door. The lasagna. What about the lasagna? We stared at the oven mutely. The lasagna had the power to hold us together as we teetered over the abyss between us. I could feel my mouth full of melted *mozzarell'*, hot clouds of *ricott'*, soft wide tongues of pasta, spiced chewy lamb, beef, soft pork. I knew we could all be okay. With the annual dose of lasagna in our systems, we would put up with each other for one whole year. I looked away from the oven door, and at my mother, niece, and girlfriend. They looked at me and one another. Then we did something we never in the history of the family had done before. We all walked out at once. We pulled away from the lasagna, the family glue. The four of us women, on Christmas Day, left. Never had we walked out on the lasagna before. After we left, even Ant'ny left. He left his own apartment. The lasagna stayed alone.

The four of us women drove around the city with nowhere to go. Down Second Avenue, around Houston Street, up First Avenue. I didn't know which direction to go in. There was nobody to "call for." My mind scoured the East Village and Lower East Side thinking, where are my friends, who still lives where, whose apartment could we show up at and have a few laughs and something good to eat? I was striking out in my brain. I had seen Alphabet City go from squatters in naked hulls of buildings to gentrified bars with three-hundred-dollar bottles of champagne. The neighborhoods were filled with my past, ex-lovers, apartments, but no door to knock on, not one window to call up at. Where was everybody? I drove over the Brooklyn Bridge. We talked about the massive lasagna waiting in the oven in the empty apartment and the love and attention and pounds of ingredients Ant'ny had put into making it. I wished we could hyperspace to *Acquaviva delle Fonte*, just blink, and be there. Could I ever explain to my Italian cousins about the dissolution of our family here in America? We glued our furniture together, we glued our food together, we ourselves were glued together, but glue hardens into a breakable bond.

Audrey mentioned one of Scaramooch's friends in the park, Buddy, a shepherd with a scar over his eye and one ear up and one ear down. Buddy's people were hosting a Christmas open house. So, that's where we ended up. We had a good time and witnessed another family's strained relationships. But, we didn't have the lasagna, and that year I didn't talk to my brother at all. The spell of *mozzarell'* had been broken.

That night, my mother felt dizzy enough to almost pass out, and for the third straight holiday, she ended up in the NYU emergency room. The ER doctor was an astute Italian American woman. She reviewed my mother's cardiac conditions, her history of the ascending aortic arch repair, looked her in the eye, and asked the only pertinent medical question: "So, how was your Christmas?"

Three Days from Eternity

Aunt Patty opened the front door. She wore sunglasses inside the house, dark-green lenses in oversize tortoiseshell frames. There was no way we were ever going to connect. She wore a nasal cannula attached to an oxygen machine, the fifty feet of tubing snaked around her floor. That's the only reason we were let in the front door. It was a level plain for her to walk to the front door. The back door had four steps. She wasn't going up and down anymore. Aunt Patty had congestive heart failure, but still sneaked cigarettes and swigs of whiskey. She hid this from my mother, but to me she seemed done with life a long time ago. I remember a comment she made to me when GranmaRose was a hundred and still wanted a fresh-cooked four-course supper.

"People are living too goddamn long these days. It's not medicine that keeps us alive, it's spite, we live on, spite."

I put on hot water for tea and took her boxes of cookies out of the closet. Stella D'oro Anisette Cookies. Nabisco Honey Graham Crackers. Nabisco Royal Lunch Milk Crackers. The strip of veneer wood pulled off around the edge of her table. The teapot began to whistle. I poured the tea and sat down with her. As easily as unbuttoning a blouse, Aunt Patty told me what I'd waited to hear for a lifetime.

"I remember the day your Mother fell out the window. I always told her, 'Don't go near the window.' Mamma was in the kitchen. Lucy and Rachel were up in Massachusetts for the summer, because Rachel had problems with her lungs. When she was a baby your mother loved the airplanes. She fixated on them. When she heard them over the house, she'd run to the windows and point up at the sky. *'Air-pain! Air-pain!'* She'd run clear across the apartment from one end to the other to follow the plane. She was two years old. I was four. Your mother pushed this bench we had over to the window. It was maroon leather with hammered brass buttons. This *paesan* made it for us. I told her not to climb up there. But she had it in her mind. Did she listen? No. She didn't listen. She climbed up on it to look out the window. She leaned against the screen. Then she was gone."

Aunt Patty finished the story and broke into a deep coughing fit. The congestive heart failure made every breath an effort. This story was a lot to get off her chest. She coughed so hard her eyes teared up, and she lifted a napkin underneath her sunglasses to wipe the tears. I thought to myself, is that it?

No mystery, no culpability, no negligence, no crime? Then why all the secrecy all these years? Why eighty years of silence? Why couldn't she tell me this years ago? I thought of something that had stuck with me through college. I thought of Kierkegaard's words—the opposite of freedom is guilt. Aunt Patty was the big sister. She was supposed to watch her baby sister. Her whole life she lived with this inside her. Now, she finally let it go, right out of her mouth, so simply, and without me even asking. I thanked her for telling me what she remembered.

Three days later, Aunt Patty slumped over in her chair and died, alone.

It took my mother a couple of months before she was able to walk back into her sister's house. Audrey, Lina, and I accompanied her. Aunt Patty's kids had taken what they wanted; the rest was to be dumped. When my mother saw Patty's wedding album, she became very sad and incensed. "No one wants their mother's wedding album? Don't they want to save it to show their grandchildren?" She rifled through the clothes hanging in the closet. "Thank God they had the sense to take the wedding dress," she said, "it's not here."

She opened up the door to the pantry. "It'd be a sin to leave all these canned goods to waste." And so, Lina, Audrey and I dragged bags of canned goods out to the car. Cannellini beans six cans, anchovies six cans, a gallon and a half of olive oil, assorted canned peas and soups, jars of prune juice and cranberry, a desktop Saint Anthony, the four bullfighting paintings, and a box of papers that belonged to GranmaRose. Taking cannellini beans felt symbolic of my teenage years on welfare after my parents' divorce, when my mother struggled to tear the bright food stamps out of their awkward booklets.

As I packed the beans, I heard a knock at the back door. It was Aunt Patty's neighbor Harper, a man she played poker with, and who lived in the mansion behind her, his rolling lawn adjoined her backyard. Harper gave my mother a warm hello and delivered fateful news: "Your sister died a multimillionaire." My mother squinched her face up, she looked betrayed, dumbfounded.

"I don't believe it," she said.

"You don't believe it? Or you refuse to believe it. Figure it out," Harper continued. "Her husband left her with a mighty pretty penny, and she had it all stashed away all these years gaining interest. Every year she handed out the annual exclusion gift, the maximum allowed under the law to avoid taxes, ten grand each to her grandchildren, year after year, like it was nothing. How do you think the grandson bought a Mercedes cash in hand?"

"What?" my mother seemed truly taken aback. "I can't believe it. Last week she had me run to buy her the butter on sale in Pathmark. I took the bus. What a jackass I am."

"You watch," Harper said. "Her kids will run away like thieves. Don't expect to be hearing from them. The daughter already purchased a Jaguar."

My mother sat down and held her head. "The sin of it all is her children never even wanted to get an education. They had no interest. And they didn't encourage their children either to get an education."

Harper agreed, "Ignorance and opulence. Not a pretty picture. What can I tell you."

As Lina, Audrey, and I dragged the black Hefty bags of canned goods out to the car, all the years hit me like one crisp smack in the face. Aunt Patty was the reason me and Mom ended up in Yonkers in the first place. This story was over. I got into the driver's seat and slammed the door. We were driving away with the beans.

"Whattaya'do?" the deaf *Napolitán* neighbor shouted at us, as Audrey and Lina finished packing the car.

"We're the poor side of the family," I yelled across the street, "we're leaving with the beans." He was a good soul. He had been kind to Aunt Patty, he brought her his backyard grapes and figs and made conversation.

"She got any liquor in there?"

"Yeah, hold on," I said. I hollered to Audrey, "*Oggi*, do me a favor. There's a new bottle of Sambuca behind the chair in the living room that looks like a throne."

"Okay alright," she said, "I'm making one more trip. I'll get your mother, and that's it. We're outta here."

"Thank you *Oggi*, you're the best."

The three of them got into the car and I handed the *Napolitán* Aunt Patty's last bottle of *Sambuca Romano*.

We left with the beans.

Don't Make 'Em Burn

Mom telephoned Aunt Patty's kids to ask about the wedding dress. I heard her say, "I wore that dress too. It was beautiful. I'd like a piece of the silk, you know, to make something for my grandchildren's weddings: a pillowcase or a wedding album cover or *whathaveyou*." She hung up the phone in disbelief. "They threw the wedding dress down the steps into the basement with the trash," she said, "they claimed it was soiled." My mother was so sad, I didn't know what to do. I sat at the maple table and opened the box of papers that belonged to GranmaRose.

It was a treasure of GranmaRose's recipes, handwritten like cut into stone, blue ink dug through the good thick paper of church envelopes, her 2s and *q*'s curly and studiously cursive. This was the penmanship of illiteracy, every letter wrought with slow deliberate care. All the *t*'s crossed, every *i* dotted by a hand that held a pen tentatively, a hand shaped around roots and soil, vines and branches, needles and thread. My grandmother lived the century, from 1900 to 2001. She never purchased paper to write on, never read a book, she wrote only on confiscated, found, recycled paper. Recipe after recipe on numbered church envelopes embossed, "This is my weekly sacrifice for Church Support" from the Church of the Blessed Sacrament, Bronx, New York 10472. Recipes on cut paper bags the whole rim and cylinder intact so you could wear it like a sleeve. A recipe on the back of an electric bill, prescription paper, an envelope with a postmarked Christmas stamp. I held each paper, and began to translate the recipes word by word by word. But what good would recipes do? I looked at my mother. We had the same exact thought. Our hands couldn't make what her hands made. We could attempt to follow recipes. We could take clues from them about who we had become. The heat of my hands could ruin the crust for the calzone.

Her recipes she writes as "Regulations." *Regole dei biscotti a l'aniso*, regulations for anisette biscotti. I broke the code. I studied them, sounded out the words. Showed them to my mother. Carried them around with me in my knapsack for weeks, protected by plastic sheets. I showed them to Italian women who took an interest in my deciphering. The regulations for biscotti calls for "*3 tispunno begn polvere.*" GranmaRose wrote in a combination of phonetic English and Italian. She wrote words down, as she heard them. *3 tispunno*, 3 teaspoons was easy. But what was *begn polvere*? I repeated the sounds, "*Begn*" to try to hear it the way Granma heard it. I read "*Begn*," as Granma would say it. "*BEHgenAH*," I said over and over.

One day at my friend Linda Mancini's house, her mother, Gina Marino Mancini, helped me crack some phrases. "*Begenah*. That's how she heard the English word *baking*," Mrs Mancini said. "The first word is *baking*. *Polvere* is *powder* in Italian. *Begn polvere* is baking powder. You have to understand, they didn't use baking powder in Italy back then. It was new to her in America. She had no word for it."

I was so excited. Granma's recipes were my own private Rosetta Stone. The regulations for *cartellato* call for, "*1 bottiglia di pruno giuse*, and *1 bottiglia di greppe giuse.*" *Bottiglia*, I knew, Italian for *bottle*. *Pruno*, I guessed was phonetic English for *prune*, as was *giuse*, for *juice*. I laughed with a sense of intrigue as I figured out, one bottle of prune juice, one bottle of grape juice, because I could hear GranmaRose's voice alive again.

"Sure, cooked wine will put you right to sleep when you have a cold," Mrs. Mancini understood.

I never saw GranmaRose follow a recipe, so these papers confused me. Who did she write them for? On the bottom of many recipes she wrote, *non li fare bruciare*, don't make them burn. Who is she talking to? Does she think one day we'll read these, we, the inept *Americahn'* hands that she never wanted to touch her dough? *Non li fate bruciare*. I can't imagine her reminding herself this. She doesn't give the time or the temperature, just the warning. Her measurements for flour translate as *ponte*, mounts, or in other recipes "put enough flour how much it will take."

My mother and I mourned the loss of GranmaRose's plain circle cookies, which we could never get enough of. How would we make them?

"She never measured," my mother moaned, "she made a well of flour and pulled it as needed. And her directions for spices have no specificity: "*è conderle*," and spice them up. I have no idea how much of anything she used. She measured all by eye and touch."

"Let's try Ma."

"Okay."

We set out to follow the unfollowable regulations. We chose a *biscotti* recipe and the one for *ricotta* cake. The work! I took for granted that as a kid I could eat all the *biscott'* I wanted. On Holy Days, there were endless hills of GranmaRose's signature unglazed circles of *biscott'*. How much work it was! My mother and I shopped, carried everything up the steps, washed the rolling board, and stood for hours. She pulled GranmaRose's rolling board out from deep within the back of her closet. I rolled up my sleeves and donned an apron. We washed our hands with the half bar of brown soap at the kitchen sink. I wiped my hands on the *mappine* that would accompany me the whole afternoon, slung over my right shoulder. I took care to work the dough around the board and not to waste any bit of flour, just as GranmaRose would have done. In the middle of the work, it struck me. Who am I doing this for? Who will eat these? Who is all this work for? My brothers on Christmas? And as soon as I asked, the answer came: No. I am doing this for my own communion with my mother, grandmother, and great-grandmother. To repeat with my hands, the circular motions on the rolling board that I saw GranmaRose make for years. My hands were engaged in a sacred act of remembering. I worked the dough.

My mother peeked under each *biscott'* with a spatula, and offered me a hot one.

"No, you. You get the first taste."

Her eyes watered up. She broke a *biscott'* and put it into her mouth. "I never thought I'd taste these again in my life. The first thing that struck me is, I'm used to somebody so small, I see the hands flying, but there's someone so tall. That's my daughter. The dough, the rolling board is so familiar and there are the flying hands, but I can't see the face at the same time 'cause you have to look up to see the face."

A month later my mother took out a tin of the *biscott'* from her bedroom.

"You still have some of these, Mom? How could you still have the *biscott'*? Didn't you bring any to Christmas?"

"No," she said, as she cradled the tin. "I guess it was subconscious. With their no-carbohydrate diets, I don't trust them. I should take a chance they're gonna throw out GranmaRose's cookies? Never!"

"You mean nobody tasted them for Christmas?"

"I guess not."

Pipe Dreams

My father comes to me in a dream. His face hovers over my face. His brown eyes look into my eyes. He looks like Omar Sharif in *Doctor Zhivago*.

"Twenty-six hundred dollars," he says. I wake up Audrey and tell her. She pulls my head into her shoulder and rocks me back to sleep. *"Shhhhhhssshhhhh."*

I heard the opening screech of the gate. I had installed a gate in our hallway so Scaramooch and Cherub could have the run of the floor without terrorizing the downstairs neighbors. I heard the gate and thought back to

Saint Raymonds Avenue, and the thought raced through me: the dogs are here, I am safe. I looked at the light coming in from the window. A large steel S-shaped meat hook hung from the curtain rod. One of the butchers from Arthur Avenue gave it to me so we could mount our heavy props. Namely, hundreds of pounds of block ice. In my half-awake state, all these elements hit me at once, the squeak of the gate, the long-brown-haired hippie girl next to me in bed, the dog-guardians, the meat hook. I realized I had constructed an exact replica of the psyche of my youth. Where the opening screech of the gate had forewarned me as a child when my father came home, I had built a squeaky gate at the top of our stairs. Where Rosemarie and Penny made me feel safe as a child, I had created a family with Audrey, Scaramooch and Cherub who protected me as an adult. Where my grandfather's meat hook expressed the gestalt of my terror as a child, I had added the butcher's meat hook to my home decor. There must be a word for this phenomenon in German, I thought. Since I don't *sprechen sie Deutsch* I made it up. *Jugenpsyche,* when you wake up one morning and realize you've recreated the elements of your psyche from your youth.

The next night Audrey woke me and said, "Annie, your father came to me in a dream. Twenty-six hundred dollars," he said.

"You know Audrey, I never went back to get his things. I feel bad about that. And he always told me, when I die, look in the pipe. How many times did he show me the stack of pipes in the basement, and the one pipe covered with electric tape with money rolled up inside the medicine vial?"

"I'll take a ride out there with you. I can go Saturday."

"Okay. One last ride to Babylon. I guess we had pipe dreams, huh?"

"Weird."

"Yeah."

We drove along the slow route, Sunrise Highway. Eventually I took the left onto Fire Island Avenue. The house was nowhere in sight.

"I always get confused out here," I said, "maybe this is the wrong corner?"

"Well, this ain't it. Let's go around the block once."

"This looks like the corner. This is it. Here's the Marconi sign. This is the corner. The house is gone."

"How could it be gone?"

"It's gone. Not even a trace. *Poof!*"

"What!"

I was stunned. I felt as if none of it ever happened, as if life was one great mirage, and I had dreamed it all up, a mansion turned into a mental home on the lot where Marconi sent ship to shore radio waves a hundred years before. I got out of the car and ran my hand along the Marconi sign over the words: ". . . the birth . . . with ships at sea." In the mansion's place werc five pre-fab houses. A German Shepherd barked into the daylight from the shade of a pre-fab doghouse. I could hear the dog, for blocks away, as we drove to go stare into the ocean.

The Little Fish and the Big Ocean

RHODE ISLAND

Seven a.m. The air is creamy with sunrise. The whole beach aches with oncoming light. Rosemarie and Peter had taken me and Mom on vacation with them and their kids, to a beach house in Rhode Island. I had two hours left before we began the drive back home. An old friend named Carbone came to take me for a morning walk on the beach. Carbone had a beautiful countenance that reminded me of the old timers who had spent a life in the fields. He was a guitarist who played in my project at Arthur Avenue. I remember he came up to the Bronx in his poncho and beautiful smile with moustache and beard and wool peaked cap as if he just walked over from *la campagna*. As we walk along the beach, Carbone strips to his boxer shorts and walks into the water with his arms open wide. He hugs the ocean as it swells over him. He ducks under a wave and rises up on the other side of it. "Mother Ocean!" he calls, as the swell of water lifts his smile up toward the sky. Another swell followed. I stood in the water up to my shins. Since that day I almost drowned after visiting my father, I never went into the ocean without a life jacket. One wave hit me. "Here take my hand," Carbone said. He reached his wet hand out to me. If I am holding his hand, I thought, I don't need a life jacket. Do I tell him that I grew up with fire hydrants and never learned to swim, or that I'd almost drowned in an ocean riptide after visiting my father in a mental home? The next wave rushed toward us. I held Carbone's hand and took the hit of the curve like a linebacker. He let go. The wave lifted my whole body and knocked me down onto the sand. I tumbled and lost my breath, dragged back through the sand as the water pulled back to the sea. I got to my knees to push my head above the foam. Before the next wave came, I got on my feet and staggered up to the shore.

"You had to go," Carbone laughed, water dripping off his beard. "I'm not as strong as Mother Ocean." We walked down the beach. "I like to walk to take it in," he said. His chest shivered. Carbone wanted to feel being alive the way an animal feels it, the wind on his skin and the hair on his chest with droplets of water.

"Look at that," I said. "They should toss him back in the water." There was a fat fisherman and his fat fisherman wife. They smiled as we walked past their fishing pole stuck vertical in the sand. The fisherman pulled the bright line, and a fish the size of his forearm dragged through the sand. The fish's gulls, crusted with sand, swelled in the air. I became silent. The fish must be shocked to be pulled out of water.

"What do you need to say?" Carbone asked.

"I just want the fish to go back in the water."

"I know you're feeling that fish. Can we walk back by the fish?"

"Okay."

We turned and walked back down the beach. The fisherman stuck the fish in the sand, tail down, head up, next to the rod. The fish stood straight up. The fisherman took the fish's photo with his cell phone. He and his wife laughed. I wanted to grab the fish and toss him in the water. I wanted to swim far out in the ocean and release him deep, so he would never have to hear about the shore again. I'd never seen a scene quite like this. I know there are angels. I know renaissance paintings didn't make them up, angels watching life, angels sitting on the roofs of buildings. Angels all around driving fate, pushing humans. I know angels make all things happen. After all this is part of the genius of *La Rinascimento*, right? This is part of what made me halt and weep in *Firenze*. Every time I pick a peach from Granma Peach Tree I know it to be true. We walked down the beach. Carbone talked about being a vegetarian.

"Do you eat fish?" I asked.

"I eat a fish here and there. It's a life. Ahh, Mother Ocean's resplendency. I give thanks for her vastness."

We both turned our heads at the same time to look back at the fish.

The fisherman waved his arms at the water, then he backed up quickly as a wave broke at his shins. He stepped forward again, bent down, lifted the forearm-size fish up and tossed him over the crest of the wave. He waved at the sea as if he could push the fish back into the depths.

I thought of the fish getting hit by the blast of rolling water, and turning and making it out past the roll. The fish couldn't know what had just happened to him exactly, but he was aware now of hooks and air and sun and sand and one man's hands.

Three Hundred Cream Puffs and the Illusion Veil

My father's sister, my Aunt Tessie, set out sandwiches and trays of cookies and tea, as soon as I walked into her house. There was no way I could convince her to "not fuss," so I didn't even try. She had a bag prepared for me.

"Your father gave me these and he said, 'Tess, save this for Annie. One day she may want to write a book.'"

I looked through the bag. My father had handwritten a memoir. All the periods of his life, he organized with tabs. "Van Buren Street. Okinawa. Atomic Bomb. Bainbridge." I was stunned. After all that had been lost in life, I couldn't believe that these notebooks existed. That my father had actually written a memoir while he was in the mental home.

"I removed a few pages," Aunt Tess said, "I hope you don't mind. They were about me."

"Okay, Aunt Tess, whatever you want."

"I feel bad. It's just that, you know, he writes about everything."

"Don't feel bad. It's okay. Thank you for saving these for me. This is a treasure. Aunt Tess, I have to ask you something. I don't have a wedding photo of my parents."

I took a cookie. "Do you have one?"

I never saw my parents embrace, or kiss, or hold hands. I thought maybe, somewhere there was a photo of the good times they had as a young handsome couple madly in love.

"Ooh, Annie, I think I have one somewhere, if I could find it. Maybe you can help me pull some papers out of the closet. I have so many piles, I have to think where to look."

She pulled papers out and then asked me to move the bed and she reached into a drawer. She found Aunt Apollonia's and Uncle Tony's wedding photo; they walk down an aisle of crossed swords. Then she pulled out a manila envelope marked "Joey's Wedding." I've wanted all my life to see a photo like this. It is the groom's family photo: my mother the bride, my father the groom, his parents, his four sisters, the "Four Roses," and his two brothers. The stunning Apollonia stands with her husband Tony in military dress. Apollonia and Tony were the first to get married. My father and mother were the second. I stare at these central four people, Rachel, Joseph, Apollonia, Tony. I see all their gorgeous looks. Apollonia and her almond-shaped eyes, thick brunette mane, full lips. Tony's tall, slender self, soulful eyes. My father all spicy and sharp. My mother, not smiling, but beautiful, gorgeous, and scared, braced as if she sensed that my father's brutal childhood and trauma from the war would one day catch up to him and quite literally smack her in the face. I look at these four Bronx Italian beauties in the lone surviving wedding photo, and I think: suicide, paranoid schizophrenia, wife-beating, depression, war trauma, shell shock, battle fatigue, post-traumatic stress disorder, order of protection, plaintiff, defendant, divorce. In this one glorious moment of the war hero's wedding, did some part of themselves sense their inner fragmentation? Did they sense each others? That all was not as it looked to the camera? In my mother, I see a survivor. I want to tell her this, to tell her young twenty-one-year-old self, "You will survive, and have many happy years. You, young Rachel, will be blessed many times over. *Coraggio!*"

I thought back to the night my mother announced that we would move away to Yonkers and the lentils shot out my nose. I sat with Johnny Denaro and we laughed in front of the television as we ate on snack tables. I didn't know that my father had already put the house up for sale while we were all still living in it. I didn't know that he'd tortured her until she signed her half of the house over to him. I didn't know that my mother's parents paid the down payment on the house, I didn't know that my father swindled her out of the house altogether. I had seen him yank her head back over the living room radiator, steak knife at her throat. I had seen him swing the wagon wheel chandelier over the maple table into the back of her head. I had seen him backhand smack her in the face. I had seen her hold back her tears, and most miraculously I'd seen her eyes learn again their fierce most determinate sparkle. I was home with them alone; I was the only witness to the bulk of the violence.

I was nine when my father sat with me at the maple table with a scissor and cut out paper dolls. He had a box and a big book with gold lettering. He whistled the tune, *"You made me love you, I didn't want to do it. I didn't want to do it."*

I knew what paper dolls were because my mother so often described them. "We grew up cutting paper dolls. We had no toys, but on Sunday we'd all chip in a penny apiece and buy the *Sunday News* for four cents. We'd cut paper dolls and play for hours."

A few times, she folded paper and taught me to cut the shapes of girls, that when unfolded, all held hands. The paper dolls my father cut had my mother's face on them. I watched my mother's face in the photos, being cut out by my father's slow deliberate scissors. First he drew a sharp X over her face with his pen. He X-ed her face out. Then he stabbed a hole through the thick album paper with the point of the scissor and he sliced the oval around her head. The sound of the scissors clipping was final. The oval pieces of her faces fluttered to the floor. The afternoon light rained on the maple table.

My mother stood in front of the stove screaming, "Good. Ga'head. Good. Who needs a wedding album."

His scissors were decisive. "Lies. Lies. It is all lies."

The bride lay in pieces on the floor.

He could have just burned the whole thing, tossed it in his old tar bucket and set it afire, but no, he sat there in her kitchen with his big black handled steel scissors. In some photos he cut a perfect rectangle around her figure. Empty rectangles indicated where the bride had been. I picked up one piece of her face off the floor underneath the table that had no pen mark on it, and I hid it away in my pocket. My father cut my mother out of their whole wedding album. Then he stood up, lit another cigarette, then swept her pieces all up in the copper dustpan and shook the faces and bodies into the trash.

The wedding album he kept. The sound of the scissor, the oval pieces of her face as she fluttered to the kitchen floor, the afternoon light on the maple table, haunt me and me alone.

The wedding album had photos of him with cut-off arms, and bridal photos with the bride missing. Who keeps a wedding album with the bride cut out? I know what my father was thinking. I know what my father's last words on earth about my mother were. But I'm not printing them here. Let them stay silent within me and with my father in his grave under his undecorated stone carved with the words "Bless Them All," in Calverton National Cemetery, where he lies, red and green hat on his skull, with hundreds of thousands of soldiers.

"Annie you want more cookies?"

"No, thank you Aunt Tessie thank you."

"Come on, what else can I give you?"

"Could I borrow this photo to make a scan? I'll bring it back."

"I can't let that one go. You can go to CVS and get it copied. It's just a mile and a half down the road."

So, that's exactly what I did. I even bought a frame. I didn't want any harm to come to this one photo. I wanted to see my parents as they were once, a hot young Bronx couple, a gorgeous bride and her fantastically handsome and promising young groom.

I come home and hesitantly show the wedding photo to my mother.

"What a cake, huh?" I say to divert my sadness.

"Not a cake," she corrects me, "a tremendous tray of cream puffs topped by a bride and groom. Our first wedding task as a bride and groom. After we collected *la boost*. We went table to table. We carried this tremendous tray of cream puffs. Our reception was in the Audubon Ballroom where hoodycall was assassinated."

"Malcolm X?"

"Malcolm X. But this of course was years before. Nineteen forty-seven. We had a Football Wedding. That was the best part, the night before, we stayed up all night making sandwiches. It was so much fun."

"Why'd they call it a Football Wedding?"

"I don't know. I guess the guys used to toss a hero to each other. Hey, who wants a salami?"

"Look how gorgeous you are."

"Look how gorgeous Apollonia was. She had almond-shaped eyes like Merle Oberon. What eyes! Poor Apollonia. She was ahead of her time. She opened a donut shop, imagine? Ahead of Dunkin' Donuts and all the rest."

"Where was it?"

"In the train station. Must have been 180th Street. In Morris Park. Unheard of back then. Everyone told her this would never catch on, that people had their morning coffee *a casa*, at home, but she insisted New Yorkers would learn to grab a coffee and a donut on their way to work. She believed it would catch on."

"Look how gorgeous you are," I said.

"I wore an illusion veil. It was my best friend Mary Como's sister's veil. It was so long, and you barely saw it. It was like a whisper. Yards and yards long. A veil like a whisper."

She pulled the photo closer to her eyes.

"And this dress was my sister Patty's wedding dress. It had an illusion neckline, and it fit me perfectly. I was in an illusion."

Lingua Madre

*I*o *vengo* **da** *New York. Io sono* **di** *New York. Habito* **a** *New York. Vengo* **dall'***America. Nato* **nel** *Bronx*. It is the small words that throw me. *da, di, a, nel, nello, nella, nell', nei, negli, nelle, nell'*. I am thirty-seven when I sit in my first Italian class inside Our Lady of Pompeii Catholic School on Bleecker Street. I am a *cittadina*. Now I want words. I want grammar. I want to be able to speak to my all my cousins in *Acquaviva* about life. I want to write them letters. I want to read the Italian newspapers. I want to read Dante. I want to *capishe* who I am. We are all adults, sitting at night, in small kids' desks. The teacher is a young, hot beauty from Milan. She wears red lipstick, tight red pants, a low-cut red crocheted top over a red bra that shows her *scolatura*. Sitting in the small wooden chair at the small wooden desk with carved pencil groove makes me want to misbehave.

"*Lancialotto*," the teacher says, "I always wondered when I would meet my *Lancialotto*; I didn't know he would be a woman."

I am the only student she doesn't call by a first name. She calls my name with the dignity that fits the noble legacy of Lancelot. Lanzillotto, *Lancillotto, Lancialotta*, Lancelot. *Lancia*, lance. *Lotta*, fight, struggle, contest. Lancelot, the lover knight, the steadfast warrior, the perfect knight, of whom nothing bad can be said, except that he falls to love, a love bigger than life itself. *Lancillotto's* shield was split in two until he kissed *Ginevra*, his queen, the wife of the King, and the shield became whole again. Devotion, destiny, ardor, all consuming passion; for *Ginevra, Lancillotto* would fight any battle. *Cavaliere innamorato, Lancillotto* suffers love, serves love, sacrifices for love, is overtaken by love. Happily ever after is not for Lancelot. My father too, did not believe in happiness. My father was a Lancelot in his own right. In foxholes in Okinawa and Guadalcanal he read my mother's love letters. Knee deep in mud, with malaria, on quinine, in the rain. "Her letters were heavy with perfume," he wrote in his memoirs, "having a life was a castle in the sky." And even I, know how to run circles around a femme.

The teacher gives us a lesson in possessives. She says, "*figlia mia,*" my child, and it sounds like it came off a violin. The voices of my great grandmothers were more sharp and staccato, "*Figghe migghe.*" The breaking of stone with a chisel. "*Figghe migghe pensaich a Mamma mo a Rosine.*" Rosine, listen to your Mother, my child. *Acquavivesi* punches inside me, cut phrases close to the heart. The teeth of lions. *Dente di lione.* Dandelion. In my youth, it was the language of curses, prayers, secrets, card playing maneuvers, and keening. My mother and grandmother spoke it when they didn't want me to *capishe*, or when they couldn't understand life as it were. When I think of my GranmaRose's life, I think in the rhythms of her language. When her mother told her to go to America instead of her elder sister Maria, I cannot hear it at all in plain English. It is 1919. World War I has been over for just a few short months. My great-grandmother Rachele turns to Rosa, then a girl of nineteen, and here is where all kinds of syllables tumble in my mind. How did my grandmother Rachele tell her youngest daughter to go to America? "*Si va in America! Vai, vai, figghe migghe.*" Go, go. You go my child. You go to America. I hear her directive with the simple clarity with which my own mother told me to go to the corner store for milk and bread. I see my great-grandmother's finger swirl over the heads of her children until, like a compass needle it settles on the head of the youngest. You. You go. You go instead. When I divine this scene, I cannot hear it in plain English. English is so plain in my ear, so separate, each word with finality. No echoes around consonant endings. Each word, its own room. I long for flowing interlocking phrases with multiple meanings, where nothing said is straightforward. I climb through books to learn who I am. Verb tenses snag me, conjugation my nemesis; then, when? before, no *dopodomani*, after tomorrow, not now, not now, now. "It's all one day," Janis Joplin sings, and I add, why, why, why conjugate at all?

"*Lancillotto, come se dice* rainbow *in Italiano?*"

"*Boh. No lo so.*" Uh, I don't know.

"*L'arcobaleno,*" she said *faccia contenta*, the face of contentment.

L'arcobaleno was the word I repeated to myself as I walked down the four flights of stairs after class. I would learn to be *una Italiana* one word one phrase at a time, just like GranmaRose had learned to be an American. My mother told me that Granma taught herself English by reading the lettering on all the trucks that went by. As a child, I taught my grandmother some English words and she taught me some Italian. We did single words, mostly. GranmaRose had trouble with homonyms; here/hear, our/hour, flour/flower, ant/aunt, buy/bye. One day we did antonyms, opposites. Good/bad, ugly/ beautiful, hot/cold, near/far, old/new. Then she asked me: *"Qual è il contrario di zuccheen'?"* What's the opposite of *zucchini*? I was stumped. I revisit this question from time to time. Granma's whole life, it seems to me, was the opposite of zucchini, the opposite of kicking up dust as a peasant child and being asked to walk the rocky roads to the shriveled fields and grab what the chickens left, or give the skinny goat some water. I imagine her looking at the endless fields and seeing predictability and starvation in her future, and I see her getting on that boat the blessed *Duca degli Abruzzi*, and I see the boat arriving in Ellis Island, and I see her walking onto the land and with her perceptive and protective blue eyes, her eyes that contain churning oceans, I see her looking all around at everything and everybody. The opposite of *zucchini*. I thought about the tumors that had grown rampant inside my body, the mass that used to creep around inside my chest squeezing my superior vena cava, and my throat, and I thought, this Granma, this also is the opposite of *zucchini*. It's what I grow. And it's not in a field, but in my body. And it's unpredictable. There is something in the unpredictable that I now crave.

I crossed Bleecker Street and walked into *Pasticceria Rocco*. I ordered in Italian. *Pasticiotti, cappuccino, taralli di finocchio.* The server wore a nametag that said, Axel. I repeated my order in English, and later when I bit into the *taralli*, I realized he gave me the wrong ones, the black pepper biscuits. I went next door into the gourmet pet shop. I wanted to go home with treats for everyone. *Pasticiotti* for me and Audrey, and bones filled with marrow for Scaramooch and Cherub. I walked toward the subway. My inner Judy Garland came out as I belted up Sixth Avenue, "Somewhere over *l'arcobaleno*, way up high. There's a land that I heard of once in a lullabye. Somewhere over *l'arcobaleno* . . ."

Sì o No?

My maroon *passoporto* came in the mail. I smell it, hold it, stare at it, and carry it around for everyone to see. I want to stitch a century-long scar together since my grandparents were babies in Bari. We've been split from our family and homeland for sixty-odd years. I want a ceremony. I want to be sworn in. I want to memorize Italian tenets and Garibaldi quotes. I want a ritual. I want to raise my right hand, bite into a liver for a contract like I imagine my ancestors did.

Referendum voting papers on oversized pastel paper arrived in the mail. I unfolded the light blue square like a poster. I opened the pink one. I sat with my mother at the maple table and read them aloud in my most flourished Italian pronunciation with trilled *rrr*'s. I read every word aloud and said, "Ma, how do you want to vote? *Sì o no?*"

My mother paused, looked at the two boxes we had to X off. One said *Sì* and one said *No*.

Unequivocally she said, *"A No!"*

This was the first time I heard her say *no* that strongly. I heard everything in her no. I heard her saying no to Italy, no to not being able to understand her own mother's language, no to all the pain in life, no to how quickly life passed, no to growing old, no to the maple table, no to me, no to my father, no to her marriage, no to the suitors she'd refused, no to the court judge, no to the cops, no to the surgeon, no to the priest, no to her fall out the tenement window, no to citizenship, to politicians, to Italy to Italy to Italy, to the world, to the Bronx, to her whole life, she said strongly, "No!"

Weeks later I found out we voted to send the women's movement backward a hundred years. I read the referendums correctly, but misunderstood the word *abrogazione*, repeal.

A Couple of Teaspoons of Coffee and a Couple of Drops of Milk

One winter morning I am well into my oatmeal when my mother says, "Is there by any chance a little spoon of–" and she leaves the sentence hanging as if she can't remember the word for what she wants.

"Yoghurt," I offer, finishing her sentence.

"Yoghurt," she affirms.

I pass her the yoghurt and she walks to the maple table. Her words echo in my head. *Is there by any chance a little spoon of*—. "Ma," I say, "Come back here. Try saying, 'Gimme the yoghurt.'"

"Gimme the yoghurt."

"There. How does that feel?"

"Good."

We walk through the kitchen doorway at the same time, she turns her body into the wall to let me pass. I wave my hand so she goes first. I walk big like a bull. I hit middle age and my gut expanded like a *focaccia* dough that never stopped rising.

I make a pot of coffee. I said, "Ma, do you want a coffee or Gatorade?"

She says the telltale phrase, "A couple of teaspoons of coffee and a couple of drops of milk."

We head out on the road for the two hour drive to Rosemarie's house.

I play Sinatra's "Come Fly with Me" and we take off, northbound.

"You know Mom it's time we have this discussion about our relationship and how you always want less and I always want more."

"What are you talking about?"

"Like we sit in the cafe. You don't order a thing. I get a cream donut and a cappuccino."

"What's there to say?"

"What's there to say!"

"You're badgering."

"Okay I'll shut up."

"You don't have to shut up. It was being a single parent. I had to learn to be conservative to survive. Your father never paid child support."

"I don't think I'm talking about that. If you were having this conversation in therapy, they'd ask you what you remember from your childhood. Did you feel you had enough, or not enough, with food or in general?"

"Oh, not enough. I remember my Aunt 'Tse telling my mother that me and my sister ate too much, that we ate more than Lucy and Rachel. She was always saying what good eaters we were. I felt so self-conscious at the table. Then one day they separated their food in the refrigerator."

"The icebox."

"Right, the icebox."

"How do you separate food in an icebox?"

"Whatever. Things were tough. Papa wasn't working for a while."

Waves of compassion opened in my heart toward my mother. She never allowed herself any indulgence in life. It's not that she's been sparse or withholding; on the contrary, she has cooked and cleaned and listened to all our crap and knitted for every one of us and given of herself in a thousand ways, a million times. It's just that she is withheld. So many things suddenly made sense. How she reluctantly spoons food onto her plate, saying, "only a little," to how she lets someone pour her wine, "just a drop," to how she laughs, folds over and begins a coughing fit, to how she acquiesces for coffee "just a couple of teaspoons of coffee and a couple of drops of milk," to how she never let me rope her into my own brand of extravagance and grandiosity.

Up to this point I thought I inherited all that from my father, his devil may care—throw it to the wind—one day my horse will come in attitude. But now I see it is my reaction to my mother, and her paralysis around having enough and taking too much. It hits me that my overeating and grandiosity is reactionary to my mother's paucity, which is a direct result of a comment made in 1932 over a divided icebox.

So, this is what I felt in the rocking chair all those years ago, this thing about my mother that I had never understood, but that pained me. This rocking as if there wasn't enough; enough breath, enough minutes, enough years, enough milk, enough enough enough, as if the rocking chair would run out if we rocked too long, as if we shouldn't sit in the chair cause we'd surely wear it out. That chair that is still in my mother's apartment. The one chair whose dowels never pull out. The one chair that creaks and whines and cracks but will never, never pull out from underneath you.

We watch Rosemarie's granddaughter lift her first chickpea to her mouth. "Mmmmm," Caroline Rose says, and picks up another chickpea with her thumb and index finger. With that one bean, she is taking in the whole of our family's culture. Melissa has given her daughters *Rose* and *Rachele* as their middle names to connect them with their great-great-grandmother *Rose*, and their great-grandmother *Rachele*. Holding the chickpea, Caroline Rose's eyes are open as wide as her mouth. The cycle of life begins again with a little girl's delight over a single chickpea. Elizabeth Rachele has my sister's eyes, which are my mother's eyes, which are GranmaRose's eyes, this deep blue that notices everything and understands all of life. My mother is the happiest I have ever seen her in my life.

"It's time we give away the maple table," she says, "Your brother always wanted the table." She telephones Ant'ny and tells him to go take it. He asks if she is sure. "Yes," she says into the telephone, "the apartment was always too small. The table was always too big. The apartment was supposed to be temporary. That was thirty years ago."

When my mother and I get home, the table is gone. We dance in the empty space. She plays Sinatra, "That Old Black Magic," and we dance and sing. This is the first time in my life we are together without the maple table. The space feels immense. "We have a dance hall," I shout and spin her with my hand.

"You know the first time I heard Sinatra was this song. I was sitting on my bed by the window. The music came in from somewhere on the block and filled the air. I thought wow who is this? I must have been about fifteen. Listen. '*In a spin. Loving the spin I'm in.*'"

Becoming GranmaRose Peach Tree

I look up at the full moon out beyond GranmaRose Peach Tree. The man in the moon is a woman. I don't know how I've missed this before. I sit under GranmaRose Peachtree and I understand. It doesn't matter where you are or what you have. You can make and give what you need. GranmaRose became a peach tree, two stories tall, on top of a hollow parking garage full of fumes, when there were no other trees around, and it's easy to say well a tree needs other trees to protect it from the wind for when storms come around a tree will fall down, get uprooted, there's not a lot of soil. She's not on top of Manhattan schist or Bronx gneiss or *Barese* limestone with aquifers. Granma's lesson is this: I am this one tree. I can grow a thousand peaches. *Faccio io.* I do it myself. I can bear fruit. Grow. Give peaches. *Fruttificare.* To make fruit.

As a woman named Khadija kneeling in a garden outside a mosque in Providence once told me: "Be like the tree, my love, be like the tree."

I connect my soul to the soil.

Soul = See + All

I sit under the peaches in moonlight and ripen.

glossary

LINGO I HEARD AS A KID IN THE BRONX

bunked into	met by chance
call for me	stand outside my window and shout my nickname
chestnut	stupid
the choose	childhood methodology for picking sides for games
ding hao	thumbs-up (word my father learned in World War II, during R&R in Peiping, 1946)
don't leave me hangin'	my hand waits open for your hand to slide, palm to palm
English	slice you put on a ball
fresh head	stupidity
fungo	to pitch the ball to yourself
gimme five	slide the palm of your hand on mine
gung-ho	enthused (word my father taught me that he learned in World War II)
hood	a shady character
hoodycallit	someone whose name you forgot or don't want to mention or don't want to put in the effort to remember

hoodycall	hoodycallit
I'll call for you	I will stand outside your window and shout your nickname
in cahoots	to be partners in causing trouble, or crime
Itchy Balls	hard spiky balls that fall off an Itchy Ball tree
johnnypump	fire hydrant
knucks	game; you slam a deck of cards on your opponent's knuckles 'til they bleed
left me flat	stood me up
mark it on the ice	Forget it (If an iceman marked the money owed on the ice, the price would melt away.)
no skin off my back	No problem, I'll help you anytime
peashooter	a fat straw, you blow lentils through it at opponent's eyes
pipsqueak	tiny, insignificant, you can beat him in a fight
scootch	a whiny pain in the ass; rhymes with butch
Spaldeen	small pink "Spalding" ball
skullycap	street game; melt crayons in bottle caps
"to do"	"a big to do" is a giant event
you got a shot	life has given you a cosmic opportunity
whaddycallit	something you forgot the name of
whaddycall	whaddycallit
whoosiwhats	hoodycallit

LINGO WITH AN ITALIAN ETIOLOGY

acida	indigestion; from *acidare* to make acid, Latin *acidus*

agita	indigestion; from *agitare,* to agitate, Latin *agitatio*
acasi acasa	a person who flip-flops; not loyal
a'schapett	the little shoe, when you sop up the juices of the dish, after the meal with the heel of the bread; savor the end, the best part
baccalai	a jackass
bafanabala	from *va fa Napoli;* go to Naples.
ba fangool	from *va' a fa 'n culo,* go make it in the ass
cazzamarole	a series of errors, caused by one bad decision after another
chibobi	a pompous jerk; from *cipolla,* onion
chooch	a big dopey guy; from *u ciucc,* donkey
ciambott'	a soup or stew where you throw everything in
famaith	of hunger
gavone	someone with no manners; from *cafone,* landless peasant
imbroglio	a mess of a situation
miseratz	miserable, chronically
oongatz	when you have less than nothing; from *un cazzo,* ass
madonn'	Mother of God, *Madonnamia*
mannaggia	damn it
mappine	dishtowel
mavatheen	get outta here
piglia pifesse	smart enough to act stupid; *pigliare per fesso,* take for a fool
pishadu	piss place; from *pisciaturr,* chamber pot

ꜱᴄʜᴀᴛʜ	someone makes you choke; from *sciacciale*, to squash
scumbari	a beggar
scustamaith	without customs, ill mannered
sfaccimme	stupid face; from *faccia*, face
shangaith	off kilter; from *siancatto*, cripple
stunaith	out of it, literally out of tune

THINGS GRANMAROSE SAID

Bah!	I've had enough of you, I don't want to hear anymore.
"Cosa mangia oggi!"	A greeting. Thing you eat today! What'd you eat today? List the things you ate today!
Dingeel a me.	*Acquavivese.* Tell me.
Disch a ked.	*Acquavivese.* Tell her.
Eeeee.	Are you kidding me? You're out of your mind. (Sounded like a shrill alarm. Accompanied by the right arm shooting straight up.)
Ke de ditt a me.	*Acquavivese.* She told it to me.
Ye tutta fatt.	*Acquavivese.* It's done.

acknowledgments: exquisite pleasure

Writing this book was a solitary act done in community. I remain eternally grateful to all those who've made this book a reality, made my life into something you can gently hold in the palm of your hands and understand on your own time. If I were a racehorse I'd want to be called Exquisite Pleasure. That's what we say upon meeting someone, *"Piacere Squisito."* And it is. We meet. We kiss twice. We bite into the fruit of each other. I thank you all who have kept me alive and in the game. My mother, Rachele Claire Petruzzelli Lanzillotto, stuck by me every single day of my life and taught me how to survive and keep sparkling. Her effervescent soul and resilience is truly beyond words. My father, Joseph Rocco Lanzillotto, taught me imagination. May all fathers teach their daughters metallurgy, magnetism, electricity, and the properties inherent in ice and batteries. My sister Rosemarie protected me when I was very young and is a continual source of love and support. With great honor I name my grandparents: Rosa Marsico Petruzzelli and Giuseppe Petruzzelli, Anna Cianciotta Lanzillotto and Carmine Lanzillotto, and my great-grandparents: Rachele Lerario and Nicola Marsico, Michele Petruzzellis and Lucia Armienti, Saverio Cianciotta and Arcangela Scigliuto, Giuseppe Lanzillotta and Apollonia Sorranno. Honor to all the ancestors.

Joanna Clapps Herman made this book happen. She double parked on Broadway when I couldn't go a step farther, took me home, bathed and fed me, gave me her husband's bathrobe, tucked me in for a sunset nap, then sat me down at her computer to write my book pitch to her editor. Her husband Bill Herman polished that letter, we hit the send button together then raised a glass of *Chianti*. Better friends, no writer could have. My editor, James Peltz of SUNY Press took me on. I am profoundly grateful to him and everyone at the press who made it a gentle, loving, and magnificent ride: Amanda Lanne, Ryan Morris, Fran Keneston, Emily Keneston, Chris Mangini, Laura Glenn, Fred Gardaphé, Kelli Williams-LeRoux, Sue Morreale, and Laurie Searl. Thanks to Todd Shuster for sending me to Gail Leondar-Wright and glprbooks.com, and thanks to the all-powerful Gail for taking me on. My friend Rosette Capotorto is the editorial midwife of this book. She gave the manuscript her devotion and her hard-earned Bronx wisdom and made me laugh wildly over an otherwise overwhelming barrage of life's detail. To her I am eternally indebted. This would have been a very different book were it not for her ability to enter scenes and know exactly what was going on as if she had been there. Rose Imperato rendered the spirit of my grandmother's peaches and pit and tree in ink and graphite, an artistic feat only Rose could do. Jean Feraca came at the manuscript with ferocious passion and saw through to the core of several scenes and gave me treasured feedback. LuLu LoLo performed midnight readings of new passages over the telephone; having a friend who is up all night is the best gift a writer can have. Edvige Giunta urged me on and would not let me rest until I completed this book. I thank her for her single-minded drive. She is a voice of consistency, healing, and accomplishment, is the hub of my memoir writing community, and has brought me the additional friendship and sage council of Joshua Fausty, the brilliant and generous Margaux Fragoso, Gina DiRenzi and Krystal Sital. Audrey Kindred taught me to be an artist. Her constant love has carried me through decades of adventure, creativity, and travail, along with our beloved guardian-knights Scaramooch and Cherub. Audrey is my family and rock. It is because of her love and "enlightened witnessing" that I have thrived. Johnny Denaro is my friend for life, and I'm grateful to have this journey in tandem with him. Joseph Papaleo, my "Don Giusepp" at Sarah Lawrence College, taught me that I was an Italian-American writer, introduced me to his beloved Toni Papleo who became one of my trusted readers and guides, and brought me by the hand to Bob Viscusi and the Italian American Writers' Association. Bob Viscusi taught me just how wild a book can be. Shirley Kaplan taught me that I was a consummate artist.

Dr. Sanford Kempin saved my life when I was eighteen and told me, "Go write the great American novel." I didn't do that but I hope this book will suffice for now. He was the first man I ever met who truly listened and made me feel loved on an intellectual level. Dr. Diane Stover is the embodiment of compassion. Deep thanks go to the surgeons whose brilliant focus and steady hands kept me alive: Dr. Nicholas Daniello, Dr. Nael Martini, Dr. Alan Turnbull, Dr. Jatin Shah, Dr. Dennis Kraus, Dr. Carolyn E. Reed, and Dr. Virgilio Sacchini. *Grazie eterna* to everyone at Memorial Sloan-Kettering Cancer Center, especially the cleaning ladies who hum spirituals in the elevators, the wise and wonderful pharmacists, and Phyllis Capello, clown and *cantastoria* extraordinaire, who sang to me with her ukulele while I was waiting to get a nuclear medicine test; and Dr. Kevin Oeffinger, Beth Whittam, RoseAnne Tucci, Dr. Jennifer Ford, Dr. Jimmie Holland, Dr. Anna Marcelli, Dr. M. H. Heinemann, Dr. Debra Mangino, Dr. Mercedes Castiel, Dr. Sherri Donat, Dr. Michael Baum, Dr. Hans Gerdes, Dr. Lourdes Niece, Dr. Michael Tuttle, Dr. Michael Stubblefield, Flavio Martinez, Donna Andrus, Cecil Rowe,

Janet Bermudez, Nick Medley, Ivelisse Belardo, Jim Brooks, Genevieve Medina, Sister Elaine Goodell, Uletha, Annette Galassi, Ugo Majori, and the hundreds of others, including the stellar 15th Floor Nurses, and staff who saved me in 2012. All the love in the world to Dr. Mack Sullivan, T-Bone, Kalil, and everyone at Fitness & Recovery. Special thanks to Dr. Stuart Neidle, Emily and Margo. Dr. Clark Sugg at the White Institute wrote me the best prescription in the world, "Write every day." Hedgebrook women's writing residency gave me the profound and unique experience, where to be a woman writer is to be queen; I thank all the staff for their lavish treatment. Hedgebrook gave me owls. Santa Fe Art Institute gave me ravens, and months of focused time to piece the bulk of this book together. I thank the visionaries who founded these havens, and all the staff and artists who are the keepers of the vision and the land. Noted thanks to Evie Wilson-Lingbloom for her eagle-eye research and Julie Rosten for her spiritual nourishment, as well as Robin Cole Henderson and Anthony Henderson, Vito Zingarelli, Cathy Bruemmer, and Denise Barr.

Lucia and John Mudd, in memory of Peggy Mudd, generously funded my work. In addition I thank the many individuals, families and institutions who have supported my work, bought tickets to my shows where I unearthed many of these stories and downloaded my albums online. A few super generous supporters are: Ellyne Skove, Micki Wesson, John Denaro, Maria Grace LaRusso, Annie Hauck-Lawson and family, Indrani DeSilva, Kerry Scheidt and David Freeman, Laraaji, Antonia Kirkland and Mark Gelman and Helena and Esther, and Min Brassman, Eliza Ladd, Alina Lundry, Ralph Lewis, Rick Trizano, Chris Casanova, Pete Esser, Kitty Loving, Roe and Pete, David Packer, Jude Rubin, Suzy Wahmann, Joseph Novi, Lori Starace Beresford, Roy Campolongo, Jon Ebinger and all those who funded my "Book Promo and Tour Fund."

Graziemille to all the Sarah Lawrence College librarians, and to Susan Guma, Shirley Kaplan, and Allen Lang and the Sarah Lawrence College Theater Outreach Program. Carolina Kroon Photography (www.carolinakroonphotography.com) lovingly documented my work since 1993. Hope Savvides of Duggal Visual Solutions expertly processed the photos for this book. Larry Weiss, Rosette Capotorto, Sophia Capotorto-Weiss and Full House Printing (www.fullhouseprinting.com) printed manuscripts and designed postcards along the way. Rosemary Cappello and Philadelphia Poets. Elise Bernhardt and Tony Giovanetti, The Kitchen, and *Dancing in the Streets*. Ellie Covan and Dixon Place. Martha Wilson and Franklin Furnace Archive Inc. Steve Zeitlin, Amanda Dargan and City Lore curated me for the Smithsonian Folklife Festival, and provided fiscal sponsorship and spirited support. Jeannie Lovetri and the Voice Workshop. Michael Legg and Amy Attaway and all the Apprentices at the Actors Theatre of Louisville. Thanks to all my students over the years for teaching me everything, especially Emily Jordan Agnes

Kunkel and Courtney Moors, Lisa Dring, Sean Mellot, and Sarah Grace Welbourn. Jean Feraca and the staff of Here on Earth: Radio Without Borders at Wisconsin Public Radio. Judith Kelman and Visible Ink at Sloan-Kettering give me chardonnay instead of chemo. I call on my *sorelle* of the MALIA Collective of Italian American Women in all kinds of situations, love to all, including Jennifer Guglielmo, Samantha DeMuro, Tiziana Rinaldi, Carmelina Cartei, Vincenza Lorenza, Valerie Vitale, Claire Ultimo, Nancy Carnevale, Mary Cappello, Maria Laurino, Mary Ciuffitelli, Dina Gerasia, Adele Regina La Barre, Gabriella Belfiglio, Margarita Suarez, Procopia Corso, Stefania Taviano, Mary Anne Trasciatti, Chiara Montalto, Joanne Robertozzi. Gennaro Pecchia, Angelo Zeolla. Linda Petta. Cara De Silva. Italian American Writers Association. Italian American Studies Association. Italian Americana and Christine Palamidessi Moore and Carol Bonomo Albright. Remember the Triangle Fire Coalition. ACT-UP. Claudia Horwitz and the Stone House, Cancer and Careers. LifeLab. Yael Raviv and Umami Festival of Food and Performance. Puffin Foundation. New York Foundation for the Arts. The Rockefeller Foundation MAP Grant, and Next Generation Leadership Program, especially the Arts and Activism Group: Cara Page, Kathie DeNobriga, Pam McMichael, Liz Canner, and Timothea Howard. Will MacAdams, Tufara Waller Muhammad, Gina Marino Mancini, Simba Yangala, Eddie Gormley, Ronnie Mae Painter, Joan Spota, Yuko Takeda, Mark Prezorski, Artie Rothschild, Barbara Imperato, Joseph Bosco and Anthony's Restaurant, Pasquale Cangiano and cleanandhumble. com, David Greco and the merchants at the Arthur Avenue Retail Market, Valerie Jiminez, Asimina Chremos, Karen Cellini Corcoran and Joe Corcoran, David Michalek, Wendy Whelan, Kay Whelan, Anthony Tamburri and the Calandra Italian American Institute at CUNY, Lisa Cichetti, Lucia Grillo, Stefano Albertini and Casa Italiana Zerilli/Marimò NYU, Maria Lisella and Gil Fagiani, Maria Mazziotti Gillan, Louise DeSalvo, Roseangela Briscese, Patrizia Calce and Westchester Italian Cultural Center, Ottorino Cappelli and i-italy.com, Joseph Sciorra, George Guida, Bill Schemp, Diane Fortuna, Rob Stupay, Lori Goldston and Kyle Hanson, Mark Ameen, Adeel Salman, Mitria DiGiacomo, Maria Fama, Al Tacconelli, Rosie Goldensohn, The Kindred and Goldensohn family: Wendy, Michael, Pam, Thomas, Karen (RIP), Jessie, Steve, Ellen and Ben. Valerie Jimenez, Elizabeth Messina, Jen Miller, James Periconi and Alice McCarthy, Nancy Youngblood, Tamra Plotnick, Jonathan Deutsch.

For housing me during writing periods and taking me in as family, uber thanks to Jenny Bass, Trisha Gorman and Andrew Holmes, Marc Choyt and Helen Chantler, Jean Caliendo, John Gennari and Emily Bernard, Tim Z. Hernandez and Dayanna Sevilla, Lexie Honiotes and family, John Denaro and Joel Van Liew, and Gale Lockland.

My key mentors: Sister Raymond Aloysius, Denya Cascio, Anthony Caliendo, Dr. Alfred Senft, Dr. Michael Scala, Karen Romer, Dr. Stanley

Aronson, Joseph Papaleo, Dom Malandro, Anthony Chiappelloni, Neil Goldberg, Shirley Kaplan, James Head III who taught me about bedrock and outer space. Intrepid individuals show up at the hardest times in life: Susan Elizabeth Samuels. Alexandra Hartmann whose healing powers made me live again. Salley May created a spiritual performance art playground where I became free. Rachel Blumenfeld brought the most steadfast friendship in the world and gave me a trunk full of literature to start me off. Dr. Stephanie LaFarge and Dr. James Crowley helped me create the class at Brown, Everything You Always Wanted to Know About Cancer but Were Afraid to Ask.

In loving memory of Amelia King, Al Paoletta, Chrystyna Hubickyj, Peter Franklin Findlay, Connie Robinson, Melody Stappas, Mindy Nissenfeld, Safiya Henderson-Holmes. RIP, for never hating Mondays . . .

Thanks to all my aunts, uncles, and cousins here and in *Acquaviva delle Fonti*, *Cassano delle Murge*, and *Bitetto*, and to my siblings and their spouses. Being an aunt is a grand gift in life, being a Godmother is divine. The honor is mine. *Grazie* Melissa, Rob, Caroline Rose, Elizabeth Rachele; Rachel; Charlie, Margo, Charles; Nicole, Emily; Jonathan, and the dazzling Catherine Rose. And to all those whose lives are part of this book, thank you.

Forever,
Annie Rachele Lanzillotto,
2012, Yonkers

credits

I gratefully acknowledge these editors and presses for publishing earlier versions of the following chapters and sections:

Bachelor, Lace, Butch, Trousseau, in "Embroidered Stories: Interpreting Women's Domestic Needlework from the Italian Diaspora," edited by Edvige Giunta and Joseph Sciorra, University of Mississippi Press, forthcoming

Post-Mortem Peach Surprise, in "Storied Dishes: What Our Family Recipes Tell Us About Who We Are and Where We've Been," edited by Linda Murray Berzok, Praeger Press, An Imprint of ABC-CLIO, LLC, California 2011

Madeleine and the Magic Biscotti appeared in an earlier version as *Catatonia Blues*, in "Italian Americana, Music of Affection," edited by Christine Palamidessi Moore and Carol Bonomo Albright, University of Rhode Island, Providence, Rhode Island Winter 2011

Rachele's Pocketbook Frittata in "Avanti-Popolo: Italian American Writers Sail Beyond Columbus," edited by The Italian American Political Solidarity Club, Manic D Press, San Francisco California 2008

The Names of Horses in Creative Nonfiction #30/*Our Roots Are Deep With Passion: Creative Nonfiction Collects New Essays by Italian American Writers*, edited by Lee Gutkind and Joanna Clapps Herman, New York, Other Press 2006

How To Catch A Flyball in Oncoming Traffic in Hidden New York: A Guide To Places That Matter, edited by Marci Reaven and Steve Zeitlin, Rutgers University Press, New Jersey 2006

Cosa Mangia Oggi, in Gastropolis: Food and New York City, edited by Annie Hauck-Lawson and Jonathan Deutsch, Columbia University Press 2007

Triple Bypass, in The Milk of Almonds: Italian American Women Writers on Food and Culture. Editors: Louise DeSalvo and Edvige Giunta, The Feminist Press at The City University of New York 2000

Wallid Walla Bint, in "Politics of Water, A Confluence of Women's Voices," *Water and Women* Issue 9.4, Guest Edited by Paola Corso and Nandita Ghosh, International Feminist Journal of Politics, Centre for International and Security Studies, Toronto Ontario, Canada, York University, 2007 Taylor & Francis Ltd., http://www.informaworld.com

The Doctor's Touch, in "Women, Health, and Medicine: Transforming Perspectives and Practice," Women's Studies Quarterly, volume XXXI, Numbers 1 & 2, New York: The Feminist Press at the City University of New York in Cooperation with Rochester Institute of Technology

Strike One, in "Italian American Writers on New Jersey: An Anthology of Poetry and Prose," edited by Jennifer Gillan, Maria Mazziotti Gillan and Edvige Giunta. Rutgers University Press, New Jersey, 2003

The Lasagna Stands Alone, as *9/11 Breadballs*, in "Italian Americana: Cultural and Historical Review," Vol XXVII, Number 2, edited by Christine Palamidessi Moore and Carol Bonomo Albright, University of Rhode Island, Providence, Rhode Island, Summer 2008

about the author

Annie Rachele Lanzillotto is the author of the book of poetry *Schistsong* (Bordighera Press, 2013), songwriter and vocalist of the albums *Blue Pill, Eleven Recitations*, and *Carry My Coffee*. Lanzillotto was born and raised in the Westchester Square neighborhood of the Bronx, and in Yonkers, New York. She received a B.A. with honors in medical anthropology from Brown University and an MFA in writing from Sarah Lawrence College. Her poem *Triple Bypass* won the Italian American Writers' Association Paolucci Award in Poetry. Her poems *Manhattan Schist*, and *My Grandmother's Hands* both won Rose and John Petracca Awards second place from *Philadelphia Poets*. Lanzillotto made her acting debut in 1993 with her solo show, *Confessions of a Bronx Tomboy: My Throwing Arm, This Useless Expertise* at Under One Roof Theater and Manhattan Class Company in New York City. She's received fellowships and performance commissions from New York Foundation for the Arts, *Dancing In The Streets*, Dixon Place, Franklin Furnace Archive Inc., and The Rockefeller Foundation where she was a Next Generation Leadership Fellow. Lanzillotto teaches master classes in solo performance for the Acting Apprentice Company at Actors Theatre of Louisville, and guest lectures in Theatre Outreach at Sarah Lawrence College. For more information and contact: www.annielanzillotto.com